Language Arts 100
Teacher's Guide Part 1

CONTENTS

Revision Editor: Alan Christopherson, M.S.

Alpha Omega Publications®

804 N. 2nd Ave. E., Rock Rapids, IA 51246-1759

CURRICULUM

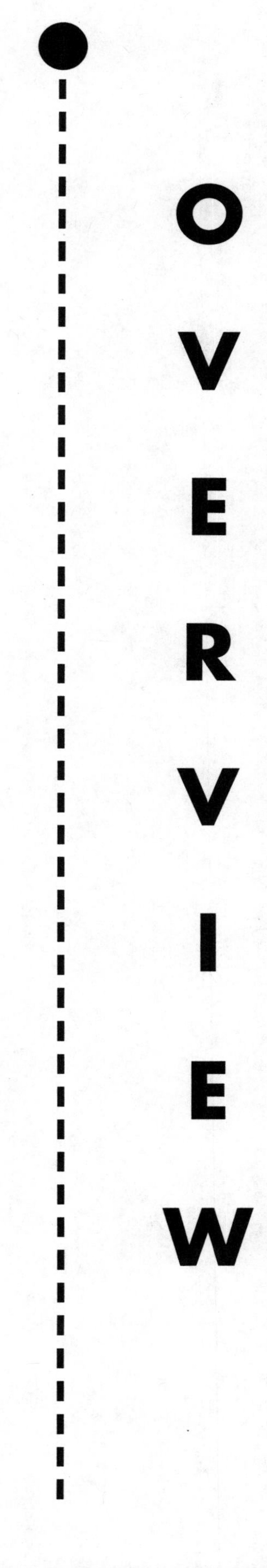

LANGUAGE ARTS

Curriculum Overview
Grades K–12

Language Arts Lessons

1-40	41-80	81-120	121-160
Alphabet-say the alphabet **Colors-**recognize colors **Directions**-left to right **Following directions-**given once **Grammar-**form simple sentences **Listening skills** **Personal recognition-**read and write first name -know age and address -recognize names of family members **Phonics-**short *a, e, i* vowels -initial: *b, t, m, r, s, n, d, p, l* -form and read simple words -form rhyming words **Shapes-**circle, square, triangle, and rectangle -recognize shapes in objects **Stories and Poems-**create simple stories and poems **Writing-**form circle and lines -*Aa, Bb, Dd, Ee, Ii, Ll, Mm, Nn, Pp, Rr, Ss, and Tt*	**Grammar-**sentences begin with capital, end with period **Patterns-**simple shape, color patterns **Personal recognition-**read and write first and last name **Phonics-**short *a, e, i, o, and u* vowels -initial: *k, c, ck, f, h, g, j, v, w, y, z, qu, and x* -read simple sentences **Position/direction concepts-** in/out, in front of/behind, up/down, on/off, open/closed, over/under **Sequencing-**alphabetical order -simple story **Shapes-**oval **Size concepts-**big/little, large/small **Writing-***Kk, Cc, Ff, Hh, Oo, Gg, Jj, Vv, Ww, Uu, Yy, Zz, Qq, and Xx*	**Phonics-**recognize the short vowel sounds -recognize all initial consonant sounds -recognize long *a, e, i, o,* and *u* sounds -silent *e* -initial consonant digraphs: *sh, ch,* both soft and hard *th* -final consonant sounds: *_b, _ck, _k, _l* **Word recognition-**color words, number words & shape words **Writing-**name -complete alphabet, capital and small letters -all color words -number words: *one, two, three, four, five, six* -shape words: *circle, square, triangle*	**Phonics-**recognize the long vowel sounds -initial consonant diagraphs: *wh;* review *ch, sh, th* -recognize all final consonant sounds: **Stories and poems-**create, tell, and recite stories and poems **Word recognition-** position/direction words: *up/down, high/low, in, inside, out, outside, top/bottom* -number words: *seven, eight, nine, ten* -shape words: *rectangle, oval, star* **Writing-**number words: *seven, eight, nine, ten* -shape words: *rectangle, oval, star* -position/direction words: *up/down, high/low, in, inside, out, outside, top/bottom*

	Grade 1	Grade 2	Grade 3
LIFEPAC 1	FUN WITH PHONICS • Short vowel sounds • Consonants • Main ideas • Rhyming words	KNOW YOUR NOUNS • Review vowels & consonants • Beginning, middle, ending sounds • Singular & plural nouns • Common & proper nouns	OLD AND NEW SKILLS • Vowels • Consonants • Sentence phrases • Capital letters • Reading skills
LIFEPAC 2	FUN WITH PHONICS • Kinds of sentences • Cardinal & ordinal numbers • Suffixes • Plurals • Classifying	ACTION VERBS • Vowel digraphs • Action words – verbs • Following directions • The dictionary • ABC order	BUILDING WORDS • SENTENCES • Vowels – long, short • Questions • ABC order • Capital letters
LIFEPAC 3	FUN WITH PHONICS • Consonant digraphs • Compounds • Syllables • Possessives • Contractions • Soft c and g	SIMPLE SENTENCES • r-controlled vowels • Consonant blends • Using capital letters • Subjects & verbs in sentences	WORDS • GETTING TO THE ROOTS • Root words • Dictionary guide words • Synonyms • Antonyms • Capital letters
LIFEPAC 4	FUN WITH PHONICS • Paragraphs • Silent letters • Sequencing • Subject-verb agreement	TYPES OF SENTENCES • Consonant digraphs • Statement, question, exclamation sentences • Using capital letters • The library	WORDS • HOW TO USE THEM • Noun • Verb • Adjective • Adverb • Irregular vowels • Composition
LIFEPAC 5	FUN WITH PHONICS • Long vowels • Homonyms • Poetry • Syllables • Possessives • Contractions • Plurals • Suffixes	USING PUNCTUATION • Diphthongs • Punctuation review • Using a comma • Rules for making words plural • Writing a biography • Contractions	SENTENCE • START TO FINISH • Main idea • Capital letters and punctuation • Paragraphs • Making words plural
LIFEPAC 6	FUN WITH PHONICS • R-controlled vowels • Writing stories • Pronouns • Following directions	ADJECTIVES • Rhyming words • Biblical poetry • Adjectives in sentences • Synonyms, antonyms • Thesaurus • Comparative, superlative adjectives	ALL ABOUT BOOKS • Main idea • Books • Stories • Poems • Critical thinking
LIFEPAC 7	FUN WITH PHONICS • Vowel digraphs • Letters - business, friendly, invitations • Syllables	POSSESSIVE NOUNS • Introduction to letter writing • Pronunciation key • Possessive nouns • Silent consonants • Homonyms	READING AND WRITING • For directions • Friendly letters • Pronouns • Fact • Fiction
LIFEPAC 8	FUN WITH PHONICS • Vowel digraphs • Subject-verb agreement • Compounds • Contractions • Possessives • Pronouns	PRONOUNS • Author's intent & use of titles • Predicting content • Suffixes • Character, setting, & plot • Analogies • Writing in cursive	READING SKILLS • For sequence • For detail • Verbs - being, compound • Drama
LIFEPAC 9	FUN WITH PHONICS • Vowel digraphs • Titles • Main ideas • Sentences • Paragraphs • Proper nouns	VERB TYPES AND TENSES • Review action verbs • Dividing words into syllables • State of being verbs • Past & present verb tenses	MORE READING & WRITING • For information • Thank you letters • Book reports • Reference books
LIFEPAC 10	LOOKING BACK • Letters and sounds • Contractions • Plurals • Possessives • Sentences • Stories	LOOKING BACK • Nouns & verbs • Word division • Consonant blends, digraphs • Prefixes, suffixes, root words • Possessives • Pronouns, adjectives	LOOKING BACK • Reading for comprehension • Sentence punctuation • Writing letters • Parts of Speech

	Grade 4	Grade 5	Grade 6
LIFEPAC 1	WRITTEN COMMUNICATION • Word derivations • Story sequence • Writing an outline • Writing a report	STORY MESSAGES • Main idea • Plot • Character • Setting • Dialogue • Diphthong • Digraph	READING FOR A PURPOSE • Critical thinking • Research data • Parables • Synonyms
LIFEPAC 2	SOUNDS TO WORDS • Hard and soft – c and g • Parts of dictionary • Accented syllables • Haiku Poetry	MAIN IDEAS • Poetry • Story • Synonyms • Compounds • Topic sentence • Adjectives • Nouns	FORMING NEW WORDS • Prefixes • Suffixes • Synonyms • Antonyms • Adjectives • Adverbs • Critical thinking
LIFEPAC 3	WORDS • HOW TO USE THEM • Prefixes • Suffixes • Homonyms • Antonyms • Poetry • Stories • Writing an outline	WORDS TO STORIES • Subject • Predicate • Adverbs • Idioms • Critical thinking • Writing a short story	BETTER READING • Story elements • Author's purpose • Information sources • Outline
LIFEPAC 4	MORE WORDS • HOW TO USE THEM • Parts of speech • Possession • Written directions • Verb tenses	WRITTEN REPORT • Outline • Four types of sentences • Metaphor • Simile • Writing the report	SENTENCES • Capitals • Punctuation • Four types of sentences • Author's purpose • Propaganda
LIFEPAC 5	WRITING FOR CLARITY • Figures of speech • Capital letters • Punctuation marks • Writing stories	STORY ELEMENTS • Legend • Implied meaning • Dialogue and quotations • Word order and usage • Story elements • Implied meaning	READING SKILLS • Following directions • Literary forms • Phrases • Nouns • Verbs • Paragraph structure
LIFEPAC 6	FUN WITH FICTION • Book reports • Fiction • Nonfiction • Parables • Fables • Poetry	POETRY • Rhythm • Symbolism • Personification • Irregular plurals • Stanza	POETRY • Similes • Metaphors • Alliteration • Homonyms • Palindromes • Acronyms • Figures of speech
LIFEPAC 7	FACT AND FICTION • Nouns • Verbs • Contractions • Biography • Fables • Tall Tales	WORD USAGE • Nouns - common, plural, possessive • Fact • Opinion • Story • Main idea	STORIES • Story elements • Nouns • Pronouns • Vowel digraphs • Business letter
LIFEPAC 8	GRAMMAR AND WRITING • Adjectives to compare • Adverbs • Figurative language • Paragraphs	ALL ABOUT VERBS • Tense • Action • Participles • Of being • Regular • Irregular • Singular • Plural	NEWSPAPERS • Propaganda • News stories • Verbs – auxiliary, tenses • Adverbs
LIFEPAC 9	THE WRITTEN REPORT • Planning a report • Finding information • Outline • Writing a report	READING FLUENCY • Speed reading • Graphic aids • Study skills • Literary forms	READING THE BIBLE • Parables • Proverbs • Hebrew - poetry, prophecy • Bible history • Old Testament law
LIFEPAC 10	LOOKING BACK • Reading skills • Nouns • Adverbs • Written communication • Literary forms	LOOKING BACK • Literary forms • Parts of speech • Writing skills • Study skills	LOOKING BACK • Literary forms • Writing letters • Parts of speech • Punctuation

	Grade 7	Grade 8	Grade 9
LIFEPAC 1	WORD USAGE • Nouns – proper, common • Pronouns • Prefixes • Suffixes • Synonyms • Antonyms	IMPROVE COMMUNICATION • Roots • Inflections • Affixes • Interjections • Directions – oral, written • Non-verbal communication	STRUCTURE OF LANGUAGE • Nouns • Adjectives • Verbs • Prepositions • Adverbs • Conjunctions • Sentence parts
LIFEPAC 2	MORE WORD USAGE • Speech – stress, pitch • Verbs – tenses • Principle parts • Story telling	ALL ABOUT ENGLISH • Origin of language • Classification– nouns, pronouns, verbs, adjectives, adverbs	NATURE OF LANGUAGE • Origin of language • Use – oral and written • Dictionary • Writing a paper
LIFEPAC 3	BIOGRAPHIES • Biography as a form • Flashback technique • Deductive reasoning • Words – base, root	PUNCTUATION AND WRITING • Connecting and interrupting • The Essay • Thesis Statement	PRACTICAL ENGLISH • Dictionary use • Mnemonics • Writing a paper • Five minute speech
LIFEPAC 4	LANGUAGE STRUCTURE • Verbs – tenses • Principle parts • Sentence creativity • Speech – pitch, accent	WORDS • HOW TO USE THEM • Dictionary • Thesaurus • Accent • Diacritical mark • Standard • Nonstandard	SHORT STORY FUNDAMENTALS • Plot • Setting • Characterization • Conflict • Symbolism
LIFEPAC 5	NATURE OF ENGLISH • Formal • Informal • Redundant expressions • Verb tenses • Subject–verb agreement	CORRECT LANGUAGE • Using good form • Synonyms • Antonyms • Homonyms • Good speaking qualities	LANGUAGE IN LITERATURE • Collective Nouns • Verbs • Use of comparisons • Gerunds • Participles • Literary genres
LIFEPAC 6	MECHANICS OF ENGLISH • Punctuation • Complements • Modifiers • Clauses – subordinate, coordinate	LANGUAGE AND LITERATURE • History of English • Coordination and subordination • Autobiography	STRUCTURE AND MEANING IN LITERATURE • Reading for purpose • Reading for meaning • Reading persuasion • Understanding poetry
LIFEPAC 7	THE NOVEL • The Hiding Place • Sequence of events • Author's purpose • Character sketch	CRITICAL THINKING • Word evaluation • The Paragraph – structure, coherence, introductory, concluding	COMMUNICATION • Planning a speech • Listening comprehension • Letters – business, informal, social
LIFEPAC 8	LITERATURE • Nonfiction • Listening skills • Commas • Semicolons • Nonverbal communications	WRITE • LISTEN • READ • Business letters • Personal letters • Four steps to listen • Nonfiction	LIBRARY AND DRAMA • Library resources • Drama – history, elements, reading • The Miracle Worker
LIFEPAC 9	COMPOSITIONS • Sentence types • Quality of paragraph • Pronunciation • Nonsense literature	SPEAK AND WRITE • Etymology • Modifiers • Person • Number • Tense • Oral report	STUDIES IN THE NOVEL • History • Define • Write • Critical essay • Twenty Thousand Leagues Under the Sea
LIFEPAC 10	LOOKING BACK • Parts of speech • Sentence structure • Punctuation • How to communicate	LOOKING BACK • Composition structure • Parts of speech • Critical thinking • Literary forms	LOOKING BACK • Communication – writing speaking, listening • Using resources • Literature review

	Grade 10	Grade 11	Grade 12
LIFEPAC 1	EVOLUTION OF ENGLISH • Historical development • Varieties of English • Substandard & standard • Changes in English	STANDARD ENGLISH • Need for standard English • Guardians of the standard • Dictionaries • Types of standard English text	THE WORTH OF WORDS • Word categories • Expository writing • Sentence structure • Diction
LIFEPAC 2	LISTENING AND SPEAKING • Noun plurals • Suffixes • Creating a speech • Nature of listening	EFFECTIVE SENTENCES • Subordinate – clauses, conjunctions • Relative pronouns • Verbals • Appositives	STRUCTURE OF LANGUAGE • Parts of speech • Sentence structure • Subordinate phrases • Subordinate clauses
LIFEPAC 3	EFFECTIVE SENTENCES • Participles • Infinitives • Prepositions • Gerunds • Sentences – simple, compound, complex	SENTENCE WORKSHOP • Understanding pronouns • Using pronouns correctly • Using modifiers correctly • Parallel sentence structure	READ, RESEARCH, LISTEN • Reading skills • Resources for research • Taking notes • Drawing conclusions
LIFEPAC 4	POWER OF WORDS • Etymology • Connotations • Poetic devices • Poetry – literal, figurative, symbolic	WHY STUDY READING? • Greek and Latin roots • Diacritical markings • Finding the main idea • Analyzing a textbook	GIFT OF LANGUAGE • Origin–Biblical, • Koine Greek • Purpose of Grammar • Semantics
LIFEPAC 5	ELEMENTS OF COMPOSITION • Paragraphs • Connectives • Transitions • Expository writing – elements, ideas	POETRY • Metrical feet • Sets • Musical effects • Universality • Imagery • Connotation	ENGLISH LITERATURE • Early England • Medieval England • Fourteenth century • Chaucer
LIFEPAC 6	STRUCTURE AND READING • Subordinate clauses • Pronouns – gender, case, agreement • Reading for recognition	NONFICTION • Elements • Types – essays, diaries, newspaper, biography • Composition	ELIZABETHAN LITERATURE • Poetry • Prose • Drama • Essay
LIFEPAC 7	ORAL READING AND DRAMA • Skills of oral reading • Drama – history, irony elements, allegory • Everyman	AMERICAN DRAMA • Development • History • Structure • Purpose • Our Town	17TH—18TH CENTURY LITERATURE • Historical background • Puritan literature • Common sense – satire • Sensibility
LIFEPAC 8	THE SHORT STORY • Elements • Enjoying • Writing • The Literary Critique	AMERICAN NOVEL • Eighteenth, nineteenth twentieth century • The Old Man and the Sea • The Critical Essay	WRITING • SHORT STORY, POETRY • Fundamentals • Inspiration • Technique and style • Form and process
LIFEPAC 9	THE NOVEL • Elements • In His Steps • The Critical Essay • The Book Review	COMPOSITION • Stating the thesis • Research • Outline • Writing the paper	POETRY • ROMANTIC , VICTORIAN • Wordsworth • Coleridge • Gordon • Byron • Shelley • Keats • Tennyson • Hopkins • Robert and Elizabeth B Browning
LIFEPAC 10	LOOKING BACK • Writing skills • Speech skills • Poetry • Drama • Short stories • Novel	LOOKING BACK • Analyzing written word • Effective sentences • Expository prose • Genres of American literature	LOOKING BACK • Creative writing • English literature – Medieval to Victorian

LIFEPAC

MANAGEMENT

STRUCTURE OF THE LIFEPAC CURRICULUM

The LIFEPAC curriculum is conveniently structured to provide one teacher's guide containing teacher support material with answer keys and ten student worktexts for each subject at grade levels two through twelve. The worktext format of the LIFEPACs allows the student to read the textual information and complete workbook activities all in the same booklet. The easy to follow LIFEPAC numbering system lists the grade as the first number(s) and the last two digits as the number of the series. For example, the Language Arts LIFEPAC at the 6th grade level, 5th book in the series would be LAN0605.

Each LIFEPAC is divided into 3 to 5 sections and begins with an introduction or overview of the booklet as well as a series of specific learning objectives to give a purpose to the study of the LIFEPAC. The introduction and objectives are followed by a vocabulary section which may be found at the beginning of each section at the lower levels, at the beginning of the LIFEPAC in the middle grades, or in the glossary at the high school level. Vocabulary words are used to develop word recognition and should not be confused with the spelling words introduced later in the LIFEPAC. The student should learn all vocabulary words before working the LIFEPAC sections to improve comprehension, retention, and reading skills.

Each activity or written assignment has a number for easy identification, such as 1.1. The first number corresponds to the LIFEPAC section and the number to the right of the decimal is the number of the activity.

Teacher checkpoints, which are essential to maintain quality learning, are found at various locations throughout the LIFEPAC. The teacher should check 1) neatness of work and penmanship, 2) quality of understanding (tested with a short oral quiz), 3) thoroughness of answers (complete sentences and paragraphs, correct spelling, etc.), 4) completion of activities (no blank spaces), and 5) accuracy of answers as compared to the answer key (all answers correct).

The self test questions are also number coded for easy reference. For example, 2.015 means that this is the 15th question in the self test of Section II. The first number corresponds to the LIFEPAC section, the zero indicates that it is a self test question, and the number to the right of the zero the question number.

The LIFEPAC test is packaged at the centerfold of each LIFEPAC. It should be removed and put aside before giving the booklet to the student for study.

Answer and test keys have the same numbering system as the LIFEPACs and appear at the back of this handbook. The student may be given access to the answer keys (not the test keys) under teacher supervision so that he can score his own work.

A thorough study of the Curriculum Overview by the teacher before instruction begins is essential to the success of the student. The teacher should become familiar with expected skill mastery and understand how these grade level skills fit into the overall skill development of the curriculum. The teacher should also preview the objectives that appear at the beginning of each LIFEPAC for additional preparation and planning.

TEST SCORING and GRADING

Answer keys and test keys give examples of correct answers. They convey the idea, but the student may use many ways to express a correct answer. The teacher should check for the essence of the answer, not for the exact wording. Many questions are high level and require thinking and creativity on the part of the student. Each answer should be scored based on whether or not the main idea written by the student matches the model example. "Any Order" or "Either Order" in a key indicates that no particular order is necessary to be correct.

Most self tests and LIFEPAC tests at the lower elementary levels are scored at 1 point per answer; however, the upper levels may have a point system awarding 2 to 5 points for various answers or questions. Further, the total test points will vary; they may not always equal 100 points. They may be 78, 85, 100, 105, etc.

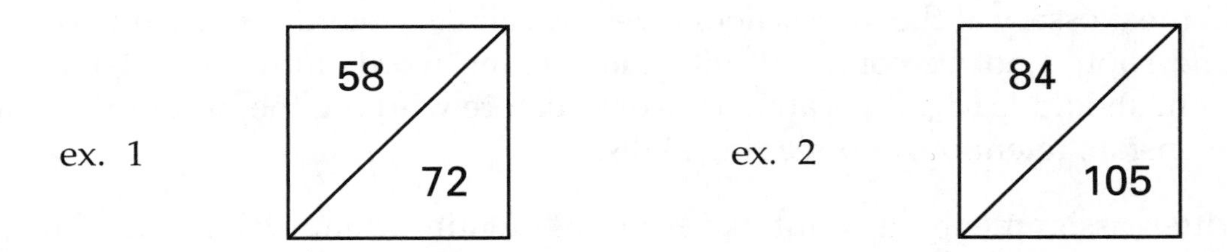

A score box similar to ex.1 above is located at the end of each self test and on the front of the LIFEPAC test. The bottom score, 72, represents the total number of points possible on the test. The upper score, 58, represents the number of points your student will need to receive an 80% or passing grade. If you wish to establish the exact percentage that your student has achieved, find the total points of his correct answers and divide it by the bottom number (in this case 72.) For example, if your student has a point total of 65, divide 65 by 72 for a grade of 90%. Referring to ex. 2, on a test with a total of 105 possible points, the student would have to receive a minimum of 84 correct points for an 80% or passing grade. If your student has received 93 points, simply divide the 93 by 105 for a percentage grade of 89%. Students who receive a score below 80% should review the LIFEPAC and retest using the appropriate Alternate Test found in the Teacher's Guide.

The following is a guideline to assign letter grades for completed LIFEPACs based on a maximum total score of 100 points.

LIFEPAC Test	=	60% of the Total Score (or percent grade)
Self Test	=	25% of the Total Score (average percent of self tests)
Reports	=	10% or 10* points per LIFEPAC
Oral Work	=	5% or 5* points per LIFEPAC

*Determined by the teacher's subjective evaluation of the student's daily work.

Example:

LIFEPAC Test Score	=	92%	92 x .60	=	55 points
Self Test Average	=	90%	90 x .25	=	23 points
Reports				=	8 points
Oral Work				=	4 points
TOTAL POINTS				=	90 points

Grade Scale based on point system:

100	–	94	=	A
93	–	86	=	B
85	–	77	=	C
76	–	70	=	D
Below		70	=	F

TEACHER HINTS and STUDYING TECHNIQUES

LIFEPAC Activities are written to check the level of understanding of the preceding text. The student may look back to the text as necessary to complete these activities; however, a student should never attempt to do the activities without reading (studying) the text first. Self tests and LIFEPAC tests are never open book tests.

Language arts activities (skill integration) often appear within other subject curriculum. The purpose is to give the student an opportunity to test his skill mastery outside of the context in which it was presented.

Writing complete answers (paragraphs) to some questions is an integral part of the LIFEPAC Curriculum in all subjects. This builds communication and organization skills, increases understanding and retention of ideas, and helps enforce good penmanship. Complete sentences should be encouraged for this type of activity. Obviously, single words or phrases do not meet the intent of the activity, since multiple lines are given for the response.

Review is essential to student success. Time invested in review where review is suggested will be time saved in correcting errors later. Self tests, unlike the section activities, are closed book. This procedure helps to identify weaknesses before they become too great to overcome. Certain objectives from self tests are cumulative and test previous sections; therefore, good preparation for a self test must include all material studied up to that testing point.

The following procedure checklist has been found to be successful in developing good study habits in the LIFEPAC curriculum.

1. Read the introduction and Table of Contents.
2. Read the objectives.
3. Recite and study the entire vocabulary (glossary) list.
4. Study each section as follows:
    a. Read the introduction and study the section objectives.
    b. Read all the text for the entire section, but answer none of the activities.
    c. Return to the beginning of the section and memorize each vocabulary word and definition.
    d. Reread the section, complete the activities, check the answers with the answer key, correct all errors, and have the teacher check.
    e. Read the self test but do not answer the questions.
    f. Go to the beginning of the first section and reread the text and answers to the activities up to the self test you have not yet done.
    g. Answer the questions to the self test without looking back.
    h. Have the self test checked by the teacher.
    i. Correct the self test and have the teacher check the corrections.
    j. Repeat steps a–i for each section.

5. Use the SQ3R* method to prepare for the LIFEPAC test.
6. Take the LIFEPAC test as a closed book test.
7. LIFEPAC tests are administered and scored under direct teacher supervision. Students who receive scores below 80% should review the LIFEPAC using the SQ3R* study method and take the Alternate Test located in the Teacher Handbook. The final test grade may be the grade on the Alternate Test or an average of the grades from the original LIFEPAC test and the Alternate Test.

   *SQ3R: **S**can the whole LIFEPAC.
   Question yourself on the objectives.
   Read the whole LIFEPAC again.
   Recite through an oral examination.
   Review weak areas.

GOAL SETTING and SCHEDULES

Each school must develop its own schedule, because no single set of procedures will fit every situation. The following is an example of a daily schedule that includes the five LIFEPAC subjects as well as time slotted for special activities.

Possible Daily Schedule

8:15	–	8:25	Pledges, prayer, songs, devotions, etc.
8:25	–	9:10	Bible
9:10	–	9:55	Language Arts
9:55	–	10:15	Recess (juice break)
10:15	–	11:00	Mathematics
11:00	–	11:45	Social Studies
11:45	–	12:30	Lunch, recess, quiet time
12:30	–	1:15	Science
1:15	–		Drill, remedial work, enrichment*

*Enrichment: Computer time, physical education, field trips, fun reading, games and puzzles, family business, hobbies, resource persons, guests, crafts, creative work, electives, music appreciation, projects.

Basically, two factors need to be considered when assigning work to a student in the LIFEPAC curriculum.

The first is time. An average of 45 minutes should be devoted to each subject, each day. Remember, this is only an average. Because of extenuating circumstances a student may spend only 15 minutes on a subject one day and the next day spend 90 minutes on the same subject.

The second factor is the number of pages to be worked in each subject. A single LIFEPAC is designed to take 3 to 4 weeks to complete. Allowing about 3-4 days for LIFEPAC introduction, review, and tests, the student has approximately 15 days to complete the LIFEPAC pages. Simply take the number of pages in the LIFEPAC, divide it by 15 and you will have the number of pages that must be completed on a daily basis to keep the student on schedule. For example, a LIFEPAC containing 45 pages will require 3 completed pages per day. Again, this is only an average. While working a 45 page LIFEPAC, the student may complete only 1 page the first day if the text has a lot of activities or reports, but go on to complete 5 pages the next day.

Long range planning requires some organization. Because the traditional school year originates in the early fall of one year and continues to late spring of the following year, a calendar should be devised that covers this period of time. Approximate beginning and completion dates can be noted on the calendar as well as special occasions such as holidays, vacations and birthdays. Since each LIFEPAC takes 3-4 weeks or eighteen days to complete, it should take about 180 school days to finish a set of ten LIFEPACs. Starting at the beginning school date, mark off eighteen school days on the calendar and that will become the targeted completion date for the first LIFEPAC. Continue marking the calendar until you have established dates for the remaining nine LIFEPACs making adjustments for previously noted holidays and vacations. If all five subjects are being used, the ten established target dates should be the same for the LIFEPACs in each subject.

FORMS

The sample weekly lesson plan and student grading sheet forms are included in this section as teacher support materials and may be duplicated at the convenience of the teacher.

The student grading sheet is provided for those who desire to follow the suggested guidelines for assignment of letter grades found on page 3 of this section. The student's self test scores should be posted as percentage grades. When the LIFEPAC is completed the teacher should average the self test grades, multiply the average by .25 and post the points in the box marked self test points. The LIFEPAC percentage grade should be multiplied by .60 and posted. Next, the teacher should award and post points for written reports and oral work. A report may be any type of written work assigned to the student whether it is a LIFEPAC or additional learning activity. Oral work includes the student's ability to respond orally to questions which may or may not be related to LIFEPAC activities or any type of oral report assigned by the teacher. The points may then be totaled and a final grade entered along with the date that the LIFEPAC was completed.

The Student Record Book which was specifically designed for use with the Alpha Omega curriculum provides space to record weekly progress for one student over a nine week period as well as a place to post self test and LIFEPAC scores. The Student Record Books are available through the current Alpha Omega catalog; however, unlike the enclosed forms these books are not for duplication and should be purchased in sets of four to cover a full academic year.

Reproducible page.

WEEKLY LESSON PLANNER

Week of:

Subject	Subject	Subject	Subject
Monday			
Subject	Subject	Subject	Subject
Tuesday			
Subject	Subject	Subject	Subject
Wednesday			
Subject	Subject	Subject	Subject
Thursday			
Subject	Subject	Subject	Subject
Friday			

WEEKLY LESSON PLANNER

Week of:

	Subject	Subject	Subject	Subject
Monday				
	Subject	Subject	Subject	Subject
Tuesday				
	Subject	Subject	Subject	Subject
Wednesday				
	Subject	Subject	Subject	Subject
Thursday				
	Subject	Subject	Subject	Subject
Friday				

Student Name ______________________ Year ____________

Bible

LP #	Self Test Scores by Sections 1	2	3	4	5	Self Test Points	LIFEPAC Test	Oral Points	Report Points	Final Grade	Date
01											
02											
03											
04											
05											
06											
07											
08											
09											
10											

History & Geography

LP #	Self Test Scores by Sections 1	2	3	4	5	Self Test Points	LIFEPAC Test	Oral Points	Report Points	Final Grade	Date
01											
02											
03											
04											
05											
06											
07											
08											
09											
10											

Language Arts

LP #	Self Test Scores by Sections 1	2	3	4	5	Self Test Points	LIFEPAC Test	Oral Points	Report Points	Final Grade	Date
01											
02											
03											
04											
05											
06											
07											
08											
09											
10											

Student Name ______________________ Year ____________

Mathematics

LP #	Self Test Scores by Sections 1	2	3	4	5	Self Test Points	LIFEPAC Test	Oral Points	Report Points	Final Grade	Date
01											
02											
03											
04											
05											
06											
07											
08											
09											
10											

Science

LP #	Self Test Scores by Sections 1	2	3	4	5	Self Test Points	LIFEPAC Test	Oral Points	Report Points	Final Grade	Date
01											
02											
03											
04											
05											
06											
07											
08											
09											
10											

Spelling/Electives

LP #	Self Test Scores by Sections 1	2	3	4	5	Self Test Points	LIFEPAC Test	Oral Points	Report Points	Final Grade	Date
01											
02											
03											
04											
05											
06											
07											
08											
09											
10											

TEACHER

NOTES

LANGUAGE ARTS

Teacher Notes

Concepts

Phonics/Spelling/Syllable Rules

Teaching Pages

INSTRUCTIONS FOR FIRST GRADE LANGUAGE ARTS

The first grade handbooks of the LIFEPAC curriculum are designed to provide a step-by step procedure that will help the teacher prepare for and present each lesson effectively. In the early LIFEPACs the teacher should read the directions and any other sentences to the children. However, as the school year progresses, the student should be encouraged to begin reading and following his own instructional material in preparation for the independent study approach that begins at the second grade level.

Language Arts includes those subjects that develop the student's communication skills. The LIFEPAC approach to combining reading, spelling, penmanship, composition, grammar, speech and literature in a single unit allows the teacher to integrate the study of these various language arts subject areas. The variety and scope of the curriculum may make it difficult for students to complete the required material within the suggested daily scheduled time of forty-five minutes. Spelling, reading and various forms of composition may need to be completed during the afternoon enrichment period.

This section of the teacher's guide includes the following teacher aids: 1) Index of Concepts 2) Phonics/Spelling/Syllable Guidelines 3) Teacher Instruction Pages.

The Index of Concepts is a quick reference guide for the teacher who may be looking for a rule or explanation that applies to a particular concept. It does not identify each use of the concept in the various LIFEPACs. The Phonics/Spelling/Syllable Guidelines are another convenient reference guide.

The Teacher Instruction Pages list the Concept to be taught as well as Student Objectives and Goals for the Teacher. Sight words are words that either are needed before their phonetic presentation or do not follow the standard phonetic rules. The Vocabulary Lists are made up of sight words that are needed by the student for better understanding of the subject content. These words need to be learned through memorization and children should be drilled on them frequently. The Teaching Page contains directions for teaching that page. Worksheet pages contained in some lessons follow this section and may be duplicated for individual student use. The Activities section at the end of each lesson is optional and may be used to reinforce or expand the concepts taught.

Materials needed are usually items such as pencils and crayons which are readily available. Additional items that may be required are Alphabet-Penmanship Charts (purchased through the catalog), alphabet cards, color and number charts, and flash cards for vocabulary words, and writing tablets (reproducible writing line pages are provided on pages 10, 20, and 375-378 if you would like to create your own writing tablet) or you may substitue a writing tablet with any lined paper.

Five Readers are necessary for the first grade Language Arts curriculum. Each Reader gives the student an opportunity to practice concepts that have been taught in the LIFEPAC in which it appears as well as the one that precedes it. For example, Reader 1 is used for both LIFEPACs 101 and 102. Before the stories in each of the readers is a list of 'Instant Words' which may need to be introduced to the student as sight words. Readers are an effective tool to develop the student's reading vocabulary and when they are no longer directly associated with a lesson may be used throughout the school year for independent reading purposes.

The Spelling Words are on the self test and LIFEPAC test Teacher Instruction Pages in the Teacher's Guide and may be written by the student on writing tablet pages. Unlike the upper grade levels, there are no spelling lists for the student to study. Instead, the spelling tests, for both self tests and LIFEPAC tests, are designed to test the student's auditory phonics. The teacher should stress the sound of the word when administering the test. A student who spells the word *sat* as *sad* has not learned to discriminate between the phonetic sounds of *t* and *d* and should receive further drill on these sounds. Words such as *road* and *rode* should be presented to the student in sentences. A misspelled word suggests the teacher should review the concepts of vowel digraph *oa*, silent *e* and homonyms with the student.

Concept	LIFEPAC	Section
Abbreviations and Titles	109	3
Alphabetical Order	108	1
Composition		
letters - invitation, business, friendly	107	3
paragraph definition	108	2
writing a report	109	2
writing a story	103	2
Compound words	103	3
Contractions	103	1
Following Directions		
oral and written	102	1
Homonyms	105	1
	106	2
	107	3
Introductions	108	2
Oral Expression		
discussion boxes	108	3
tell a story rules	102	3
Phonics		
c - soft	103	2
consonants	101	all
consonant blends	104	1,2
	106	2
	108	2,3
consonant digraphs	103	1
consonants - silent	101	2
	104	2
consonants - special blends	104	2
g-soft	103	3
letter groups - gh,ph,igh	104	2
	105	1
r-controlled vowels	106	1
vowels - long	105	1,2
	107	all
vowels - short	101	all
vowel digraphs	105	1
	107	1
	108	1,3
	109	1,2
y as long i and e	105	1
Parts of Speech		
nouns	107	3
pronouns	106	3
verbs		
forms	102	3
	107	2
definition	107	3
tense	104	1
	108	2
Plurals	102	1
	103	1,3
Poetry	105	1
	109	1
Possessives	103	2
Sentences		
definition	108	2
quotations	106	1
types		
exclamation	102	3
question	102	2
statement	102	1
Suffixes	102	3
	105	3
Syllables	103	3
Telephone Use	106	2
	108	2

Reader	LIFEPAC	Page in LP
Reader 1 *Dog in the Tub*		
A Map	101	2
The Sun	101	15
Dog in the Tub	101	29
Dad	101	30
Wet	101	31
	102	5
Getting Dressed To Go Out in the Rain	102	2
Sis	102	6
My Bible	102	7
What Is In The Pot?	102	8
My Rag Doll	102	10
Tom	102	11
A Very Big Mess	102	14
Our Pet	102	15
Jesus	102	16
Run	102	17
Little Red Fox	102	18
Bzz	102	21
Mom	102	22
The Big Fat Hen	102	24
Tim Kicks	102	25
Ball Fun	102	26
Fast Jim	102	27
Little Black Ants	102	30
Bug	102	31
Reader 2 *Cotton Candy*		
The Red Ball	103	2
The Mess	103	4
Three Missing Pups	103	7
Clickety Clack	103	9
The Twins Fix Lunch	103	12
Fun!	103	14
The New Little Bug	103	19
Pets	103	21
The Cowboy	103	26
Betty the Bat	103	27
Black and White Keys	103	31
A Big Problem	104	2
The Pup and the Box	104	7
Pigs	104	13
Fish, Fish, Fish	104	16
Ann and the Fish	104	18
Little Lamb	104	20
Glad Tammy	104	22
Cotton Candy	104	23
The Last Trick	104	24
The Lemonade Stand	104	26
I Talk to God	104	29
Stuck Again	104	31
The Gift	104	33
Reader 3 *Oats Are For Goats*		
Kelly's Daisies	105	2
Nonsense Poem	105	3
I Don't Know About Snow	105	6
The Tree Fort	105	7
Mike's Light Bites	105	11
A Tale of a Tail	105	12
Adam and Eve	105	14
Oats Are For Goats	105	15
Clean Machine	105	16
The Ball Game	105	18
Just Like Jesus	105	28
Jack's Table	105	29
Lion Fun	106	2
Rose's Rose	106	6
Working	106	7
The Cross	106	12
Fun with Words	106	13
That Buzzing Sound	106	16
I Like Stripes	106	17
Big Blue	106	20
Jesus Prays	106	25
A Sea Horse is a Fish	106	27
My Little Black Pony	106	28
A Sea Horse is Not a Race Horse	106	29

Reader	LIFEPAC	Page in LP
Reader 4 *Flying My Kite*		
Sisters	107	2
Waiting For Grandma	107	2
Julie's Painting	107	3
Sheep	107	4
Steven and Taylor	107	5
What Do You Want To Be?	107	8
Surprise! Surprise!	107	9 & 10
Casey's First Lesson	107	10
The Pet Show	107	17 & 18
Going to Florida	107	18
Flying My Kite	107	22
The Lazy Little Train	107	31
No More Alligator Fear	108	5
Friends	108	6
A Little About Alligators	108	7
Joan's New School	108	14
The Bee Chase	108	16
Baby Zebra	108	21
Playing	108	24
Busy Bees	108	26
Leaves	108	28
The Quilt	108	29
I Am Always With You	108	30
Snow	108	32
Reader 5 *The Gold Coin*		
Bobo, the Clown	109	3 & 4
Snoopers	109	4
My Gift	109	6
Thank You, God	109	7
Building a Town	109	12 & 13
The Gold Coin	109	14
The Pony Show	109	15
Nurse Jane	109	15
Tornado	109	16
Old, Old Goat	109	24
Animals	109	27
Playmates of the Sea	109	28
Building Rockets	109	30
God is our Rock	110	5
The Old Red Barn	110	6
Joseph's Dream	110	7
Cory's Kitten	110	8
The Kitten Gets a Name	110	9
Clouds	110	10
Dolphin	110	17
My Father and Mother	110	18
Little Garden	110	21
The Wait	110	24
What is Tall?	110	29

This listing is for those instructors who would like to reference the Teaching Page for each one of the stories. For example, the activities for *Ball Fun* are in the Teacher Notes for Page 26 of LIFEPAC 102.

PHONICS for Language Arts 100

The following letter and letter combinations are introduced in Language Arts 100. They may be put on cards for drilling purposes.

a e i o u

b c d f g h j k l m n p q r s t v w x y z

th wh sh ch, ng nk, ck mb lk gn kn gh

ar er ir or ur, ai ay, au aw, ei ey, ea ee, ie

oa, oo, ew, ou, ow, oi, oy

gh ph, igh

				Teacher Notes
1.	short vowels	-	a (bat) e (bet) i (bit) o (cot) u (but)	101
2.	long vowels	-	a (bait) e (beat) i (bite) o (coat) u (use)	105
3.	consonants	-	b d f h j k l m n p r s t v w x z	101
4.	c and g	-	hard sound before a, o, u 101	
		-	soft sound before e, i	103
5.	q (qu)	-	always has the sound of kw	101
6.	y	-	as y (yard) 101	
		-	as e (baby) 105	
		-	as i (cry)	105
7.	consonant digraphs	-	th, wh, sh, ch	103
8.	special blends	-	ng (sing) nk (sank)	104
9.	silent consonants	-	ck (lock)	101
		-	mb (lamb) lk (talk) gn (sign)	104
		-	kn (know) gh (though) t (often)	104
10.	r-controlled vowels	-	ar (car) or (for)	106
		-	er (her) ir (sir) ur (fur)	106
11.	vowel digraphs	-	ai, ay as long a (pail) (pay)	107
		-	au, aw (Paul) (paw)	107
		-	ei, ey as long a (veil) (they)	105
				107
		-	ea, ee as long e (beat) (feet)	107
		-	ie as long e (piece)	107
		-	as long i (pie)	107
		-	oa as long o (boat)	108
		-	oo long sound (boot)	108
			short sound (book)	108
		-	ew as long u (few)	108

		-	ou as long u (soup)	108
				109
		-	as `ow' (cloud)*	109
		-	ow as long o (slow)	108
			as `ow' (clown)*	109
		-	oi, oy (boil) (boy)*	109
12.	letter groups	-	gh ph as f (laugh) (phone)	104
		-	igh as long i (sigh)	105
			*sometimes referred to as diphthongs	

DIRECTION WORD FLASHCARDS for Language Arts 100
Begin constructing a set of direction words flashcards—Circle, Say, Write, Listen, Cut and Paste, etc.—for key words in the activity instructions. Add to this set of direction words as new ones are encountered in the activities.

SPELLING RULES for Language Arts 100

1. Double the final consonant of a short vowel word before adding *er, ed* and *ing,* and drop the final *e i*n long vowel words and some short vowel words before adding *er, ed* and *ing*.(102 p. 32).
2. Even though the sound is the same, some words with the *ch* sound are spelled *tch* (103 p. 6). In *ch* words, if the letter right after the *h* is an *l* or *r,* the *ch* will usually have the sound of *k* as in *Christmas* or *chlorine* (103 p. 6).
3. Words ending in *s, x, sh* or *ch* must have the *es* ending to make them plural (103 p. 30).
4. *Y* is used at the end of short words to make the sound of *i*. *Y* is used at the end of long words (those with two or more syllables) to make the sound of *e*.
5 A word that has a long vowel sound may have a silent *e* at the end of the word (105 p. 10).
6. Because *er, ir, ur* and sometimes *or* all have the same sound, it becomes necessary to remember how the word is spelled (106 p. 9).
7. Words that end in *y,* change the *y* to *i* before adding *es*. Words that end in *f,* change the *f* to *v* before adding *es* (106 p. 18).

THE SYLLABLE RULE for Language Arts 100

There are as many syllables in a word as the number of vowels you can hear (103 p. 27).

Example: boat: One vowel is heard. (*oa* is a vowel digraph)
This is a one-syllable word.

basket: Two vowels are heard - *a* and *e*.
This is a two syllable word.

difference: Three vowels are heard - *i, e, e*.
(The final *e* simply makes the *c* a soft sound.)
This is a three-syllable word.

Page 1: FUN WITH WORDS

CONCEPTS: purpose of LIFEPAC, objectives, writing first name

TEACHER GOALS: To teach the children
To know what is expected of them in the LIFEPAC, and
To write their first names correctly in manuscript.

VOCABULARY: objectives, write, name

TEACHING PAGE 1:

Point to the title and read it. Tell the children that the name of a book is called its title. Have the children follow along as you read. Ask what the title means. Ask what kind of letters are found in the title (all capitals).

Read the three paragraphs one at a time and discuss. Check to see how many children have an idea of what they will learn.

Write the word *OBJECTIVES* on the board. Say it. Have the children repeat it. Have the children find the word on the page.

Explain that objectives tell the things they will be expected to do in the LIFEPAC. Ask them how many objectives are listed for this LIFEPAC. Read each one. Have the children repeat each one as they run their fingers under the sentence from left to right. Talk about each objective so that the children will understand what they will be doing.

Write the direction *Write your name* on the board. Read it to the children. Have them repeat it. Put an icon on the board in front of the direction. Explain to the children that the pencil icon points to work they must do. Have the children find the icon and the direction on the page. Have them read the direction with you.

Have each child write his first name on the line at the bottom of the page. Check the formation of letters and the spelling to determine which children need help.

FUN WITH WORDS

Learning to listen, read, and write
is fun for you.

In this LIFEPAC you will learn
about short vowels.

You will learn about consonants.
You will learn to write the letters of
the alphabet.

Objectives

1. I can listen and follow directions.
2. I can tell the sound of short vowels.
3. I can tell the sound of consonants.
4. I can write the letters of the alphabet.

Write your name.

page 1 (one)

ACTIVITIES:

Have the children practice their names in their writing tablet if they are having difficulty.

I. PART ONE

Page 2: Aa

CONCEPTS: sound of short *a*, telling a story

TEACHER GOALS: To teach the children
To identify things in the picture with the short /a/ sound,
To tell a story about the picture,
To make inferences about what is happening in the picture,
To tell what might happen next in the picture,
To recall details about the picture, and
To write the letter *a*.

BIBLE REFERENCE: Genesis 2:19, 20

VOCABULARY: listen, find, circle, pictures, short

MATERIALS NEEDED: crayons, Worksheet 1, alphabet flash cards, Bible

Alphabet flash cards are cards with the letters of the alphabet on them. They can include picture cues and/or writing guidelines. They can be used individually for letter recognition practice or you can hang them together on a clothesline to spell words for the students to read.

TEACHING PAGE 2:

Write the letters *Aa* on the board. Read them. Have the children repeat them after you and find them on the page.

Read the sentence and have the children repeat it.

Read the Bible verses (Genesis 2:19,20). Emphasize especially the first part "And Adam gave names to all cattle...." Repeat this part slowly and ask the children to repeat all the short *a* words (*And, Adam, cattle*).

Ask the children to look at the picture and find some of the things that Adam might have named (rabbit, cat, butterfly). Ask which of these animals have a short /a/ sound in their name (rabbit, cat). Have them circle these animals.

Ask the children if they can find any other short *a* pictures of things God made (apples, sand, grass). Have them circle these things.

Read the story to the children. Ask them to find other things in the picture that have the short /a/ sound (cap, hat, basket, bat, hand, fan, nap (cat), ladder, "catch"—two girls playing, pants, Sam, branch).

If the children have difficulty finding all of the things, give them some clues.

Have the children choose a part of the picture and tell a story about it. Ask them what might have happened before the action in the picture. Ask them what might happen next.

If, for example, a child chooses the portion with the man sitting under the tree, his story should include what the man is doing (resting, cooling off, using a fan), what the man was doing to make him hot or tired (picking apples), and what the man will do (finishing picking the apples). The child's deductive abilities are tested in this story as well because he must see connections between the ladder, the bushel of apples, the man, and the tree.

Read the second direction.

Name the pictures (cap, hand, lamp, basket).

Have the children write the letter *a* and say the words.

ACTIVITIES:

1. Let the children who are able write or draw their story.
2. Let the children dictate the story to an aide and then illustrate it.
3. Color the picture.
4. Add more short *a* pictures to the picture if they fit.
5. Do Worksheet 1.

Write the word *Circle* on the board. Read it. Have the children repeat it and find it on the page.

Read the first direction to the children. Have them repeat it while running their fingers under the sentence from left to right.

Have the children name the pictures and listen for the short /a/ sound (cat, rat, dog, man, cake, rabbit, apple, bee). Have the children name all the pictures that they circled. Have them correct any that are wrong.

Read the second direction and have the children read it with you. Tell the children to listen, then to read the list of *an* words. Ask the children if they noticed anything about the words (short /a/ sound, rhyme). If no one can tell, say the words again, emphasizing the *an*.

Explain that the rhyming words sound the same at the end. Emphasize the short /a/ sound.

Name ______________

Circle each picture with the short a sound.

Say each short a word with your teacher.

can	cat	ham
ran	bat	dam
pan	pat	tam
tan	rat	Sam
man	fat	ram
fan	hat	jam
dad	cab	back
pad	dab	sack
sad	jab	tack

Language Arts 101
Worksheet 1
with page 2

Teacher check ______________
Initial Date

Have the children repeat the words as you read them the second time. Be sure the children know the meaning of each word. Have the children add to each list if they are able.

6. Begin making an alphabet Bible booklet. Each time a letter is introduced or reviewed add a new page or pages with words and pictures from the Bible that begin with the letter, the blend, and so on being studied.
7. Practice writing letter *Aa* in the writing tablet.

TEACHING READING:

Talk with the children about their new readers. Tell them that these will be different than their work pages. The children will not be writing on their readers. Tell them that they will want to keep the readers as nice as they can. They can keep them in a special place. They will want to read the stories again and again.

Give *Reader 1* to the children and give them a few minutes to look at the pictures. They will want to talk about what they see.

Tell students you need to go somewhere, but you don't know how to get there. What should you do? Have them share ideas and list them. If map isn't suggested, give hints or suggest it. Show examples of different kinds of real maps.

Read the story "A Map" then ask the following questions:

"What kind of map was found?" (flat)

"Where do you think it was found?" (varied answers)

"What will the map do?" (tell me where to go) Discuss parts of a map. (direction, symbols, etc) Draw map on the board or a piece of paper. Have students contribute ideas.

Have the students find the short vowel words.

READING BASICS:

Instant Words

Ways to Use:

• The first goal should be for the student to properly pronounce each word without having to attack it several times.

• When the student can accurately read every word orally without error, the next goal should be increasing speed while maintaining accuracy, a reasonable goal should be at a rate of approximately 120 syllables per minute. Reading with a metronome set at the student's starting rate and increasing it in 10 beat increments works very well.

• Tracking is another skill which can be developed through the use of Instant Words. Play follow-the-leader, by instructing student to read down column one, up column two, down column three, and up column four. Create your own pattern both vertical and lateral; even give them names.

• Scanning for quick find is another skill to be developed through use of these lists. Have the student read every other word, every third word, etc. Read every word with a "th"sound, short "a" sound. Read the words which have another shorter word in them (e.g. "as" in has; "or" in work; "on" in one.

• The word lists can also be used for sentence building. Have your student make up sentences using words from the list. See how many they can create.

Enjoy the Enrichment Provided by Instant Words.

ACTIVITY:

Teach North, East, South, and West. (chants, movement, or other ways) Provide other maps and sources for further reinforcement. Talk about the globe being a type of map. Have students create their own map on paper. (neighborhood, treasure map, etc)

Page 3: Bb

Concept: sound of *b*

TEACHER GOALS: To teach the children
To identify pictures beginning with the */b/* sound,
To identify pictures ending with the */b/* sound,
To write b as the beginning sound of a word, and
To write the one-syllable short *a* words on the page.

VOCABULARY: sound, letter, read, words

MATERIALS NEEDED: alphabet flash cards, picture cards, crayons

Picture cards are similar to the alphabet flash cards but they do not include the letter. Each card should have of one item that is used for a beginning sound. For the letter (b) use items like the ones pictured on page 3. Add to the set of cards as new letters are introduced.

TEACHING PAGE 3:

Read the first direction with the children. Have the children name the pictures (bow, bat, shovel, box, bear, tree, bed, butter). Have the children circle all the pictures beginning with the */b/* sound.

Read the second direction with the children. Tell the children to say the name of the picture, to write the letter *b,* and then to sound out the word. Have the children say the name of the picture, write *b,* and then sound out the word for each of the other pictures. Check (bat, bad, ban).

ACTIVITIES:

1. Have the children who need more work on the */b/* sound work with the picture cards.
2. Have children work in pairs with the picture cards and alphabet cards.
3. Add to the *Bb* page in the Bible booklet.
4. Have students make up *Bb* stories. *(Example:* Big Bear buys books for baby.)
5. Practice writing letter *Bb* in the writing tablet.

Page 4: Mm

CONCEPT: sound of *m*

TEACHER GOALS: To teach the children

To identify the sound of *m* at the beginning of a word or picture and

To identify the sound of *m* at the end of a word or picture.

MATERIALS NEEDED: picture cards, alphabet cards, Worksheet 2

TEACHING PAGE 4:

Put *m*______ on the board and tell the children that this symbol means that they are to look for words or pictures beginning with the /*m*/ sound. Ask children to give words that begin with *m*.

Put ______*m* on the board and tell the children that this symbol means that they are to look for words or pictures ending in /*m*/ sound. Ask children to give words ending in *m*.

Read the directions. Have the children repeat and follow along. Ask the children to point to the word *Circle*.

Have the children name the pictures on the page and circle those beginning with *m* (moon, sun, nut, mouse, mailbox, table, monkey, mirror).

Read the direction and have the children repeat it as they follow along. Ask what the first picture is. Ask what sound the children hear at the beginning of *milk*. Ask what letter has that sound. Have the children trace the *m* and say the word.

Name the remaining pictures on the page (milk, mailman, money, mouse).

Tell the children to say the name of the picture and listen for the sound at the beginning of the word. Tell them to write the letter *m* on the lines under the pictures.

Check by having the children say the name of the pictures and by giving the beginning letter.

ACTIVITIES:

1. Have the children whose names begin or end with *m* write their names on the board. Read them over several times.
2. Children who need more help should match the picture and alphabet cards or should sort out all picture cards beginning or ending with *m*.
3. Do Worksheet 2.

Ask the children to give words beginning and ending with /b/ sound.

Read directions with the children. Be sure they understand what they are to do. Have the children name the pictures (bird, crab, ball, bicycle, crib, bus, bug, knob).

Tell the children to say the name of the picture and listen for the sound at the beginning of the word. Tell them to write the letter *m* on the lines under the pictures that begin with the /m/ sound. Let the children finish the page independently. Some children may need help.

4. Practice writing letter *Mm* in the writing tablet.

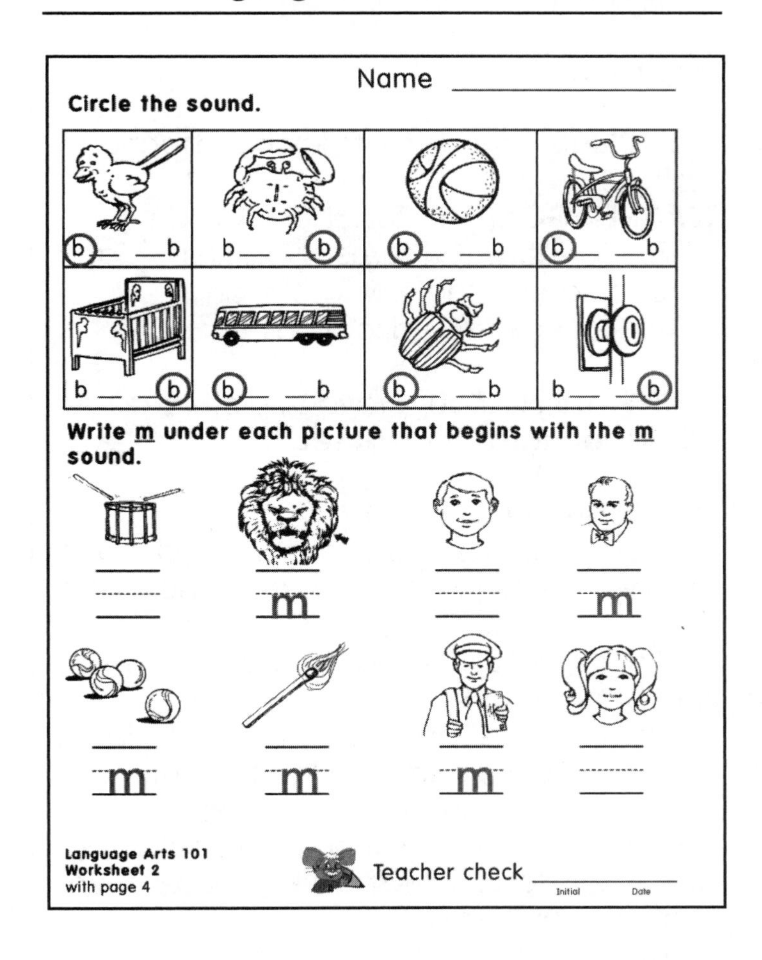

Name ______________

Circle the sound.

(b)__ __b	b__ __(b)	(b)__ __b	(b)__ __b
b__ __(b)	(b)__ __b	(b)__ __b	b__ __(b)

Write m under each picture that begins with the m sound.

____	m	____	m
m	m	m	____

Language Arts 101
Worksheet 2
with page 4

Teacher check ______________
Initial Date

Page 5: Rr

CONCEPTS: sound of *r*, following directions

TEACHER GOALS: To teach the children
To identify pictures beginning and ending with the sound of *r*, and
To follow written directions.

MATERIALS NEEDED: crayons, picture cards, alphabet cards, Worksheet 3.

TEACHING PAGE 5:

Say the words *roar, rear,* and *runner* and ask the children where they hear the sound of *r*.

Ask them to give words beginning with *r* and ending with *r*.

Read the first direction with the children as they follow along from left to right.

Have the children name the pictures and listen for the /r/ sound (rake, cake, rag, car, chair, cat, newspaper). Have them circle the pictures. Check.

Name the pictures. Write the letter *r* under the pictures.

ACTIVITIES:

1. Sort out all picture cards beginning with the /r/ sound.
2. Add to the *Rr* page in the Bible booklet.
3. Do Worksheet 3.

Read the direction with the children as they follow along.

Ask a child to tell the name of the first picture. Ask what sound it begins with and what letter. Have the children trace the circle around the picture of a rake. Have the children name the rest of the pictures in the first section and circle those which begin with *r* (rug, shovel, rose, rainbow, rocking chair, radio, door). Check by having the children name the pictures they circled. Have the children name the pictures and circle those with *r* in the middle in the second section. Check (barrel, cherries, ball, grapes).

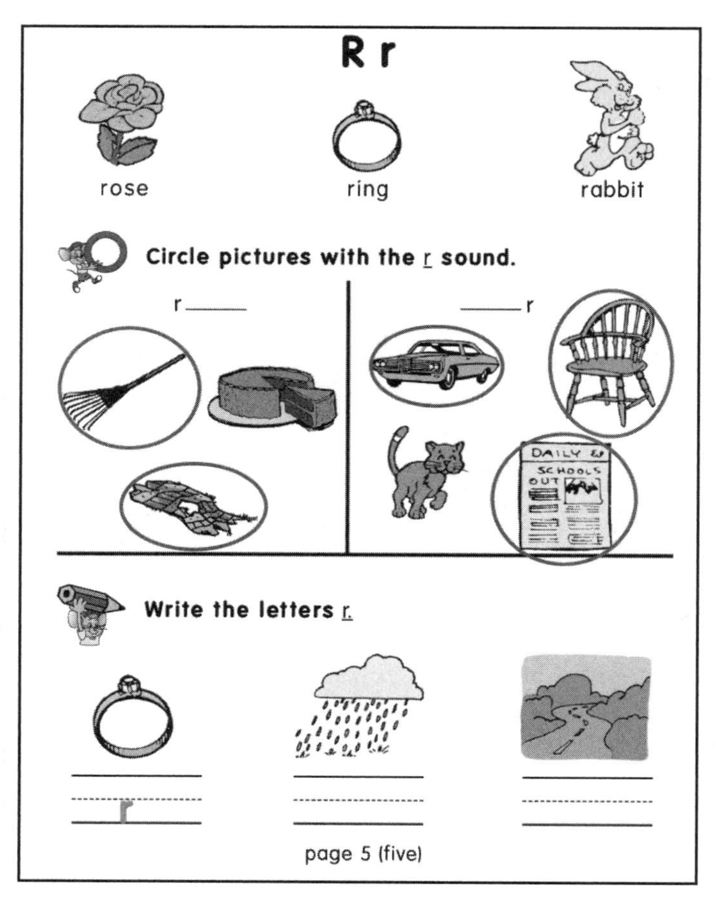

Have the children name the pictures and circle those with *r* at the end in the last section. Check. (car, ladder, truck, door, crate, chair, star, picture)

Help the children who seem to be having trouble with the /r/ sound.

4. Practice writing letter *Rr* in the writing tablet.

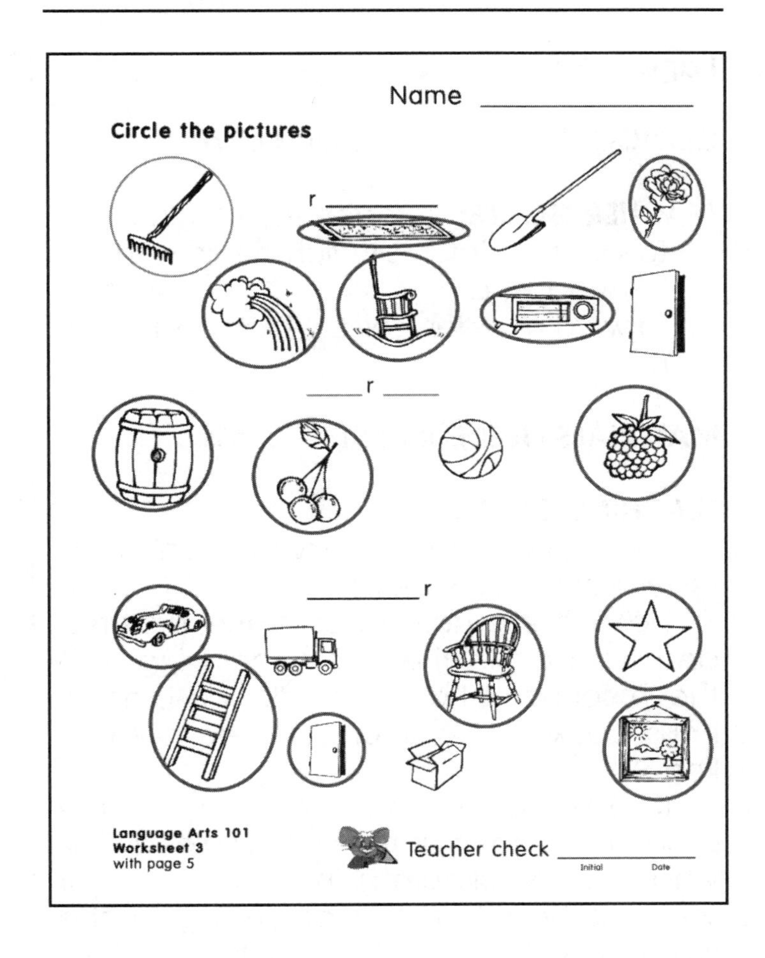
Name
Circle the pictures
r
r
r
Language Arts 101
Worksheet 3
with page 5
Teacher check
Initial
Date

Page 6: Nn

CONCEPTS: beginning sound of *n*

TEACHER GOALS: To teach the children
To identify pictures which begin with the *n* sound, and
To write *n* under words which begin with *n*.

MATERIALS NEEDED: picture cards

TEACHING PAGE 6:

Read the directions. Have the children repeat and follow along.

Have the children name the pictures, and then circle the ones beginning with the *n* sound. Check (needle, nest, neck, house, newspaper, kitten, nail, tree, net, nut, knee).

Read the direction and have the children repeat it as they follow along. Ask what the first picture is (nickel). Ask what sound is heard at the beginning of the word nickel, and what letter has that sound. Have the children trace the *n* and say the word.

Name the rest of the pictures on the pictures on the page.

Tell the children to say the name of the picture and listen for the beginning sound. Tell them to write the letter that makes that sound on the lines below the picture.

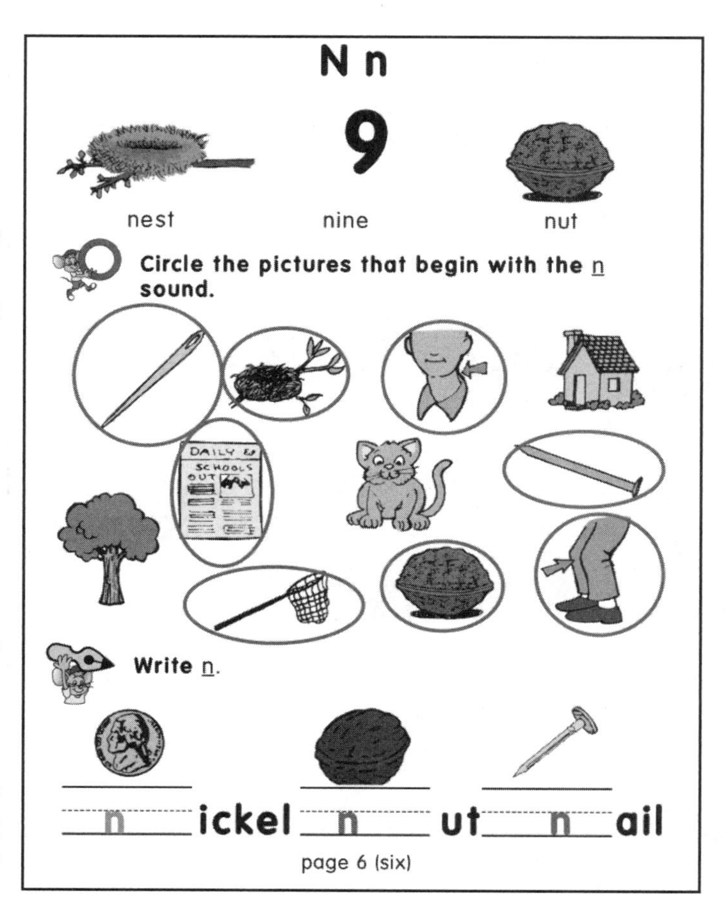

ACTIVITIES:

1. Use the letter charts or picture cards. Add pictures to the *Nn* chart that have the *n* sound at the end or in the middle.
2. Review and add to the *Nn* page of the Bible booklet
3. Practice writing letter *Nn* in the writing tablet.

Page 7: Ss

CONCEPTS: sound of *s*

TEACHER GOALS: To teach the children
To identify pictures beginning with the sounds of *s,* and
To write the letter *Ss.*

MATERIALS NEEDED: crayons, alphabet cards

TEACHING PAGE 7:

Have the children give words that have *s* as the beginning, middle, or ending sound.

Read the first direction with the children. Have the children circle the pictures with the *s* sound (sailboat, pan, sun, bus, saddle, sink).

Read the directions. Name the pictures (saddle, sink, sun). Have the children write *s* under each picture.

Have the children put their pencils away when they finish an exercise and correct their mistakes with a crayon. This procedure gives you a quick way to find the children who will need more help.

ACTIVITIES:

1. Write the letter *s* on the board and see who can be first to give a word with that sound at the beginning.
2. Do the same as Activity 1 but have them give words with the sound in the middle or at the end.
3. Add to the *Ss* page of the Bible booklet.

Give individual help if the children seem to be having trouble.

4. Practice writing letter *Ss* in the writing tablet.

Page 8: Tt

CONCEPTS: sound of *t*

TEACHER GOALS: To teach the children
To identify pictures beginning with the sound of *t*, and
To identify pictures ending with the sound of *t*.

VOCABULARY: beginning, ending

MATERIALS NEEDED: Worksheet 4, crayons, alphabet cards

TEACHING PAGE 8:

Have the children give words that have *t* as the beginning, middle, or ending sound.

Read the directions. Ask what the name of the picture is. Ask what towel begins with. Have the children draw a circle around the picture of the towel. Name the rest of the pictures and tell the children to circle all those that begin with *t*. Check by having the children name the pictures they have circled (trunk, table, nest, tree, truck, towel).

Use the same procedure of each of the other sections.

Have the children name the pictures before they begin (nest, hat, coat, letter, goat, skirt).

Have the children give words that have *t* as the beginning, middle, or ending sound.

Read the directions. Have the children repeat them and follow along. Remind the children what *t*____ and ____*t* mean.

Have the children name the picture (top). Have the children tell you the name of the letter at the beginning of top. Have them write the letter *T*.

Have the children put their pencils away when they finish an exercise and correct their mistakes with a crayon. This procedure gives you a quick way to find the children who will need more help.

ACTIVITIES:

1. In a small group write the letter *t* on the board and see who can be first to give a word with that sound at the beginning.
2. Do the same as Activity 1 but have them give words with the sound in the middle or at the end.
3. Add to the *Tt* chart and to the *Tt* page of the Bible booklet.
4. Do Worksheet 4.

Read the first direction with the children. Have them trace the *a* in the first word. Ask if anyone can read the word. Do each word in the exercise the same way. Have the children read all the words several times.

Have the children give words that have *s, n, m,* or *t* as the beginning, middle, or ending sound.

Read the directions. Have the children repeat them and follow along. Have the children circle the pictures that begin with the sound of the letter shown. Name the pictures (top, street, flower, mouse, nose, nickel).

5. Practice writing letter *Tt* in the writing tablet.

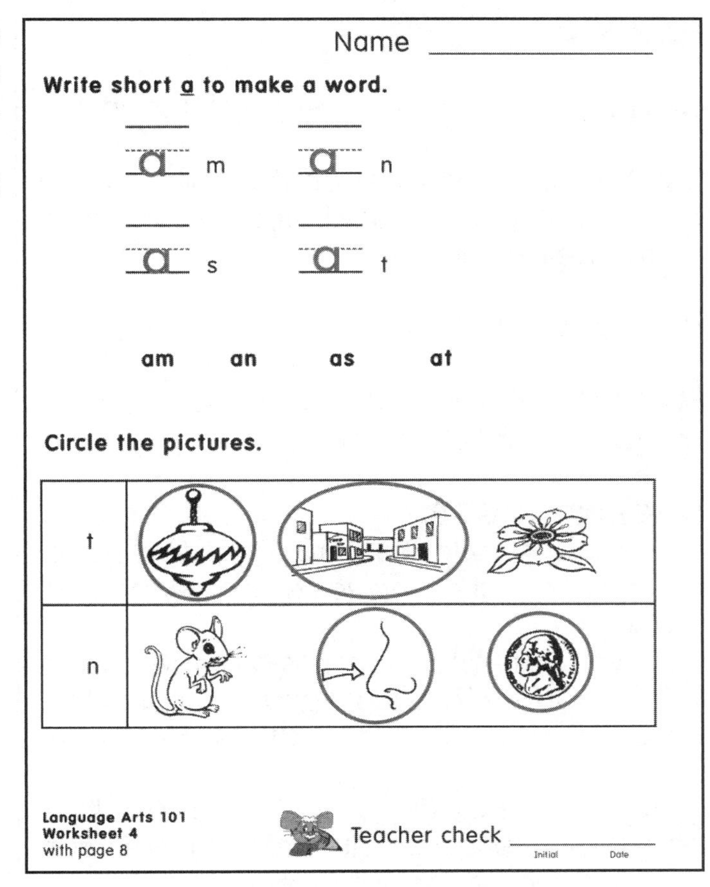
Name ______________

Write short a to make a word.

a m a n

a s a t

am an as at

Circle the pictures.

t			
n			

Language Arts 101
Worksheet 4
with page 8

Teacher check ______________
Initial Date

Page 9: Dd

CONCEPTS: sound of *d*, beginning sounds

TEACHER GOALS: To teach the children
To identify pictures with the */d/* sound at the beginning.

VOCABULARY: story

MATERIALS NEEDED: picture cards, alphabet cards, Worksheet 5

TEACHING PAGE 9:

Hold up the letter card for *d* and have the children give the letter name and its sound.

Give a direction, such as *d* at the end, *d* in the middle, *d* at the beginning. Have the children give words that have those sounds.

Review the *Dd* page in the Bible booklet. Have the children recall the stories of David, Daniel, or Deborah.

Read the directions with the children as they follow along. Have the children name the pictures (dinner, dog, dime, duck, dustpan, banana, bell). Have them circle the pictures with the *d* sound. Check.

Read the second direction. Name the pictures (dam, dad, dab). Have them write the letter *d* and say the words.

ACTIVITIES:

1. Have children work matching picture and letter cards.
2. Add to *Dd* page of Bible booklet.
3. Do Worksheet 5.

Read the direction with the children as they follow along from left to right.

Tell the children to say the name of the first picture (doll). Ask what sound they hear at the beginning of the word. Ask what the letter is for that sound. Have the children write the *d* on the lines under the picture of the doll.

Have the children name the rest of the pictures in the first section and tell the children to write the letter *d* under each one that begins with the *d* sound (doll,dog, dime).

Read this list of words and have the children give the beginning and ending sound for each.

sit	mud	sun	dad
tar	bus	net	sin
bat	ran	bid	

Read the directions with the children.

Have the children name the pictures (raft, nest, bird, mailbox, sun, book, bus, car).

Have the children circle the letter in the correct beginning or ending position.

4. Practice writing letter *Dd* in the writing tablet.

Name ______________

Write d.

d ______

d d d

Circle the letters.

(r) __ __ r	t __ __ (t)	d __ __ (d)	(m) __ __ m
n __ __ (n)	(b) __ __ b	s __ __ (s)	r __ __ (r)

Language Arts 101
Worksheet 5
with page 9

Teacher check ______________
Initial Date

Page 10: Ee

CONCEPTS: listening, following oral directions, sound of short *e*

TEACHER GOALS: To teach the children

To listen and follow oral directions,

To recognize the sound of short *e* in words, and

To identify pictures with the sound of short *e*.

MATERIALS NEEDED: crayons, Worksheet 6, alphabet flash cards

TEACHING PAGE 10:

Hold up the flash card for the letter *e*. Ask the children to give the name of the letter and the short sound. If a child should give the long sound of *e*, tell them they will learn about long *e* later. In this one the sound of *e* will be the short sound.

Have the children give words that have the short /e/ sound. Have them use these words in sentences. Go through the flash cards several times.

Read the title and directions to the children. Have them read them with you as they follow along from left to right.

Have the children look at the picture and tell what they think is happening. Then read the story to them. Have them point to things that have the short /e/ sound (tent, bed, desk, chest, pencil, peg on wall, shed, fence).

Have the children circle all the things in the picture that have the short /e/ sound.

Note: If you have the children keep their pencils inside their desks until you are ready to have them begin marking the page, they will be much better listeners.

Read the first direction and have the children repeat and follow along with their fingers. Point out the words *write* and *read*. Have the children read them.

E e

Circle the pictures with the short /e/ sound.

Ben was excited.
He was going to write a great story today.
He had a pencil next to him on the bed.
What would he write about?
Maybe he could write about Uncle Ted.
Or he could tell about his turtle, Ed.
He could write about his new bike that was red.
Ben couldn't decide. What would you write about?

Write e. Read the words.

p e n m e n

t e n h e n

page 10 (ten)

Ask what the first picture is. Have the children point to it. Tell them that the letters beside the picture spell *pen*, but one letter is missing. Ask them to say the word and to tell you which letter should go in the blank space. Have them trace the letter *e*. Have them run their fingers under the word and read it.

Do the same for the other words in the exercise. Ask which words rhyme.

When all have finished marking, have them put their pencils away and take out a crayon. Have the children tell which things in the picture they circled. Have them circle any they have missed with a crayon. This quick check tells you which children will need more help with the short /e/ sound.

ACTIVITIES:

1. Add to and review the *Ee* page in the Bible booklet.

2. Write ____en on the board. Read it with the children and ask them to give words which end in *en*. Write them on the board under the ending. Read the list of words several times.
3. Have the children write or dictate sentences for each picture.
4. Do Worksheet 6.

Use the flash cards to review the words *circle* and *pictures*.

Read the direction with the children as they follow along.

Have the children name the pictures. Have them point to the words *circle* and *pictures*.

Have the children name the pictures in the two rows at the top of the page. Ask the children if they hear the short /e/ sound in the first picture. Where do they hear it? Have them trace the circle around the bed. Let them finish the exercise. Have the children tell which pictures they circled and correct any they have missed. (bed, sled, cup, jet, bench, bat, pencil, ten)

Read the first list of words, then read it again and have the children repeat it after you. Ask what is the same about all the words (ending, short *e*). Ask what you call it when the ending of the word is the same (rhyming). Ask if they can give any more words that rhyme with *hen* and *ten*.

Do each list the same way. Point out that *said* is spelled differently but pronounced the same as the other *ed* words. Point out the other words that are spelled differently (meant, friend). Point out also that the words *read, head,* and *bread* have a silent *a*.

Have the children write some of the short *e* words in their writing tablet.

5. Practice writing letter *Ee* in their writing tablet.

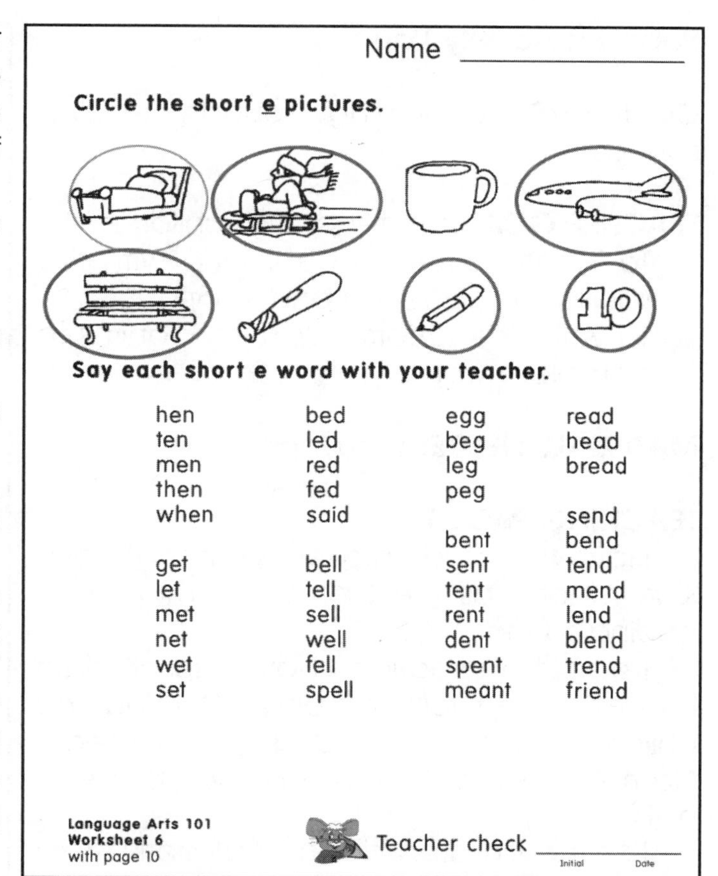
Name ______________

Circle the short e pictures.

Say each short e word with your teacher.

hen
ten
men
then
when

get
let
met
net
wet
set

bed
led
red
fed
said

bell
tell
sell
well
fell
spell

egg
beg
leg
peg

bent
sent
tent
rent
dent
spent
meant

read
head
bread

send
bend
tend
mend
lend
blend
trend
friend

Language Arts 101
Worksheet 6
with page 10

Teacher check ______________
Initial Date

Page 11: Activity Page

CONCEPTS: beginning sounds, ending sounds

TEACHER GOALS: To teach the children
To identify pictures beginning with the sounds of *t, d, n, m, r* and *s* and
To write the letters *t, d, n, m, r,* and *s* to complete words.

MATERIALS NEEDED: crayons

TEACHING PAGE 11:

Have the children give words that have *s, n, m,* or *t* as the beginning, middle, or ending sound.

Read the direction. Have the children repeat it and follow along. Remind the children what *m*____ and ____*m* mean. Name the pictures (milk, cat, nail, bus, sun, hat).

Let the children do the first activity by themselves. Check.

Put this diagram on the board.

_________*a*_______

Fill in the letters to make words and have the children give the sounds and say the words (can, hat, lad, tab, etc.).

Read the second direction.

Ask the children what the picture is, what the middle letter is, and what the sound of *a* is.

Ask the children to tell what the first letter should be and what the last letter should be. Write them in. Sound out the word. Say the word and have the children spell it.

Do the first word together. Then let the children finish the page by themselves. Check. (rat, mat, man, sad)

Have the children read the words they have made.

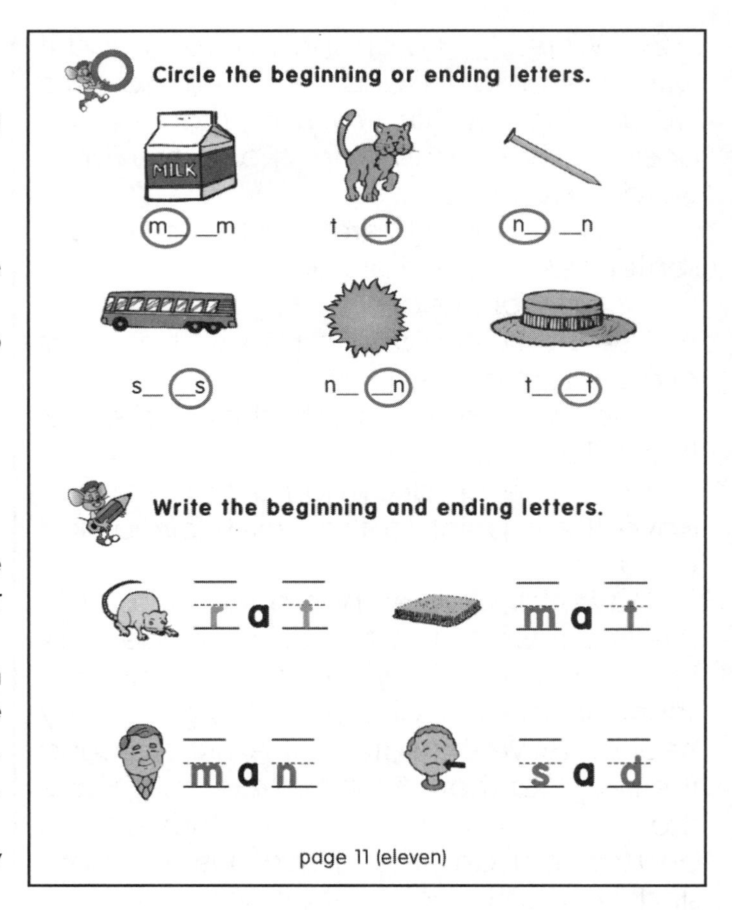

ACTIVITIES:

1. Dictate the words *rat, man, sad,* and *mat* and have the children write them in their writing tablets.
2. Dictate the following words and have the children write them in their writing tablets ((ban, ran, mad, sat, bad, bat).
3. Dictate a word and have the children make the word on their desks with alphabet cards.

Page 12: Pp

CONCEPT: sound of *p*

TEACHER GOAL: To teach the children
To recognize the sound of *p* at the beginning, in the middle, or at the end of words.

MATERIALS NEEDED: three empty boxes all the same size, picture cards, alphabet cards

TEACHING PAGE 12:

Hold up the flash card for *p* and ask for the name and sound of the letter.

Ask the children to give words that begin with the /*p*/ sound.

Name the pictures and read the words at the top of the page.

Put p____, ___p___, ___p on the chalkboard and ask what each means. Do several examples for each position.

Name the pictures in the boxes (pear, apple, bump, flipper, rip, princess, nipple, stamp).

Tell the children to say each word carefully, listen for the *p* sound and circle the right position.

Read the second direction. Name the pictures (pony, pocket, piano, pitcher).

Ask for the beginning sound of *pony*. Have children trace the *p*. Let the children complete the page. Check and have children correct any mistakes.

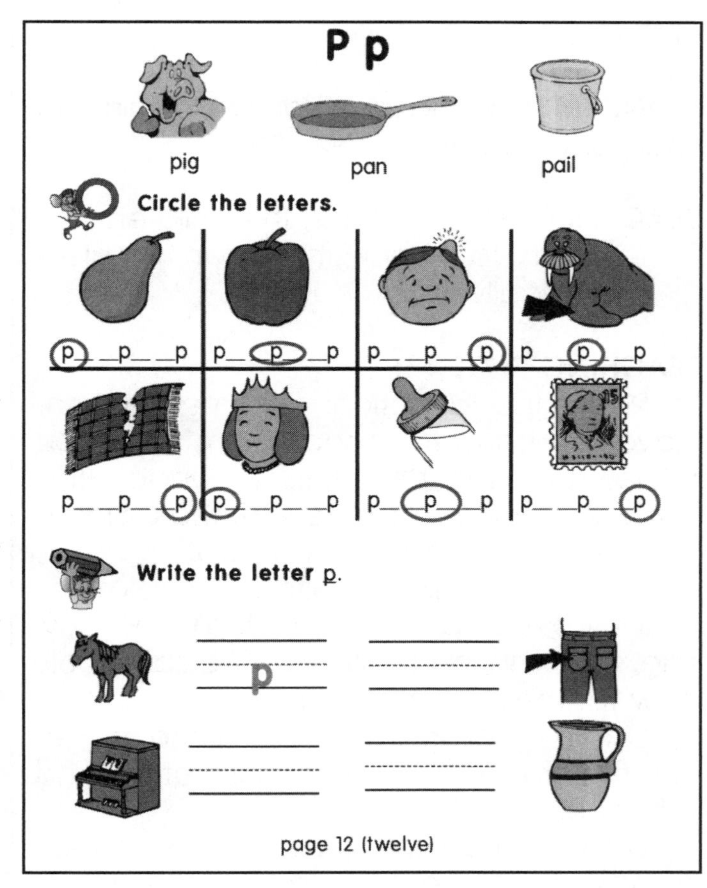

ACTIVITIES:

1. Find three boxes all the same size (shoe boxes would be fine), cover with adhesive-backed paper and put one of the following labels on each box.
•____, ____•____, ____•.

Have the children sort picture cards into the boxes. If you put the position of the sound on the back of the picture cards, the children should be able to check their own work.

2. Add to the picture-card collection. Have the children find pictures that have the *p* sound in the middle or at the end in old magazines or catalogs and paste them on tag board.

3. Review and add to the *Pp* page in the Bible booklet.

4. Practice writing letter *Pp* in the writing tablet.

SELF TEST 1

CONCEPTS: sound of short a, beginning sounds, sound of short e

TEACHER GOAL: To teach the children
To learn to check their own progress periodically.

TEACHING PAGE 13:

Read the directions to the children. Have the children repeat them after you while running their fingers under the sentence being read. Be sure the children understand what they are to do.

Have the children name the pictures (ham, cow, cap, hat, bat, dog) (monkey, ring, tent, sun, nest, ball, duck, baby) (bell, cow, feather, belt, bed, tent).

Let the children complete the page. You may repeat the directions but give no other help.

Do not have the children check their own work. Check it as soon as you can and go over it with each child. Show him where he did well and where he needs extra help.

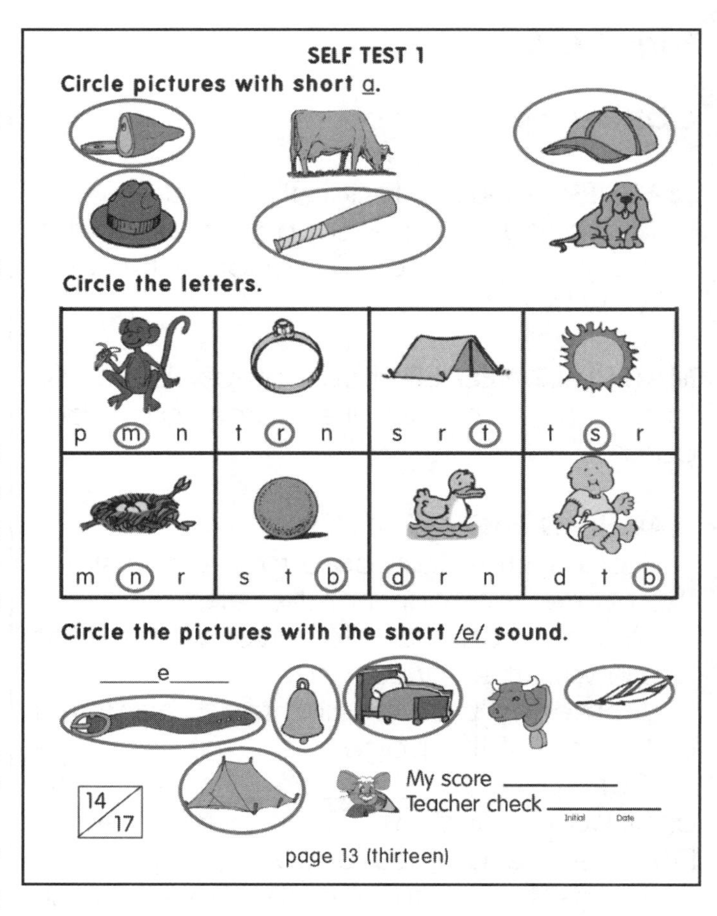

ACTIVITIES:

1. Give each child help on items he misses.
2. If several children miss the same things, reteach the skill (in a small group session, if possible).

SPELLING WORDS:

rat
sat
red
ten
men

II. PART TWO

Page 14: Ii

CONCEPTS: sound of short *i*, verb forms, telling a story, sentences, subject-verb agreement

Teacher Goals: To teach the children

To identify pictures with the sound of short *i*,
To tell a story from a picture,
To identify the main idea of a story or picture,
To note and recall details of a picture,
To make inferences from a picture, and
To predict what might happen next in a situation.

MATERIALS NEEDED: crayons, alphabet cards

TEACHING PAGE 14:

Read the story to the children. Then read the directions. Have them follow along under the sentence with their fingers, going from left to right.

Tell the children to look at the picture carefully and circle everything they can find that has the sound of short *i*. Ask one or two children to name something in the picture that has the sound of short *i*; then let the children complete the page by themselves. Allow children to work about five or six minutes; then ask the children to name what they have circled. Give each child a chance to name something even if you have to give him clues. Have the children circle anything they missed.

The children should circle (windmill, hill, children, digging, singing, twigs, family having a picnic, picnic table, charcoal grill, kitten, boy fishing in a river with a stick, fish).

Have several children tell a story about all or part of the picture. Remind them to use complete sentences.

II. Part Two

I i

Circle the pictures with the short /i/ sound.

Tim sat on the little hill and fished in the river.
His kitten, Little Miss, sat beside him, eyeing the fish jumping in the water.
His brother, Jim, was digging in the soft earth, trying to find worms.
Dad was grilling hot dogs on the charcoal grill.
Mom was setting up the picnic table.
What a wonderful day for a picnic!
Far away, Tim saw the windmill blowing in the wind.
Nearby, he heard a bird singing.
Tim thought he must be the happiest boy in the world.
He was thankful for this beautiful day.

page 14 (fourteen)

Ask these questions: "What might have happened just before what they see? What might happen after? What time of day is it? How do you know? What is the weather like? What is a windmill used for?"

Have the children tell which of the following sentences sound right.

A boy *is* fishing. *or*
A boy *are* fishing.

I *seen* the windmill. *or*
I *saw* the windmill.

The children are *dig* in the sand. *or*
The children are *digging* in the sand.

The tree *have* leaves. *or*
The tree *has* leaves.

The boy *fish* with a stick. *or*
The boy *fished* with a stick.

The children *are* having fun. *or*
The children *is* having fun.

ACTIVITIES:

1. Have the children close their books and name as many things in the pictures as they can remember.
2. Practice writing letter *Ii* in the writing tablet.

Page 15: Short i

CONCEPTS: sounds of short *i*, rhyming words

TEACHER GOALS: To teach the children
To identify words and pictures with the sound of short *i*,
To identify rhyming words,
To write the letter *i* to complete a word, and
To read the words with the short /i/ sound.

MATERIALS NEEDED: alphabet cards Worksheet 7

TEACHING PAGE 15:

Read the direction with the children. Ask what the first picture is. Ask what sound is in the middle of *pig*. Have the children draw a circle around the picture of the pig.

Name the rest of the pictures and have the children circle those with short *i* (pig, kitten, fish, lid, nest, stick).

Check by having the children name the pictures they have circled.

Read the directions with the children as they follow along from left to right. Ask the children to give you the sound for short *i*.

Ask what is in the first picture. "What letter does *fin* start with? What letter does it end with? With what sound does *fin* begin? . . . end? What sound should go in the middle? What letter stands for that sound?" Have the children trace the *i* and read the word.

Use the same procedure for all the words. Help the children sound out the words.

Have the children read all the words several times.

ACTIVITIES:

1. Have the children who need more practice with short *i* sort out the picture cards for short *i* and say them over several times.
2. Have those children who are able to write a sentence for each word.

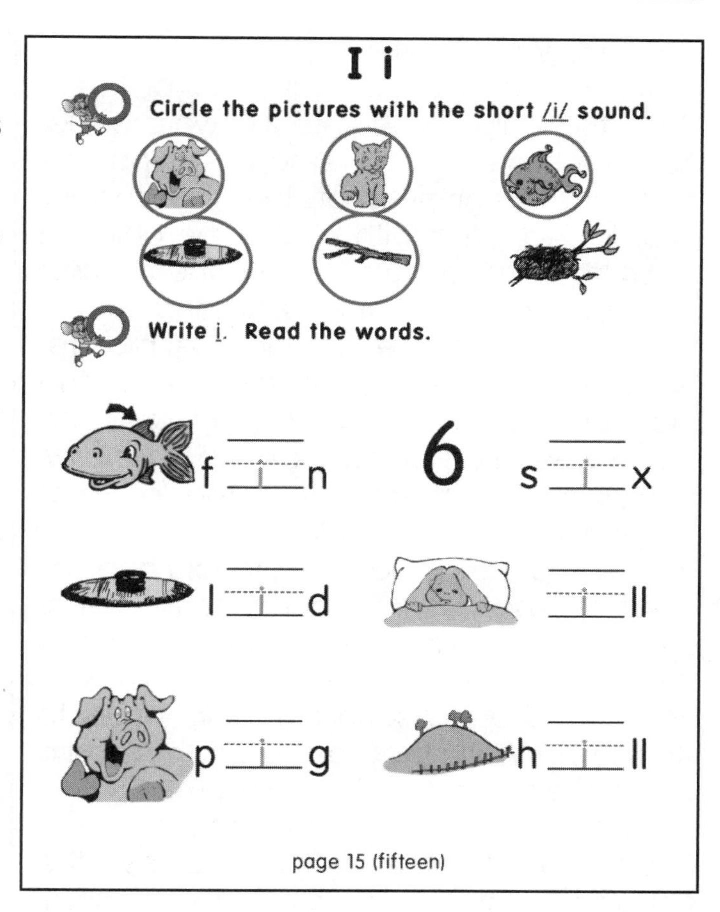

3. Do Worksheet 7.

Read the direction with the children. Have the children point to the word circle. Ask the children if they remember what the *p* at the beginning of the line means (words beginning with *p*). Ask the children what the first picture is. Ask them what sound they hear at the beginning. Have them trace the line around the picture. Have the children name the rest of the pictures in the two rows at the top of the page (penny, puppy, cat, boat, pillow, pumpkin). Let them circle the pictures beginning with *p*. Check.

Hold up the alphabet card for *i* and ask what the name and sound of the letter are. Ask the children to give words with the short /i/ sound. Ask all the children who have the short /i/ sound in their names to stand up. Write the names on the board and have the children read them.

Read the direction with the children. Read the list of *in* words and ask the children what they noticed about them. Ask how rhyming words are alike. Read each list and have the children give the part that is the same in each word.

TEACHING READING:

Ask students to describe the sun. List their answers. Ask them what kind of activities they like to do when it is hot and sunny outside. Survey students: How many like to be outside when it is hot? Record answers.

Read the story "The Sun" together then ask the following questions:

"What is this story about?" (the sun)

"Where will the speaker sit?" (on a mat in the sun)

"Why does the speaker say the sun is NOT fun?" (hot)

"What does the speaker do to make the sun fun again?" (hat, fan)

Have students find the short vowel words.

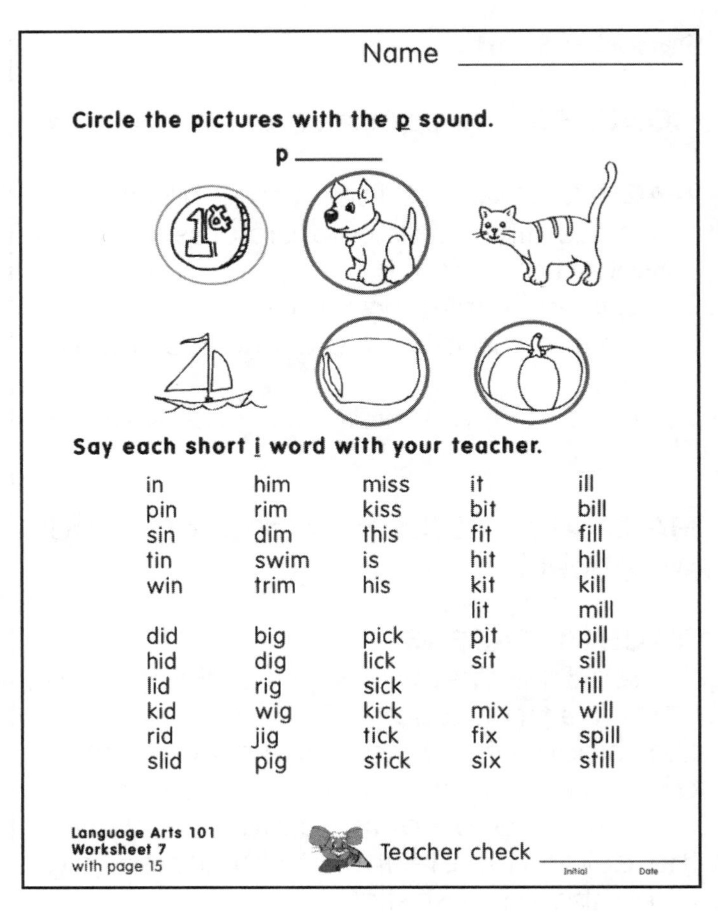

Name ______________

Circle the pictures with the p sound.

p ______

Say each short i word with your teacher.

in	him	miss	it	ill
pin	rim	kiss	bit	bill
sin	dim	this	fit	fill
tin	swim	is	hit	hill
win	trim	his	kit	kill
			lit	mill
did	big	pick	pit	pill
hid	dig	lick	sit	sill
lid	rig	sick		till
kid	wig	kick	mix	will
rid	jig	tick	fix	spill
slid	pig	stick	six	still

Language Arts 101
Worksheet 7
with page 15

Teacher check ______________
Initial Date

ACTIVITY:

What else could you do in the hot sun to make it fun? Draw a picture of something you like to do in the hot sun.

Page 16: Ll

CONCEPT: sound of *l*

TEACHER GOAL: To teach the children
To identify the sound of *l* at the beginning, in the middle, or at the end of words.

MATERIALS NEEDED: Worksheet 8, alphabet cards

TEACHING PAGE 16:

Hold up the flash card for *l* and ask for the name and sound of the letter. Read these words and ask the children to tell where they hear the sound of *l*.

lake	village	lip
leaf	seal	cattle
million	long	single
camel	allow	willow

Read the direction with the children. Have them name the pictures in each section.

Let them do the page independently. Check. (log, pillow, cup handle, lemon, lamp, bell, ball, lion, lid, whale, apple)

Read the second direction with the children. Ask what the first picture is. Ask what sound they hear at the beginning of leaves. What letter makes this sound. Have them trace the *l*. Name the rest of the pictures (leaves, legs, lions, lid).

Have the children write the beginning letters on the lines. Check.

ACTIVITIES:

1. Add pictures with the /l/ sound at the beginning, in the middle, and at the end to the picture-card collection. Have the children sort the pictures into the proper box. Have them check their own work by looking on the back of the card for the letter position.
2. Add to the *Ll* page in the Bible booklet.
3. Do Worksheet 8.

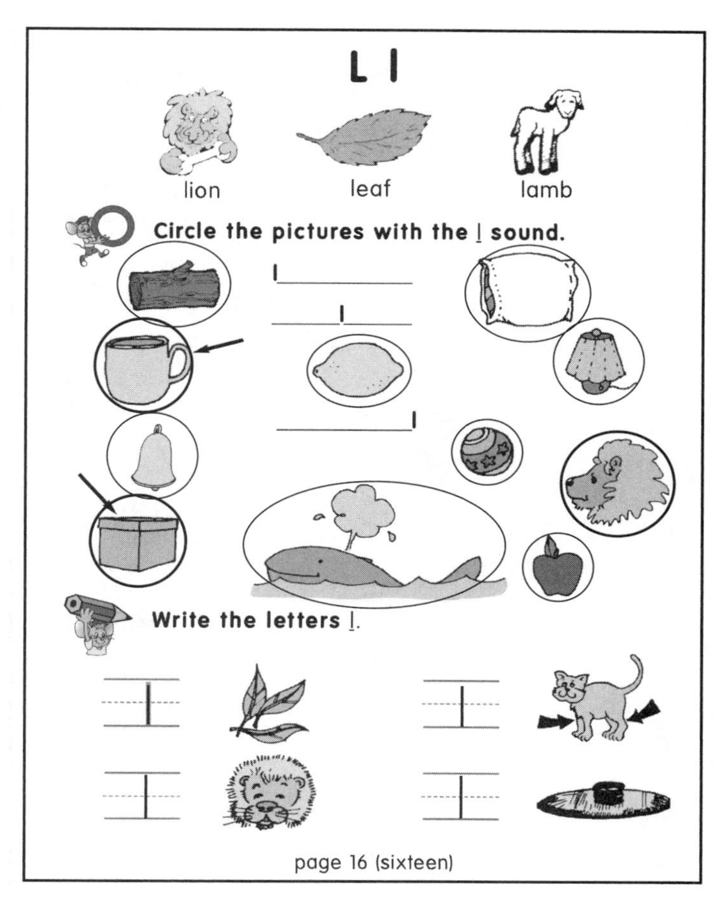

Read the first direction with the children as they follow along. Ask the children to name the first picture.

Ask where they hear the *l* sound in *dollar.* Have them draw a circle around the middle *l* in the box.

Name the pictures in the two rows of boxes (lake, tail, letter, halo, collar, camel, school).

Have the children do the rest of the exercise. Check.

Have the children match the upper and lower-case letters. Then read the words together and have the children match the words. Tell them that the only difference will be the beginning upper and lower-case letter.

4. Practice writing letter *Ll* in the writing tablet.

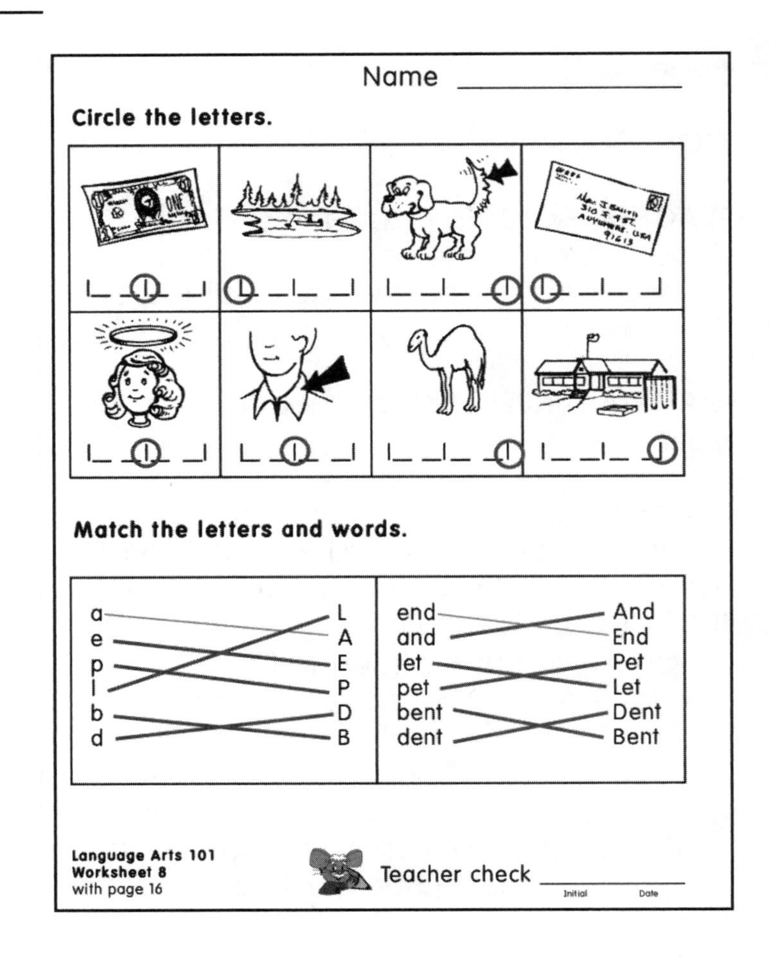
Name
Circle the letters.
Match the letters and words.
a
e
p
l
b
d
L
A
E
P
D
B
end
and
let
pet
bent
dent
And
End
Pet
Let
Dent
Bent
Language Arts 101
Worksheet 8
with page 16
Teacher check
Initial
Date

Page 17: Kk, Cc, (ck)

CONCEPT: *c* as the sound of *k, k, ck*

TEACHER GOALS: To teach the children
To recognize the sound of *k* at the beginning, in the middle, or at the end of pictures or words,
To recognize the */k/* sound for *c* at the beginning of pictures or words, and
To recognize the */k/* sound for *ck* in the middle or at the end of pictures or words.

MATERIALS NEEDED: picture cards, alphabet cards

TEACHING PAGE 17:

Write c, *k,* and *ck* on the board. Have the children read the letters. Tell the children that all three have the same sound. Ask the children to give the sound. *Tell the children:*

The */k/* sound of *c* is usually at the beginning of a word like *cat* or *candy.* A few words have a *c* in the middle or at the end like *picnic* or *mimic.*

The *k* may be at the beginning of a word as in *kick* or *kitten,* in the middle as in *tinkle* or *donkey,* or at the end as in *bank* or *desk.*

The *ck* may be in the middle of a word as in *buckle* or *tackle,* at the end of a word as in *truck* or *sack,* but not at the beginning of a word.

Read the direction and have the children follow along. Because of the variety of */k/* sounds, work through the page together. As you finish each section, write the words on the board so that the children may see how they are spelled. Call attention to the *c, k,* or *ck.*

Have the children name all the pictures in each section as you begin it.

c____ candle, dog, cup,
k____ king, tree, key

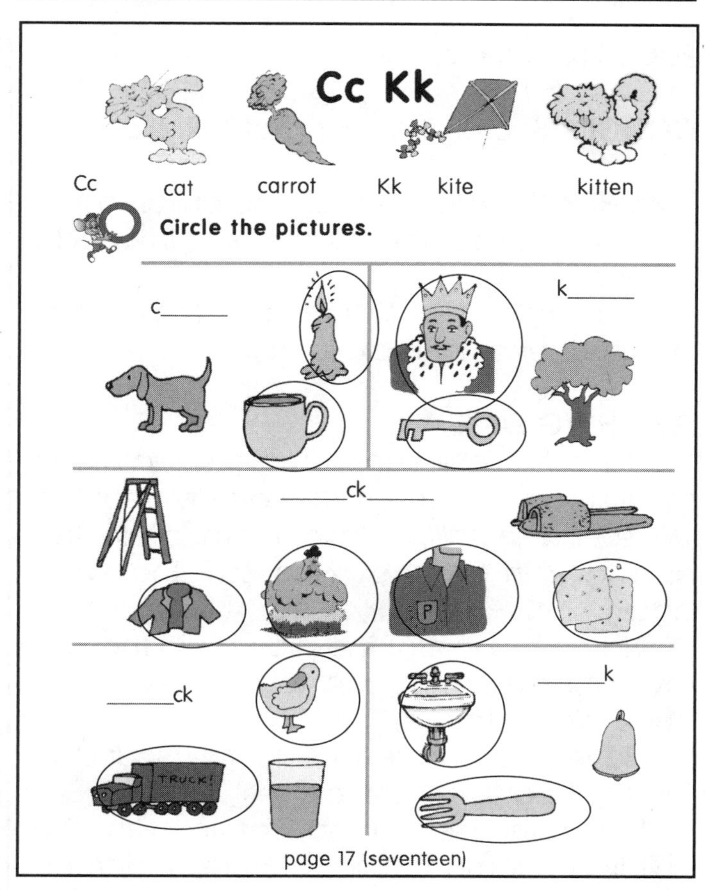

___ck___ ladder, jacket, chicken, pocket, crackers, slippers
___ck duck, truck, glass
___k sink, fork, bell

Have the children circle the pictures in each section. Check.

ACTIVITIES:

1. Add picture cards for *c, k,* and *ck* to the picture-card collection.
2. Add to the *Cc* and *Kk* pages in the Bible booklet. Make a new page for *ck.*
3. Practice writing letter *Kk* in the writing tablet.

Page 18: Kk, Cc, (ck)

CONCEPTS: *c* as the sound of *k, k, ck.*

TEACHER GOALS: To teach the children
To recognize the sound of *k* in words, and
To identify the */k/* sound at the end of words ending in *ck.*

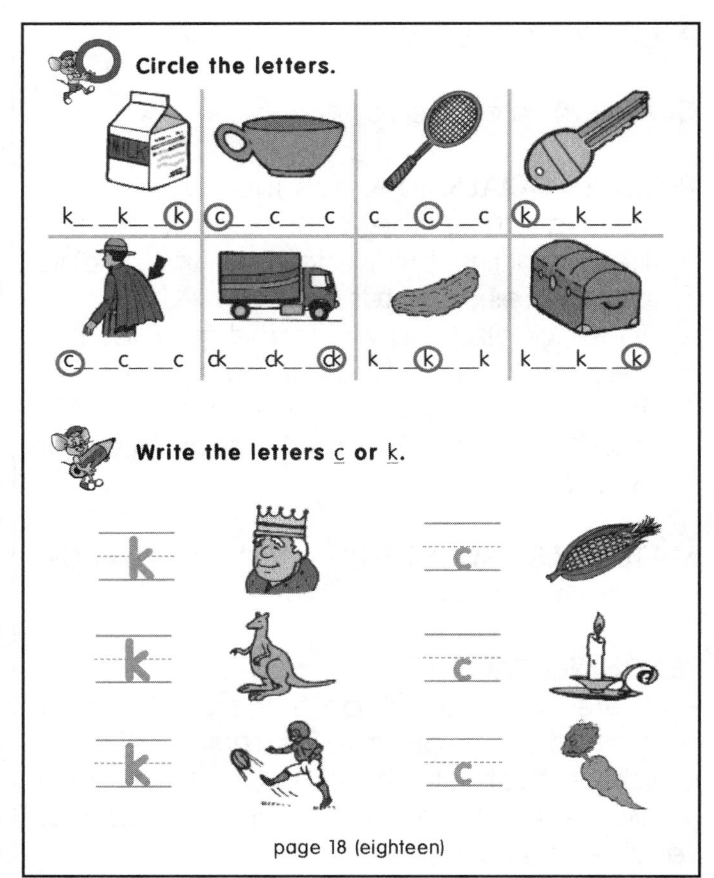

TEACHING PAGE 18:

Have the children name the picture in the first box. Ask them where they hear the */k/* sound in *milk.* Have them circle the ending *k* in the box and say the word again.

Name the rest of the pictures in the two rows of boxes (milk, cup, racket, key, cape, truck, pickle, trunk).

Have the children circle the sound in the right position. Check.

Read the second direction with the children. Name the first picture and trace the *k.* Name the picture of the corn and trace the *c.* Have the children name the other pictures and write *k* or c in the spaces (kangaroo, candle, kick, carrot). Check.

ACTIVITIES:

1. Practice writing letter *Cc* and *Kk* in the writing tablet.

Page 19: Ff

CONCEPTS: sound of *f*

TEACHER GOALS: To teach the children

To identify the sound of *Ff* at the beginning, in the middle, and at the end of a word or picture,

To write the letter *Ff* at the beginning of a word, and

To review the sound of c, k, ck.

MATERIALS NEEDED: picture cards, Worksheet 9, alphabet cards

TEACHING PAGE 19:

Hold up the flash card for *Ff* and ask for the name of the letter and its sound. Have the children give several words that begin with *Ff.*

Note: If the children should give words such as *phone* or *phonograph,* write them on the board and explain that they begin with the */f/* sound but are spelled with a *ph.*

Read these words one at a time and have the children tell where they hear the sound of *f.*

fall	puffy	sniff
muffin	waffle	flower
scarf	half	feet
buff	gift	cliff

Read the directions with the children.

Ask what the first picture is (feather). Ask where they hear the */f/* sound. Have them circle the beginning *f* symbol.

Name the rest of the pictures (scarf, muffin, calf, fan, raft, fork, ruffle, roof).

Let the children finish the exercise independently. Check.

Read the second direction with the children. Ask what the first picture is. Ask where they hear the */f/* sound. Trace the *f* and have them read the word.

Do the same for the other two pictures. Check.

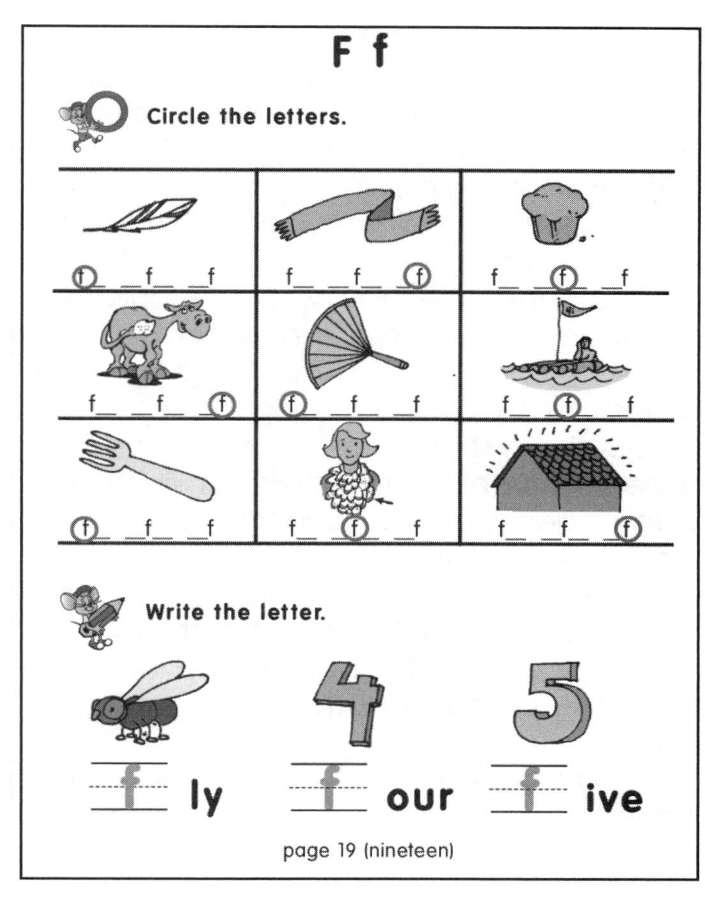

ACTIVITIES:

1. Add pictures with *f* in the middle or at the end to the picture-card collection. Have the children work with them alone or in small groups.

2. Play a Game.

Stack all cards that have the */f/* sound face up on a table or on the floor. Each child draws a card. If he can name the picture and tell where the */f/* sound is in the word, he can keep the card and the next child draws a card. If he cannot tell where the */f/* sound is, another child may help him and the card is returned to the bottom of the stack. Two, three, or four children may play.

3. Add *Ff* pictures and words to the Bible booklet.

4. Do Worksheet 9.

Read the first direction with the children. Have them name the pictures and listen for the /*k*/ sound at the end of each (duck, cup, stick, crack, clock).

Have the children complete the exercise. Check.

Read the direction with the children. Ask them to tell what the symbols •____, ____•____, and ____• stand for (beginning sound, middle sound, ending sound).

Do the first example in each column together, then let the children finish the page independently. Have them name the pictures before they begin.

Check by having the children name the picture and tell where the letter they wrote comes in the picture. (fan, hand, king, leaf, slipper, sailor, muffin, button, ball, roof, track, trap)

5. Practice writing letter *Ff* in the writing tablet.

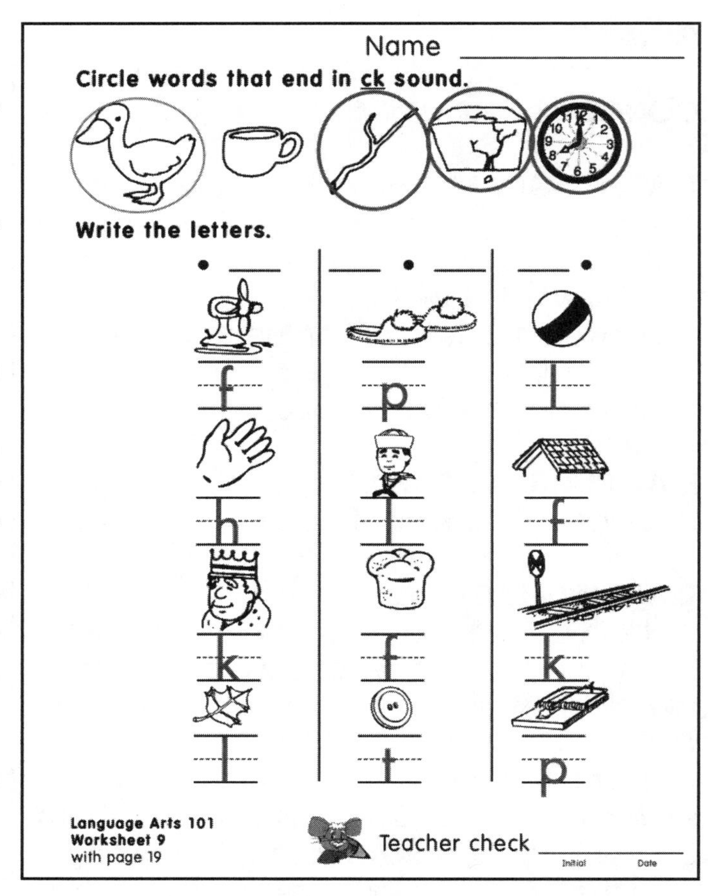

Name ____________

Circle words that end in ck sound.

Write the letters.

• ___	___ • ___	___ •
f	p	l
h	l	f
k	f	k
l	t	p

Language Arts 101
Worksheet 9
with page 19

Teacher check ____________
Initial Date

Page 20: Hh

CONCEPTS: sound of *h*

TEACHER GOALS: To teach the children
To identify the */h/* sound at the beginning of words and pictures.

MATERIALS NEEDED: picture cards, alphabet cards

TEACHING PAGE 20:
Have the children give the sound of *Hh* and read the words under the pictures.
Have the children read the first direction. Name the pictures (hat, kite, log, horse, hair, heart).
Ask the children to tell where the sound of *h* is in the first picture. Tell them that very few words have the sound of *h* anywhere else in the word. Work only with the beginning sound of *h*.
Have the children circle the pictures and check.
Have the children write the beginning letter on the lines. Check by having the children tell what letter they wrote for each picture.

ACTIVITIES:
1. Add pictures to the *Hh* chart. Choose a child to work with a small group naming the pictures and telling where they hear the sound of *h*.
2. Add more pictures to the picture-card collection. Have the children who need help work with the cards alone or in pairs.
3. Add to the *Hh* page in the Bible booklet.
4. Practice writing letter *Hh* in the writing tablet.

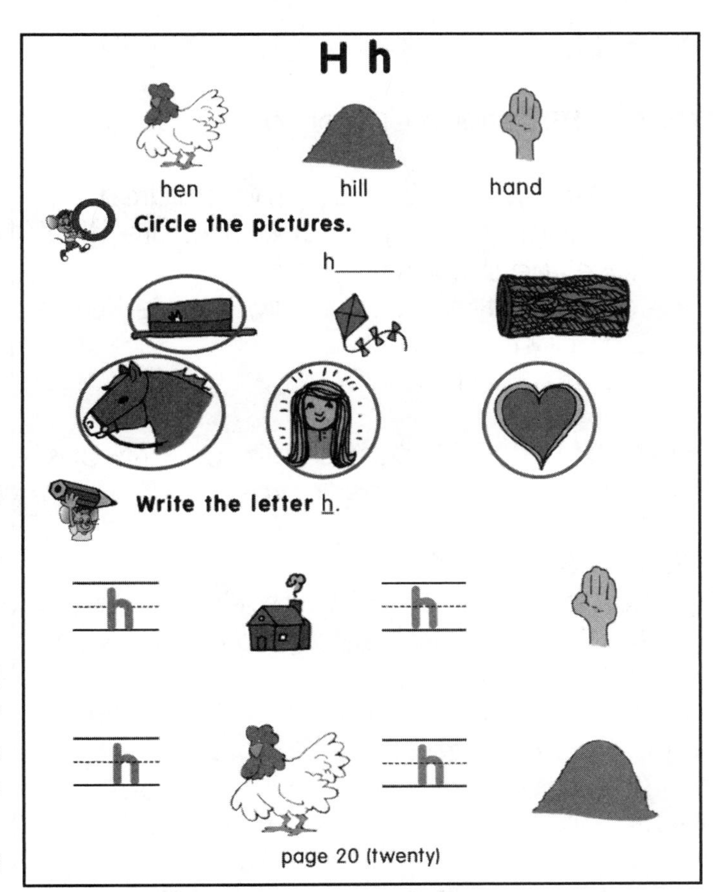

Page 21: Oo

CONCEPTS: sound of short *o*

TEACHER GOALS: To teach the children
To identify things in the picture that have the short /o/ sound,
To repeat the rhyme "Polly, Put the Kettle On," and
To write the letter *Oo*.

MATERIALS NEEDED: pencils or crayons, Worksheet 10, alphabet cards

TEACHING PAGE 21:

Read the title with the children.

Ask the children which words have the short /o/ sound.

Ask if anyone can say the rhyme. Have all the children say it.

Polly, put the kettle on. Polly, put the kettle on. Polly, put the kettle on, We'll all have tea.

Ask the children how many times they heard the words *Polly* and *on*. Ask what is the vowel sound. What letter makes that sound?

Have children look at the picture and find things with the short /o/ sound. Have them name them. Tell them to put an X on all of the things with the short /o/ sound. Check by having them name them (Polly, the girl pouring tea, dolls, teapot, top, blocks, socks).

Read the first directions with the children. Ask the children to name the first picture, to read the word, and to tell what the missing letter should be. Ask what the sound of the letter is. Have them write the *o* and read the word again. Have the children name the other picture. Write the *o* on the lines. Read the words several times (hop, stop).

ACTIVITIES:

1. Ask the children to say nursery rhymes they especially like.
2. Do Worksheet 10

Have the children read the columns of letters in the first box. Be sure the letters are read as small *a*, small *c*, capital *A*, and so on.

Have the children draw a line between the small *a* and the capital *A*. Let the children do the rest of the box by themselves.

Do the first letter in the second box together after reading the columns of letters. Then let the children finish the box by themselves. Collect the paper and check. Have the children correct their mistakes. If a child makes more than five or six mistakes on the page, work with him on the alphabet flash cards for several days and then let him do the worksheet again.

Hold up the flash card *o* and ask for the name of the letter and its sound. Ask the children to tell how rhyming words are alike.

Read the direction with the children. Read the word *bob,* have the children point to it and read it. Have them point to the word *cob* and tell how it is like *bob.* Have them point to each word, sound it out, and read it. Then have them read the entire list.

Do the same with each list of rhyming words. Call attention to the silent *k* in knob, and the silent *h* in *John.*

3. Practice writing letter *Oo* in the writing tablet.

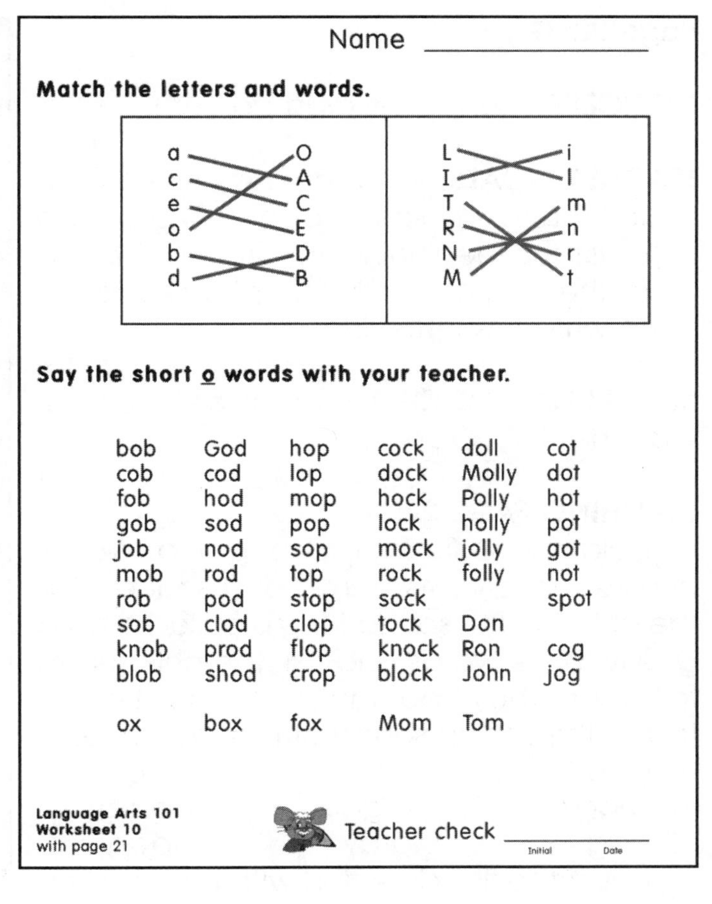

Name ____________

Match the letters and words.

a c e o b d — O A C E D B

L I T R N M — i l m n r t

Say the short o words with your teacher.

bob	God	hop	cock	doll	cot
cob	cod	lop	dock	Molly	dot
fob	hod	mop	hock	Polly	hot
gob	sod	pop	lock	holly	pot
job	nod	sop	mock	jolly	got
mob	rod	top	rock	folly	not
rob	pod	stop	sock		spot
sob	clod	clop	tock	Don	
knob	prod	flop	knock	Ron	cog
blob	shod	crop	block	John	jog
ox	box	fox	Mom	Tom	

Language Arts 101
Worksheet 10
with page 21

Teacher check ____________
Initial Date

Page 22: Gg

CONCEPT: sound of *g* as in *go*

TEACHER GOALS: To teach the children
To identify the sound of *g* as in *go* (hard *g*) at the beginning, in the middle, and at the end of words and pictures, and
To write the letter *Gg*.

MATERIALS NEEDED: alphabet cards, Worksheet 11, crayons

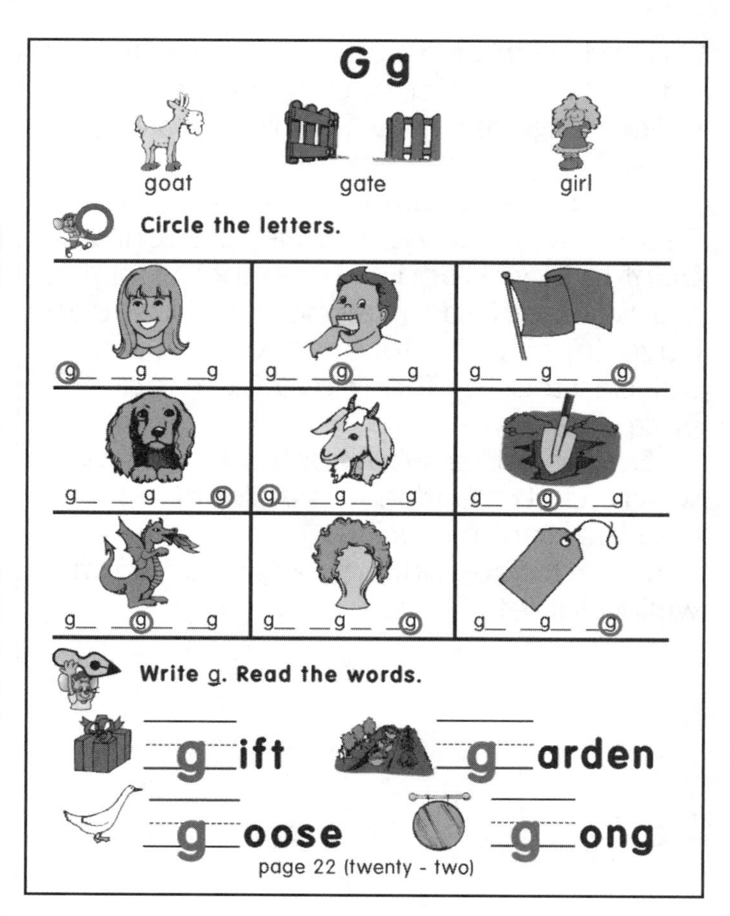

TEACHING PAGE 22:

Hold up the flash card for *g* and ask the children to give its name and sound. Tell the children this sound for *g* is called a hard *g*. Say these words and ask the children to tell where they hear the /g/ sound. Do not teach the soft /j/ sound of *g* at this time.

give	game	jug
wiggle	giggle	drag
bag	gray	gag

Read the first direction with the children as they follow along or have a child read the direction. Do the first three examples together. Ask the children to name the picture and tell where they hear the /g/ sound. Circle the letters. Have the children name the remaining pictures and finish the exercise independently (girl, wiggling a tooth, flag, dog, goat, digging, dragon, wig, tag).

Check by having the children name the picture and tell which *g* they circled.

Read the second direction with the children. Have the children name the first picture and tell what the first sound is. Ask what letter makes that sound. Have them write the *g* on the lines; then read the word. Do the same for the other three pictures.

Read all the words again.

ACTIVITIES:

1. Do Worksheet 11.

Read the direction with the children. Ask what the first picture is and where the sound of *g* is in it. Have them circle the garden. Have the children name the remaining pictures in the section and circle those with the /g/ sound (hammer, garage, gift, guitar, goose).

Do the first example in each of the other sections with the children in the same way. Have them circle the pictures. Name the pictures in each section *before* the children circle them (rug, girl, pig, leg, mug, log).

Check each section by having the children name the pictures they circled. If your children are doing well on their sounds, they may do the entire page independently.

Tell the children to look at the first group of letters in the block and read the letters. Ask which letter should come first. Have them write it in the first blank. Ask which letter should come next and have it written in the next blank. Finish the box with the children.

Let them finish the rest of the page. The teacher should check this page. Have the children correct any mistakes.

2. Add the pictures with the /*g*/ sound in the middle and at the end to the set of picture cards. Children may work with these pictures by themselves if the position of the sound is on the back of the card. Have them sort the *g* cards into the proper boxes.

3. Have the children who know the /*g*/ sound work with those who do not on the *Gg* chart or with the picture cards.

4. Add to the *Gg* page in the Bible booklet. Look for pictures or words with the /*g*/ sound in the middle or at the end.

5. Practice writing letter *Gg* in the writing tablet.

Name ____________

Circle pictures with the g sound.

g___

___g

Write letters in order.

C A D B

A B C D

H E G F

E F G H

J L I K

I J K L

Language Arts 101
Worksheet 11
with page 22

Teacher check ____________
Initial Date

Page 23: Jj

CONCEPTS: sound of *j*, writing capital *J*, Jesus and His disciples

TEACHER GOALS: To teach the children
To identify pictures with the sound of *j* at the beginning, in the middle, or at the end,
To understand that all names begin with capital letters,
To write the capital *J* at the beginning of names, and
To tell about Jesus and His disciples.

BIBLE REFERENCES: Any references to Jesus and His disciples and to Joseph.

MATERIALS NEEDED: picture cards, alphabet cards

TEACHING PAGE 23:

Hold up the flash card for *j* and ask for the name and sound of the letter. Read this list of words and have the children tell where the /j/ sound is heard.

jump	hinge	judge
budge	badge	ledger
rigid	jingle	joy
Jesus	range	jelly

Read the first direction with the children as they follow along from left to right. Ask the children what the picture in the first box is. Ask where they hear the /j/ sound in *jungle*. Have them draw a circle around the beginning *j* symbol. Have them say the word again. Have the children name the remaining pictures and circle the symbol that shows where the /j/ sound is found in the word. Check by having the children tell which symbol they circled. Have them say the word again (pajamas, jar, jacket, jacks, jar of jam, jug, jet, jewelry).

Have them trace the capital *J* and read the name Jesus. Ask the children to tell who Jesus is.

Have the children write the capital *J* in each of the other spaces and read the names if they can. Tell them any they do not know and have the children repeat them.

Read all four names and ask the children why they think those four names are together. Someone may know that John and James were Jesus' disciples. Have the children tell what they know about the disciples and what Jesus meant to them.

Ask the children who Joseph was. Ask them how many Josephs they know about in the Bible. Discuss the story of Jesus' foster father.

ACTIVITIES:

1. Add to the *Jj* pages of the Bible booklet.
2. Put the words *Jesus* and *joy* on the board and ask the children to tell why those two words go together.

3. Read Bible stories or books about Jesus, John, James, and Joseph.
4. Practice writing letter *Jj* in the writing tablet.

Page 24: Rhyming Words

CONCEPTS: beginning sounds, rhyming words

TEACHER GOALS: To teach the children
To write a beginning letter to make a short *e* word,
To read the rhyming words he has made, and
To match words that rhyme.

VOCABULARY: match, rhyming

TEACHING PAGE 24:

Read the first direction with the children. Have them first read the ending ___*en* and the first word *pen*, then trace the letter *p*. Have them write letters to make two more *en* words. To check their work, have them read their words while you write them on the board.

Some children will be able to write *-et* words by themselves. Use the same procedure as with the *-en* words for those who need more help. Check by writing the list on the board.

Read the question and second direction to the children and have them repeat.

Fold a sheet of writing tablet paper in half lengthwise. Write *en* at the top of the first half and ___*et* at the top of the second half. Have the children write more rhyming words for each ending. Write the lists on the board and let the children check their own papers. Have them add any words they missed. If you prefer, have the children do this exercise after they have done the matching exercise on the page.

Read the third direction with the children. Have them point to the word *match* and read it.

Have the children sound out the word *peg* and find the word that rhymes with it. Draw the line between the two words.

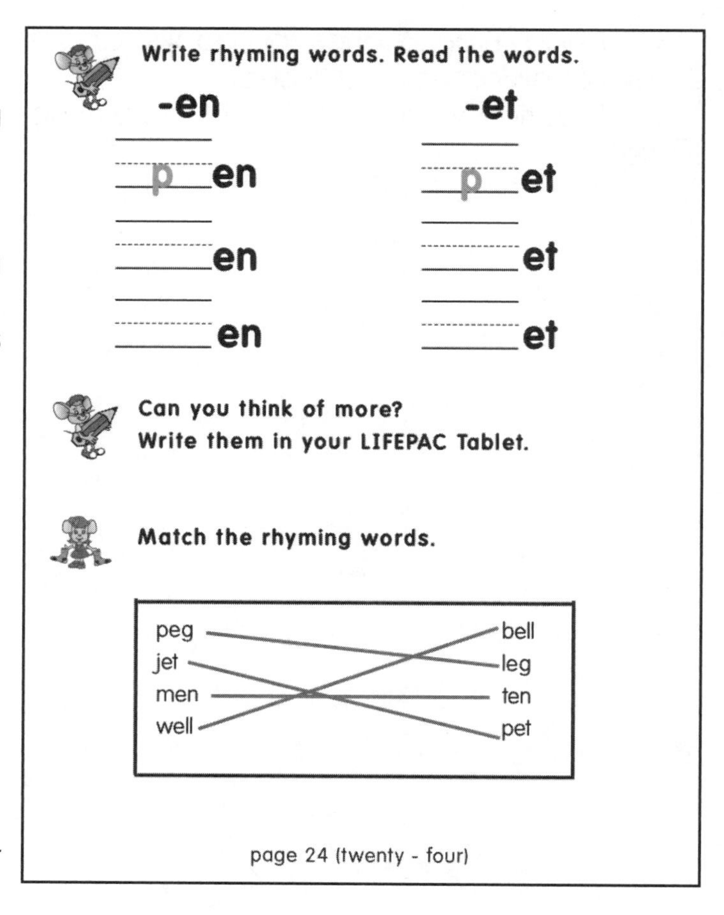

Read them. Tell the children to sound out the rest of the words and to match them. Have the children read each pair.

ACTIVITIES:

1. Say a short *e* word and have the children give a rhyming word.
2. Do the ___*en* and *et* exercises again in a small group with children who had difficulty .
3. Some students can write sentences for their *en* and *et* words.

SELF TEST 2

CONCEPTS: matching upper and lower case letters, short /i/ sound, short /o/ sound, identify sounds at the beginning, in the middle, or at the end of a word

TEACHER GOAL: To teach the children
To check their own progress periodically.

TEACHING PAGE 25:

Do not stress that this page is a test. Some children are frightened by the word *test* because of what they hear older children say about taking tests. Tell them that this page will help them to check themselves to see how well they have learned what is in the LIFEPAC.

Read all the directions and have the children repeat them. Be sure they understand what they are to do.

Let the children do the entire page independently. You may read the directions for the children who forget them but give them no other help. (bed, fish, brick)

Do not have the children check this page. Check it as soon as possible and go over it with each child so that he can see where he did well and where he needs extra help.

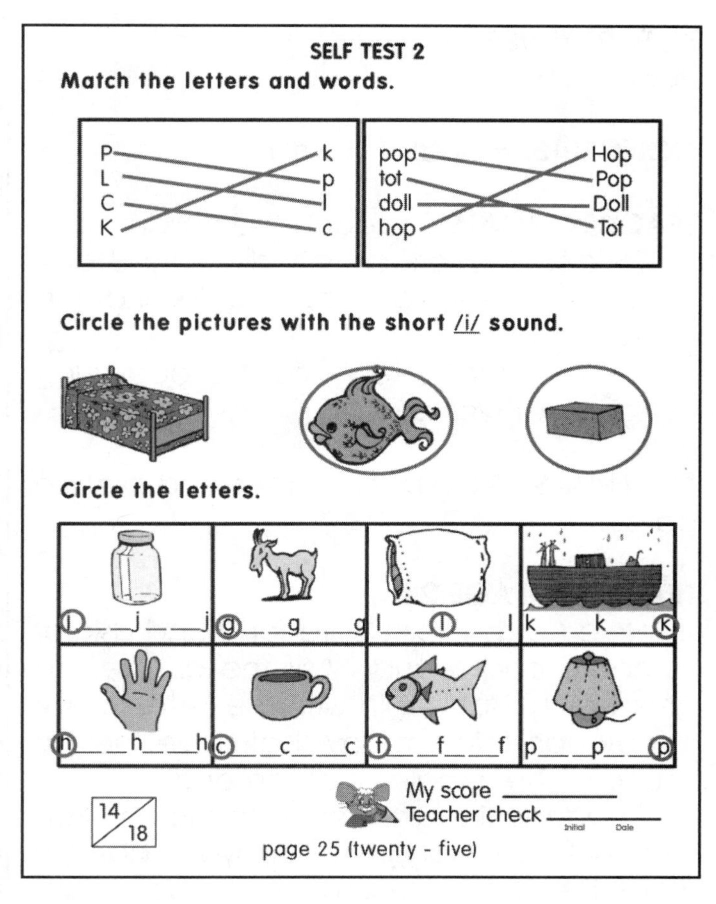
SELF TEST 2

Match the letters and words.

P L C K — k p l c

pop tot doll hop — Hop Pop Doll Tot

Circle the pictures with the short /i/ sound.

Circle the letters.

j___j___j g___g___g l___l___l k___k___k

h___h___h c___c___c f___f___f p___p___p

14/18

My score ________

Teacher check ________ Initial Date

page 25 (twenty - five)

ACTIVITIES:

1. Give individual help on items missed.
2. If several children miss the same sounds, reteach them (in small groups, if possible).

SPELLING WORDS:

kit
dip
pop
hot
kick

III. PART THREE
Page 26: Vv

CONCEPTS: sound of *v*, writing *v*

TEACHER GOALS: To teach the children
To identify pictures with the sound of *v* at the beginning, in the middle, or at the end, and
To write the letter *v* as the beginning sound of words.

MATERIALS NEEDED: alphabet and picture cards

TEACHING PAGE 26:

Hold up the flash card for *v* and ask for its name and sound. Ask the children to give words that begin with the letter *v*. Ask if they can think of any that have the /*v*/ sound in the middle or at the end.

Read the first direction with the children as they follow along. Ask if anyone can tell what the first picture is. Ask where they hear the /*v*/ sound. Have them circle the beginning *v* symbol.

Name the rest of the pictures and have the children finish the exercise (seven, wave, five, hive, eleven, vegetables, violin, clover).

Be sure the children know the meaning of all the words.

Read the direction with the children and name all the pictures (valentine, vine, vase, volcano).

Ask the children where they heard the sound of *v* in all the words. Have them write the letter *v* on the lines after each picture.

ACTIVITIES:

1. Add pictures with the /*v*/ sound in the middle and at the end to the picture-card collection. Have the children sort the pictures into the right boxes.

2. Add pictures or words with the /*v*/ sound in the middle and at the end to the Bible booklet.
3. Practice writing letter *Vv* in the writing tablet.

Page 27: Ww

CONCEPT: sound of *w*

TEACHER GOAL: To teach the children
To identify pictures with the sound of *w* at the beginning, in the middle, or at the end, and
To review the sound of *g*.

MATERIALS NEEDED: alphabet cards, picture cards, Worksheet 12, crayons

TEACHING PAGE 27:

Hold up the flash card for the letter *w* and ask for its name and sound. Ask the children to give words that begin with the sound of *w*.

Read the following list of words and have the children tell where they hear the sound of *w*.

want	lower	cow
fewer	how	we
now	were	mower
jewel	chow	wet

Read the direction with the children as they follow along from left to right. Call attention to the symbol that tells where the /*w*/ sound is to be found in the picture. Have the children name the first picture in each column and tell where they hear the /*w*/ sound. Have the children name all the pictures on the page and then complete the page independently. Check by having the children name the pictures they circled in each column (wing, wagon, wood, owl, tower, towel, pew, plow, screw).

Read the second direction. Have the children name the first picture (wagon). Have the children write the letter they hear at the beginning of wagon. Name the other pictures and have them write *w* under each one (wing, well).

ACTIVITIES:

1. Do Worksheet 12.

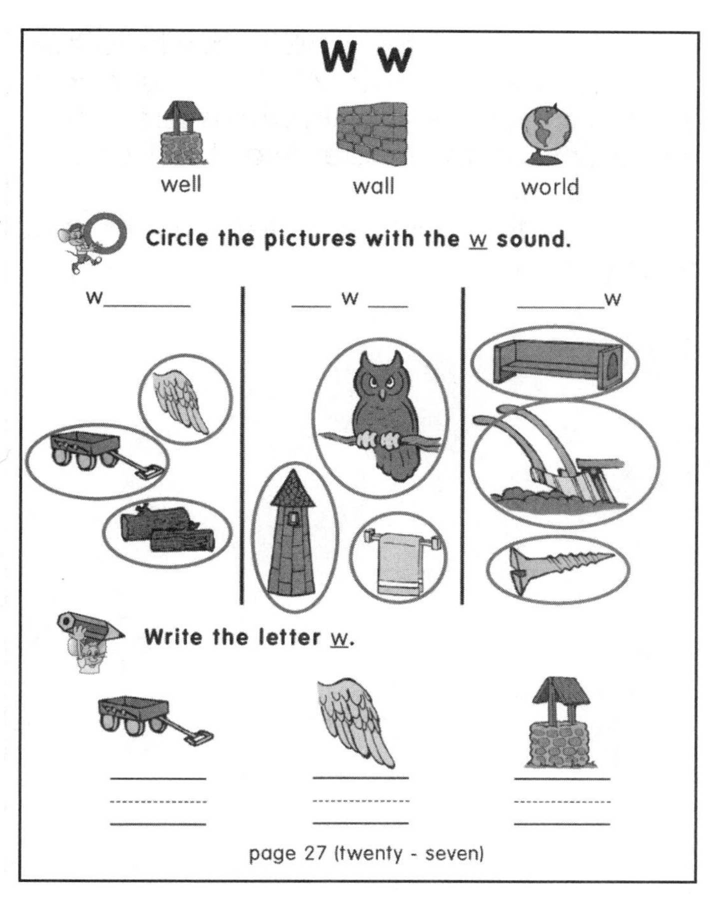

Have the children read the direction and name all the pictures on the page. Ask what sound *grass* begins with and what letter makes that sound. Have them trace the *g* on the lines and read the word. Let children finish the page independently. Check by having the children name the picture, give the beginning sound, and name the letter they wrote on the lines.

Read the lists of words over again.

2. Add pictures with the /*w*/ sound in the middle or at the end to the picture-card collection. Have the child sort the pictures into the proper boxes and check by looking at the position symbol on the back of the card.

3. Play the letter game. Stack all the picture cards with *w* face up. Have the children take turns choosing a card and telling where they hear the sound of *w*. If correct, they keep the card; if not, they replace it at the bottom of the stack after

the leader or another child tells where the /*w*/ sound is. The child with the most cards is the winner. Have a child who is sure of the /*w*/ sound be the leader. Two, three, or four may play.

5. Practice writing letter *Ww* in the writing tablet.

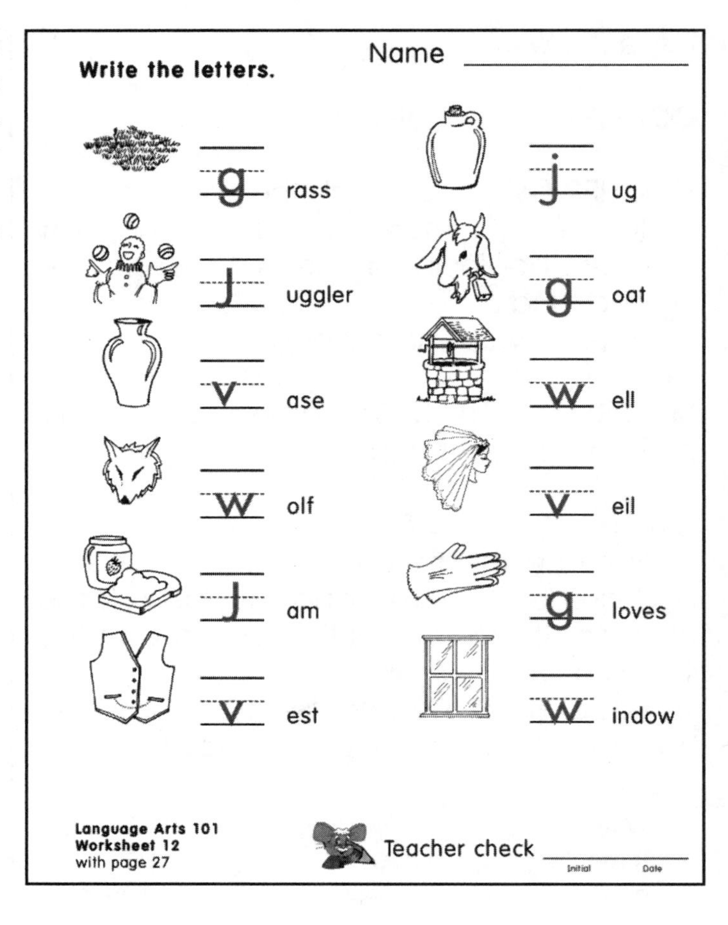

Write the letters.

Name ____________

g rass

j ug

j uggler

g oat

v ase

w ell

w olf

v eil

j am

g loves

v est

w indow

Language Arts 101
Worksheet 12
with page 27

Teacher check ____________
Initial Date

Page 28: Xx

CONCEPTS: sound of *x*

TEACHER GOALS: To teach the children
To identify the sound of *x* at the beginning, in the middle, and at the end of words.

MATERIALS NEEDED: alphabet cards, picture cards

TEACHING PAGE 28:

Hold up the flash card for the *x* and ask for its name and sound. Tell children that the /*x*/ sound is not found at the beginning of many words. They will hear it in the middle of such words as *mixer* and *boxer* and at the end of such words as *six* and *fix*. The /*x*/ sound is the same as the /*ks*/ sound.

Read the first direction with the children. Have them write an *x* on the lines and read the word. Have them write the *x* in exit and read the word. Tell the children to write an *x* in the rest of the spaces and sound out the words. Have children read them.

Read the last direction and do the matching exercises. Check.

ACTIVITIES:

1. Add pictures that have the *x* sound to the picture collection. Have the children sort them into the proper boxes.
2. Add pictures or words with the /*x*/ sounds in the middle and at the end to the Bible booklet.
3. Practice writing letter *Xx* in the writing tablet.

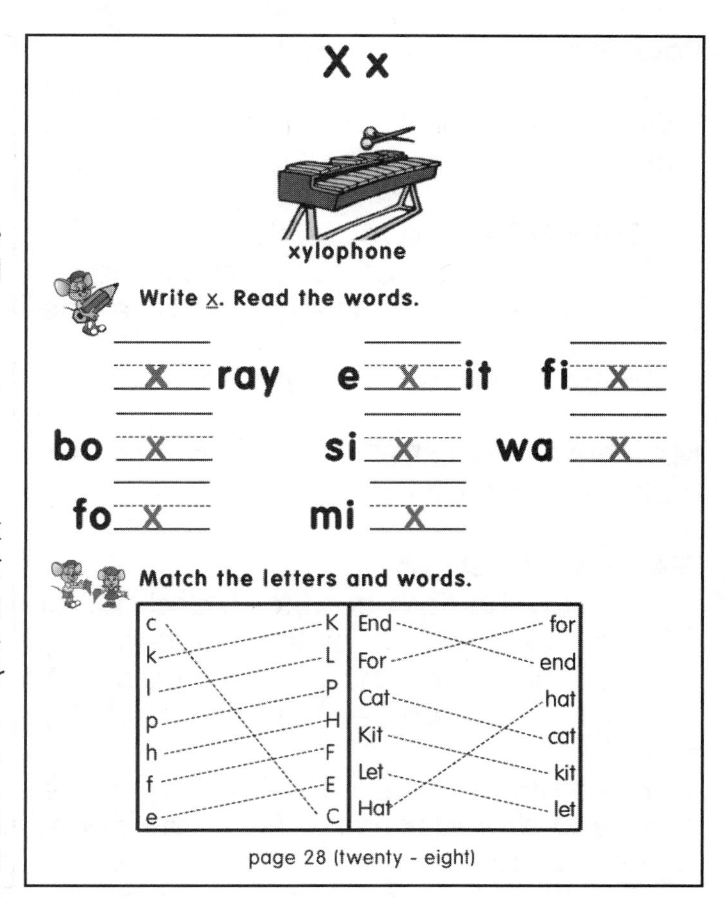

Page 29: Uu

CONCEPTS: sound of short *u*, rhyming words

TEACHER GOALS: To teach the children
To identify the sound of short *u* in words,
To identify the rhyming words in the poem, and
To review the sound of *j*.

MATERIALS NEEDED: Worksheet 13, alphabet flash cards

TEACHING PAGE 29:

Hold up the flash card for *u* and ask for its name and sound. Tell the children they will learn about the short sound of *u* on this page. Have them repeat the short /u/ sound.

Have the children tell who is in the picture and read the title. Read the poem to the children.

Have the children tell which words have the short /u/ sound. Have them tell which words rhyme.

Read the first directions with the children. Have them say the rhyme. Read the questions and have the children answer if they can.

What is a tuffet?

What are curds and whey?

You may have to tell them that a tuffet is a kind of stool and that curds and whey is like cottage cheese.

Have the children say the entire rhyme several times.

Have the children read the second direction. Ask the children to look at the first picture and tell what it is. Have them read the word after the picture and tell what the missing letter should be. Have them trace the *u* and read the word again. Have the children name the rest of the picture and write in the letter *u*. Have them read the words they have made and use each of them in a sentence.

ACTIVITIES:

1. Read more nursery rhymes or stories.
2. Do worksheet 13

Read the first direction with the children as they follow along or have a child read the direction. Do the first three examples together. Ask the children to name the picture (jet) and to tell where they hear the /j/ sound. Have them draw a circle around the first j. Have the children name the rest of the pictures and finish the exercise independently (jet, jeep, jacks, jungle, banjo, janitor).

Check by having the children name the picture and tell which *j* they circled.

Read the second direction to the children. Read the list of *ub* words and ask the children to tell how they are alike. Ask if they can think of any other words that end with *ub* or have *ub* in the middle.

Do the same with each list of rhyming words.

TEACHING READING:

Survey students to find out how many have a dog. Ask them what they need to do to care for their dog. List their responses. If giving their dog a bath isn't shared, then add it to the list as your idea. Discuss experiences with giving a dog a bath.

Read the story "Dog in the Tub" then ask the following questions:

"Who is going to get a bath?" (the dog)

"Do you think it's a big dog or a little dog?"

"How do you know?" (big, Bill offered to help)

"What does the word "kerplop" tell?" (the sound of being dropped in the tub)

"Who do you think got wet?" (answers may vary - all of them)

"What will happen next?" (accept all reasonable answers)

Have students find the short vowel words.

ACTIVITY:

Use the prior response list and make a classroom book of ways to care for a dog. As a writing exercise, have students write a story continuation. Invite students to share their own pets with pictures or a visit to the classroom.

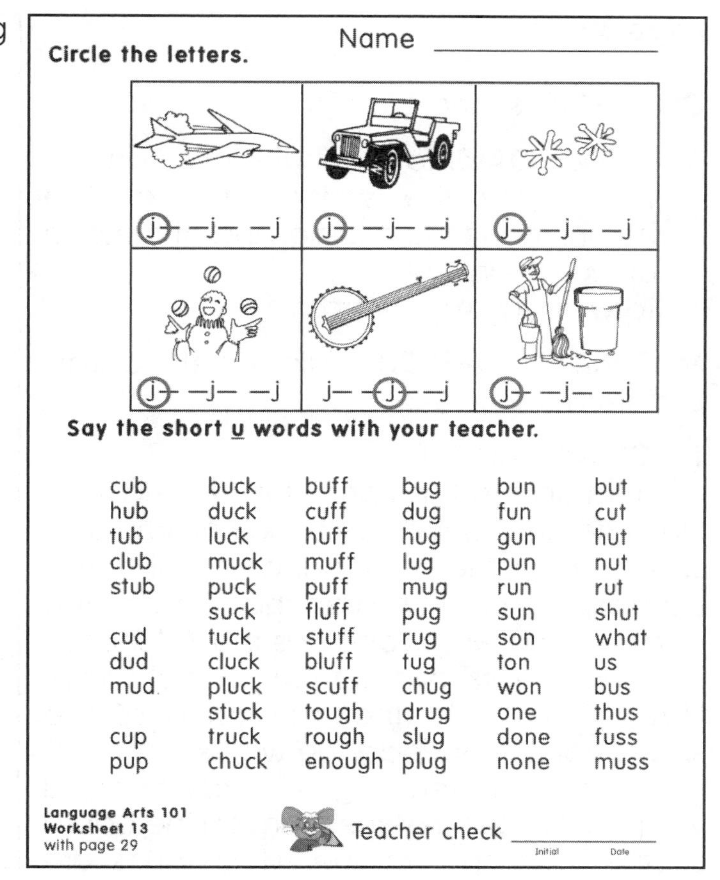

Name ______________

Circle the letters.

j– –j– –j | j– –j– –j | j– –j– –j

j– –j– –j | j– –j– –j | j– –j– –j

Say the short u words with your teacher.

cub	buck	buff	bug	bun	but
hub	duck	cuff	dug	fun	cut
tub	luck	huff	hug	gun	hut
club	muck	muff	lug	pun	nut
stub	puck	puff	mug	run	rut
	suck	fluff	pug	sun	shut
cud	tuck	stuff	rug	son	what
dud	cluck	bluff	tug	ton	us
mud	pluck	scuff	chug	won	bus
	stuck	tough	drug	one	thus
cup	truck	rough	slug	done	fuss
pup	chuck	enough	plug	none	muss

Language Arts 101
Worksheet 13
with page 29

Teacher check ______________
Initial Date

Page 30: Zz

CONCEPTS: sound of *z*

TEACHER GOALS: To teach the children

To identify the sound of *z* at the beginning, in the middle, and at the end of words, and

To write rhyming words.

MATERIALS NEEDED: alphabet cards, picture cards

TEACHING PAGE 30:

Hold up the flash card for *z* and ask for its name and sound. Have the children give words with the */z/* sound in all three positions. Tell the children that the *s* at the end of some words also has the */z/* sound.

Read the first direction with the children. Have them write the *z* in each of the spaces and then read the words.

Ask the children to give words that end with the */z/* sound. Write them on the board so the children can see which ones are spelled with a *z* and which end with an *s*.

Read the last direction with the children. Have the children read each word and give one or two words that rhyme with it. Let them write rhyming words on the lines.

ACTIVITIES:

1. Add more pictures with the */z/* sounds in the middle and at the end to the *Zz* charts. Have the children work with the charts in small groups.
2. List words that end in *s* but that have the */z/* sound in one corner of the *Zz* flashcard. Children may refer to this list when they need to spell the words in their written work. Include such words as *is, was, has, these,* and so on.
3. Add pictures that have the *z* sounds to the picture collection. Have the children sort them into the proper boxes.
4. Add pictures or words with the */z/* sounds in the middle and at the end to the Bible booklet.

Z z 0 zero zebra zipper

Write z. Read the words.

z oo z ag z ig

z ero di z z y

z ipper bu z z

Write rhyming words.

pin rim

sit hid

will hiss

page 30 (thirty)

5. Practice writing letter *Zz* in the writing tablet.

TEACHING READING:

Find the story "Dad" in *Reader 1.*

Have the children look at the picture and tell what is happening. Have several children tell about a time when they needed a hug. Allow as many children to tell their experience as time allows.

Read the story together.

Ask these questions:

"How will the little girl get to Dad?"

"What will she do when she gets to Dad?"

"Where does she fit?"

"Will she still fit when she grows?"

"Do you think the Dad loves the little girl?"

Have the children find the short /a/, short /i/, and short /u/ words. Write them on the board.

Page 31: Yy

CONCEPTS: sound of *y*, beginning sounds

TEACHER GOALS: To teach the children
To identify the sound of y at the beginning of words, and
To identify the beginning sounds: *x, y, z.*

MATERIALS NEEDED: alphabet cards, picture cards

TEACHING PAGE 31:
Hold up the flash card for *y* and ask for its name and sound. Ask the children if they can think of any words beginning with that sound.

Read the first direction with the children. Have them write a *y* in the space and read the word. Do all the words the same way. Have the children read the words several times. Be sure they know what each word means.

Read the second direction or have a child read it.

Name all the pictures in the boxes and have the children circle the beginning sound of each. Check by having the children name the picture and give the name of the beginning letter and its sound (zipper, yarn, vest, wall, zero, gate, jacket, wagon, yard).

Y y

yarn yo-yo

Write y. Read the words.

y es y ell y et

y am y arn y ear

Circle the letters.

x y z | x y z | v w r
w v j | x y z | g j v
j w g | v w g | x y z

page 31 (thirty - one)

ACTIVITIES:
1. Add pictures to the picture cards. Have children sort the cards into the proper box.
2. For a review game, pick five or six letter flash cards. Hold up a card and say "beginning," "ending," or "middle." Have the children give words with the sound on the card in the position you have called.
3. Add *Yy* pictures on words to the Bible booklet.
4. Practice writing letter *Yy* in the writing tablet.

TEACHING READING:
Read the story "Wet" in *Reader 1.*

Have the children look at the picture. Have them tell what is happening. Have the children tell about a time when they were caught in the rain.

Have the children read the story silently. Read the story aloud.

Ask questions similar to these:

"What were the people in the story doing?"

"What happened to stop their picnic?"

"Who will get wet?"

"Why will the fat cat and Jan be dry?"

"Will the food get wet?"

Have the children find the short /a/, short /e/, short /i/, and short /o/ words in the story. Write them on the board.

ACTIVITY:
Have the children draw a rainy day picture with chalk on black paper.

Page 32 Qq

CONCEPT: sound of *qu*

TEACHER GOALS: To teach the children
To identify pictures with the sound of *qu* at the beginning, and
To write *qu* as the beginning letters of words.

MATERIALS NEEDED: alphabet cards, picture cards

TEACHING PAGE 32:

Hold up the flash card for *q* and ask for its name and sound. Tell the children that we never find a *q* alone at the beginning of a word, that it always has the letter *u* with it. Hold up the flash card for *u*. The two letters together have the sound of *kw*. Have the children say it several times.

You may tell them that some words have the *q* in the middle. These words may have either the */k/* sound as in *lacquer, croquet,* or *Marquette,* or the */kw/* sound as in *request, require, liquid,* or *equal.* Words with the *q* at the end have the */k/* sound as in *Iraq, technique,* or *antique.* Do not expect the children to remember the middle and ending spellings. They will learn these spellings when the words become part of their writing vocabulary. They should begin learning to spell words with the *qu* at the beginning, however.

Read the first direction and sentence at the top of the page with the children.

Ask what the first picture is. Ask what a queen does. Have the children circle the picture of the queen. Have the children name the rest of the pictures and circle those beginning with *qu* (quail, kite, candle, question mark, quarter).

Read the directions with the children. Ask what the sound of *qu* is.

Have the children write the *qu* at the beginning of the first word and pronounce it. Have them repeat it after you. Have the children write *qu* at the beginning of the next word. Say the word and have the children repeat it. Repeat for each of the other words. Then read the list of words and have the children listen for the */kw/* sound. Be sure the children know the meanings of all the pictures and words.

ACTIVITIES:

1. Add pictures to the picture-cards collection. Have a child pick the pictures of things beginning with *qu* out of a group of cards. Have him name the pictures.
2. Some children could make a list of words with the *qu* in the middle or at the end.
3. Add qu words to the Bible booklet.
4. Practice writing letter *Qq* in the writing tablet.

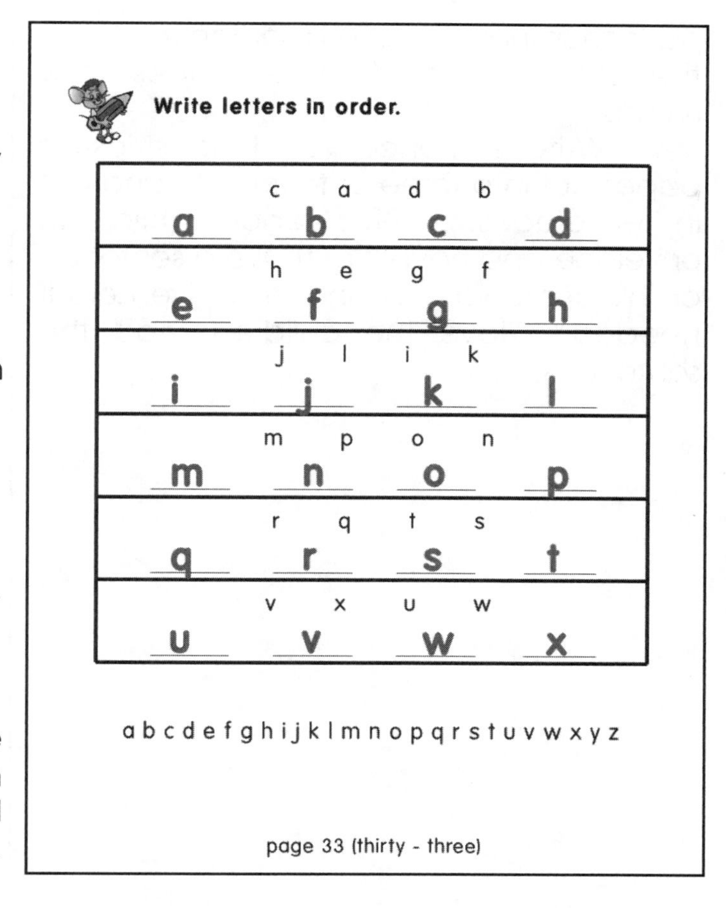

Page 33: Put in Order

CONCEPTS: sequence, telling a story, making inferences, predicting outcomes, *ABC order.*

TEACHER GOALS: To teach the children
To put pictures in proper sequence,
To tell a story from the pictures, and
To predict what might happen next in the story, and
To put letters in alphabetical order.

VOCABULARY: order

MATERIALS NEEDED: picture story cards, Worksheet 14

TEACHING PAGE 33:

Put large pictures that tell the beginning, end, and middle of a story on the chalkboard ledge out of order and have a child put them in the right order. Use several sets.

Check by having the children tell which picture should be first, second, and third.

Have the children tell the stories from the pictures.

Have them tell what they think may have happened before what they see in the pictures, what might happen after, and why they think so.

Tell the children to look at the first box and read the letters. Ask which letter should come first. Have them write it in the first blank. Ask which letter should come next and have it written in the next blank. Finish the box with the children.

Let them finish the rest of the page. Tell them to look at the alphabet at the bottom of the page if they need help. The teacher should check this page. Have the children correct any mistakes.

Tell the children that this page will be done in the same manner as the pictures they just finished, but that they will be putting letters in order instead of pictures or words.

Have the children say the alphabet.

ACTIVITIES:

1. Do Worksheet 14

Read the directions with the children. Ask them if they see a difference between this worksheet and the LIFEPAC paper they just finished. (The LIFEPAC paper was lower-case and the worksheet is upper-case letters.)

2. Have the children draw three parts of a story (either a story they know or one they make up) on three separate sheets of paper. Have them mix them up and let the other children put them in order and tell the story.

3. Have the children write a sentence on a long strip of paper. Cut it in three parts and let the other children put the

parts together to make a sentence. Have the children read the sentences they make.

4. Write sentences on long strips of paper, cut into three or four parts, and put in envelopes. Give each child an envelope and have him make a sentence on his desk. Walk around and give help if needed. Have the children read the sentences.

Name ____________

Write letters in order.

	C	A	D	B	
A	B		C		D
	H	E	G	F	
E	F		G		H
	J	L	I	K	
I	J		K		L
	M	P	O	N	
M	N		O		P
	R	Q	T	S	
Q	R		S		T
	V	X	U	W	
U	V		W		X

A B C D E F G H I J K L M N O P Q R S T U V W X Y Z

Language Arts 101
Worksheet 14
with page 33

Teacher check ____________
Initial Date

SELF TEST 3

CONCEPTS: short /u/ sound, beginning sounds, sequencing letters

TEACHER GOAL: To teach the children

To check their own progress periodically.

TEACHING PAGE 34:

Read all the directions on the page with the children and be sure they understand everything they are to do.

Let them do the entire page without help. If a child cannot name a picture, tell him what it is.

Check the page as soon as possible. Go over it with the child so he can see where he did well and where he needs extra work. (cup, pig, truck, car, tub, muffin, umbrella, cot, drum, nut)

SELF TEST 3

Circle the pictures with the short /u/ sound.

Circle the letters.

v g z	v x y	v x y	j y r
x w z	z v w	g qu p	j b g

Write the letters in order.

w v y x z

v w x y z

My score

Teacher check Initial Date

16/20

page 34 (thirty - four)

ACTIVITIES:

1. Give each child help on items he misses.
2. If several children miss the same things, reteach the skill (in a small group session, if possible).

SPELLING WORDS:

sun
bus
bun
cup
tuck

LIFEPAC TEST AND ALTERNATE TEST 101

CONCEPTS: consonant sounds, short /a/ sounds, short /e/ sounds, short /i/ sounds, short /o/ sounds, short /u/ sounds, matching letters and words, rhyming words, and consonant sounds in the beginning, middle, or end of a word

TEACHER GOAL: To teach the children
To learn to check their own progress periodically.

TEACHING the LIFEPAC TEST:

Administer this test in at least three sessions.

Read all the directions on each page as the children prepare to do it. Name all the pictures (Page 1: gate, valentine, jar, wave, zero, wing, goat, vase, wall, garden, zebra, jet, cat, cup, match, man, desk; Page 2: otter, October, rock, cat, blocks, pin, pods, box; Page 3: cup, candle, log, ruffle, fork, hand, mug, sun, queen, cup, sun, cap, tub, bread, bus, bump, drum).

Alternate LIFEPAC Test (Page 2: wing, hill, igloo, windmill, bat, lid, cup, kitten, octopus, sock, cob, bat, top, teapot, bed, ox; Page 3: pin, cup, bed, duck, nut, brush, top, hut, roof, apple, queen, pillow, corn, feather, kite, car, cup, hill, lion, pocket). Be sure they understand everything they are to do. Let them finish the page independently.

Give no help except with directions.

Go over each page with the child as soon as possible after you check it so that he can see where he did well and where he needs more work.

Evaluate the tests and review areas where the children have done poorly. Review the pages and activities that stress the concepts tested.

If necessary, when the children have reviewed sufficiently, administer the Alternate LIFEPAC Test. Follow the same procedures as used for the LIFEPAC Test.

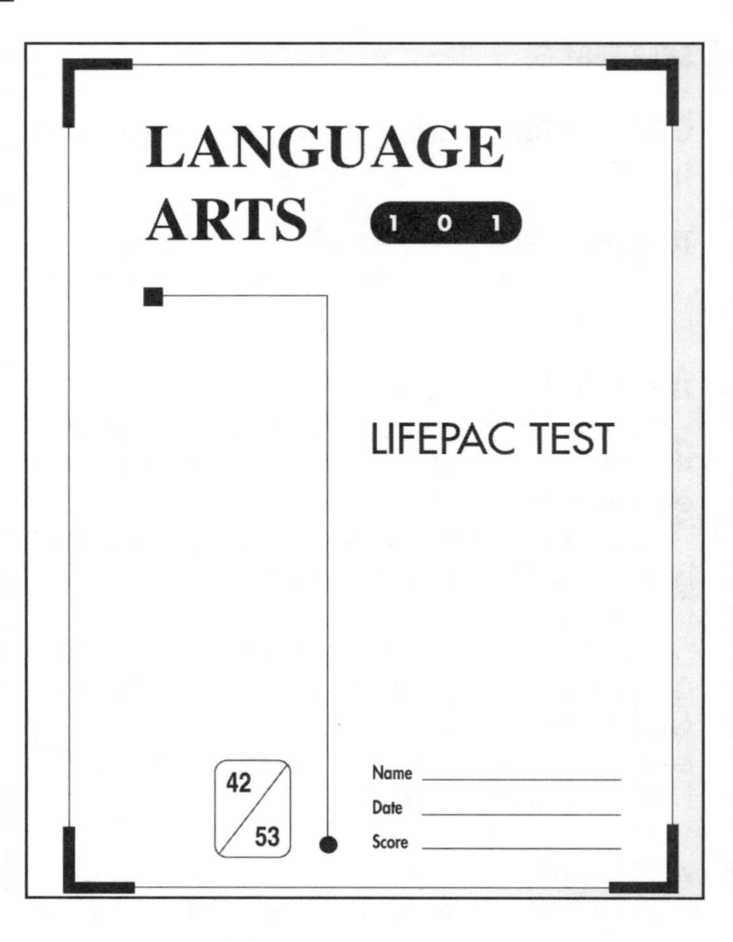

SPELLING WORDS:

LIFEPAC words	Alternate words
rat	ten
sat	men
red	dip
kit	hot
pop	pop
kick	sun
sun	bun
bun	kick
cup	tuck
tuck	bus

LANGUAGE ARTS 101: LIFEPAC TEST

Circle the letters.

g j v	w v r	t c j	w v j
y z x	x y w	h g j	t b v
h j w	g d b	x z w	j t d

Circle the pictures with the short /a/ sound.

page 1 (one)

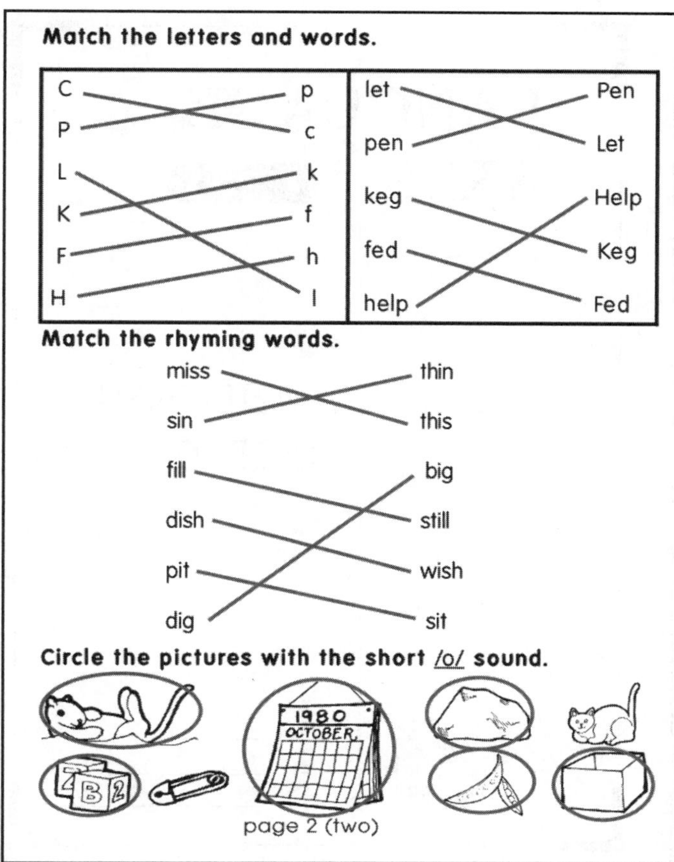

Match the letters and words.

C	p	let	Pen
P	c	pen	Let
L	k	keg	Help
K	f	fed	Keg
F	h	help	Fed
H	l		

Match the rhyming words.

miss	thin
sin	this
fill	big
dish	still
pit	wish
dig	sit

Circle the pictures with the short /o/ sound.

page 2 (two)

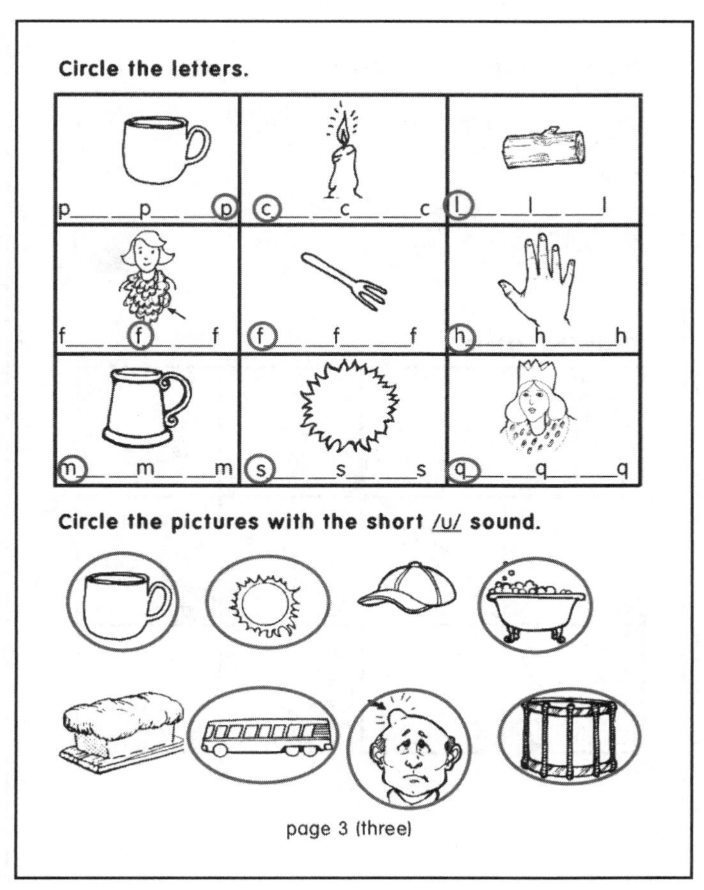

Circle the letters.

p p p	c c c	l l l
f f f	f f f	h h h
m m m	s s s	q q q

Circle the pictures with the short /u/ sound.

page 3 (three)

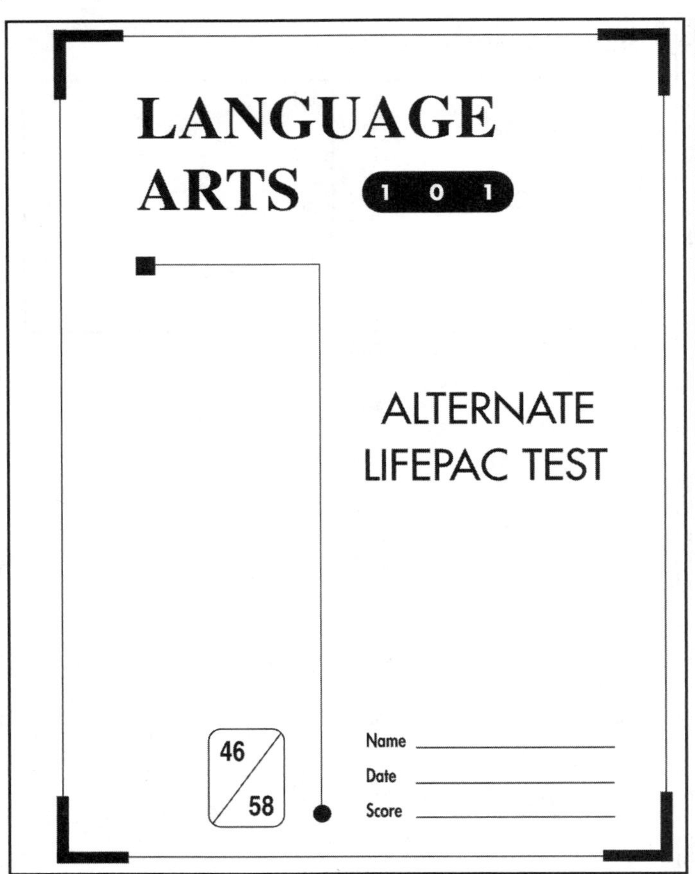

LANGUAGE ARTS 1 0 1

ALTERNATE LIFEPAC TEST

46/58

Name ______

Date ______

Score ______

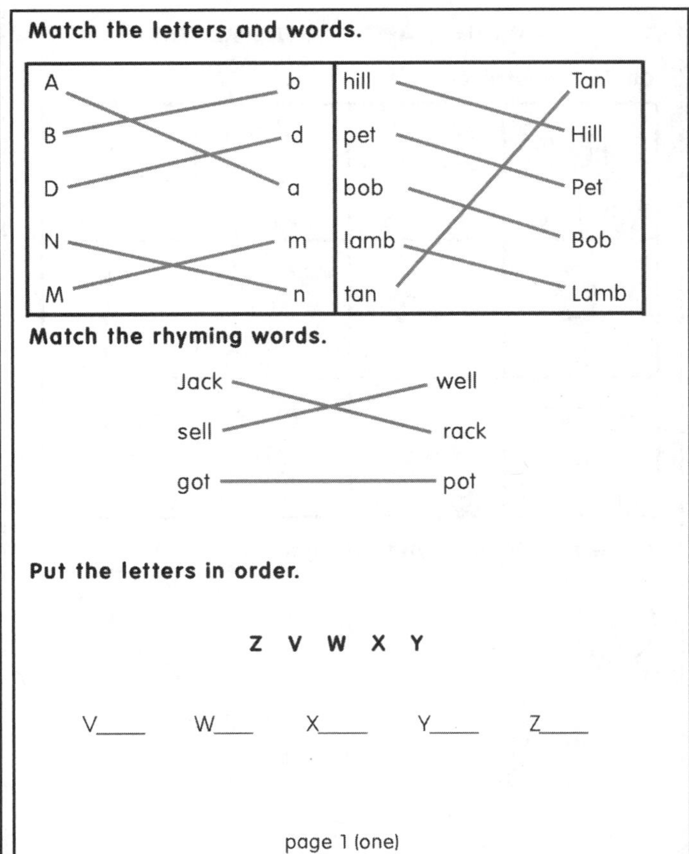

Match the letters and words.

A	b	hill	Tan
B	d	pet	Hill
D	a	bob	Pet
N	m	lamb	Bob
M	n	tan	Lamb

Match the rhyming words.

Jack — well

sell — rack

got — pot

Put the letters in order.

Z V W X Y

V___ W___ X___ Y___ Z___

page 1 (one)

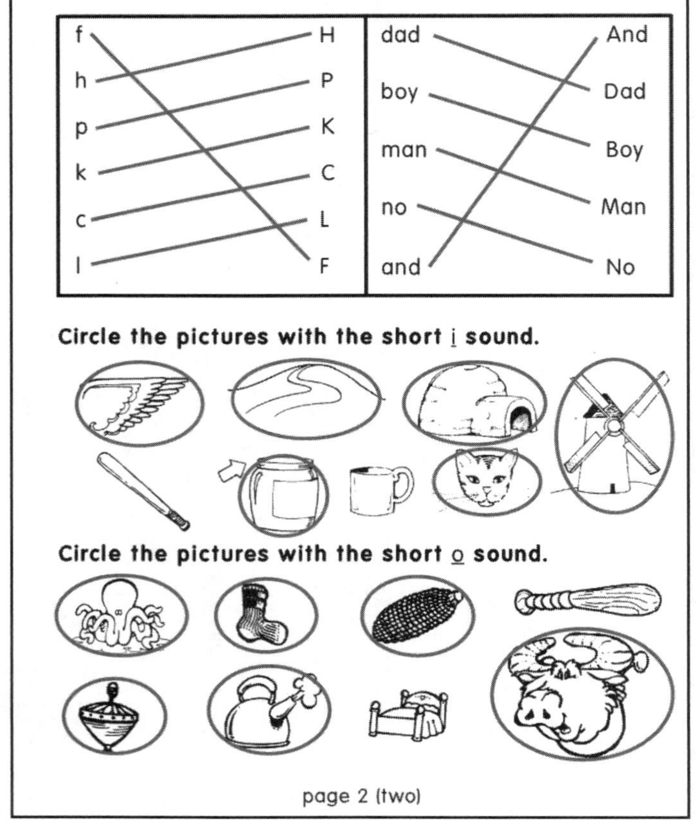

Match the letters and words.

f	H	dad	And
h	P	boy	Dad
p	K	man	Boy
k	C	no	Man
c	L	and	No
l	F		

Circle the pictures with the short i sound.

Circle the pictures with the short o sound.

page 2 (two)

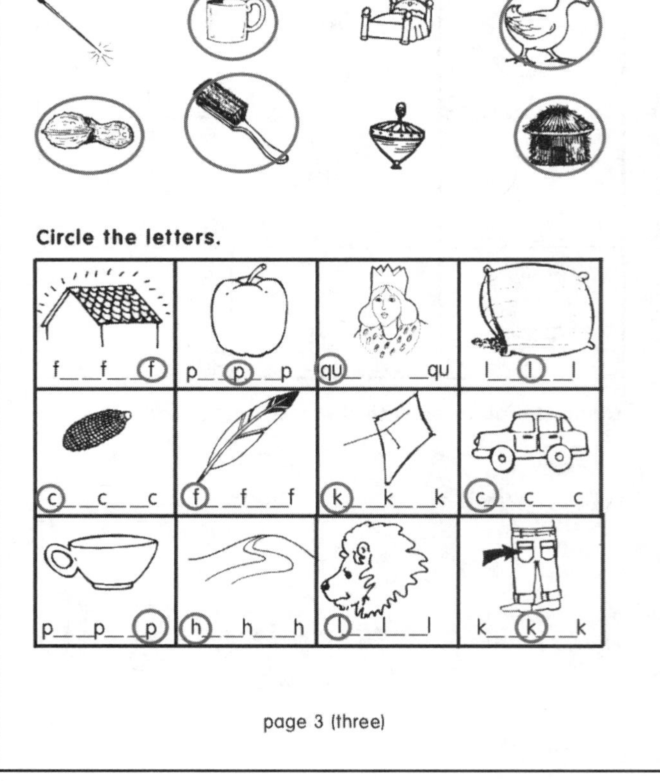

Circle the pictures with the short u sound.

Circle the letters.

f _ f _ f	p _ p _ p	qu _ _ qu	l _ l _ l
c _ c _ c	f _ f _ f	k _ k _ k	c _ c _ c
p _ p _ p	h _ h _ h	l _ l _ l	k _ k _ k

page 3 (three)

Page 1: FUN WITH WORDS

CONCEPTS: purpose of LIFEPAC, objectives, writing first name

TEACHER GOALS: To teach the children
To know what is expected of them in the LIFEPAC, and
To write their first names correctly in manuscript.

VOCABULARY: objectives, write, name

TEACHING PAGE 1:

Point to the title and read it. Tell the children that the name of a book is called its title. Have the children follow along as you read. Ask what the title means. Ask what kind of letters are found in the title (all capitals).

Read the three paragraphs one at a time and discuss. Check to see how many children have an idea of what they will learn.

Write the word *OBJECTIVES* on the board. Say it. Have the children repeat it. Have the children find the word on the page.

Explain that objectives tell the things they will be expected to do in the LIFEPAC. Ask them how many objectives are listed for this LIFEPAC. Read each one. Have the children repeat each one as they run their fingers under the sentence from left to right. Talk about each objective so that the children will understand what they will be doing.

Write the direction *Write your name* on the board. Read it to the children. Have them repeat it. Put a pencil icon on the board in front of the direction. Explain to the children that the pencil icon points to work they must do. Have the children find the icon and the direction on the page. Have them read the direction with you.

Have each child write his name on the line at the bottom of the page. Check the formation of letters and the spelling to determine which children need help.

FUN WITH WORDS

In this LIFEPAC you will learn to read and to write new words.
In this LIFEPAC you will learn to listen and to follow directions well.
You will learn to put words together to make a sentence.
You will learn about statements, questions, and exclamations.

1. I can learn to read the number words. (1-6)
2. I can listen and remember.
3. I can follow directions.
4. I can write new words.
5. I can tell what will happen next.
6. I can tell what is first, next, and last.

Write your name.

page 1 (one)

ACTIVITIES:

Have the children practice their names in the writing tablet if they are having difficulty.

I. PART ONE

THE TWINS

Listen to the story.

Janet and Nancy were twins. They looked alike, they talked alike, they dressed alike. They liked the same things to eat. Even their dolls were exactly alike.

In one way, however, the twins were not alike. Janet liked to jump rope, but Nancy did not. Janet jumped rope every day while Nancy went roller skating.

Jumping rope was fun for Janet, but not for Nancy.

Circle the pictures.

page 2 (two)

I. PART ONE

Page 2: Twins

CONCEPTS: listening, telling a story, following directions

TEACHER GOALS: To teach the children
To listen carefully,
To follow directions given only once,
To tell a story from pictures,
To tell the main idea of a story,
To note and recall details of a story,
To speak in a group with confidence, and
To understand more about twins.

VOCABULARY: twins

MATERIALS NEEDED: pictures of twins, Worksheet 1

TEACHING PAGE 2:

Show the pictures of the twins and ask if anyone can tell what is in the pictures.

Let the children share their experience with twins. If you have twins in your classroom, let them tell about being twins.

Write the word *twins* on the board and pronounce it.

Read the title and direction and have the children repeat and follow along from left to right with their fingers.

Tell the children to listen carefully as you read because you will only read the story and each sentence once. Then they must circle the picture that the sentence describes.

Read this story only once.

The Twins

Janet and Nancy were twins. They looked alike, they talked alike, they dressed alike. They liked the same things to eat. Even their dolls were exactly alike.

In one way, however, the twins were not alike. Janet liked to jump rope, but Nancy did not. Janet jumped rope every day while Nancy went roller skating.

Jumping rope was fun for Janet, but not for Nancy.

Read each of the following directions only once.

Look at all three of the pictures before you circle the one that shows what the sentence is about.

Put your finger on the fork. Circle the picture of Janet and Nancy.

Put your finger on the spoon. Circle the picture of Janet and Nancy's dolls.

Put your finger on the cup. Circle the picture that shows what Janet liked to do.

Have the children put their pencils away when they finish. Read the story and sentences again. If the children have made mistakes, have them correct them with a crayon.

Have the children retell the story.

ACTIVITY:

Do Worksheet 1.

Read the directions with the children.

Let the children find and circle the objects. Have them color the picture and take it home.

TEACHING READING:

Create a "rainstorm" in the classroom. Have students tap lightly then gradually louder and faster. Have one student flick the lights on and off to create lightning. Survey students to find out who likes to play in the rain. Develop this into a discussion about when it is not good to be out in the rain (lightning, etc,)

Read the story"Getting Dressed to Go Out in the Rain" together then ask the following questions:

"What does this person need to go out in the rain?" (jacket, hat, umbrella)

"Do you think there is thunder and lightning?" Why or why not?

"What color is the jacket?" (green)

"What color is the hat?" (blue)

"What color is the umbrella?" (red)

Have students find the short vowel words.

ACTIVITY:

Have students draw a picture about this story. Look for accuracy in coloring the jacket, hat and umbrella. Make a list of rainy day activities. Graph the weather for one month: sunny days, cloudy, rainy, etc.

Page 3: Things That Are Alike

CONCEPTS: putting into groups, identifying beginning sounds

TEACHER GOALS: To teach the children
To choose the three things that are alike in some way, and
To tell the beginning sound of each picture.

BIBLE REFERENCE: Genesis, Chapters 1 and 2

VOCABULARY: alike, things, are

MATERIALS NEEDED: letter charts for consonants, drawing paper, construction paper, old magazines or catalogs, Bible, Worksheet 2

TEACHING PAGE 3:

To prepare for this page, read Genesis, Chapters 1 and 2, from the Bible or from a children's Bible. Talk about all the things that God has made. Ask the children to name things that are alike (animals, plants, etc.). Ask how all animals that God made are alike. Ask how they are different. Ask how plants are alike and different.

Ask the children to put things into groups (plants, animals, objects in the room). If they choose to group animals, for example, explain that animals can be put into many groups (wild/tame, four-legged/two-legged, winged, furry, horned, etc.). See how many groupings they can find.

The same type of activity can be done with plants (flowers, vegetables, etc.), objects (size, shape, color, etc.), furniture, and so on.

Write the word *alike* on the board. Read it. Have the children repeat it and find it on the page. It appears three times in three different types. See if the children have difficulty spotting all three.

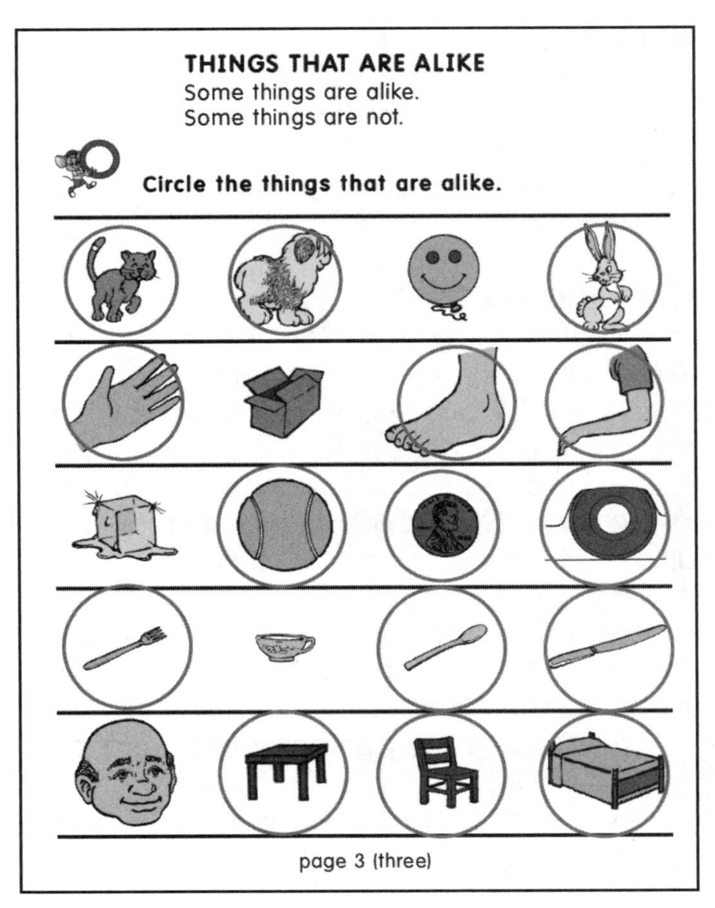

Read the title, the text, and the direction to the children and have them repeat each one.

Have the children name the pictures in the first box (cat, dog, balloon, rabbit). Ask which three are alike, and which one is different. Have the children tell why the three are alike. Draw a circle around the cat, the dog, and the rabbit.

Let the children finish the page by themselves. Check by asking which three are alike in each box and why. (hand, box, foot, arm (body), Ice cube, ball, penny, wheel (round), fork, cup, spoon, knife (utensil), man, table, chair, bed (furniture).

Have the children name each picture and give the name of the letter and its sound for those that have single initial consonants.

ACTIVITIES:

1. Do Worksheet 2.

Read the title and the direction with the children.

Tell the children to look at the three pictures carefully and to choose the two that are alike. Have them tell why two are alike and one is different. Have them circle the two that are alike. (two happy faces)

Have the children finish the page by themselves. Check by having the children tell which two pictures they circled and why. Circle: (two vehicles with wheels, two vegetables, two vehicles that go on roads, two flowers, two fruits, orange and banana).

Name ______

Circle the things that are alike.

Language Arts 102
Worksheet 2
with page 3

Teacher check ______
Initial Date

2. Put groups of four things on a table and ask the children to look at them and tell how three of them are alike and why the one is different.

To encourage children to see likenesses and differences that are not as noticeable, try something like the following example:

Line up four girls, three of whom are wearing the same color and one who has none of that color on.

Line up four children with curly hair and one with straight hair or three with long hair and one with short hair.

If the children take more than a minute or two to find the difference, give them clues until someone finds it.

3. Make a plant or animal scrapbook. Let the children decide how to group them. Draw the pictures or cut them from magazines or seed catalogs.

4. Read stories about different animals. Read about animals from the science texts or from library books.

5. For the children who have difficulty, select groups of basic shapes and colors. Group them in simple arrangements (O O ❑ O) until the children can pick out similarities. Move on to more difficult combinations, to pictures of animals, plants, and so on. Have these children rework this page when they have mastered the basic patterns.

Page 4: Learning about One

CONCEPTS: following written directions, number word one, color words

TEACHER GOALS: To teach the children

To read and follow written directions,

To read and understand the number word *one*, and

To read the color words *purple, white, orange*, and *green*.

VOCABULARY: one

MATERIALS NEEDED: crayons, color chart, drawing paper

TEACHING PAGE 4:

Ask the children to look around the classroom and name all the one-of-a kind things they can find (1 teacher, 1 clock, 1 library table, etc.).

Read the direction with the children. Point out the words draw and color and have the children read them several times.

Ask how many balls are on the page and what the number is. Ask if anyone can read the word. Read again.

Ask the children to point to the first box. Tell the children that the first box is another name for the number one box and is always at the top and to the left on the page. (Later the children will learn that the first one in a row may depend on which way the row is facing.)

Ask the children to read the phrase in the first box. Help them sound out the word *bed* if necessary. Have them refer to the color chart for the color words.

Have the children read what it says in the other three boxes, helping them sound out words if necessary. Then have them take out their pencils and crayons and do what each box says. Walk around while they are working and give help as needed.

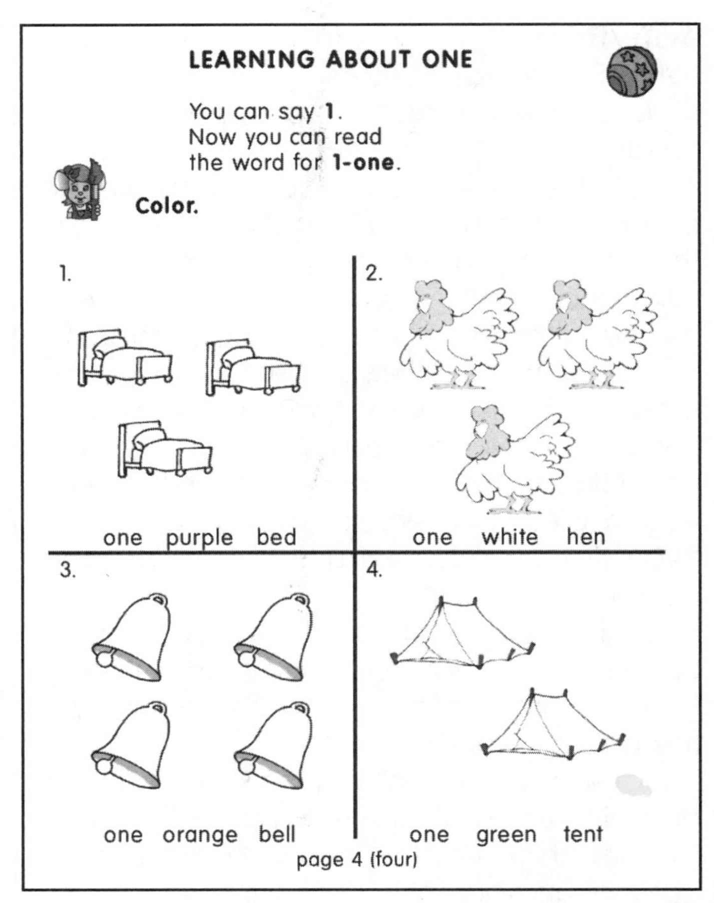

Ask the children to tell what they colored in each box. Have the children correct their work.

ACTIVITIES:

1. On the chalkboard draw a large rectangle divided into four boxes. In each box write a direction such as these: 2 blue hats, one yellow house, 3 red apples.

2. Use numbers from 2 to 5 and the word one. Have the children fold a sheet of drawing paper in fourths and copy the direction from the board into the proper box and do what it says. The teacher should correct this exercise and have the children correct any mistakes.

3. Read counting rhymes and books about colors.

Page 5: Rhyming Words

CONCEPTS: beginning sounds, rhyming words

TEACHER GOALS: To teach the children

To write a beginning letter to make a short *a* words and short *i* words,

To read rhyming words they have made, and

To match short *e* words that rhyme.

MATERIALS NEEDED: Worksheet 3

TEACHING PAGE 5:

Read the first direction with the children. Have them first read the ending ___*an* and the first word *pan,* then trace the letter *p*. Have them write letters to make two more ___*an* words. To check their work, have them read their words while you write them on the board.

Some children will be able to write ___*it* words by themselves. Use the same procedure as with the ___*an* words for those who need more help. Check by writing the list on the board.

Read the question and second direction to the children and have them repeat.

Fold a sheet of writing tablet paper in half lengthwise. Write ___*an* at the top of the first half and ___*it* at the top of the second half. Have the children write more rhyming words for each ending. Write the lists on the board and let the children check their own papers. Have them add any words they missed. If you prefer, have the children do this exercise after they have done the matching exercise on the page.

Read the third direction with the children. Have them point to the word *match* and read it.

Have the children sound out the word *peg* and find the word that rhymes with it. Draw the line between the two words. Read them. Tell the children to sound out the rest of the words and to match them.

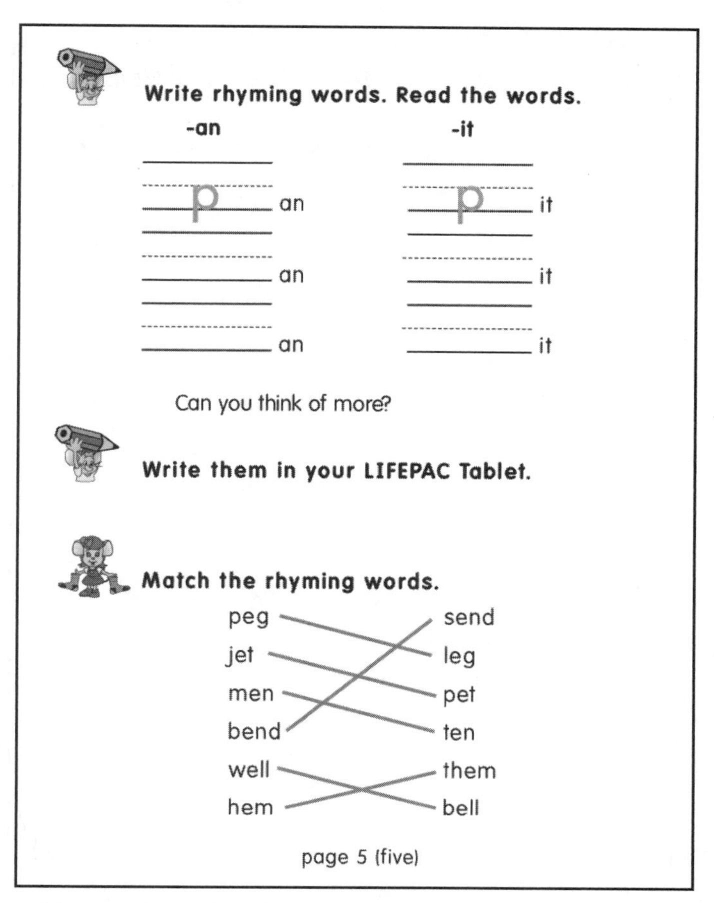
Write rhyming words. Read the words.

-an | -it

p an | p it

an | it

an | it

Can you think of more?

Write them in your LIFEPAC Tablet.

Match the rhyming words.

peg	send
jet	leg
men	pet
bend	ten
well	them
hem	bell

page 5 (five)

Have the children read each pair.

ACTIVITIES:

1. Say a short *e* word and have the children give a rhyming word.
2. Do the ___*an* and *it* exercises again in a small group with children who had difficulty.
3. Have more advanced students write sentences for their *en* and *et* words.
4. Do Worksheet 3.

Read the directions with the children and do the first example in each exercise with the children. Let them finish each section by themselves and check. The teacher may check the boxes at the top of the page while the children are writing the rhyming words. Write the words on the board and have the children give the rhyming words they have written on their pages. The children may check their words against the lists on the board and correct if necessary

TEACHING READING:

Read the story "Wet" again in *Reader 1.*

Find the words with the short /e/ sound.

Name ______________

Match the rhyming words.

ten	met	can	tag
pet	peg	mat	fat
leg	pen	bag	fan

Write rhyming words.

set ______________

beg ______________

men ______________

red ______________

tell ______________

Language Arts 102
Worksheet 3
with page 5

Teacher check ______________
Initial Date

Page 6: Which Is Real?

CONCEPTS: real or make-believe, telling a story

TEACHER GOALS: To teach the children
To tell the difference between a real situation and a make-believe one,
To tell a story from a picture,
To tell the main idea of a picture or story,
To make inferences from a picture,
To predict what might happen next,
To use complete sentences, and
To speak in a group with confidence.

VOCABULARY: real

MATERIALS NEEDED: pictures of real and make-believe situations, drawing paper, crayons

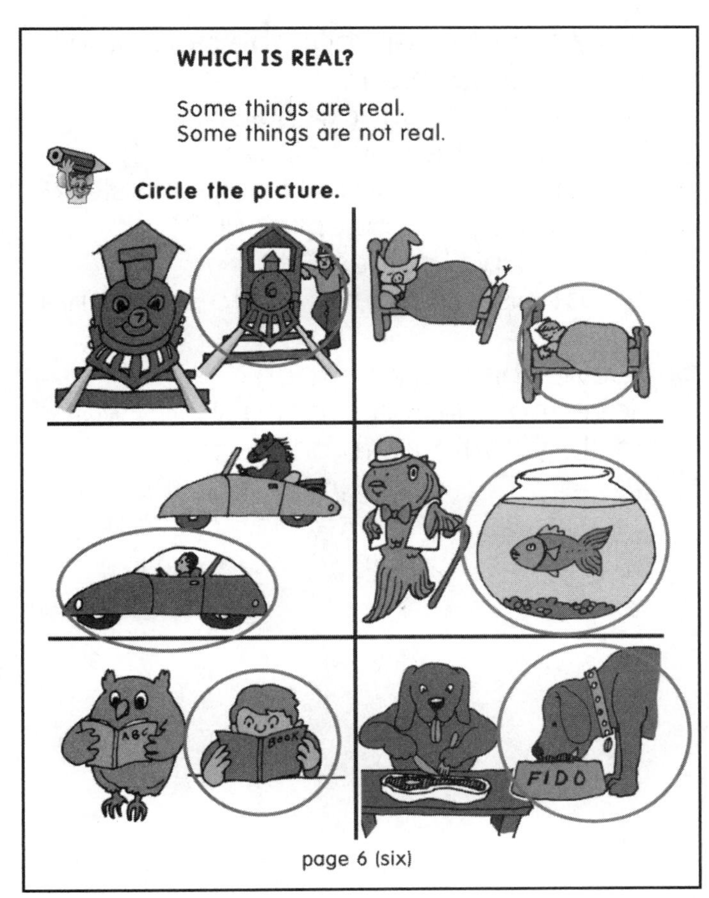

TEACHING PAGE 6:

Hold up a picture of a real situation and ask the children if what they see could really happen. Let them tell why they think so. Hold up a picture of a make-believe situation and ask if it could really happen. Let a child tell why or why not. Do this exercise with four or five pictures.

Read the title and direction with the children. Be sure they always run their fingers from left to right under what they are reading.

Ask the children to look at the first box and tell what is happening in the pictures. Encourage them to use complete sentences. Ask them to circle the picture that shows what could really happen. Check. Ask the children to tell how they know it could really happen.

Let them finish the page by themselves. Check.

ACTIVITIES:

1. Have each child draw and color either a real or pretend picture. Let the children show their pictures to the class and let them guess which they are. Then let the children tell their stories to the class.
2. Let the children dictate a story to the teacher or an aide who will then write it on a sheet of writing tablet paper and staple it to the bottom of a sheet of drawing paper. Let the child draw a picture about his story on the drawing paper. Take time to have the children read their stories either to the class or to a small group.
3. Other children may write and illustrate their own stories.
4. Read both real-life stories and make-believe stories to the children. Always ask "Could this really happen?" when you read to the children. Let them tell why or why not.

TEACHING READING:

Read the story "Sis" in *Reader 1.*

Have the children look at the picture. Have them read the title of the story. Have them tell who they think these two children might be.

Have the children read the story aloud.

Ask these questions:

"What is the matter with Sis?"

"Why does the boy call her 'Sis'?"

"What will the boy do to help his sister?"

"Will he help to cheer her up?"

"Is he a kind brother?"

"What else could he do to cheer her up?"

"Could this really happen?"

Have the children find the short *i* words in the story. Write them on the board.

Page 7: Activity Page

CONCEPTS: sequence, missing letters

TEACHER GOALS: To teach the children

To write the missing letters in the alphabet.

TEACHING PAGE 7:

Before doing the missing letter exercise have the children say the alphabet.

Say the alphabet pausing every two or three letters to let the children say the next letter.

Tell the children to look at the page carefully and write in all the missing small letters in the alphabet at the top of the page and all the missing capital letters in the alphabet at the bottom of the page.

Check by having the children read the alphabets. Collect the papers and check over quickly. Have the children correct any mistakes.

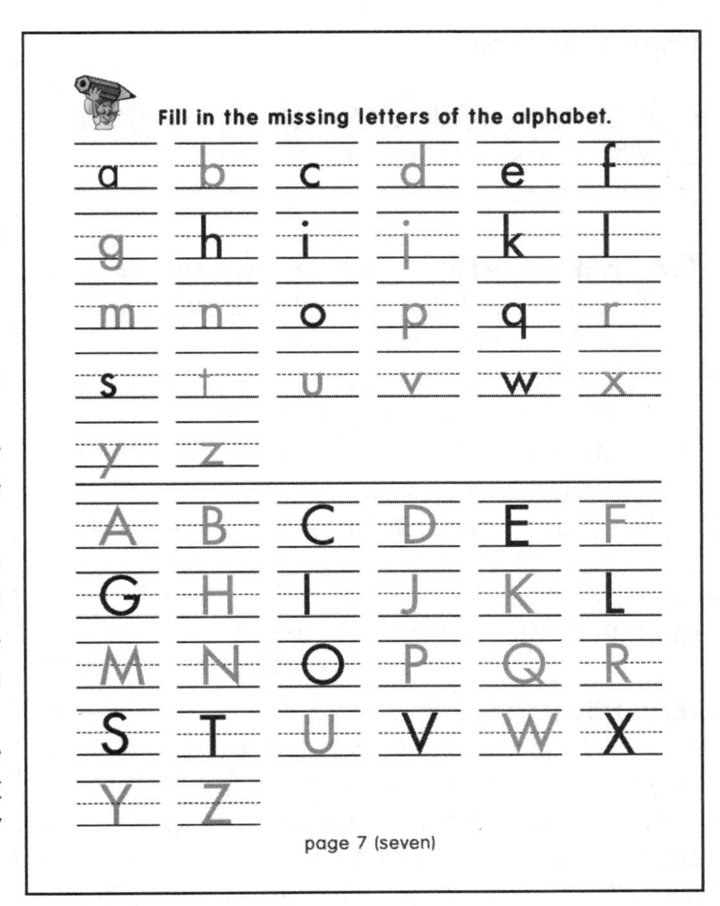

ACTIVITIES:

Have the children write the alphabet in both small letters and capitals in their writing tablets. Check formation. Have the children practice letters that are still made incorrectly.

TEACHING READING:

Read the story "My Bible" in *Reader 1*.

Have the children look at the picture. Write the title of the story on the board. Say the title and then have the children read the title. Present the word *of* and write it on the board.

Have the children tell what is happening in the story.

Have the children read the story silently, then read the story aloud.

Ask these questions:

"What does the boy have?"
"What color is his Bible?"
"Will he hold his Bible carefully?"
"What does he want to keep from happening?"
"What will he do with his Bible?"
"What will it tell him?"

Have the children find the short vowel sound of *a, e, i,* and *o.*

Page 8: Listening

CONCEPTS: listening, following directions, big/little, small/large, ordinal numbers, plural words

TEACHER GOALS: To teach the children
To listen and follow oral directions given only once,
To tell the difference between big and little, large and small objects,
To find the first, second, third, fourth, or last object in a row, and
To learn that plural means more than one.

MATERIALS NEEDED: Worksheet 4

TEACHING PAGE 8:

Hold up the flash cards for picture and pictures and ask the children to read them. Ask which word means only one and which one means more than one. Tell the children words that mean more than one are called *plurals.* We can make some plurals by adding an *s* to the word. Have the words read again.

It may be necessary to review the concepts big/little, large/small, first/last, and also first, second, third, and fourth before using this page.

Read the directions with the children. Have them point to the words *pictures* and *circle* and read them. Ask which word is a plural. Ask what the plural of *circle* would be.

Tell the children to put their fingers on the number one and look at the row of pictures. Tell them to circle the largest dog. Ask them to tell where it is. Be sure the children are counting from the left. Tell the children to put their fingers on the number 2 and to look at the row of rabbits. Tell them to circle the first *rabbit.* Check.

Follow the same procedure for the rest of the page.

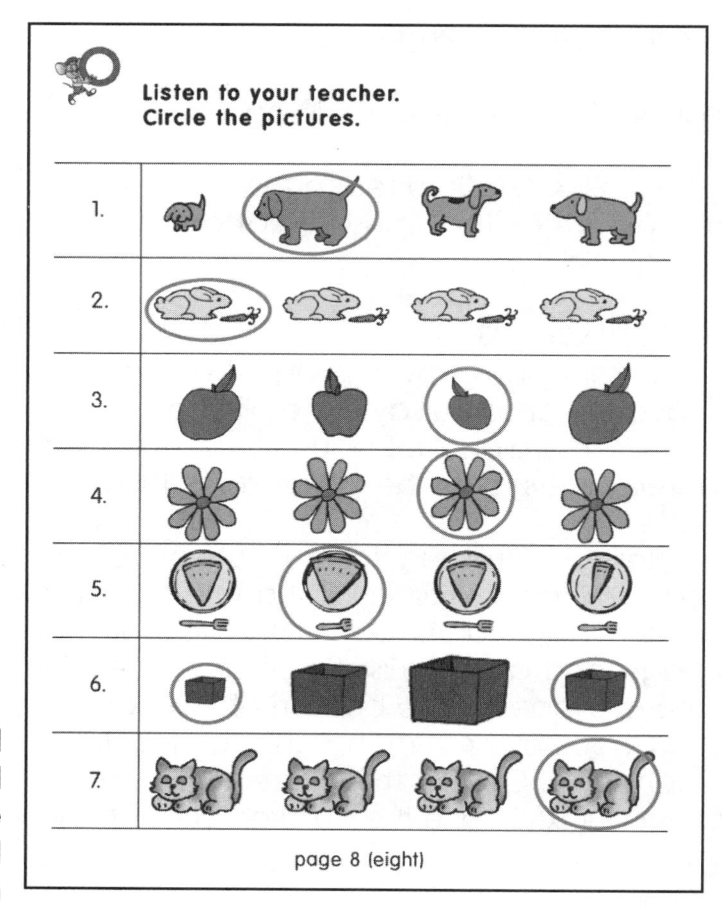

3. Circle the *smallest apple.*
4. Circle the *third flower.*
5. Circle the *largest piece* of *pie.*
6. Circle the *two smaller boxes.*
7. Circle the *last kitten.*

ACTIVITIES:

1. Review all the direction-word flash cards.
2. Do Worksheet 4.

Tell the children to listen carefully because you will tell them only once what to mark. Have them put their fingers on the numbers to keep their place on the page.

1. Circle the *third* puppy.
2. Circle the *last* basket.
3. Circle the *smallest* car.
4. Circle the *first* rabbit.
5. Circle the *largest* house.
6. Circle the *biggest* apple.
7. Circle the *second* book.
8. Circle the *next to the last* chair.

TEACHING READING:

Write the words pot, cup, sack, and box on the board or on a piece of paper as column headings. Ask students to think of words which rhyme with each of the heading words. List their answers.

Read the story "What is in the Pot?" together then ask the following questions:

"What is not in the pot?"

"What is not in the cup?"

"What is not in the sack?"

"What is not in the box?"

Ask students to identify the rhyming pairs.

Have students find the short vowel words.

ACTIVITY:

Give students a piece of paper. Ask them to put something IN each object, paying attention to the clues and what IS NOT in each object. Challenge students to think of more rhyming words for each of the rhyming pairs.

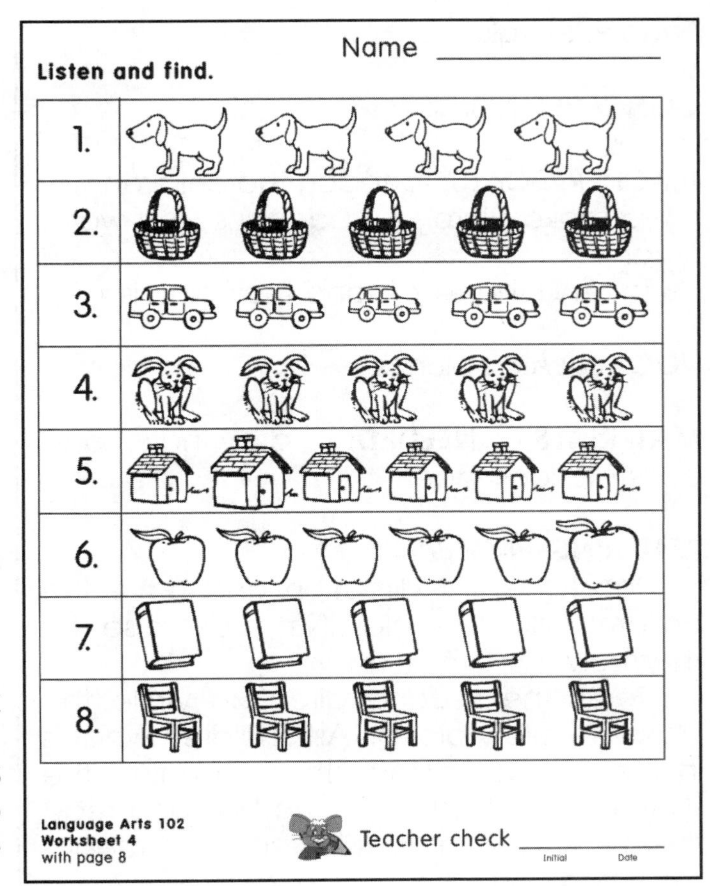

Page 9: Plurals

CONCEPTS: plurals

TEACHER GOALS: To teach the children
To make plurals by adding s to a word, and
To read the words and their plurals.

VOCABULARY: plurals

MATERIALS NEEDED: drawing and construction paper

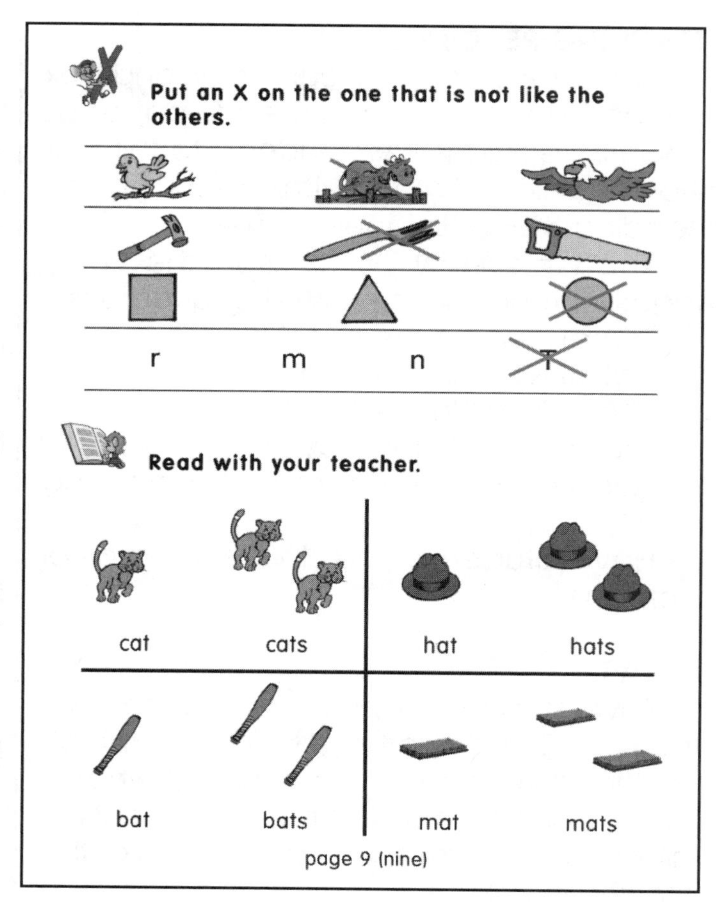

TEACHING PAGE 9:

Read the first direction and have the children do the classifying exercise by themselves.

Read the second direction while the children follow along. Ask children what is in the first box. Have them point to the words at the bottom of the box and read them if they can. Ask which word means more than one.

Ask what letter has been added to cat to make it mean more than one. Tell the children the word *cats* is a *plural* word.

Have the children spell the two words. Do the same for the other three boxes.

ACTIVITIES:

1. Make a scrapbook of plurals. Draw the pictures or cut from magazines. Write the words under the pictures.
2. Put in irregular plurals that the children use often.
3. Ask the children to give the plurals of these words: child (children), mouse (mice), man (men), house (houses), woman (women), box (boxes), you (you).

Page 10: Statements

CONCEPT: statements

TEACHER GOALS: To teach the children

To recognize a statement when they hear or read it,

To make up a statement,

To know that a statement begins with a capital letter, and

To know that a statement ends with a period, to identify a period, and to write one.

VOCABULARY: statement, capital, period

MATERIALS NEEDED: red and yellow crayons,

TEACHING PAGE 10:

Hold up the flash card for statement, read it and have the children repeat it. Tell them a statement is a sentence that tells us something.

Hold up the flash card for statements and ask the children to read it. Ask what it means (more than one statement). Have the children read the cards several times.

Ask them to listen carefully and to raise their hands if they think what you are reading is a sentence.

Read:
I am here.
The boy is walking.
Mary is
We have no
We have no cookies.

If some children raise their hands when you read *Mary is,* ask if that really tells us something. Does it tell what Mary is doing? Ask someone to make it into a sentence. Do the same with *We have no.*

Tell the children that sentences can be either short or long. Ask them to give examples of each.

Tell them again that a statement is a sentence that tells us something.

STATEMENTS

A **statement** is a sentence that tells something.

•

The first word in a statement begins with a capital letter.

A statement ends with a period.

Read these statements with your teacher.

This is a Bible.

This is a cat.

I can run.

Draw a yellow line under the capital letter at the beginning of the statement.

Draw a red circle around the period at the end of the statement.

page 10 (ten)

Read the title and the sentences at the top of the page to the children as they follow along. Identify the period.

Ask these questions:

"What is a statement?"

"How does the first word in a statement begin?"

"How does a statement end?"

"Who can make a period on the board?" (Children should learn to make a period with a single pencil or chalk dot—not a heavy scribbled dot.)

Read the first direction with the children. Have them point to the word statements and ask what it means and what that kind of word is called (plural).

Have the children look at the pictures and read each sentence. Help if necessary. Have several children read each statement.

Read the second and third directions and let the children do what they say. Check.

ACTIVITIES:

Have the children write two or three statements in their writing tablets. Have them read them to you or to an aide. Help with spelling if necessary.

TEACHING READING:

Ask students to share about their favorite doll, stuffed animal or toy. Teacher may have an example of his/her own to share.

Read the story "My Rag Doll" together then ask the following questions:

"Who will make the doll?" (Mom)

"What will the doll be made out of?" (rags, bits of cloth)

"What color is the dress, socks, hair?" (red, yellow, black)

"What is the doll's name?" (Sam)

"Where will the doll stay?" (on the bed)

Have students find short vowels and color words.

ACTIVITY:

Have students do doll cut-outs using cloth pieces for clothing, or if possible, sew rag dolls. Invite students to bring their favorite "doll" to class. As a writing exercise, have them write about where they got their favorite "doll."

Page 11: Plurals

CONCEPTS: plurals

TEACHER GOALS: To teach the children
To make plurals by adding *s* to a word, and
To read the words and their plurals,

MATERIALS NEEDED: drawing paper, construction paper

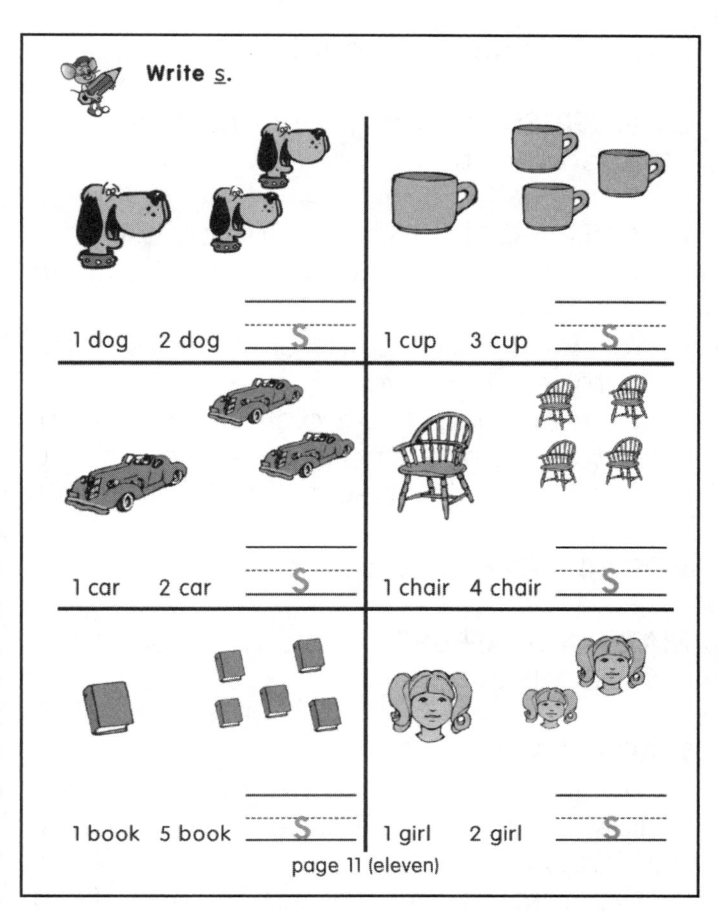

TEACHING PAGE 11

Read the direction and have the children repeat it. Ask the children what a plural is. Ask the children to tell what is in the first picture in the first box and what is in the second picture. Ask the children to read what it says under each picture. Ask what letter is missing. Have the children write the letter *s* in the space. Ask the children to read the plural word.

Have the children finish the page by themselves. Remind them to look at the pictures carefully and to read the words before writing the missing *s*.

Check by having the children read the phrases in each box. Ask them to read all the plurals on the page.

ACTIVITIES:

1. Add to your scrapbook of plurals. Draw the pictures or cut from magazines. Write the words under the pictures.
2. Put in irregular plurals that the children use often.
3. Call attention to plurals as they come up in the children's speech.

TEACHING READING:

Read the story "Tom" in *Reader 1*.

Have the children look at the picture and tell what is happening in the story. Present the word *he.* Tell the children that *he* is a pronoun that stands for *Tom* in this story. Tell them that they will be learning more about pronouns later. Present the word *pull.* Have the children tell what it means.

Have the children read the story silently.

Ask these questions:

"Who is the boy in the story?"

"Why will he huff and puff?"

"Do you remember a story about a wolf who huffed and puffed?"

"Why will he dig and pull?"

"What is Tom going to do?"

"Will the hill look nicer when he has finished?"

Have the children find the short /a/, /i/, /o/, and /u/ sounds.

Have them find the double consonants.

Page 12: Learning about Two

CONCEPTS: following written directions, number word two

TEACHER GOALS: To teach the children
To read and follow simple written directions,
To recognize and understand the number word *two,*
To recognize the color words *green, yellow, orange,* and *brown,* and
To sound out and read short *a* words.

VOCABULARY: two, draw, color

MATERIALS NEEDED: crayons, color chart, number chart

TEACHING PAGE 12:
Ask the children to name things that are usually in twos (hands, feet, eyes, twins, mittens, etc.).
Go through the direction-word flash cards several times.
Read the direction with the children. Ask them to point to the phrase draw and color and read it. Have the children read *two balls,* the number *two,* and the word *two.*
Ask the children to read the phrase in the first box silently and then ask a child to read it aloud. Have them draw what it says and then finish the page independently. Give help only if needed. Check.

ACTIVITIES:
Draw a large rectangle divided in fourths on the board. Write in directions similar to the ones on this page. Use numbers from 3 to 7 and number words *one* and *two.* Have a number chart and color chart posted for the children to refer to.

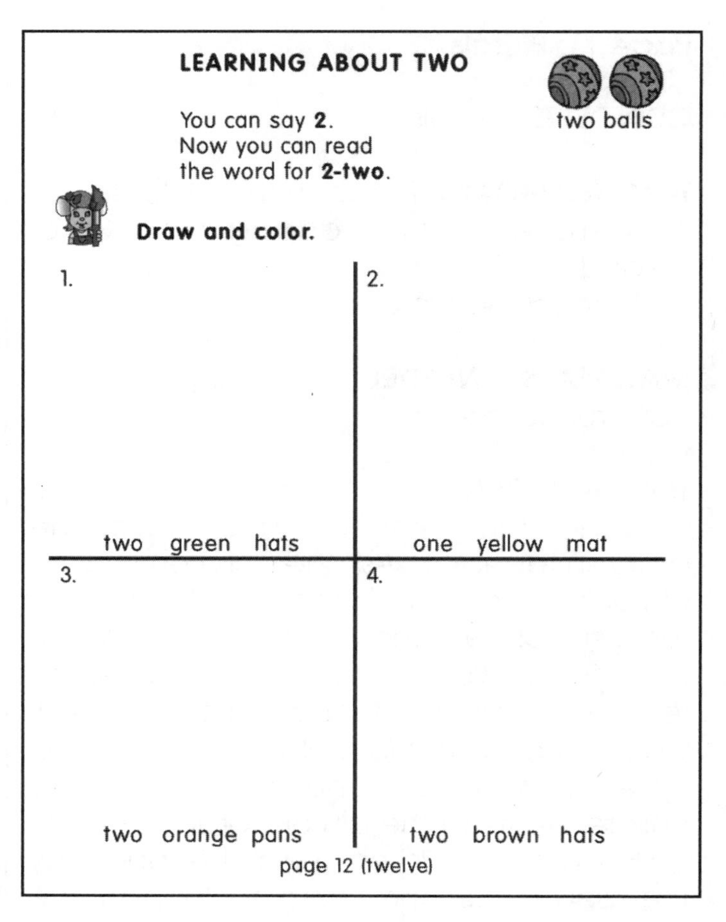

SELF TEST 1

CONCEPTS: classifying into groups, matching rhyming words, identifying plurals

TEACHER GOAL: To teach the children

To learn to check their own progress periodically.

TEACHING PAGE 13:

Read the directions to the children. Have the children repeat them after you while running their fingers under the sentence being read. Be sure the children understand what they are to do.

Let the children complete the page. You may repeat the directions but give no other help.

Do not have the children check their own work. Check it as soon as you can and go over it with the child. Show him where he did well and where he needs to work harder. (two hats, two garmets)

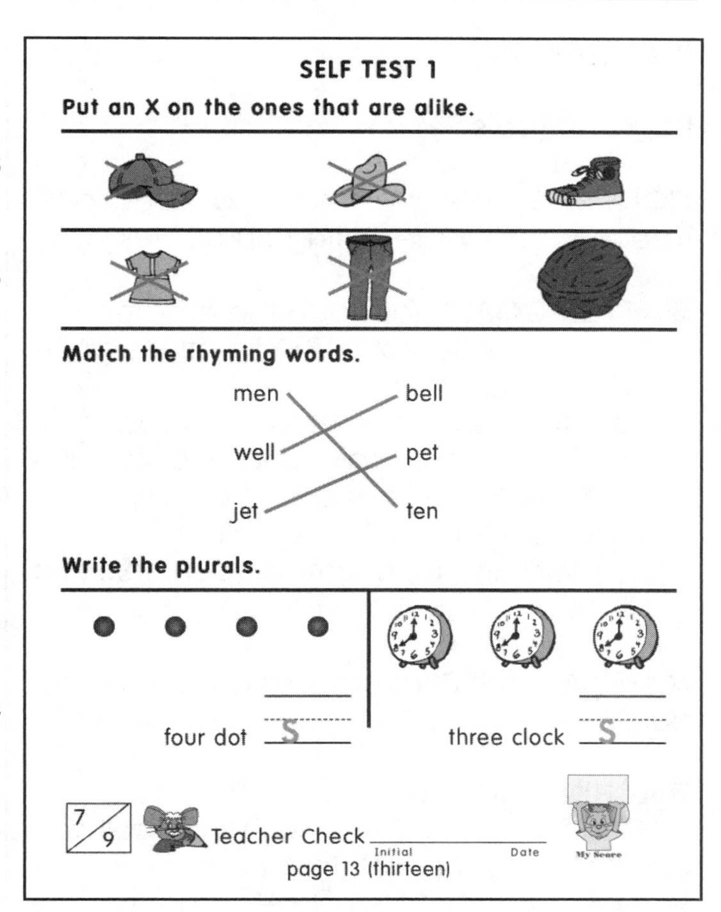

Activities:

1. Give each child help on items he misses.
2. If several children miss the same kind of things, reteach the skill (in a small group session, if possible).

SPELLING WORDS:

pens
wet
one
two
Sis

II. PART TWO

Page 14: Ted's Pet

CONCEPTS: listening, following directions, retelling a story, predicting outcomes

TEACHER GOALS: To teach the children
To listen and follow oral directions given only once,
To retell a story in their own words,
To tell what the main idea of a story is,
To make inferences about a story,
To recall details of a story, and
To predict what might happen next in a story.

MATERIALS NEEDED: crayons (blue, red and purple)

TEACHING PAGE 14:

Read the title, PART TWO, and tell the children they are starting to work in the second part of the LIFEPAC and will be learning many more things.

Read the title *Ted's Pet* and ask the children to tell what the story might be about.

Read the direction with the children. Ask them to look at the picture and listen while you read the story. Tell them you will read the story only once, then they will mark some things in the picture. Be sure the children have nothing on their desks but this LIFEPAC opened to page 14.

Read:

Ted's pet was lost. Ted had been playing with his pet out in the back yard all afternoon. Then Mother had called him in to eat dinner, and he had left his pet in the sandbox.

When Ted came back outside, his pet was gone. Ted looked and looked, but he could not find his pet anywhere. Ted looked in the sandbox, under the bushes, in the flower beds, and by the swing set. Where was his pet?

II. PART TWO

TED'S PET

Listen to the story.

Ted's pet was lost. Ted had been playing with his pet out in the backyard all afternoon. Then Mother had called him in to eat dinner, and he had left his pet in the sandbox.

When Ted came back outside, his pet was gone. Ted looked and looked, but he could not find his pet anywhere. Ted looked in the sandbox, under the bushes, in the flower beds, and by the swing set. Where was his pet?

Would you help Ted find his pet? His pet has four legs, a tail, and a shell on his back.

page 14 (fourteen)

Would you help Ted find his pet? His pet has four legs, a tail, and a shell on his back. Have the children put their crayons on their desks.

Read these directions only once:

Find Ted's pet in the picture and put a blue circle around it (the turtle). Put a red X on all the places Ted looked for his pet (sandbox, bushes, flower beds, swing set).

Draw two purple lines under two places where Ted did not look (tree, rock, house).

Read the directions again and have the children tell what they marked.

Note: If you have the children correct any mistakes in pencil, this procedure will give you a quick check on who did not listen well.

ACTIVITIES:

1. Ask the children to tell what they think will happen next and why.
2. Ask the children to think of other names for this story. Write them on the board.

3. Let several children retell the story. Encourage them to use complete sentences.
4. Ask the children to tell whether a group of words you read is a statement. Read several groups of words from the story, some that are only partial sentences.
5. Go on to page 15.

TEACHING READING:

Ask students what kind of things make messes. (paint, garbage, mud...) List theirresponses. Ask students if they have ever played in the mud. Have them share experiences. Tell them they're going to read a story about mud! (Oh, boy!)

Read the story "A Very Big Mess" together then ask the following questions:

"What kind of things can you do in the mud?" (dig, sit, kick, plop, drop, flop, run, jump, have fun)

"Why does it say mud is a mess, a very big mess?" (inference, answers will vary)

"Can you think of a time when you or someone else made a mess with mud?"

Have students identify short vowel words and rhyming words. Make a chart with the following words: dig, sit, kick, plop, run, jump, mud, mess

Have the class think of rhyming words and build a rhyming chart from this list.

ACTIVITY:

If possible, have some fun time writing in mud or making mud pies, castles or other creations. Tell students the challenge is NOT to be messy. Give students a freeform cut out of brown paper. Have them glue it on a piece of paper. Tell them the brown "blob" is mud and they are to finish the picture.

Page 15: Listening

CONCEPTS: listening, following directions, recalling details, making inferences

TEACHER GOALS: To teach the children
To listen and follow oral directions given oniy once,
To recall details about the story, and
To make inferences from the story and pictures.

VOCABULARY: question, mark

MATERIALS NEEDED: green crayons, Worksheet 5

TEACHING PAGE 15:
This page should be done in the same session as the previous page.
Have the children put green crayons on their desks.
Read the direction with the children.
Tell the children to put their fingers on the number 1 and to look at the pictures in the first box. Tell the children to listen carefully and then to draw a green circle around the picture in the box that shows what the sentence says.
Say:
Circle the picture that shows Ted's pet.
Put your finger on the number 2.
Circle the picture that shows where Ted was playing.
Put your finger on the number 3.
Circle the picture that shows what time of day it was.
Put your finger on the number 4.
Circle the pictures that show two places Ted looked for his pet. Be sure everyone is circling two pictures.
Put your finger on the number 5.
Circle the picture that shows where Mother was when Ted went in the house.
Put your finger on the number 6.
Circle the picture that shows what the weather was like that day.

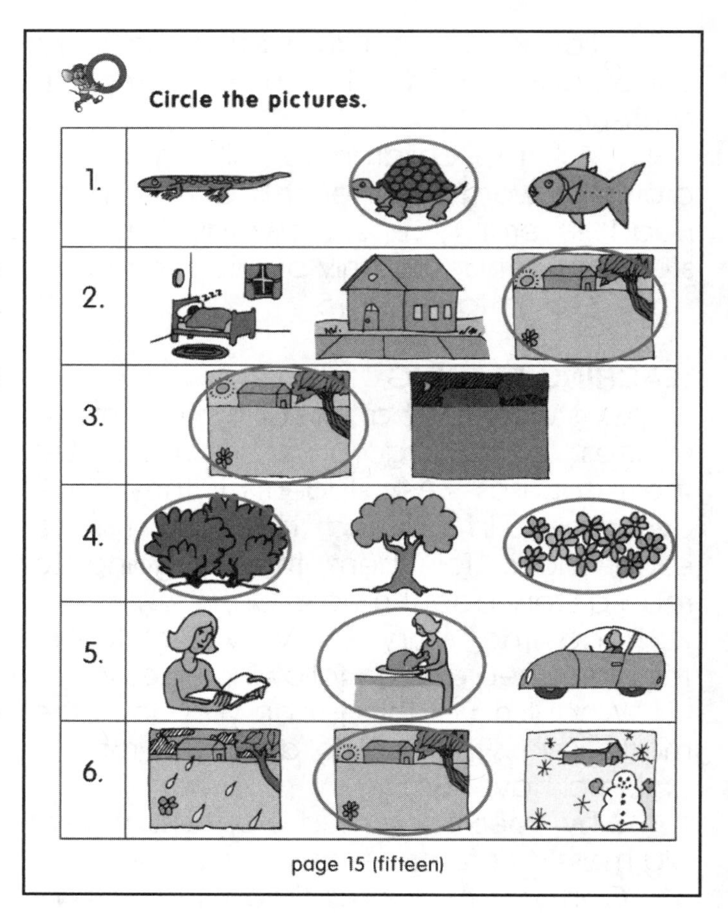

Read the sentences again and have the children tell what they marked. Have the children correct any mistakes.

ACTIVITIES:
1. If some children have trouble remembering what they are to do, give two or three oral directions at a time and have those children follow them. When they can do three without forgetting, add one more.
2. Do Worksheet 5.
Tell the children to listen carefully and then to mark the picture that is the best answer. Have the children put their fingers on the numbers to keep their places.
Read:
1. Circle the picture that shows where you would go to buy a jacket. (store)
2. Circle the picture that shows what Father uses to cut the grass in the yard. (lawnmower)

3. Circle the picture that shows something you might use at breakfast time. (toaster)

4. Circle the picture that shows how you could get to school if you lived a long way away. (bus)

5. Circle the picture that shows the slowest animal. (turtle)

6. Circle the picture that shows the fastest way to go across the ocean. (plane)

7. Read the directions again. Let children tell what they circled and why. Correct any mistakes.

TEACHING READING:

Ask students to think of an animal that would make a good pet. List their responses. Survey students to determine which pets they have. Ask students to think of an animal that would be an unusal pet. List their responses. Tell them they're going to read a story about an unusual pet.

Read the story "Our Pet" together then answer the questions:

"What kind of pet do they have? (pig)

"Who gave it to them? (Dan)

"Where did Dan get it? (vet)

"Is it a girl or a boy? (girl)

"How do you know? (it says, "it's a she and not a he)

"What is her name? (Pinky Sue)

"Why did the author write it Pinky Suuuuuuuuuue? (to make it sound like you were calling her)

Have students find short vowel and rhyming words.

ACTIVITY:

Make a Picto-Graph showing the results of the pet survey. (Students draw their pet on a small piece of paper to create the graph.) Make pig masks out of paper plates. Write a story – A Day in the Life of Pinky Sue

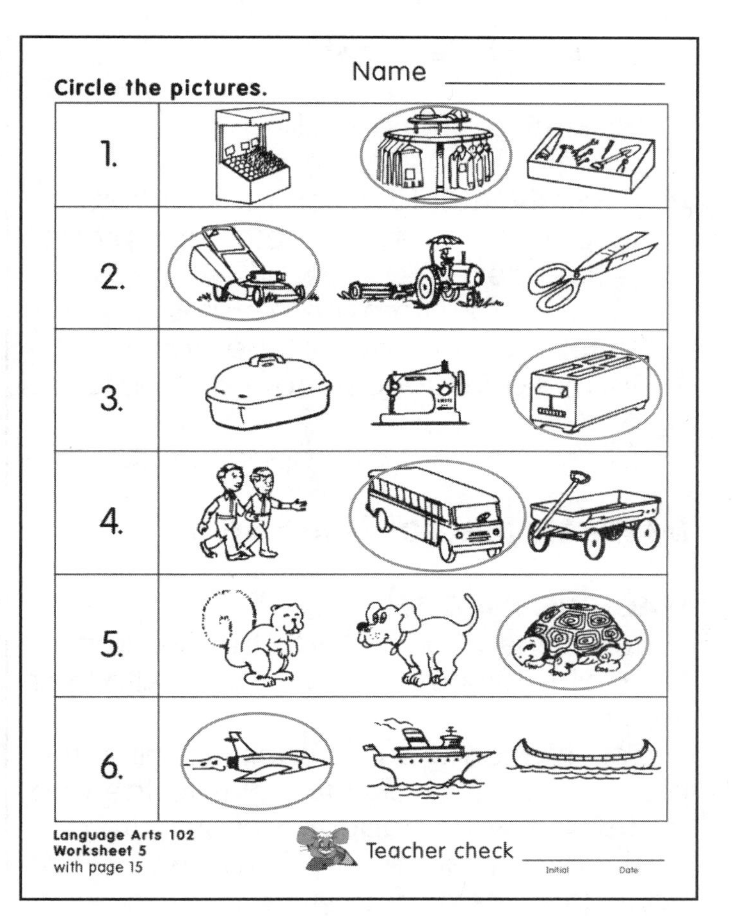

Page 16: First, Next, Last

CONCEPTS: sequence, telling stories

TEACHER GOALS: To teach the children
To put three pictures into their proper sequences,
To tell a story from the pictures,
To tell the main idea of the story,
To make inferences from the pictures, and
To predict what will happen next.

MATERIALS NEEDED: Worksheet 6

TEACHING PAGE 16:

Read the direction with the children as they follow along from left to right with their fingers.

Tell the children to look at all three pictures carefully and to point to the one that shows what happened first. Write a *1*. Find the picture that shows what happened next and write a *2* under it. Write *3* under what happened last. (Row 1: 2, 1, 3)

Ask a child to tell the story shown in the pictures.

Let the children finish the page by themselves. Check. (Row 2: 3, 2, 1 Row 3: 1, 3, 2)

Have the children tell the stories.

Remind them to use complete sentences.

ACTIVITIES:

1. Ask the children to tell what might happen next in the stories, what time of day they think it is and why, how old they think the children are, why they think the mother is calling the children, and so on.
2. Have the children fold a sheet of drawing paper in thirds. Have them draw three parts of a story, show it to the class, and tell the story.
3. Have the children talk about the prayers they say at night. Write an evening prayer together, put it on a chart, and hang it in a place where the children can see it.
4. Read stories or books about birthdays, families, or evening prayers.
5. Do Worksheet 6.

Read the title and the direction with the children.

Tell the children to look at all three pictures and to point to the one that shows what happened first. Ask how they can tell. Have them write the number one. Ask which picture shows what happened next and last and how they can tell. Have them write the numbers 2 and 3 on the lines. (Row 1: 3, 2, 1)

Let them finish the page independently. Call attention to the last two rows. These two rows are more difficult; therefore, you may have to give some help to children who do not know the words.

Check by having the children tell which word or letter should be first, second, and third. (Row 2: 2, 3, 1; Row 3:1, 3, 2; Row 4: 3, 2, 1).

Have the children tell the stories from the pictures. Encourage them to use complete sentences, correct verb forms, and correct subject verb agreement. Have them tell what they think may have happened before what they see in the pictures, what might happen after, and why they think so.

TEACHING READING:

Read the story "Jesus" in *Reader 1*.

Have the children look at the picture. Have them tell what is happening in the story. Have them tell who the man is in the picture. Write *Jesus* on the board. Write the words, *of* and *love*. Tell the children that the two words sound alike even though they are spelled differently.

Have the children read the story.

Ask these questions:

"Do the children love Jesus?"

"How will he show them He loves them?"

"What will Jesus tell the children?"

"What does the sentence, Jesus is love, mean?"

"Who is Jesus?"

Have the children tell what might have happened next.

Find the short *i* words in the story.

Name ____________

PUT IN ORDER

Can you tell
what comes first?
Can you tell
what comes last?

Write 1, 2, 3, for first, next, and last.

____ ____ ____

____ ____ ____

H **morning** **night** **noon**

____ ____ ____

H **C** **B** **A**

____ ____ ____

Language Arts 102
Worksheet 6
with page 16

Teacher check ____________
Initial Date

Page 17: Questions

CONCEPTS: questions, question mark

TEACHER GOALS: To teach the children
To recognize a question when they hear or read it,
To recognize and write a question mark, and
To know that the first word of a question begins with a capital letter and ends with a question mark.

MATERIALS NEEDED: green and blue crayons

TEACHING PAGE 17:

Ask the children if they remember what a statement is. Tell them that they are going to learn about another kind of sentence. Ask if anyone knows what a sentence that asks something is called. *Read the following sentences* and have the children raise their hands when they hear a question.

I am in school.
Am I in school?
Where are you going?
This pig is a big one.
Is this hat yours?

Ask the children to tell what a question is.

Read the title and sentences at the top of the page to the children. Call attention to the question mark. *Ask the following questions:*

"What is a question?"

"Where is the capital letter?"

"What goes at the end of the question?"

"Who can make a question mark on the board?"

Read the first direction with the children. Let the children read the questions silently. Then let several children read them aloud. Let them answer the questions in complete sentences.

QUESTIONS

A **question** is a sentence that asks something.

The first word in a question begins with a capital letter.

A question ends with a question mark.

Read these questions with your teacher.

Am I a cat?

Is this a hen?

What is this?

Draw a green line under the capital letter at the beginning of the question.

Draw a blue circle around the question mark at the end of the question.

page 17 (seventeen)

Read the second and third directions and let the children do what is asked. Check.

ACTIVITIES:

1. Write questions on the board that the class dictates and have everyone copy them.

TEACHING READING:

Read the story "Run" in *Reader 1*.

Have the children look at the picture. Have them tell what is happening.

Have the children read the story silently.

Ask questions similar to these:

"What are the names of the children in the circle?"

"What are the children doing?"

"Why are they holding hands?"

"What will happen if they run faster and faster?"

"Which boy is Ron?"

"Do you think he will fall?"

"How can they keep him from falling?"

Have the children find the capital letters in the story. Tell the children that names always begin with capital letters.

Have the children find the words that contain short /i/, /o/, and /u/ sounds. Have them find the words with double consonants.

Go on to the next page.

Page 18: Activity Page

CONCEPTS: statements, questions

TEACHER GOALS: To teach the children
- To recognize a statement when they hear or read it,
- To recognize a question when they hear or read it,
- To know that statements and questions begin with a capital letter,
- To recognize and write a period at the end of a statement, and
- To recognize and write a question mark at the end of a question.

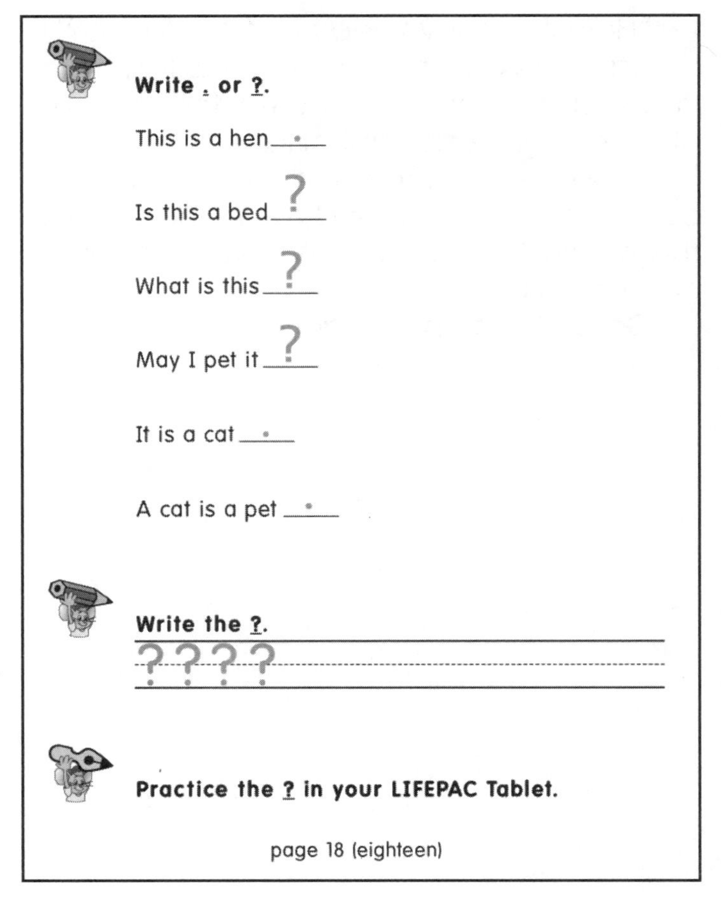

VOCABULARY: practice

MATERIALS NEEDED: magazines or newspapers, tagboard

TEACHING PAGE 18:

This page should be done in the same class period as the previous page. Ask the children to tell what a statement is, what a question is, and what the punctuation mark for each is called.

Read the first direction and have the children repeat and follow along.

Have the children read the first sentence silently. Ask if it is a question or a statement. Have a child read it aloud. Ask what mark to put in the blank space. Have the children put in the period.

Do the same for each sentence.

Read the second direction with the children. Have them practice making question marks. Trace the question marks first with their fingers and then with a pencil. Have them point to the word *practice* and read it.

Have the children practice several more rows of question marks in their writing tablets.

ACTIVITIES:

1. Give each child a page of a magazine or a quarter page of a newspaper. Have the children find questions and underline them. Have them circle the question marks. Allow about five or six minutes for this activity.
2. Have the children cut out questions and statements from magazines or papers at home and bring them to school. Tell them to look for large letters. Divide a bulletin board in half, label one side *QUESTIONS* and the other side *STATEMENTS.* Pin the sentences the children bring in the proper place.

TEACHING READING:

Tell students to listen carefully to the following clues:

I am a wild animal. I have a long bushy tail. I can be red or gray. I am about the size of a medium dog. My name rhymes with box. What am I? Have them write their answer. Yes, it is a fox. Have some nonfiction books on foxes to share.

Read the story "Little Red Fox" together, then ask the questions:

"Where did the little red fox run?" (up the hill)

"Is it a small hill?" (no, it is big)

"What time of day was it when he got to the top of the hill?" (evening, night or a reasonable time i.e. 6:00)

"How do you know?" (it says "as the sun went down)

"What do you think the little red fox sees? (answers will vary)

"Where do you think he goes when he's up and over the hill?" (answers will vary)

Have students identify short vowel sounds.

ACTIVITY:

Have several books on foxes for students to read more about them. Make a chart listing real characteristics of foxes. Have students write and draw pictures telling where little red fox goes and what he sees. Make fox puppets from construction paper and craft sticks and act out the story.

SELF TEST 2

CONCEPTS: reading comprehension, sequence, question, question mark, statement, period

TEACHER GOAL: To teach the children
To check their own progress periodically.

TEACHING PAGE 19:
Read the directions with the children and be sure they understand what they are to do.
Let them do the page independently. You may repeat the directions but give no other help.
Check the page yourself as soon as possible. Go over it with the child so he can see where he did well and where he needs extra help. (Row 3: 1, 3, 2 Row 4: turtle)

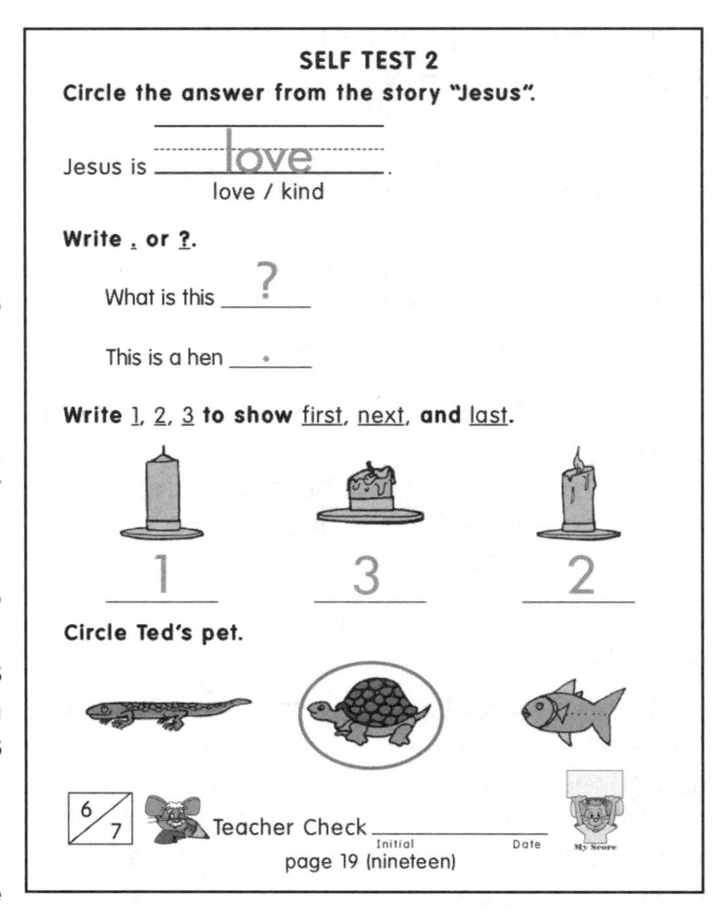

ACTIVITIES:
1. Give each child help on items he misses.
2. If several children miss the same things, reteach the skill (in a small group session, if possible).

SPELLING WORDS:

will
hug
run
tell
God

III. PART THREE

Page 20: What Will Happen Next?

CONCEPTS: listening, following directions, predicting outcomes, making value judgments

TEACHER GOALS: To teach the children

To listen and follow oral directions,

To make inferences from a picture or story,

To predict what will happen next in a situation,

To tell what is the right thing to do in a situation, and

To retell a story in their own words.

MATERIALS NEEDED: Worksheet 7

TEACHING PAGE 20:

Read the titles and talk about them. Tell the children that they will be learning more new things in PART THREE and also reviewing things they learned in the first two parts of the LIFEPAC.

Tell the children that they will be listening to a story that will not be finished. They must look at the pictures and decide which one would be the best ending for the story.

Have the children put their fingers on each row of pictures to help keep their places. Be sure everyone is on the right row before you begin reading.

Read these stories only once:

1. It was time for bed. John brushed his teeth, put on his pajamas, and said his prayers. Circle the picture that shows what John did next (went to bed).

2. Jean got up, ate her breakfast, and picked up her book. Circle the picture that shows what Jean did next (went to school).

3. Father called the family together. He took the Bible from the shelf. Circle the picture that shows what Father did next (read the Bible).

4. Father put on his work clothes. He went out to the back yard. Circle the picture that shows what he did next. (mowed the lawn)

When the children have finished marking the page, read each story again. Have them tell which picture they marked and why. If they have marked different pictures, read the story again and discuss it, then talk about all three pictures to help them choose the best one.

Children do not always know the right thing to do. They must be helped to make the right decisions and to develop a set of values for themselves. Whenever you read a story, always ask if what happened was the right thing to do or the best way to handle the situation.

ACTIVITIES:

1. Have the children retell the stories.
2. Have the children act out the stories. Have two sets of children act out two different endings and let the class choose the best ending.
3. Do Worksheet 7.

Read the title and sentence with the children and talk about them.

Read the title *Tell the Story* and ask children to tell what it means. Have children give some rules for telling stories and list them on the board.

The rules should be similar to these: Have a beginning, middle, and ending to the story. Speak clearly and loudly enough for everyone to hear. Use good English. Use complete sentences. Speak with good expression. Do not put in sentences that do not fit the story. Stand straight and keep your hands at your sides. The audience should sit quietly and listen. Talk about each of these rules and be sure the children understand the meaning of each.

Have the children look at each picture in turn and tell about it. *Ask questions such as these:* "What is happening in the picture? What might have happened just before this? How does the person feel? Would you feel the same way? What do you think will happen next? What would be the right thing to do next? Has this ever happened to you? What time of the year is it? How can you tell? What time of day is it? How can you tell? What could the person have done to keep this from happening? How could you help the person in the picture?"

Let several children tell a story about one of the pictures.

Page 21: Could This Really Happen?

CONCEPTS: real and make-believe, following directions, yes or no

TEACHER GOALS: To teach the children
To read and understand the words *yes* and *no*,
To tell if a pictured situation is real or make-believe, and
To follow directions.

VOCABULARY: yes, no

TEACHING PAGE 21:

Write the words *yes* and *no* on the board and ask children to read them. Ask them if they can answer *yes* to a question without saying anything. Ask them to answer *no* without saying anything. Ask if anyone can say *yes* or *no* in another language.

Read the title and direction and have the children repeat. Ask what kind of sentence the title is.

Ask a child to tell what is happening in the first box. Ask the children if this could really happen. How do they know? Have them circle the word *yes*.

Tell the children to look at the pictures very carefully. If what they see could really happen, circle the *yes*. If it could not really happen, circle the *no*.

When all have finished marking, have the children tell what is happening in the picture, which word they circled, and why.

page 21 (twenty-one)

ACTIVITIES:

1. Have the children make up a story for each picture. Include what might have happened before what they see in the picture and what might happen after.

TEACHING READING:

Read the story "BZZ!" in *Reader 1*.

Present the word *this* to the children. Use it in a sentence.

Have the children look at the picture. Have them tell what is happening. Have several of the children talk about experiences they have had with bees.

Have the children read the story silently. Have the children read aloud. Have each child read one sentence with expression.

Ask these questions:

"What is the noise the bug made?"

"What kind of animal does the girl think it is?"

"What does she yell to the people around her?"

"Does she think the bug is loveable?"

"What should the girl do?"

(She should stand as still as possible to keep from fightening the bee into stinging.)

Have the children find the rhyming words in the story.

Page 22: Learning about Three

CONCEPTS: following directions, number three

TEACHER GOALS: To teach the children
To read and follow written directions,
To read and understand the number word *three,*
To recognize the color words *black, orange, yellow,* and *purple,* and
To learn to sound out and read short *a* and short *e* words.

VOCABULARY: three

MATERIALS NEEDED: crayons, drawing paper,

TEACHING PAGE 22:

Ask the children to name things that usually come in threes (triplets, three points on a triangle, the Trinity, a triple in baseball, etc.).

Read the title and directions with the children. Have them read *three balls,* number *three,* and word *three.*

Ask the children to read the phrase in the first box silently. Have a child read it aloud. Ask if this expression is a sentence. Have a child tell why it is not.

Have the children draw and color what is said in the box, and then finish the page independently. Check by having the children tell what they drew.

LEARNING ABOUT THREE

You can say **3**.
Now you can read
the word for **3-three**.

three balls

Draw and color.

1.	2.
three black hats	two orange cats
3.	4.
three yellow jets	three purple beds

page 22 (twenty-two)

ACTIVITIES:

1. Put a rectangular box on the board. Divide it into four or six smaller boxes as done previously, use the number words-one, two, and three, any of the color words, and short-e words.

TEACHING READING:

Read the story "Mom" in *Reader 1.*

Present the word *we* to the children. Tell them that it is a pronoun that stands for all of the children in the story. They will talk more about pronouns later.

Have the children look at the picture. Have them read the title. Have them talk about what might be happening. The title is "Mom", but there is no Mom in the picture. Where might she be?

Have the children read the story silently.

Ask these questions:

"What is wrong with Mom?"
"What will the children do to help?"
"Will Mom get well?"
"Do you think Mom will be pleased with the children?"
"What do you think might happen next?"

Have the children tell what they do to help when someone is not well at their house. Find the words with the short /i/ sound and the short /o/ sound.

Page 23: Playing in the Backyard.

CONCEPTS: listening, following directions

TEACHER GOALS: To teach the children
To listen carefully,
To follow directions given only once, and
To note and recall details of a story,

TEACHING PAGE 23:

Ask how many children have a sandbox in their yard, what they do in a sandbox, and what kind of toys can be used in a sandbox. Tell the children they are going to listen to a story about some children playing in a sandbox.

Read the title and direction with the children as they follow along. Tell the children to listen carefully because you will read the story and directions only once. *Read this story.*

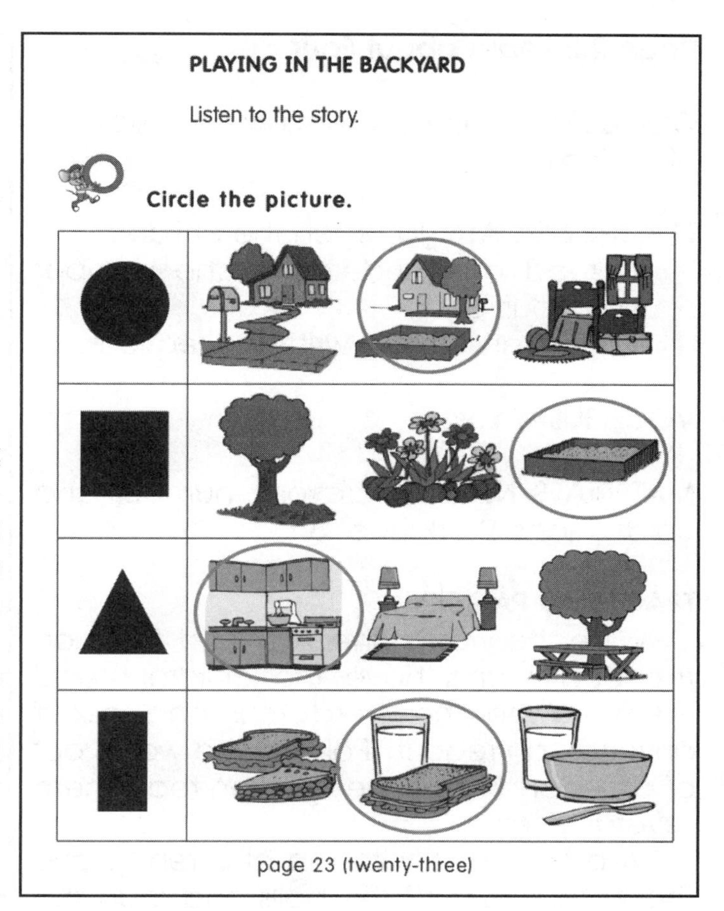

Playing in the Backyard

Dan and Ann were playing in their backyard. They were building a town in the sandbox. They had houses and roads and trees in their town.

Suddenly Ann said, "I'm hungry." The children ran into the house to get something to eat. Mother gave them each a ham sandwich and a glass of milk.

After lunch the children ran back to the sandbox. Dan made more roads for their town and Ann made another row of houses. They played in the backyard all afternoon.

Read each of these directions only once and wait for the children to circle the picture. Put your finger on the circle. Circle the picture that shows where Dan and Ann were playing (backyard). Put your finger on the square. Circle the picture that shows where they were building their town (sandbox). Put your finger on the triangle. Circle the picture that shows where the children had their lunch (kitchen). Put your finger on the rectangle. Circle the picture that shows what the children had to eat for lunch (sandwich and milk).

Have the children put their pencils away. Read each direction again and let the children tell which picture they circled. Have the children correct any mistakes with a crayon.

Let several children tell the story in their own words.

ACTIVITIES:

1. If you have a sand table in your room, let the children build a town on it.
2. Let the children build a town in one corner of the playground.
3. Let the children build a town on the floor in the classroom using construction paper for roads and boxes for houses.
4. Other students can make up stories and test each other's recall.

Page 24: Learn about Four

CONCEPTS: number word four, following directions

TEACHER GOALS: To teach the children
To read and understand the number word four, and
To read and follow written directions.

VOCABULARY: four

MATERIALS NEEDED: crayons, number and color charts, Worksheet 8

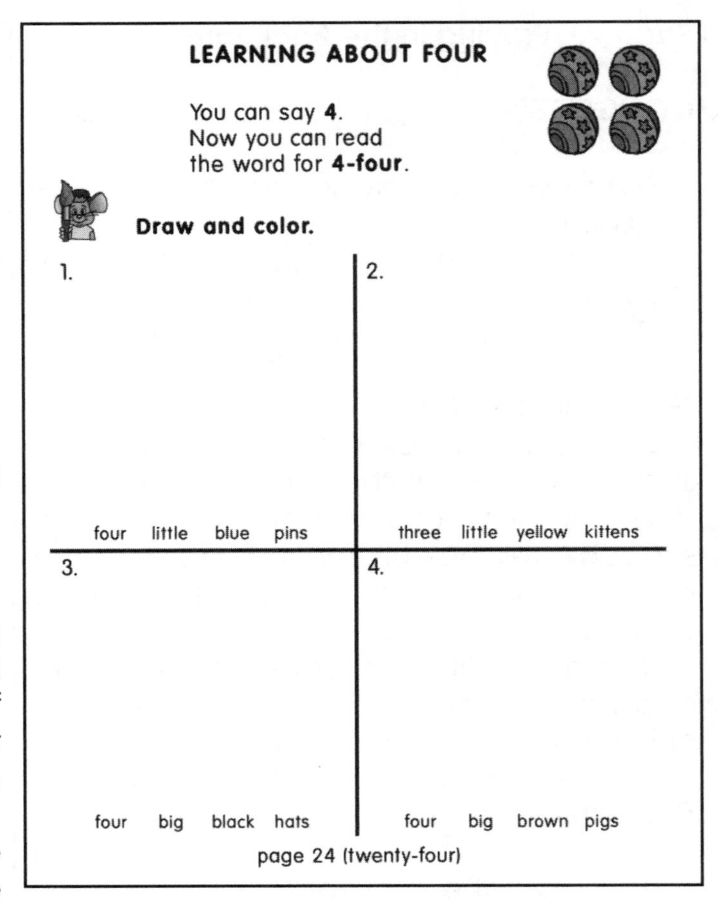

TEACHING PAGE 24:

Write the words *one, two,* and *three* on the board and have the children read them. Write the word *four* and ask if anyone can read it. Point to the words out of order and have the children read them several times.

Read the title with the children. Have the children count the balls and read the number *4* and the word *four.*

Ask the children to read the next direction. Have them read the phrase in the first box silently. Then have a child read it aloud. Ask if it is a sentence. Have a child make a complete sentence out of the phrase. (Draw and color four little blue pins.)

Have the children draw and color what it says and then complete the page by themselves. Help the children sound out words if necessary.

Check by having the children tell what they drew in each box.

ACTIVITIES:

1. Do Worksheet 8.

Read the directions with the children. Read the list of number words at the bottom of the first section.

Have the children count the dots; then write in the number word on the lines. Then let the children finish the page by matching numbers to pictures to words.

Collect the papers and check. Have the children correct any mistakes.

2. Work with the children who have difficulty reading color and number words.

TEACHING READING:

Ask students where they might see a dog, cat, pig and hen at the same time. (farm) Have each student draw and cut out a farm animal. Use them to make a class farm.

Read the story "The Big Fat Hen" together, then ask the following questions:

"What animal is this story telling about? (the big, fat hen)

"Who sees the big, fat hen? (Matt, Jan, Tom, man, cat, dog, pig)

"Who does the big, fat hen see? (Matt, Jan, Tom, man, cat, dog)

"Who doesn't she see? (the pig)

"Why do you think the big, fat hen doesn't see the pig? (answers will vary)

Have students identify short vowel and rhyming words.

ACTIVITY:

Make finger puppets of all the characters. Act out the story. The big, fat hen says, "cluck, cluck". Have students create a word list of sounds the other animals make.

Name ____________

Write the words.

I ____________

I I ____________

I I I ____________

I I I I ____________

two **four** **one** **three**

Match

1 three

3 one

4 two

2 four

Language Arts 102
Worksheet 8
with page 24

Teacher check ____________
Initial Date

Page 25: Activity Page

CONCEPTS: number words, capital and small letters, sequence

TEACHER GOALS: To teach the children
To match numbers and number words,
To match the same word, one with a capital and one with a small letter,
To put three pictures in their proper sequence, and
To tell a story from the picture sequence.

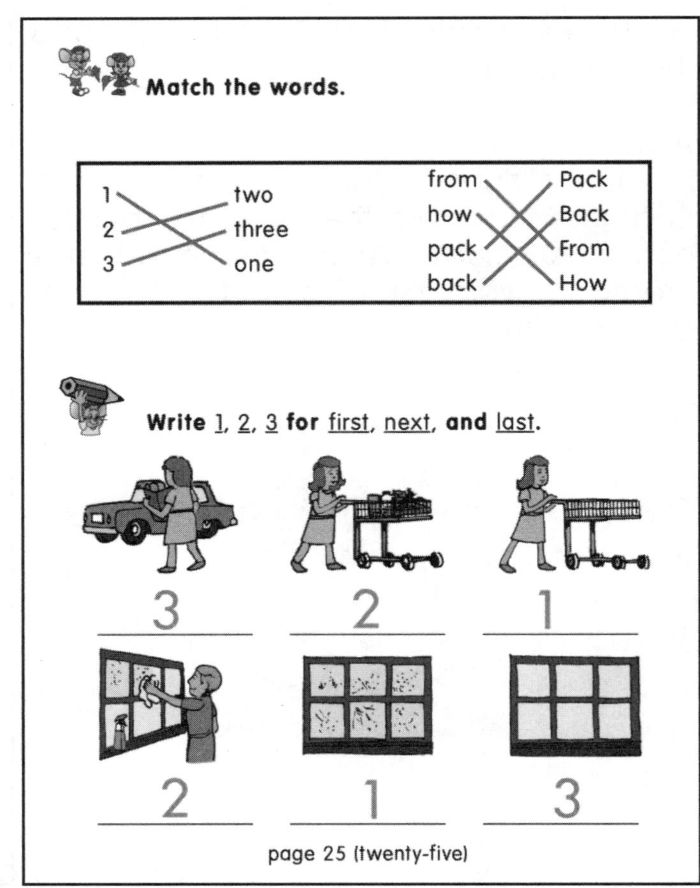

TEACHING PAGE 25:

Go through the direction-word flash cards several times and have the children read them.

Have the children read the directions.

Have the children do the matching in the two boxes. Check while the children are doing the second exercise.

Have the children read the second direction. Then have the children number the pictures in the correct order. (Row 1:3, 2, 1 Row 2: 2, 1, 3)

ACTIVITIES:

1. Use the *Cc* and *Kk* flashcards with the class to point out the words that are spelled with each of these letters. Keep the charts posted to help the children with spelling.

TEACHING READING:

Read the story "Tim Kicks" in *Reader 1*.

Have the children look at the picture. Have them read the title. Have them tell what is happening in the picture. Have them guess who Tim is.

Have them read the story silently.

Ask these questions:

"Which boy is Tim?"

"What special thing can he do?"

"What does Tim kick?"

"Can he kick the ball to Tom?"

"Who do you think taught him to kick the ball?"

"Do you think Tom is a kind brother?"

Have the children find the letter or letters that have the sound of *c*. Have them tell which sentence is a question. How can they tell it is a question?

Page 26: Exclamations

CONCEPTS: exclamations, exclamation point

TEACHER GOALS: To teach the children
To recognize and read an exclamation,
To capitalize the first word of an exclamation,
To recognize and write an exclamation point at the end of an exclamation, and
To read exclamations with good expression.

VOCABULARY: exclamation, point

MATERIALS NEEDED: brown and purple crayons, drawing paper

TEACHING PAGE 26:

Ask the children to tell what kinds of sentences they have already learned. Ask several children to give an example of a statement and a question. Ask what is at the end of each.

Present the word *exclamation* on the board and have the children read it.

Go through the flash cards for *statement, question,* and *exclamation* several times.

Read the sentences at the top of the page to the children and talk about them. Point out the exclamation point.

Ask:

"What is at the end of the exclamation?"

"What is an exclamation?"

"Is an exclamation always a complete sentence?"

"Who can make an exclamation point on the board?"

Read the sentence with the children.

Read each exclamation with good expression and have the children repeat it. Have the children tell what might have caused someone to say that.

EXCLAMATIONS

An **exclamation** shows that someone is excited.

The first word of the exclamation begins with a capital letter.

An exclamation ends with an exclamation point.

An exclamation may be very short.

Read these exclamations with your teacher.

Look at that!

Surprise! Surprise!

Oh, yes!

Draw a brown line under the capital letter at the beginning of the exclamations.

Draw a purple circle around the exclamation point at the end of the exclamations.

page 26 (twenty-six)

Read the directions at the bottom of the page with the children and have them do what they say. Check.

ACTIVITY:

Have the children choose one of the exclamations, write it at the bottom of a sheet of drawing paper, and draw a picture that fits it. Let them show their pictures and read the exclamations to the class.

TEACHING READING:

Read the story "Ball Fun" in *Reader 1*.

Present the word *ball.* Have the children give the meaning of the word.

Have the children look at the picture. Have them read the title. Have them tell what is happening in the picture.

Have them read the story silently.

Ask questions similar to these:

"Who starts out with the ball?"

"Do the boys move slowly or quickly?"

"Who ends up with the ball?"

Have the children read the story together. Remind them to read the last sentence with excitement.

Have the children list all the words that are in the story more than once. How many times do they appear?

Page 27: Activity Page

CONCEPTS: statements, questions, exclamations, punctuation marks

TEACHER GOALS: To teach the children
To recognize and read a statement,
To recognize and read a question,
To recognize and read an exclamation,
To write a period at the end of a statement,
To write a question mark at the end of a question, and
To write an exclamation point at the end of an exclamation.

MATERIALS NEEDED: crayons, Worksheet 9

TEACHING PAGE 27:

Do this page in the same class period as the previous page.

Ask the children to give an example of each kind of sentence.

Have the children read the direction. Write each symbol on the board and ask which kind of sentence it completes.

Help the children read the first sentence. Have them put in the period. Ask a child to read the statement with the proper expression.

Do each sentence the same way.

Read the directions at the bottom of the page. Have the children write the exclamation point on the lines. Have them practice both the exclamation point and the question mark in their writing tablet. Two or three lines of each should give a child enough practice.

ACTIVITY:

1. Paste examples of exclamations cut from papers on a sheet of tagboard or put them on the statement-and-question bulletin board.
2. Do Worksheet 9.

Ask the children to name the three kinds of sentences. Write the punctuation marks on the board and ask the children to tell what they are and what kind of sentence they punctuate. Ask the children to tell how a sentence should begin.

Write ., ?, or !.

This is a bed .
Is that a hen ?
This is a Bible .
Oh, look !
What is that ?
Yes, yes !
This is a pen .

Write the !.

! ! !

Practice ! and ? in your LIFEPAC Tablet.

page 27 (twenty-seven)

Read the title and directions with the children as they follow along.

Read the first sentence with the children and have them raise their hands when they can tell what kind of sentence it is. Ask which mark goes at the end of the sentence. Read the sentence and have them write the period. Do the same with the other sentences. Read all of the sentences. Have the children put in the appropriate punctuation marks.

Let several children choose a story and read it aloud to the class. Encourage them to use good expression when reading. Remind them that their voice should go up at the end of a question and that an exclamation is said louder than an ordinary sentence because they are excited about something.

TEACHING READING:

Have students listen carefully to the following clues:

I am a game. A ball is used in my game. The ball is round. Players hit the ball with a bat. What game am I? (baseball) Survey students to find out how many like baseball or play baseball. Have students tell you the rules of the game.

Read the story "Fast Jim" then ask the following questions:

Who is going to hit the ball? (Jim)

What will Don do? (toss Jim the ball)

Who knows the name of Don's position? (pitcher)

Does Jim hit the ball? (yes)

What does Don do with the ball Jim hits? (he gets it and tosses it to Pat)

Does Pat catch it? (yes)

How do you know? (it says, "the ball is in Pat's mitt.)

Is Jim safe? (yes)

How do you know? (the fans yell hurray, Jim is glad he is fast)

Have students find short vowel words and names.

ACTIVITY:

Make a class picture book of rules for baseball. Have some nonfiction books about baseball and baseball players. Have students get in groups of three and act out the story.

Read the story, "Ronald Morgan Goes to Bat." Have a special treat, cupcakes decorated like baseballs!

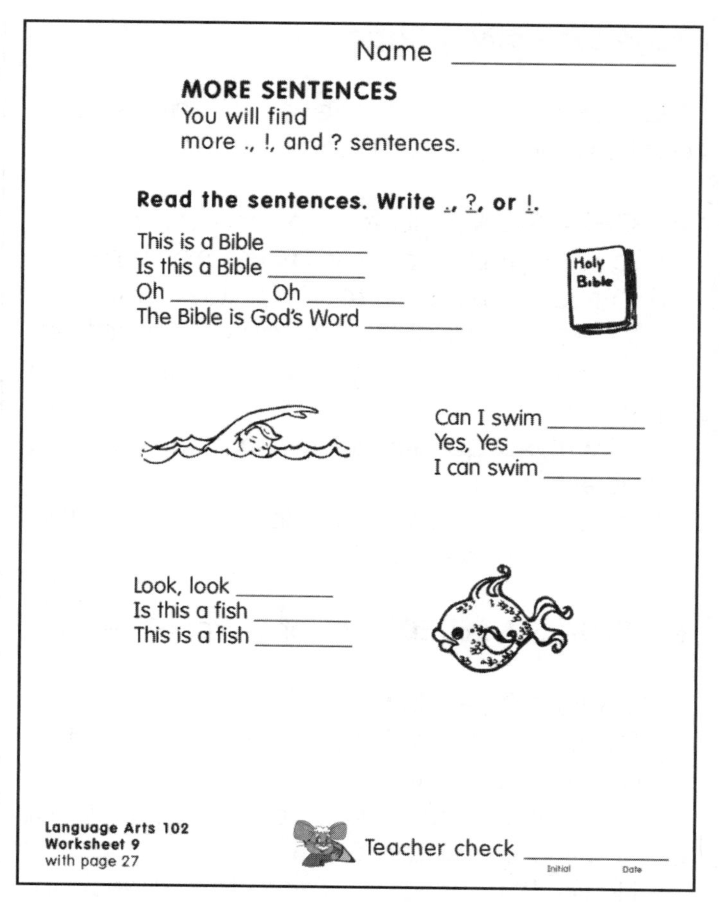

Name ____________

MORE SENTENCES

You will find
more ., !, and ? sentences.

Read the sentences. Write ., ?, or !.

This is a Bible ________
Is this a Bible ________
Oh ________ Oh ________
The Bible is God's Word ________

Can I swim ________
Yes, Yes ________
I can swim ________

Look, look ________
Is this a fish ________
This is a fish ________

Language Arts 102
Worksheet 9
with page 27

Teacher check ____________
Initial Date

Page 28: Learn about Five

CONCEPTS: number word five, following directions

TEACHER GOALS: To teach the children
To read and understand the number word *five*,
To read and follow written directions, and
To match the numeral and the number word with the right number of objects for the numbers 1 to 5.

VOCABULARY: five

MATERIALS NEEDED: crayons, number chart, number word cards

TEACHING PAGE 28:
Show the number word flash cards for the numbers *one* to *four*. Go through them several times. Show the flash card for *five* and ask what it is. Have the children read it several times, then put it with the others and go through them several more times.

Read the title with the children.

Have the children read *5* dots, number *5*, word *five*.

Have a child read the direction. Tell the children to read the phrase in each box carefully and to draw and color what it says. Check by having the children tell what they drew in the boxes. When you check, be sure they make a difference in size between the *big* hats and the *little* pigs.

Have the children read the direction and do the matching exercise. The teacher should check this exercise. Be sure children have individual color and number charts.

ACTIVITIES:
1. Have the children work in pairs with number flash cards. One child holds up a number and the other shows the number of objects it calls for.

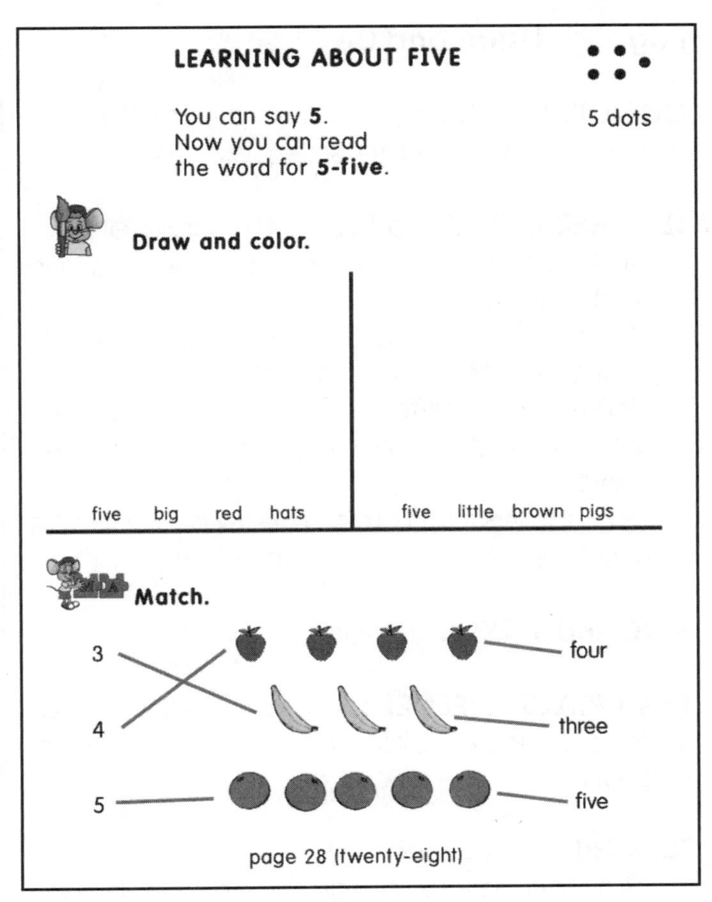

2. If you have a box of colored cubes available, say a number and a color and have the child pick them out of the box or pile. Any objects will do if you have ten or more of each kind in each color.

Page 29: Listen and Do

CONCEPTS: listening, following directions, ordinal numbers, age, size, position

TEACHER GOALS: To teach the children
To listen and follow oral directions given only once,
To read and understand the ordinal numbers *first* through *sixth*,
To tell the difference between *oldest* and *youngest* and *largest* and *smallest*, and
To understand the meanings of the positions *in*, *under*, *on*, and *around*.

VOCABULARY: directions

MATERIALS NEEDED: color charts, red, yellow, orange, blue, purple, and brown crayons,

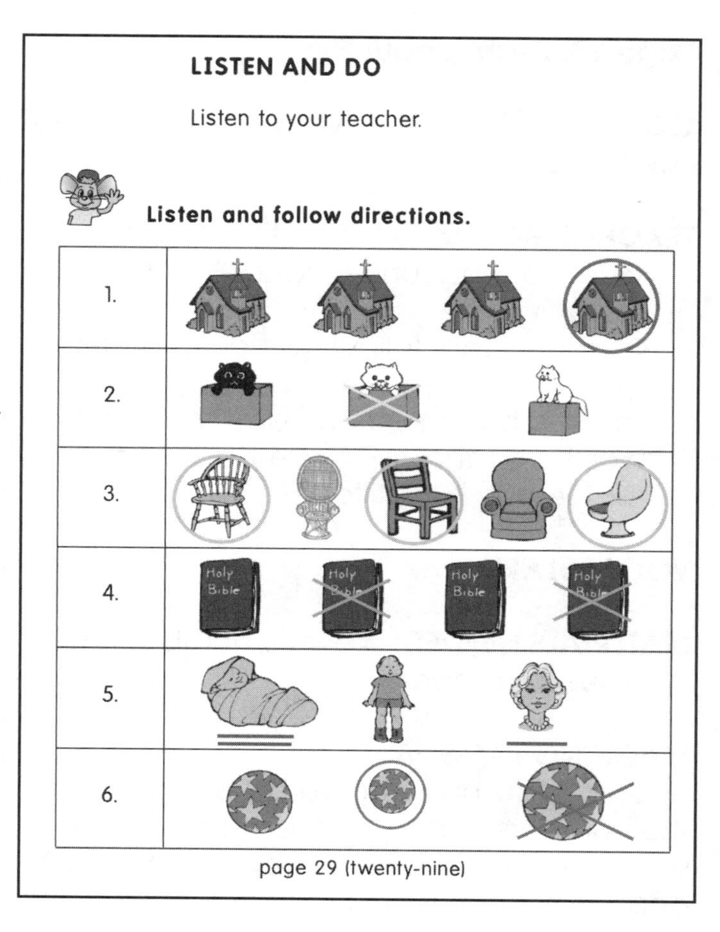

TEACHING PAGE 29:

Put the follow diagram on the board and have the children read.

❑	❑	❑	❑	❑	❑
1	2	3	4	5	6
first	second	third	fourth	fifth	sixth

Leave the diagram on the board while the children do the page.

Read the title and directions with the children as they follow along. Tell the children to listen carefully as you will read the directions only once. Be sure a color chart is nearby so that the children can see it. Have the children put their fingers on the numbers at the left of each row to help keep their places on the page.

Read once: (Emphasize the underlined words slightly.)

1. Put a red circle around the <u>fourth</u> church .
2. Put a yellow X on the picture of the white kitten <u>in</u> the box.
3. Put an orange circle around the <u>first</u>, <u>third</u>, and <u>fifth</u> chairs.
4. Put a blue X on the <u>second</u> and <u>fourth</u> Bibles.
5. Put 1 purple line under the picture of the <u>oldest</u> person and 2 purple lines under the picture of the <u>youngest</u> person.
6. Put a brown circle around the <u>smallest</u> ball and a brown X on the <u>largest</u> ball.

The teacher should check this page.

ACTIVITIES:

Use color word flash cards with children who do not know all the color words. Have the children work in pairs or small groups.

Page 30: Learn about Six

CONCEPTS: number word six, following directions

TEACHER GOALS: To teach the children
To understand and read the number word *six,*
To read and follow written directions, and
To match the numbers 1 to 6 with the same number of objects and the corresponding number word.

VOCABULARY: six

MATERIALS NEEDED: crayons, Worksheet 10

TEACHING PAGE 30:

Read the title with the children. Have them read *6* dots, number *6,* and word *six.*

Have the children read the first direction and do what it says. Check. Be sure the *suns* are different sizes.

Read the second direction and have the children match the numbers with the objects and the number words. The teacher should check this page.

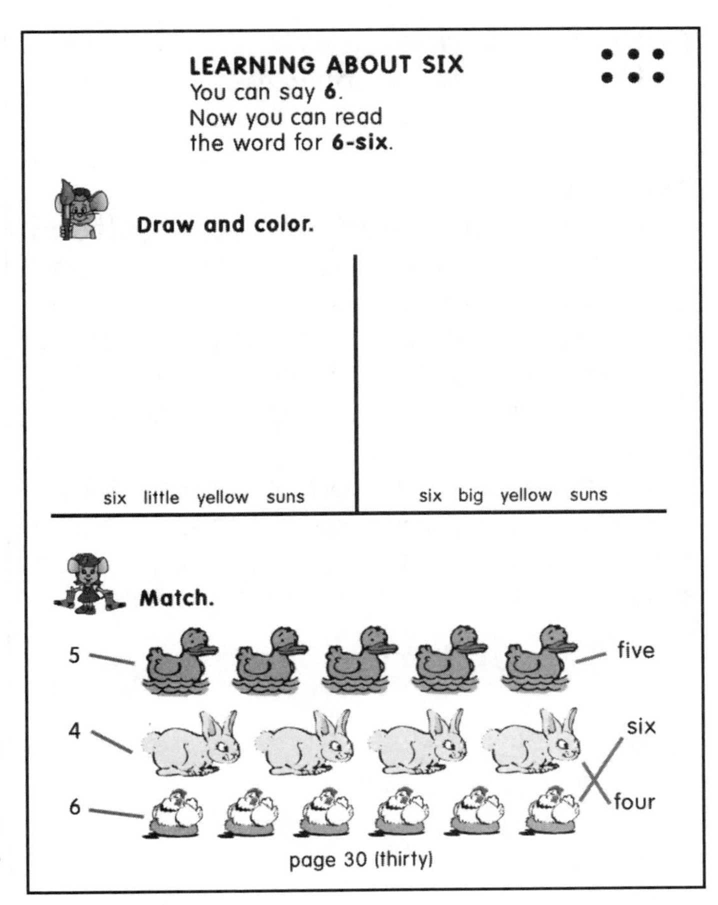

ACTIVITIES:

1. Do Worksheet 10.

Read the directions with the children. Ask the children to tell how many balls they see in the first box. Have them write the word one and read it. Have the children cross out the word one at the bottom of the page. Remind them to follow this procedure each time they use a word .

Let the children finish the page. Collect the papers and check. Have the children correct any mistakes.

This page may be used as an informal check to see how well the children know the number words.

2. If children do not know all the number words, have them work in pairs with the number word flash cards.

3. Have the children take a sheet of writing tablet paper and their crayons. Hold up a number word flash card and say a color. Children will make a row of dots on the paper having the right color and the correct number. Check each row before going on to the next.

TEACHING READING:

Ask students to share what they know about ants. List their responses. Share nonfiction books on ants. It's exciting to learn there are over 10,000 different kinds! Ask students to share about times when they have watched ants.

Read the story "Little Black Ants" then answer the following questions:

"When do the ants come out of their hill?" (when the sun comes up)

"How do they go down the path." (one by one)

"What do they do all day?" (work)

"When do they go back to their hill?"

(when the sun goes down)

Have students identify the short vowel words.

ACTIVITY:

Make ant head bands. (attach antennas to a paper band that fits around the head) Sing the song, "The Ants Go Marching....one by one hurrah, hurrah! Change the words to different actions: The Ants Go Skipping...etc. Have students do the motions and sing.

Do mini research reports on ants. Make ants out of egg cartons - cut them in three section parts, paint and add details. Have students write about an ant experience.

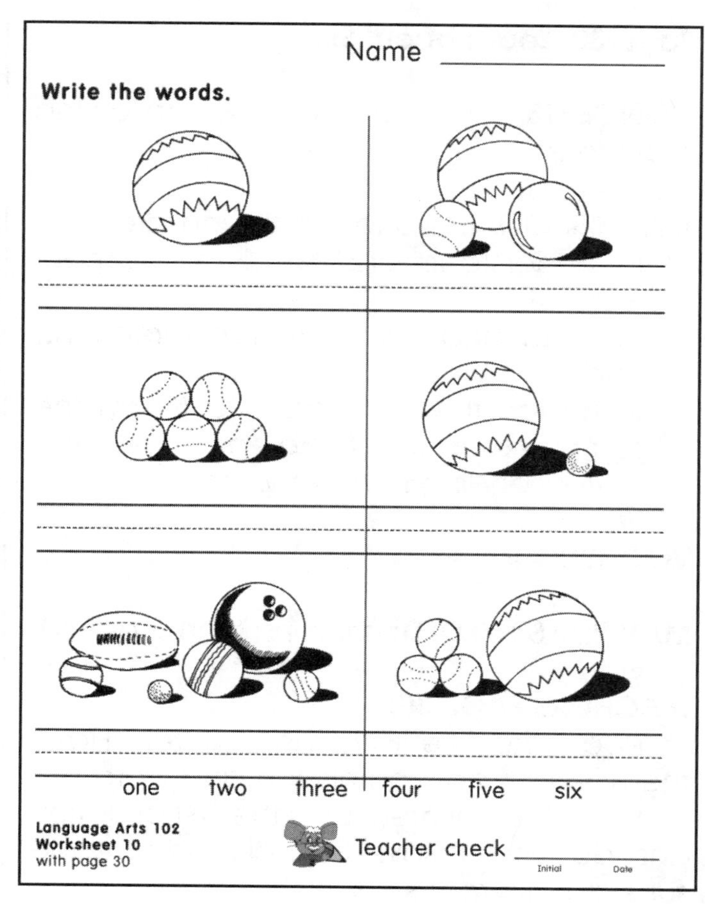

Name ____________

Write the words.

one two three four five six

Language Arts 102
Worksheet 10
with page 30

Teacher check ____________
Initial Date

Page 31: Sentences

CONCEPTS: statements and periods, questions and question marks, exclamations and exclamation points, subject-verb agreement, verb forms

TEACHER GOALS: To teach children

To recognize, read, and write a statement,

To recognize, read, and write a question,

To recognize, read, and write an exclamation,

To recognize and write a period, question mark, and exclamation point and to use them with the proper sentence,

To recognize and use correct subject-verb agreement in sentences, and

To recognize and use the correct verb form in sentences.

VOCABULARY: sentence

MATERIALS NEEDED: Worksheet 11

TEACHING PAGE 31:

Go through the flash cards for the direction words several times.

Read the title and ask the children to give the three kinds of sentences. Ask the children to tell the punctuation mark that goes with each.

Help the children read the three sentences. Have them read them with good expression. Ask which is a statement, a question, and an exclamation.

Read the directions with the children. Ask what kind of letter a sentence should always have at the beginning. Have the children write the three sentences on the lines.

The teacher should check this page and have the children recopy if necessary.

ACTIVITIES:

1. Take time for the children to write some sentences and to read their sentences to the class.

2. The children may write more sentences in their writing tablets. For children who cannot seem to get started, write three or four words on the board and suggest they use those in sentences.

3. Using sentences the children write, change the verb (from *is* to *are,* from *has to have,* etc.) and ask which sentence sounds better. Give sentences such as these and have the children tell the correct verb form:

The children *go* or *goes* to school. John *jump* or *jumped* over the box. *The* class *sing or sang* a song .

4. Do Worksheet 11

Read the title and the first directions with the children. Have the children read the sentences silently, then have the first sentence read aloud. Ask the children what kind of sentence it is and what mark should be put on the line. Do the same with the other two sentences and then have the story read with expression.

Go through the second story in the same way.

Read the directions with the children. Call attention to the three sentence types and the punctuation marks that go with each type of sentence. Tell the children to write the sentences. Have them read aloud when the children are finished.

TEACHING READING:

Read the story "Bug" in *Reader 1.*

Present the word *I* to the children. Explain that it is a pronoun that takes the place of the story teller's name. Tell them that *I* is always a capital letter when it takes the place of a person's name.

Have the children look at the picture and tell what is happening. Have them read the title of the story aloud.

Have the children read the story silently.
Ask these questions:
"Who is telling the story?"
"What happened to her?"
"What did her Mom do?'
"What did her Dad do?"
"Did she hit the bug?"
"Who hit the big, bad bug?"

Have the children find the rhyming words. Write them on the board. Have them find the short *u* words.

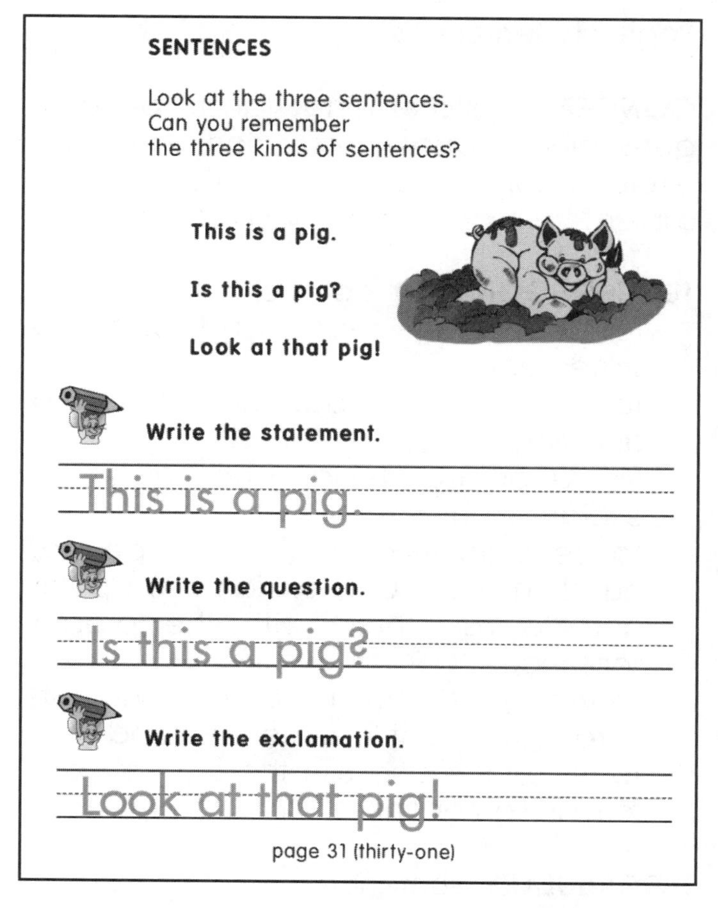

SENTENCES

Look at the three sentences.
Can you remember
the three kinds of sentences?

This is a pig.

Is this a pig?

Look at that pig!

Write the statement.

This is a pig.

Write the question.

Is this a pig?

Write the exclamation.

Look at that pig!

page 31 (thirty-one)

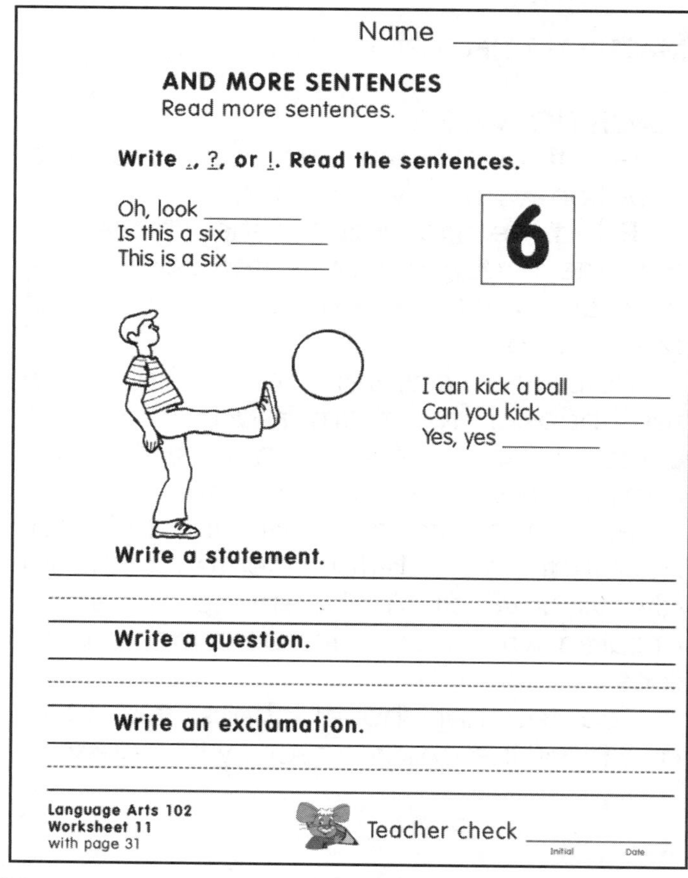

Name ____________

AND MORE SENTENCES
Read more sentences.

Write ., ?, or !. Read the sentences.

Oh, look ______
Is this a six ______
This is a six ______

I can kick a ball ______
Can you kick ______
Yes, yes ______

Write a statement.

____

Write a question.

____

Write an exclamation.

____

Language Arts 102
Worksheet 11
with page 31

Teacher check ____________
Initial Date

Page 32: Rhyming

CONCEPTS: rhyming words, word ending: *ing*

TEACHER GOALS: To teach the children
To read and write words ending in *-ing* that rhyme,
To add *-ing* to a root word to make a new word,
To double the final consonant of a short vowel word before adding *-ing*, and
To drop the final *e* in long vowel words and some short vowel words before adding *-ing*.

MATERIALS NEEDED: tagboard, Worksheet 12

TEACHING PAGE 32:

Ask the children to give words that rhyme with *sing*.

Tell the children that the letters *-ing* are also used as an ending for words, such as *run/running* and *jump/jumping*. Have them give a few more examples. Use some of the words in the sentences. Tell the children that when *-ing* is at the end of a word, the action is happening now and illustrate with such sentences as these:

I will run.	He will sit down.
I am running.	He is sitting down.
I ran.	He sat down.

Read the first direction with the children. Have them write the rhyming words on the lines. Have them write *-ing* at the top of a sheet of writing tablet paper and put aside until later (bring, king, ring, wing).

Read the second direction with the children. Have them read the word pick and the word picking. Have them trace the *-ing*. Read the other pairs of words and have the children write *-ing* on the lines. Read the words several times.

Write rhyming words.

____ ing

Add ing. Read the words.

pick	pick picking
jump	jump jumping
fish	fish fishing

Read these words with your teacher.

sit	sitting	make	making
win	winning	like	liking
hop	hopping	hope	hoping
bat	batting	give	giving
wag	wagging	love	loving
bob	bobbing	have	having
dig	digging	come	coming

page 32 (thirty-two)

Read the last direction with the children. Read the pairs of words and have the children repeat them. Write on the board the word *sit* and tell the children that the last consonant must be doubled before the *-ing* is added. Write *ting* and read the word. Write each of the other words and have the children tell you what to write at the end of each.

Read the pairs of words in the last section and have the children repeat them. Write the word *make* on the board and tell the children that the final *e* must be taken off before adding the *-ing*. Erase the *e* and write the *-ing*. Read the word. Write each of the other words the same way.

Read all the words in both sections several times.

Note: These concepts are introduced here for the children who are ready to use them in their written work. Teach the concepts again as the children need them.

ACTIVITIES:

1. Have the children finish the *-ing* words on the sheet of writing tablet paper prepared earlier.
2. Dictate five *-ing* words from each list and have the children write them on a sheet of writing tablet paper.
3. Have the children write sentences using any of the *-ing* words on this page. Have them read their sentences.
4. Cut strips of tagboard about two inches wide and eight inches long. Write the root word on one end of the strip. Write the ending on the opposite side so that when the card is folded, the ending is at the end of the root word. For words in which the final *e* must be dropped fold the strip so that the *e* is covered. The children can work these strips alone or with a child who can read all the words. Add words as they come up in materials read by the children.
5. Do Worksheet 12.

Have the children read the direction and color the picture. Be sure they understand that all petals of a flower are to be colored, not just the one indicated by the dotted line. All flower centers are to be colored black and all the leaves and stems green.

If some children still cannot read the color names, have them work with the color chart or color-word flash cards.

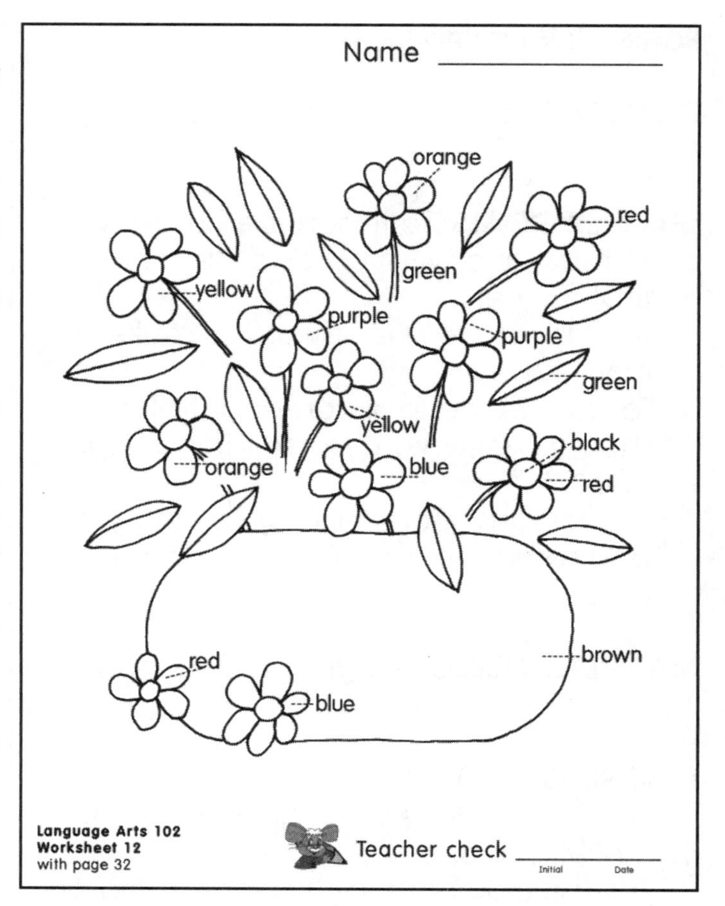

SELF TEST 3

CONCEPTS: matching numbers to number words and objects, exclamation, exclamation point, add *-ing* to words, real and not real

TEACHER GOAL: To teach the children
To check their own progress periodically.

TEACHING PAGE 33:
Read all the directions on the page with the children and be sure they understand everything they are to do.
Let them do the entire page without help.
Check the page as soon as possible. Go over it with the child so he can see where he did well and where he needs extra work. (Mom: jog with the dog)

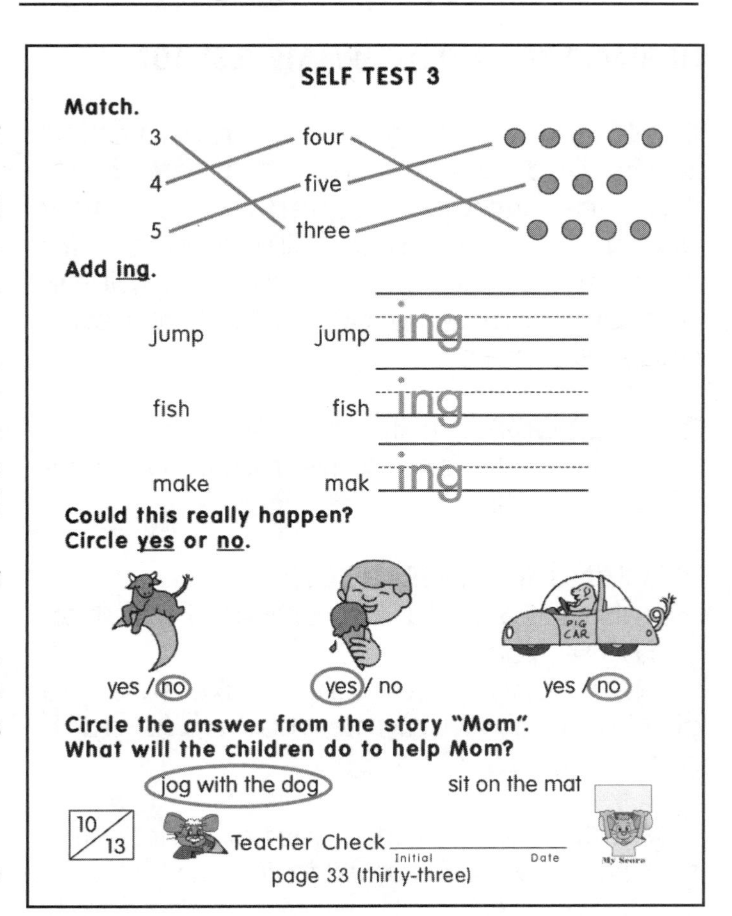
SELF TEST 3

Match.

3 four

4 five

5 three

Add ing.

jump jump ing

fish fish ing

make mak ing

Could this really happen?
Circle yes or no.

yes / no yes / no yes / no

Circle the answer from the story "Mom".
What will the children do to help Mom?

jog with the dog sit on the mat

10/13 Teacher Check ______ Initial Date

My Score

page 33 (thirty-three)

ACTIVITIES:
1. Give each child help on items he misses.
2. If several children miss the same things, reteach the skill (in a small group session if possible).

SPELLING WORDS:

three
four
five
bug
not

LIFEPAC TEST AND ALTERNATE TEST 102

CONCEPTS: real or make-believe, matching letters and words, things that are alike, rhyming words, sequence, auditory discrimination (listening skills), adding suffix *ing* to words, alphabet sequence, plurals and punctuation of question, statements, and exclamations

TEACHER GOAL: To teach the children
To learn to check their own progress periodically.

TEACHING the LIFEPAC TEST:
This test should be broken into short testing sessions.
Read each direction. Make sure the children know what they must do for each activity (Page 2: 2, 1, 3).

Audio Discrimination section (Circle the picture.)-*Read the story to the children.*
Candy Cat is alone. All of the family have gone to school and to work.
First, Candy watches the fish swim in the fish bowl. She licks her lips.
Next, Candy hears a noise and runs to see Buddy Bird perched on his swing in his cage. Candy wishes Buddy weren't in a cage.
Then Candy curls up to take a nap on her pillow.
Circle the picture that shows the first thing Candy did when she was alone (watches the fish swim in the fishbowl).

If the children do poorly on any section of the test, review the pages and activities that stress the concepts tested.
Give those children who do not achieve the 80% score additional copies of the worksheets. A parent or a classroom helper may help in the review.
When the child is ready, give the Alternate LIFEPAC Test. Use the same procedure as for the LIFEPAC Test.

Audio Discrimination section (Circle the picture.) -*Read the story to the children.*
Barb gave Jenny a beautiful new balloon. Jenny waited until after school was out. When it was time to go home, Jenny blew and blew until she had a big balloon. Next, she sat down and tied a string to the balloon so that it would not blow away. Then she walked down the sidewalk to meet her Mom. Mom liked Jenny's new balloon!
Circle the picture that shows the second thing Jenny did with her balloon (tied a string) (Page 2: 3, 1, 2).

SPELLING WORDS:

LIFEPAC words	**Alternate words**
pens	one
wet	two
will	Sis
hug	run
one	tell
two	God
three	bug
run	not
tell	four
four	five

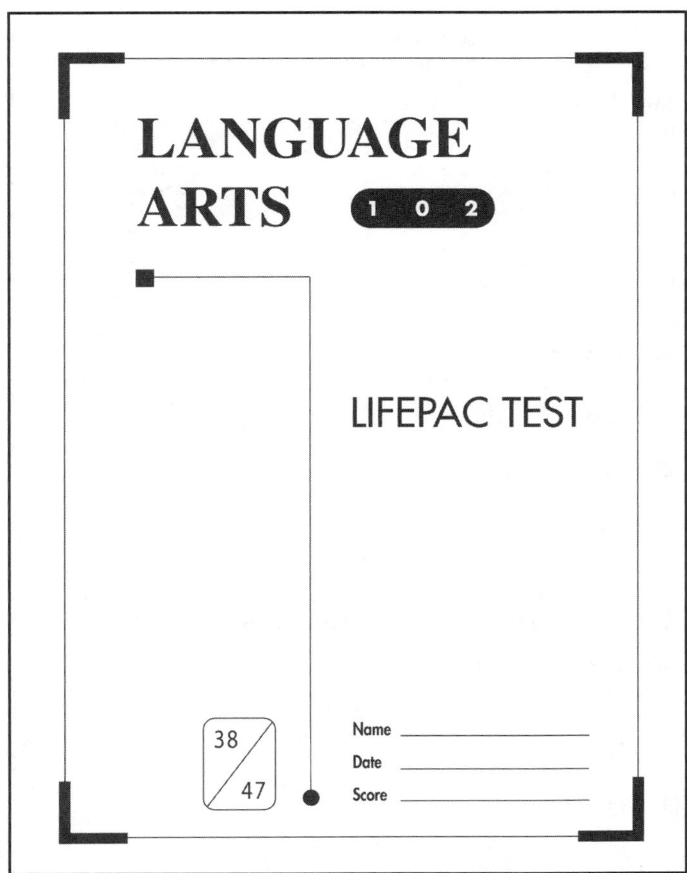

LANGUAGE ARTS 1 0 2

LIFEPAC TEST

38 / 47

Name ______

Date ______

Score ______

LANGUAGE ARTS 102: LIFEPAC TEST

Could this really happen?
Circle yes or no.

yes / no   yes / no   yes / no

Match the letters and words.

C	p	let	Pen
P	c	pen	Let
L	k	keg	Help
K	f	fed	Keg
F	h	help	Fed
H	l		

page 1 (one)

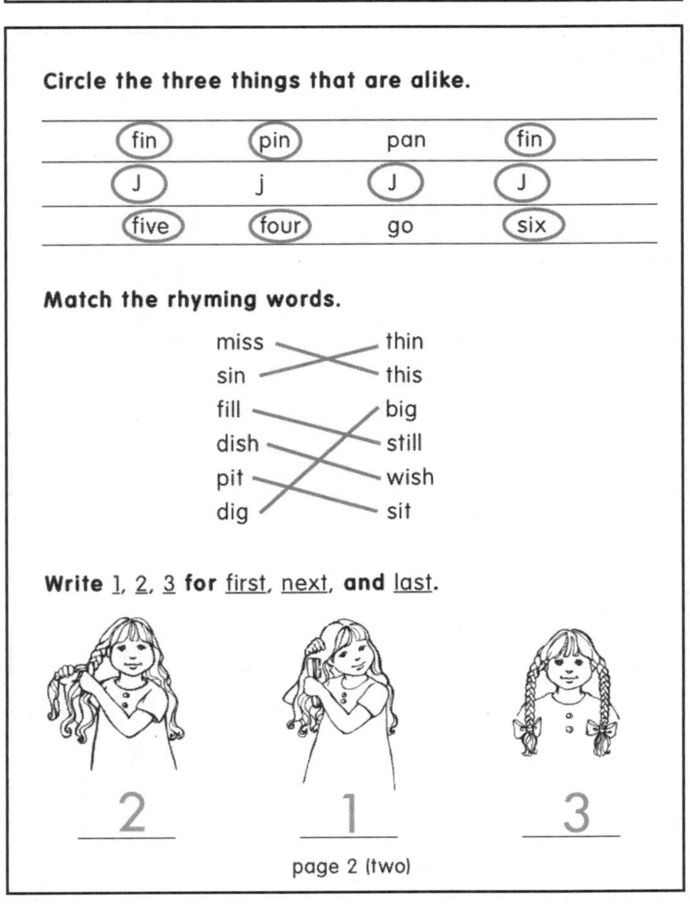

Circle the three things that are alike.

fin	pin	pan	fin
J	j	J	J
five	four	go	six

Match the rhyming words.

miss	thin
sin	this
fill	big
dish	still
pit	wish
dig	sit

Write 1, 2, 3 for first, next, and last.

2   1   3

page 2 (two)

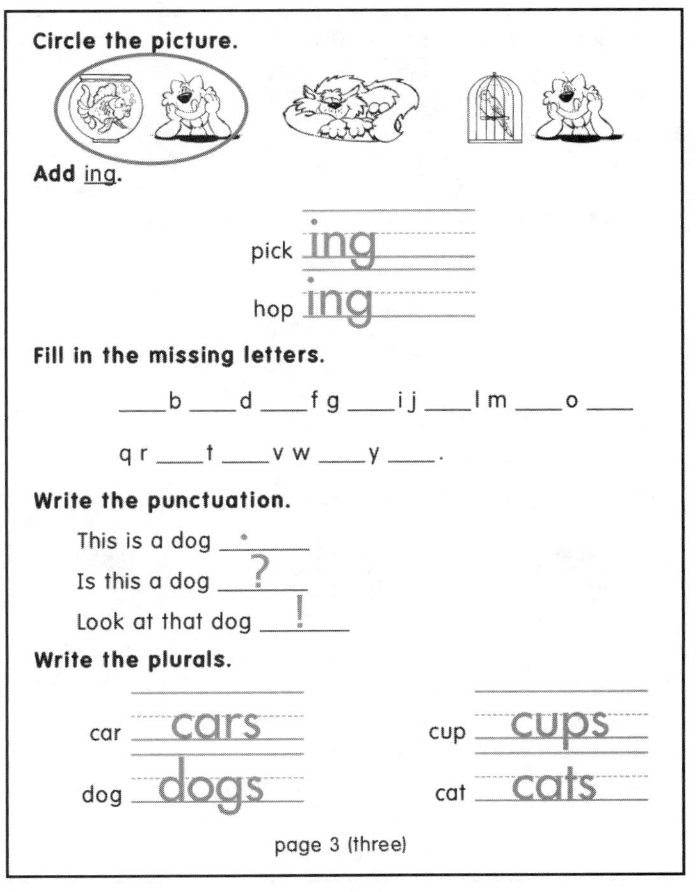

Circle the picture.

Add ing.

pick ing

hop ing

Fill in the missing letters.

___ b ___ d ___ f g ___ i j ___ l m ___ o ___

q r ___ t ___ v w ___ y ___ .

Write the punctuation.

This is a dog .

Is this a dog ?

Look at that dog !

Write the plurals.

car cars   cup cups

dog dogs   cat cats

page 3 (three)

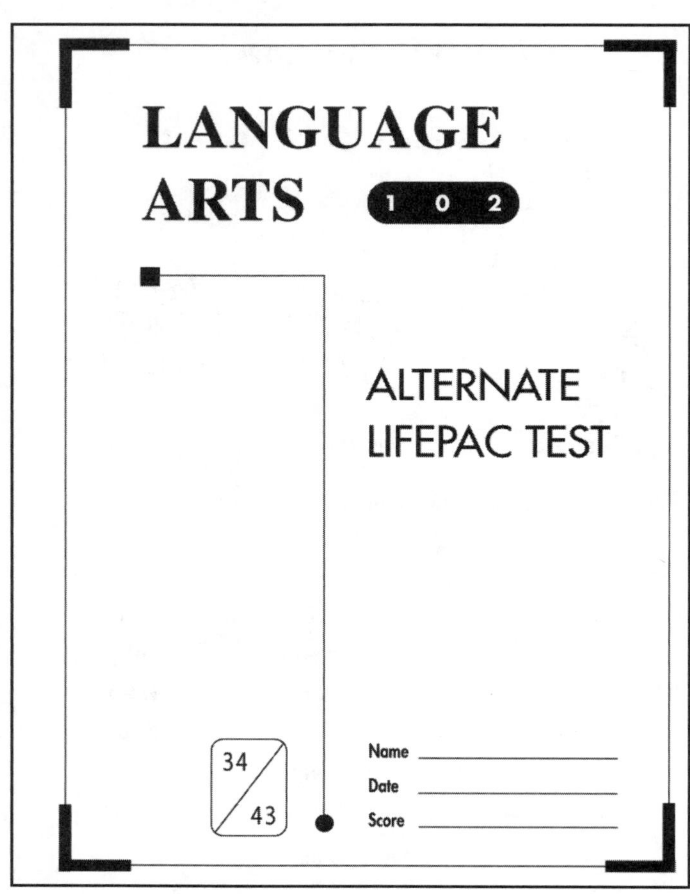

LANGUAGE ARTS 102

ALTERNATE LIFEPAC TEST

34/43

Name ______

Date ______

Score ______

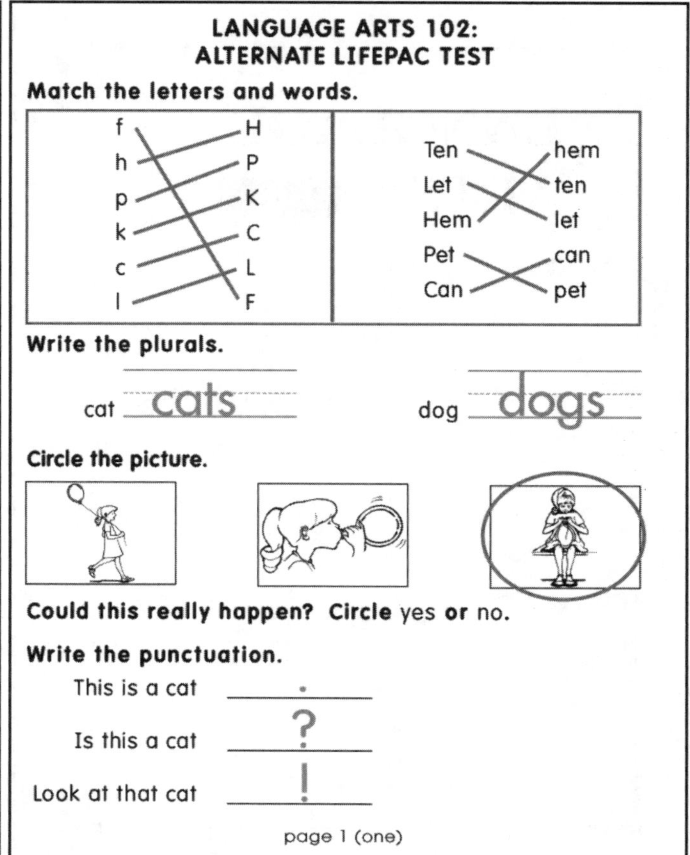

LANGUAGE ARTS 102:
ALTERNATE LIFEPAC TEST

Match the letters and words.

f	H	Ten	hem
h	P	Let	ten
p	K	Hem	let
k	C	Pet	can
c	L	Can	pet
l	F		

Write the plurals.

cat cats   dog dogs

Circle the picture.

Could this really happen? Circle yes **or** no.

Write the punctuation.

This is a cat .

Is this a cat ?

Look at that cat !

page 1 (one)

Circle the three which are alike.

dog	big	dig	rig
six	four	yes	five
g	g	g	G

Match the rhyming words.

fish	pin
thin	this
hiss	bill
sill	dish
bit	dig
fig	sit

Write 1, 2, 3 **for** first, next, **and** last.

3   1   2

page 2 (two)

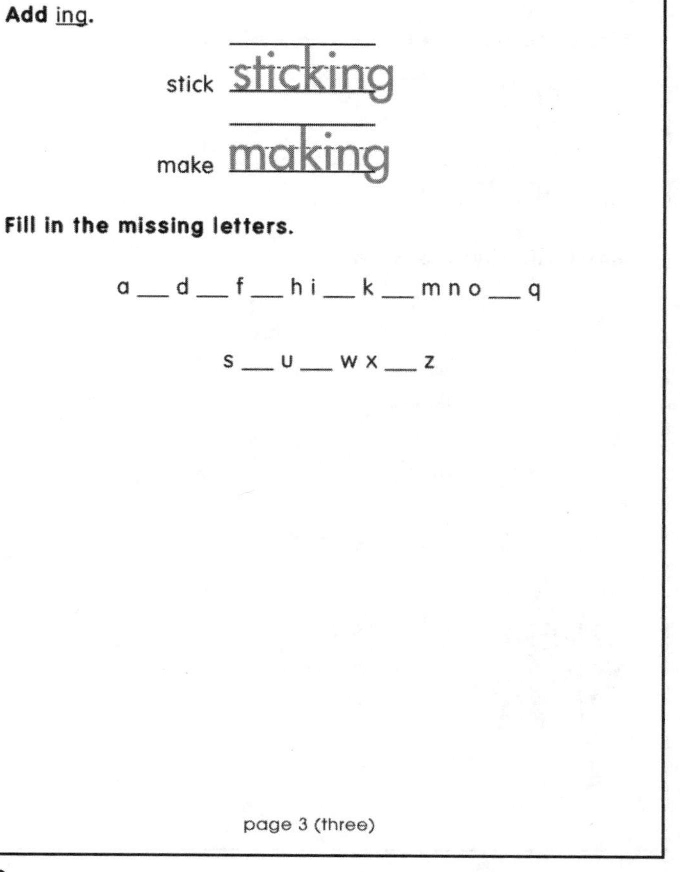

Add ing.

stick sticking

make making

Fill in the missing letters.

a __ d __ f __ h i __ k __ m n o __ q

s __ u __ w x __ z

page 3 (three)

Page 1: FUN WITH WORDS

CONCEPTS: purpose of LIFEPAC, child's objectives, writing name

TEACHER GOALS: To teach the children
To see an overview of the work in Language Arts LIFEPAC 103, and
To write their names correctly in manuscript.

TEACHING PAGE: 1:
Write the word *Objectives* on the board and ask the children if they remember seeing this word in Language Arts LIFEPAC 102. Read it with them and ask if anyone remembers what an objective is. If no one does, explain that an objective is something you decide you want to do and then you work hard to do it.

Read the title and the paragraph with the children and discuss.

Have the children point to the word *Objectives* and ask a child to tell what it means. Read each of the objectives with the children and discuss. Be sure the children understand what will be expected of them. Ask the children why making a list of things to do helps us to remember.

Read the direction and have the children write their names on the lines.

FUN WITH WORDS

In this LIFEPAC
you will learn more
about words and sentences.

You will learn
about contractions, compound words,
and words that show
that something belongs to someone.

Objectives

1. I will learn about syllables.
2. I will learn about consonant digraphs.
3. I will spell and write words.
4. I will learn about contractions.
5. I will learn about possessives.
6. I will learn about compound words.
7. I will learn about plurals.

Write your name

page 1 (one)

I. PART ONE

Page 2: Th

CONCEPT: *th* digraph

TEACHER GOALS: To teach the children
To identify and read words with the two sounds of *th*,
To identify words with the soft (unvoiced) sound of *th* at the beginning, in the middle, or at the end, and
To identify words with the hard (voiced) sound of *th* at the beginning, in the middle, or at the end.

TEACHING PAGE 2:
Have the children look at the picture and tell what is happening. Write on the board:

th	*th*
with	*the*

Have the children tell which of the *th* words from the picture should go under each heading. Write them on the board. Have the children read each list several times, listening for the /*th*/ sound. Tell the children that the *th* in *with* is called a soft *th* and that the *th* in *the* is called a hard *th*. Have them practice both sounds.

(*th* as in *with* - Thanksgiving, thankful)
(*th* as in *the* - father, brother)

Read the direction with the children. Remind them that *th* has two sounds. One sound is soft because it is not made with the voice as in *the* and *mother*.
Read the lists of words and have the children repeat them after you.
Give words from the lists and let the children tell whether the *th* sound is soft or hard.

I. PART ONE

Read these words with your teacher.

soft th		hard th	
three	with	the	bathe
third	bath	thee	mother
thirty	math	this	father
thing	hath	that	other
think	path	then	brother
thank	moth	them	gather
thirsty	Beth	they	rather
thick	Seth	those	bother
thumb	north	these	wither

page 2 (two)

TEACHING READING:
Read the story "The Red Ball" in *Reader 2*.
Have the children look at the picture and tell what is happening.
Have them read the title. Ask the children if they see a ball in the picture. Write the word *ball* on the board. Have the children read it. Write the word *go* on the board. Have a child use it in a sentence.
Have the children read the story silently. Have the children read the story aloud.
Ask these questions:
"What is the girl's name?"
"What does Jan have?"
"What color is it?"
"What does she do with it?"
"Who will call Jan?"
"What will Jan do?"
"What happens to the ball?"
"Is it a ball?"
Have the children find the short *a* words. Write them on the board. Have the children find the color word.

Page 3: Th

CONCEPT: th digraph

TEACHER GOALS: To teach the children

To identify and read words with the two sounds of *th,*

To identify words with the soft (unvoiced) sound of *th* at the beginning or at the end, and

To identify words with the hard (voiced) sound of *th* at the beginning, in the middle, or at the end.

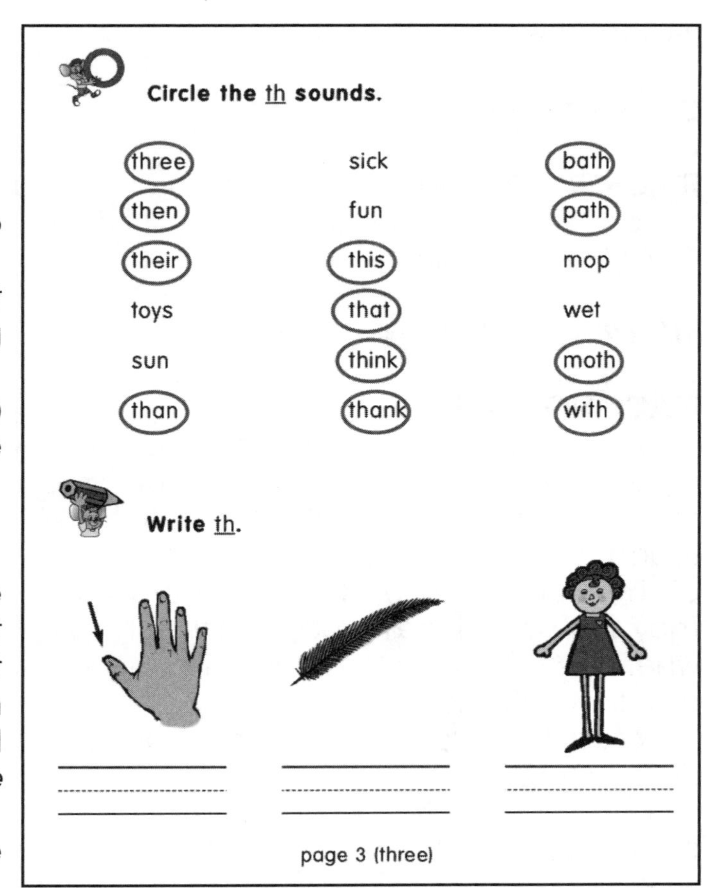

TEACHING PAGE 3:

Read the direction at the top of the page with the children. Remind them that *th* has two sounds. One sound is soft because it is not made with the voice as in *thing or with.* The other sound is hard because it is made with the voice as in *the* and *mother.*

Read the lists of words and have the children repeat them after you.

Give words from the lists and let the children tell if they hear the *th* sound. Have them circle each *th* word.

Read the second direction. Have the children name the pictures. Then have them write *th* under each picture (thumb, feather, thin).

ACTIVITY:

1. Read passages from the Bible that use the *th* ending on common words such as *putteth, hath,* or *goeth.* Write the words on the board and have children read them so they will be familiar with them when they hear them when the Bible is read.

Page 4: Wh

CONCEPT: wh digraph

TEACHER GOAL: To teach the children
To identify words with the sound of *wh* at the beginning.

MATERIALS NEEDED: Worksheet 1

TEACHING PAGE 4:

Say the sound for *wh*. Have the children repeat it several times and be sure they are making a blowing sound, not just the /w/ sound. Have them hold their hands in front of their mouths when they say the words. They should feel their breath on their hands when they say the /wh/ sound. Have them practice until they can.

Read the lists of words and have the children repeat them.

Read the sentence and words at the bottom of the page and have the children repeat the words.

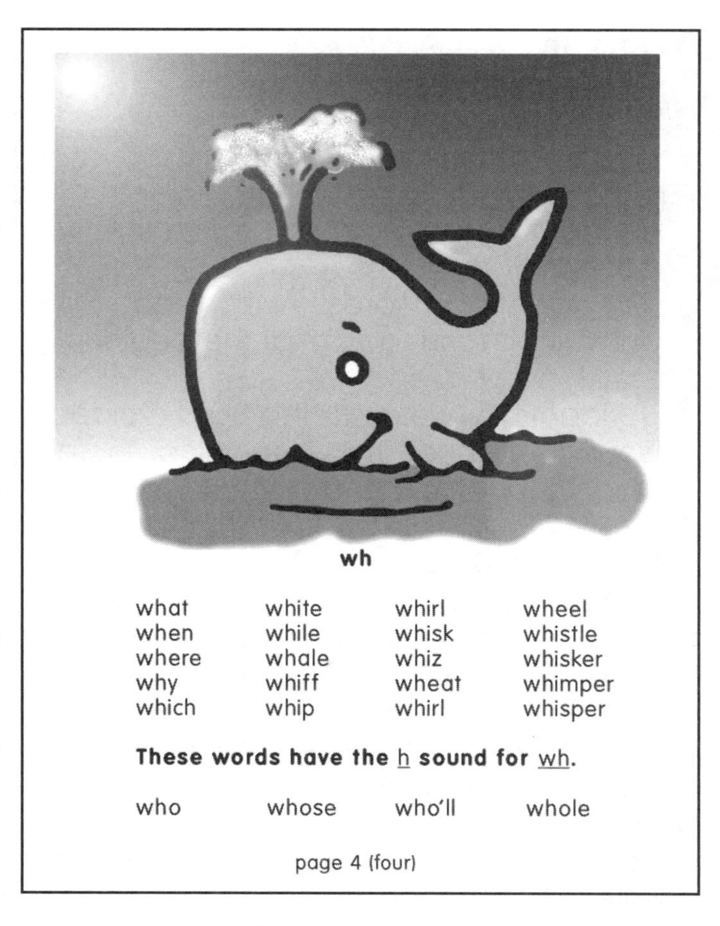

wh

what	white	whirl	wheel
when	while	whisk	whistle
where	whale	whiz	whisker
why	whiff	wheat	whimper
which	whip	whirl	whisper

These words have the h sound for wh.

who	whose	who'll	whole

page 4 (four)

ACTIVITIES:

1. Do Worksheet 1.

Have the children read the direction at the top of the page. Have them name the pictures and write *th* or *wh* on the lines.

(whale, thumb, wheat, whisper, thread, thirty, thirsty, whip, wheel, whistle, throwing, three).

Check by having the children name the picture and tell which letters they wrote on the lines. Have the children correct any mistakes.

TEACHING READING:

Read the story "The Mess" in Reader 2.

Present the word *do* to the children. Write it on the board. Have the children read it.

Have the children look at the picture. Have them tell about experiences they have had with spilling something. Have them tell if they cleaned it up.

Have the children read the story silently.

Ask these questions:

"What is the mess?"

"Do we know who did it?"

"Where was Dan?"

"Where was Kim?"

"Who do you think will clean it up?"

"Can you guess who did it?"

"How can you tell who spilled the paint?"

(These are cat tracks. Dog tracks would have claw marks showing.)

Have the children find the *wh* words. Have the children find the *th* words.

ACTIVITY:

Have the children draw a picture of the accident. Have them draw the one who did it.

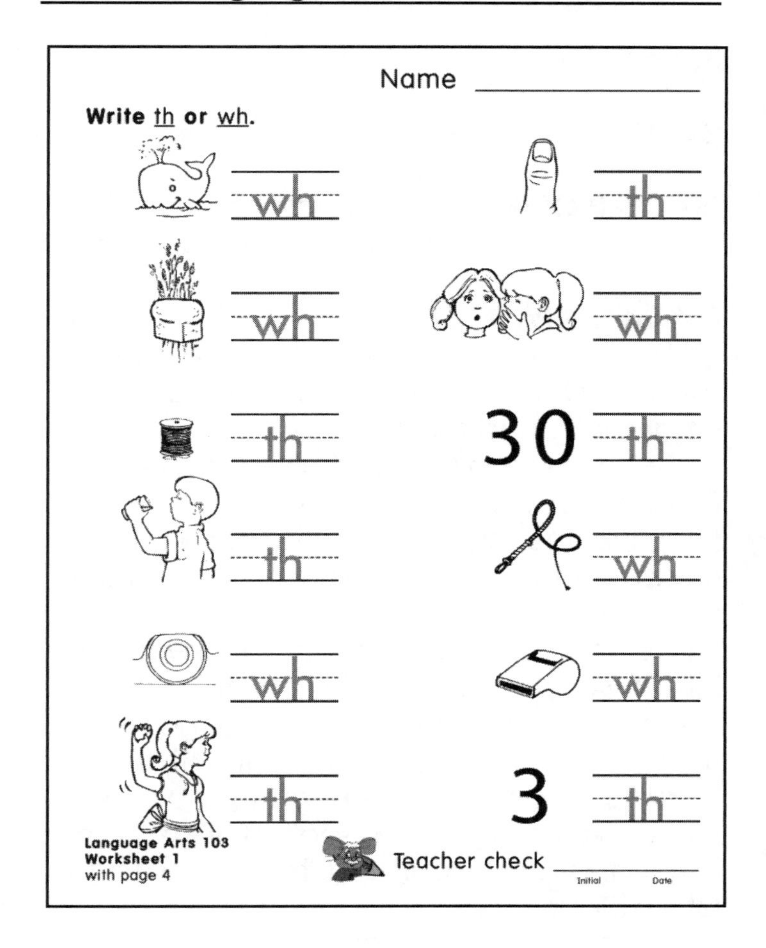

Name ____________

Write th or wh.

wh | th
wh | wh
th | 30 th
th | wh
wh | wh
th | 3 th

Language Arts 103
Worksheet 1
with page 4

Teacher check ____________
Initial Date

Page 5: Sh

CONCEPT: sh digraph

TEACHER GOAL: To teach the children
To identify words with the sound of *sh*

TEACHING PAGE 5:

Have the children read the direction at the top of the page. Ask if anyone knows what the sound for *sh* is.

Say the */sh/* sound and have the children repeat it.

Have the children name the pictures. (shade, sheep, shell) Have them write *sh* under each picture.

Read the second direction. Read the lists of words and have the children repeat them after you. Call attention to the words that have the sound of *sh* but not the *sh* spelling. Some children may know that some words that are spelled with a *ch* have the /sh/ sound (Cheryl, Chicago, Chevrolet).

Ask the children to give more words with the */sh/* sound.

Listen to the sh sound.
Write sh.

Listen to the sh sound.

sh			
she	shoe	washer	dish
sheep	shop	dasher	fish
shell	show	ashes	wish
shelf	shin		wash
shall	shirt	Russia	push
share			ash
shade		session	cash
shame	sure	emotion	rush
shale	sugar	caution	splash

page 5 (five)

Listen to the ch sound.
Circle pictures with the ch sound.

Listen to the ch sound.

ch			tch
chin	cheek	rich	catch
chill	cheese	such	match
chap	chest	much	hatch
chop	check	which	scratch
chair	chalk	touch	watch
chain	chew	pouch	ditch
change	chase	lunch	hitch
cherry	chimp	bunch	pitch

page 6 (six)

Page 6: Ch

CONCEPT: ch digraph

TEACHER GOAL: To teach the children
To identify words with the sound of *ch* .

MATERIALS NEEDED: Worksheet 2

TEACHING PAGE 6:
Read the first direction. Have the children circle each picture that has the /*ch*/ sound. (chimpanzee, checker board, sheep, chair, chin, chopping)

Ask if anyone knows what sound the *ch* has. Have the children say it several times. Read the first three lists of words. Have the children repeat each word and tell where they hear the /*ch*/ sound.

Tell the children that even though the sound is the same, some words must be spelled with a *tch* in the middle or at the end. Read the list of words. Have the children repeat each one and spell it.

Ask the children if they can think of other words with the /*ch*/ sound.

Tell the children that some words are spelled with a *ch*, but have a /*k*/ sound. Write *Christ* and *Christmas* on the board to illustrate. Tell the children an easy way to tell is to look at the letter right after the *h*. If the letter is an *l* or an *r*, the *ch* will have a /*k*/ sound. If the letter is a vowel, it will usually be the /*ch*/ sound and sometimes the /*sh*/ sound. (Words like chorus and choir are an exception to this.)

ACTIVITY:

1. Do Worksheet 2.

Have the children read the direction at the top of the Worksheet. Have them name the pictures on the page and write *ch* or *sh* on the lines (shoes, chair, sheep, shelf, chin, sugar, chopping, chimpanzee, shell, chest, checkerboard, shade).

Check by having the children name the picture and tell which letters they wrote on the lines. Have the children correct any mistakes. In this activity you are checking accuracy of sound, not spelling.

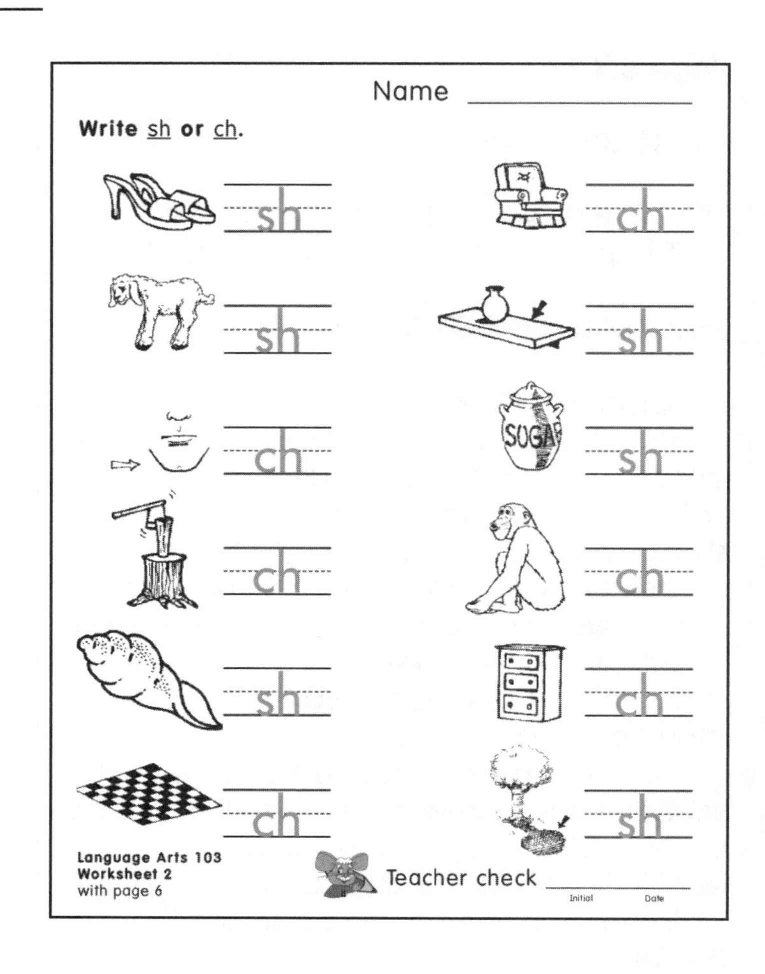

Name ____________

Write sh **or** ch.

sh ch

sh sh

ch sh

ch ch

sh ch

ch sh

Language Arts 103
Worksheet 2
with page 6

Teacher check ____________
Initial Date

Page 7: Words and Sentences

CONCEPTS: writing capital and small letters, writing words, writing sentences

TEACHER GOALS: To teach the children
To write four small letters and four capital letters,
To write two words,
To write a sentence,
To understand that a sentence may be a statement, a question, or an exclamation,
To know the proper punctuation for each kind of sentence,
To use correct verb forms in spoken or written sentences, and
To use correct subject-verb agreement in spoken or written sentences.

VOCABULARY: capital, small

MATERIALS NEEDED: Worksheet 3

Write four small letters.

Write four capital letters.

Write two words.

Write two names.

Write a sentence.

page 7 (seven)

TEACHING PAGE 7:

Ask the children to give the three kinds of sentences they have learned. Ask how each one begins and ends.

Read the direction for each part with the children and wait until they have completed it. Do not check at this time. Tell the children they may write any letters, any words they can spell, and any kind of sentence. Tell the children to be sure their sentence is complete and sounds right.

Help the children with the spelling of words in their sentences, but not with the two words they are to write.

Collect the papers and check. Correct letter forms, spelling, and punctuation in a different color and have the children write any corrections five times each on a sheet of writing tablet paper. Check the papers to be sure they wrote the words and sentences as corrected.

Note: Correct the children's written work in this way so it is easy for the children to recopy. A single line through the misspelled word lets the child see his mistake. If you make your correction in ink or in a different color pencil, the child can easily see the correct spelling. Always require a child to recopy anything he has written if a word is misspelled, if the work is messy, or if the letters are not well formed. Check over the copied work with the child if possible. Have him read it to you.

ACTIVITY:

1. Dictate the following letters, words, and sentences and have the children write them on a sheet of writing tablet paper.

r, b, k, w (Pause between letters.)
J, G, K, R, (Dictate as capital J, etc.)
him, rid, will (Pause between words.)
I am big.
Is it a pig?

Note: When dictating a sentence, read it at a normal speed the first time—*I am big*. The second time pause slightly between the words—*I am big.* Wait until the children have had time to write about half of the sentence and read it again at a normal speed.

2. Do Worksheet 3.

Read the first direction with the children. Tell them to look at the picture and read the question silently. Have a child read it aloud.

Have the children look at the next picture, trace the letters, and read the question. Let them finish the page independently. Read all the sentences again.

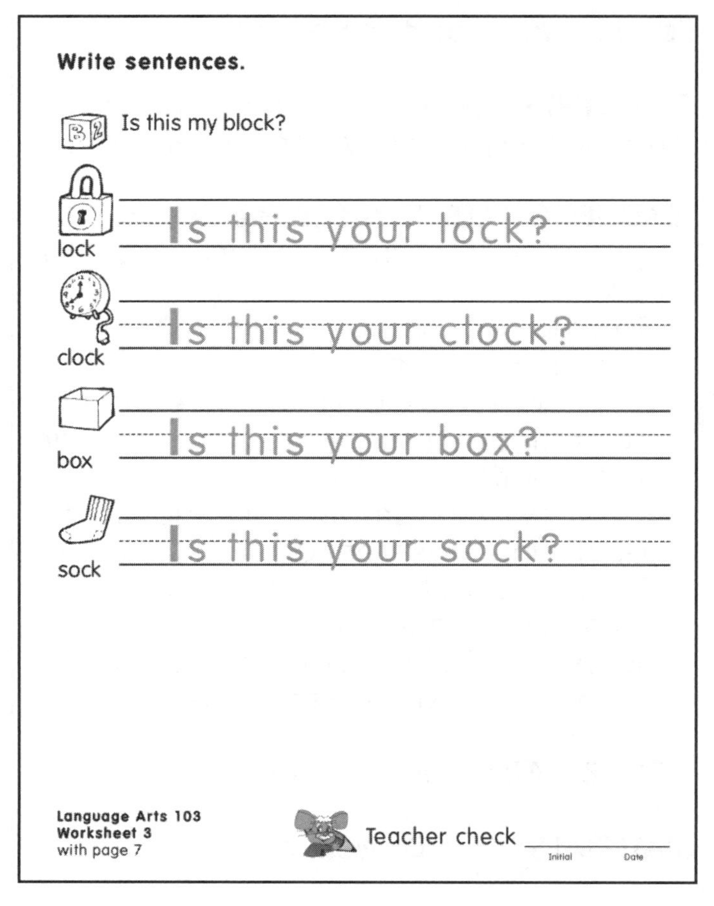

TEACHING READING:

Write the words "Boom!, Kaboom!" on the board. Read the words with students emphasizing the sound. Ask students to think of things that would make such sounds. List them on the board. If thunder isn't mentioned, give them clues and then add it to the list. Ask students what they do during a thunder storm. Discuss. Tell them they're going to read a story about some puppies and what they did during a thunderstorm.

Read the story "Three Missing Pups" together then answer the following questions:

"Who are the children in this story? (Jen, Freddie)

"How many puppies are they looking for? (three)

"Why did they have to find them fast? (answers may vary—worried because of the storm)

"Where did they look?" (in all the rooms)

"What clues helped them find the pups?" (thumping sound, three lumps on the bed)

"Why were the pups lumps on the bed?" (they were under the blanket)

"What were the five lumps Mom saw?" (Jen, Freddie, 3 pups)

Find all the the words (thunder, they, three, them, think, then, thumping). Make a list and add more.

ACTIVITY:

Give students paper and paints and have them paint a thunderstorm. Have students name the three pups and write a story about them. Make a "puppy chow" treat (Chex cereal Muddy Buddy recipe). Using the list of TH words challenge students to write a story with as many TH words as they can.

PAGE 8: Rhyming Words

CONCEPTS: sound of short *o*, rhyming words

TEACHER GOALS: To teach the children
To read and match short *o* rhyming words, and
To read and write rhyming words with the endings *od* and *ot*.

MATERIALS NEEDED: alphabet cards

TEACHING PAGE 8:

Have the children make the *ot* ending on their desks with the alphabet cards and make these words as you say them: hot, cot, lot, rot, got, spot, shot.

Say a word with a short *o* ending (od, ot, op, ock, oll, on, om, etc.) and ask the children to give a rhyming word.

Read the first direction with the children. Help the children sound out the words in the matching exercise. Have the children trace the line and read the two words it connects. Let the children match the rest of the words. Check by having the children read the pairs of words. Be sure they know the meaning of each word.

Read the second direction with the children. Read the first ending. Have the children spell the word on the first set of lines, trace the letters, and read the word. Do the same with the other ending, then let the children write rhyming words on the lines.

The teacher should check this page while the children are writing more words on their tablet paper.

Have the children read what they have written.

Have the children prepare a sheet of writing tablet paper by folding it in half lengthwise and by writing an ending on each half. Let the children write more rhyming words.

Match the rhyming words.

hot	Mom
Tom	rock
lock	got
fox	pod
sod	box

Write rhyming words. Read the words.

___ od ___ ot

Can you think of more words?

Write them in your LIFEPAC Writing Tablet.

page 8 (eight)

Check by writing the endings on the chalkboard. Let the children read words from their lists for you to write under the proper ending. Children should add to and correct their lists from the lists on the board.

ACTIVITIES:

1. Dictate five *od* words and five *ot* words. Have the children write them on a sheet of writing tablet paper. Collect the papers and correct. Have the children write each word they missed five times on the back of their paper.

   Note: Correct children's written work with a single line through the mistake.

   This method helps the children to see their mistakes more easily.

2. Have the children spell words on their desks with alphabet cards whenever you have a few minutes. Always have them spell the word aloud and say it before doing the next one.

Page 9: Learning about Seven and Eight

CONCEPTS: number words seven and eight, following directions, ordinal numbers

TEACHER GOALS: To teach the children

To read and understand the number word seven,

To read and understand the number word eight,

To read and follow written directions,

To read the color words,

To name the shapes,

To listen and follow directions, and

To understand the ordinal numbers first through eighth.

VOCABULARY: seven, eight

MATERIALS NEEDED: crayons, number word flash cards, color charts, number charts, Worksheet 4

LEARNING ABOUT SEVEN AND EIGHT

You can say **7** and **8**.
Now you can read
the words for **7 -seven**
and **8 -eight**.

Draw and color.

●●●● ●●● **seven** ●●●● ●●●● **eight**

seven blue □ **'s**
eight black ◺ **'s**
six brown ○ **'s**
eight purple ▯ **'s**

page 9 (nine)

TEACHING PAGE 9:

Make flash cards for the words *seven* and *eight*.

Go through the flash cards for the first six numbers several times. Then hold up the card for *seven* and ask what number comes after *six*. Have the children say it several times. Put it with the other cards and go through them several times.

Hold up the card for *eight* and ask what number comes after *seven*. Have the children say it several times. Put it with the others and go through the cards several times.

Read the title with the children. Have them count the dots and read the numbers and the number words. Ask which number is *one* less than *eight* or *one* more than *seven*.

Have the children read the direction. Tell them to read the phrase in each box carefully and to draw and color exactly what it says. Help only if needed. Be sure the children have individual color and number charts available. Check by having the children tell what they drew and what color it is. The teacher should check the page and have the children correct any mistakes.

Read the following directions to the children only once. Remind them to listen carefully. Use pencils.

1. Put a circle around the third square and a line under the seventh square.
2. Put X's above the first four triangles.
3. Put a line under the first and last circles.
4. Put an X on the rectangles.

The teacher should check this exercise.

ACTIVITIES:

1. Do Worksheet 4.

On a large sheet of paper show the children what is meant by: a green and orange ball, a blue and red car, and a white and yellow box. Use more examples if needed.

Read all the directions on the page with the children. Tell them to read all the words and phrases carefully and to do what they say. Let the children complete the page by themselves. Help if needed. The teacher should check this page and have children correct any mistakes.

2. The teacher should make a note of the children who missed directions on this page. Make up a worksheet with eight objects in each row and have those children work through it with you using the same directions or similar directions. Check each row as the children finish it. Reteach the position words and ordinal numbers if necessary.

TEACHING READING:

Prepare 3 (or more) bags or boxes with an object in each. Give students clues to figure out what is in each bag (or box). Have them write down their answers. Tell them they're going to read a story with clues.

Read the story "Clickety Clack" together and answer the following questions:

"What sound does this object make?" (clickety clack)

"What are the clues that tell what it looks like?" (gray, long, strong, big, black)

"What else do we know?" (fast, goes there and comes back)

"What goes down this railroad track?" (train)

Ask students if any of them have ever ridden on a train. Share stories. Can you think of something else that might make a clickety clack sound? (answers will vary)

Find rhyming words (clack, track, black, back; long, strong;). Add more words to each group.

Find words with beginning blends (cl, bl, tr, gr, str,). Arrange the words on a chart so more words can be added to each blend group.

Name ______________

Match

four	5	six	2
one	4	two	8
five	7	eight	3
seven	1	three	6

Draw and color.

four red and black balls

eight blue and yellow pots

six orange and green tops

seven purple and white socks

eight little brown rocks

Language Arts 103
Worksheet 4
with page 9

Teacher check ______________
Initial Date

ACTIVITY:

Arrange classroom chairs to look like a train. Play out a ride on a train: give out tickets, call "All Aboard", have students make the sounds—chug, chug whoooooo, whoooo, clickety clack. Decide where the train is going and add some scenic adventure. Have students each make one train car. Attach to an engine to make a classroom train. Have students write a story about where they went on a train. Have students create a picture to go with their story. If it's around Christmas time - read the story Polar Express.

Page 10: Making Contractions

CONCEPTS: contractions, apostrophe

TEACHER GOALS: To teach the children
To understand what a contraction is,
To make a contraction, and
To understand what the apostrophe is.

VOCABULARY: contractions, teacher

TEACHING PAGE 10:

Read the material at the top of the page to the children. Have them follow along from left to right with their fingers as you read. Ask them to tell you what a contraction is. Have them point to the apostrophe and say the word several times. Ask what it is used for.

Work through the illustrations with the children. Point out what the stick man must do to make a contraction out of the two words at the top.

Ask the children again what a contraction is and what the apostrophe does. Go directly to the next page.

Read this page with your teacher.

MAKING CONTRACTIONS

A **contraction** is a word made
by putting two words together and
by leaving out some letters.
It is a shorter way to say some words.

This mark is an **apostrophe**. ■
It tells you that some letters
have been left out.

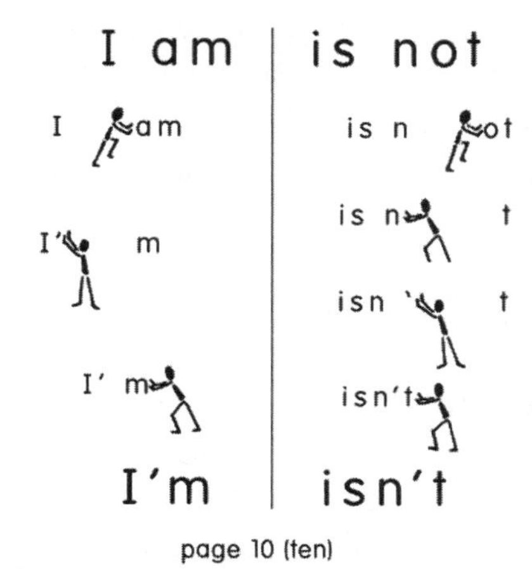

page 10 (ten)

PAGE 11: Contractions

CONCEPTS: contractions, apostrophe, sentences

TEACHER GOALS: To teach the children
To understand, make, and read contractions,
To understand the use of the apostrophe, and
To read and write sentences containing contractions.

MATERIALS NEEDED: Worksheet 5.

TEACHING PAGE 11:

Read the first direction at the top of the page with the children. Read the words in the first box and ask the children to tell how the contraction was made. They should be able to tell which letters were left out and that the apostrophe is put there to show that letters have been left out.

Do the rest of the boxes in the same way. Point out that the vowel sound in *don't* changes.

Read the second direction for the next section and point out the stick man with the apostrophe. Have the children tell why he is there.

Ask the children to read the sentences. Help them to sound out words if necessary. Let several children read each sentence. Have them point out the contractions and tell which letters were left out.

Read the last direction with the children. Have them write two or three sentences with contractions in their writing tablets. Collect the papers and correct. Have children correct and recopy sentences with mistakes.

Children who cannot write sentences yet may work with the teacher or an aide. Remind all the children to write neatly, to space their words well, to begin the first word with a capital letter, and to use the right punctuation mark at the end of the sentence.

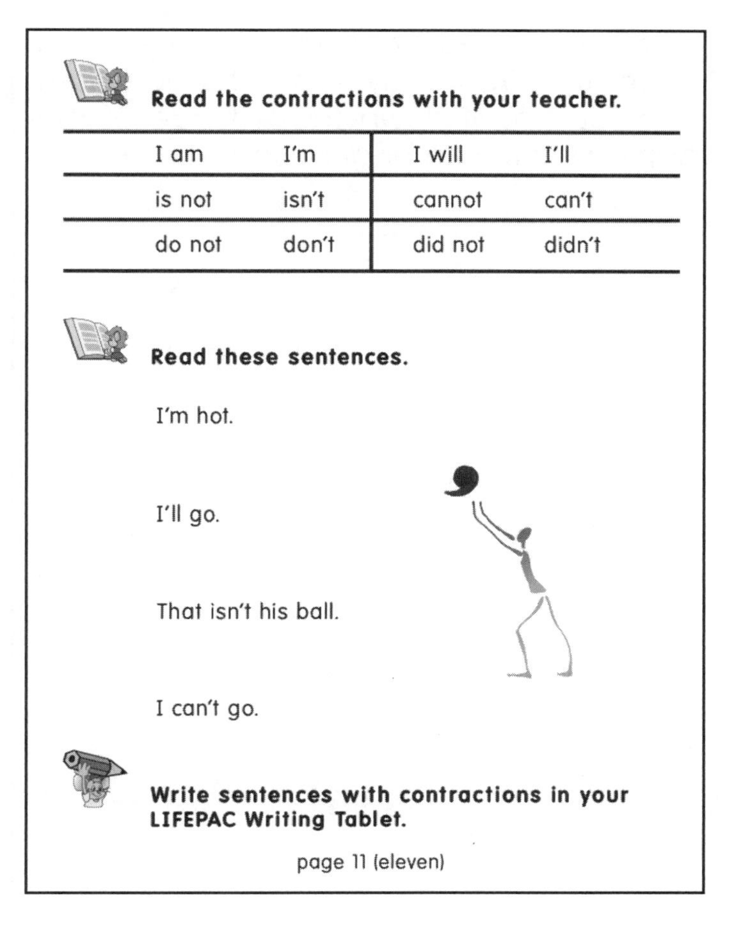

Read the contractions with your teacher.

I am	I'm	I will	I'll
is not	isn't	cannot	can't
do not	don't	did not	didn't

Read these sentences.

I'm hot.

I'll go.

That isn't his ball.

I can't go.

Write sentences with contractions in your LIFEPAC Writing Tablet.

page 11 (eleven)

ACTIVITIES:

1. Do Worksheet 5.

Read the directions with the children. Read the contraction and sentences in the first section. Ask the children to tell what kind of sentences these are and how they know. Have them point to the contraction and read it. Ask a child to tell what the apostrophe does.

Let the children finish the page by themselves. Check the page quickly to see if the words are spelled correctly and written neatly.

2. Write the contractions on this page on the chalkboard. Dictate them and have the children write them on a sheet of writing tablet paper. Check them quickly and have the children correct any mistakes.

Note: When dictating a list of words to the children, have them write the words in order down the left side of the paper. This practice makes your correcting easier and allows space for you to write the word correctly. You may have the children number *1* to *4* down the left side of the paper before you begin if you wish.

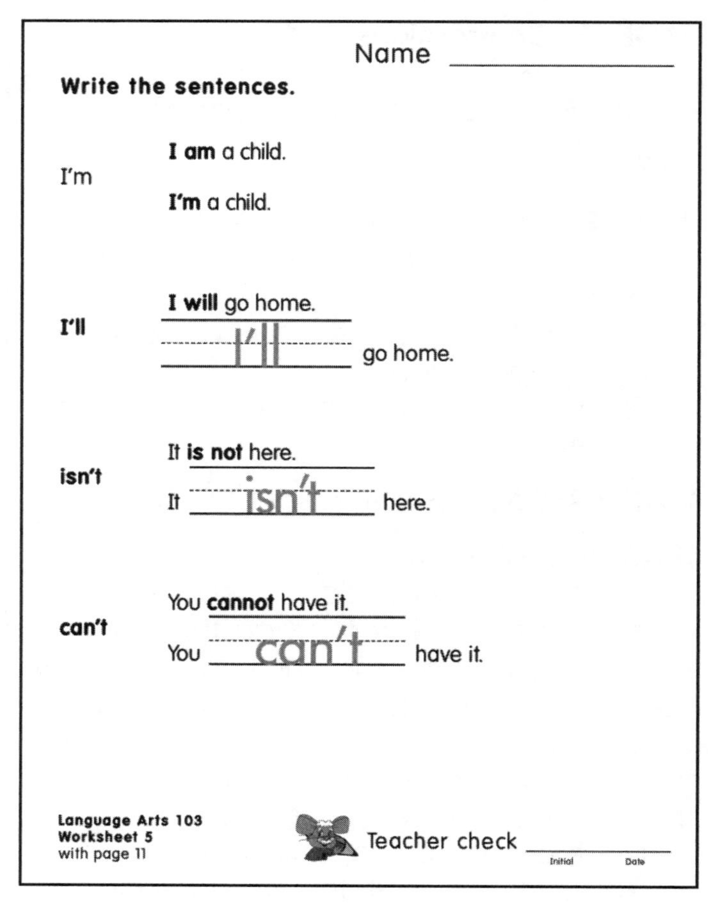
Name ______

Write the sentences.

I'm — **I am** a child. / **I'm** a child.

I'll — **I will** go home. / I'll go home.

isn't — It **is not** here. / It isn't here.

can't — You **cannot** have it. / You can't have it.

Language Arts 103
Worksheet 5
with page 11

Teacher check ______ Initial Date

Page 12: Making Plurals

CONCEPTS: plurals, number words

TEACHER GOALS: To teach the children
To add *s* to a word to form a plural,
To understand what a plural is, and
To read and understand the number words.

MATERIALS NEEDED: Worksheet 6

TEACHING PAGE 12:

Read the title and directions with the children. Ask the children what a plural is.

Explain that a phrase is a group of two or more words that means something but is not a complete sentence.

Have the children point to the first picture and read the phrase under it. Have them point to the second picture and read the phrase under it. Read both phrases again.

Have the children count the pigs in the next box, read the phrase, and write the *s*.

Have the children finish the page. Have them read all the phrases on the page again.

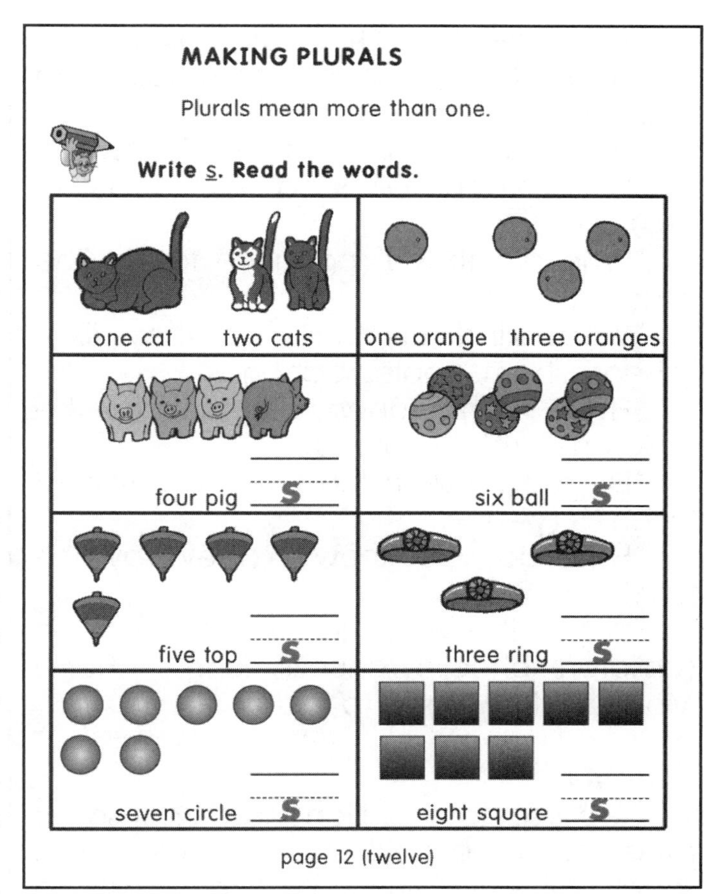

ACTIVITIES:

1. Do Worksheet 6.

Read the directions with the children or have the children read them alone. Have the children look at the pictures in the two boxes at the top of the page and read the phrases. Have them write the *s*.

Let the children finish the page by themselves. Help if needed.

The last two boxes are more difficult. Some children may need help.

Check by having the children tell what they wrote on the lines and read all the phrases. Write the words *cats* and *beds* on the board so the children can check their spelling.

Have the children use each of the phrases in a sentence. If the children use the wrong verb with the plural subjects have them say the sentence again correctly.

2. Read the following words and have the children give the plural for each.

man (men)	quail (quail)
woman (women)	house (houses)
child (children)	goose (geese)
mouse (mice)	moose (moose)
deer (deer)	foot (feet)

3. Call attention to plurals as they come up in discussions or conversations.

TEACHING READING:

Give each student a paper plate – using crayons, construction paper or other media, have them make their favorite lunch on the plate. Display. Survey students and make a graph of favorite lunches. For fun, ask the opposite – what's the worst lunch you've ever had? Tell students they'll read a story about twins who fix lunch.

Read the story "The Twins Fix Lunch" together and answer the following questions:

"How many people are twins?" (two)

"What are the twins' names?" (Ed and Ted)

"Who are they fixing lunch for?" (the children)

"What kind of foods do they fix?" (cheese, ham, apples, bananas)

"How is this lunch different to the children?" (it's in chunks)

"Do the children like their new kind of lunch?" (yes)

"How do you know?" (they say this lunch is fun)

Find all the words in the story with ch (children, cheese, chunks, lunch, cheer) Make a list and add to it.

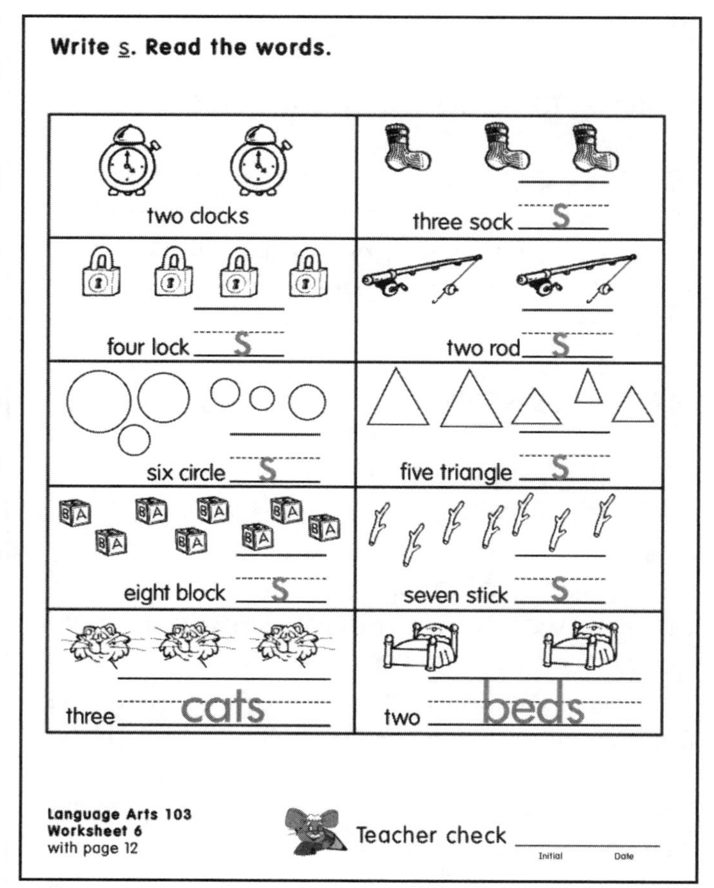

ACTIVITY:

Prepare apples, bananas, cheese or other foods in chunks and serve as a small snack. Give students a picture of twins to color exactly the same. Have students write about other things Ed and Ted do together. Do a lesson on food groups.

SELF TEST 1

CONCEPTS: consonant digraphs ch, sh, wh, th, sentences, contractions, and plurals

TEACHER GOAL: To teach the children
To check their own progress periodically.

TEACHING PAGE 13:

Read the title with the children and talk about it.

Read all the directions with the children and be sure they understand what they are to do on this page.

Let the children do the page independently.

Check the page as soon as possible. Go over it with the child so that he can see what he did well and where he needs extra work. (shell, whale, chain, thumb)

ACTIVITIES:

1. Give individual help on items missed on the page.
2. If several children miss the same things, reteach the skill (in small groups, if possible).

SPELLING WORDS:

thick
that
which
shell
chuck

II. PART TWO

Page 14: Writing Sentences

CONCEPTS: sentences, statements, paragraphs

TEACHER GOALS: To teach the children
To name the kinds of sentences and the punctuation mark for each,
To write and read a statement and to write a period,
To know that the first word of a sentence begins with a capital letter, and
To write a paragraph and a story.

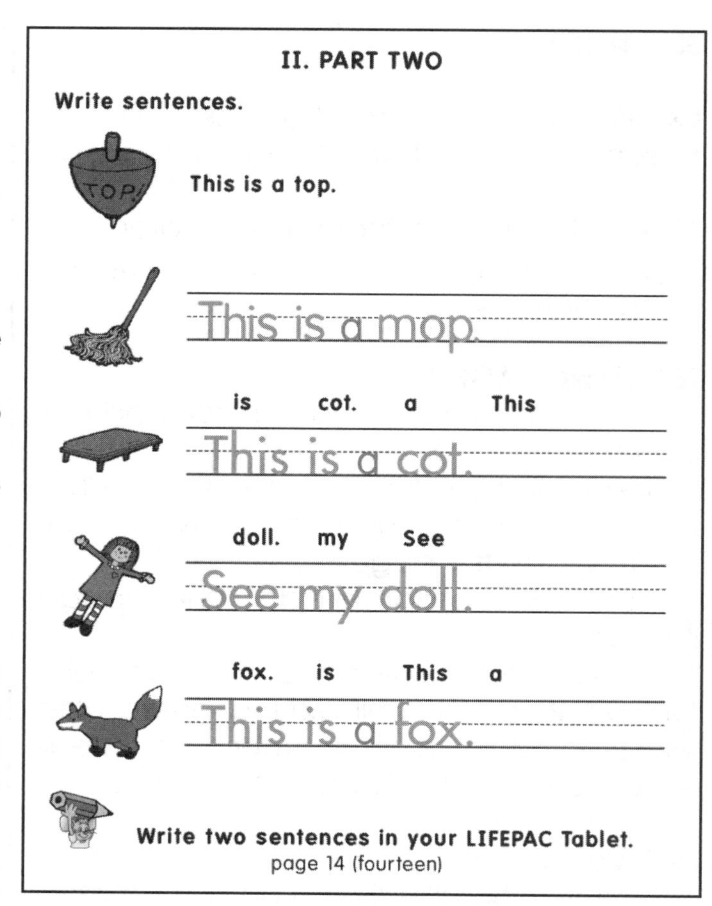

TEACHING PAGE 14:

Ask the children to name the three kinds of sentences. Ask what mark ends each sentence. Ask how the first word of each sentence begins. Have the children give an example of each kind of sentence.

Read the first direction with the children. Have them point to the first picture and tell what it is. Have them read the sentence silently, then have a child read it aloud.

Tell the children to point to the next picture (the mop) and tell what it is. Have them read the sentence silently. Have them trace the letters and have one child read the sentence.

Name the rest of the pictures and then let the children unscramble the sentences. Tell them that all the words they will need are in the sentences with the pictures. Remind them to write neatly, to space the words well, and to be sure all the words are spelled correctly.

Read the last direction with the children. Have them write two sentences in their writing tablets. They can be similar to the one on this page or anything else the children can write.

Check page 14 while the children are writing these sentences.

Collect the papers and check. Have the children recopy their sentences correctly.

Write the sentence "This is a top." on the board. Ask the children to give more sentences about the top. Write them on the board in the order the children give them. When you have four or five sentences written, read through them and ask the children if the story would sound better if some of the sentences were put in different places. Change them around and read the sentences again. Tell the children what they have written is called a paragraph. Tell them all the sentences in a paragraph will be about the same thing. Have the children give a good title for the paragraph.

ACTIVITY:

Put a list of things on the board and let the children choose one and write a paragraph about it. Have them title their paragraphs and read them to the class. Have them color or paint a picture to show as they read their paragraphs.

Suggestions: jogging, pollywogs, dolls, rocks, fishing rods

TEACHING READING:

Read the story "Fun!" in Reader 2.

Present the words *sand* and *have*. Have the children tell the meanings of the words. Write them on the board for the children to read.

Have the children look at the picture and tell them to name the things in the picture and have them tell what is happening.

Have several children tell about an experience they have had at the beach or in a sandbox. Tell what they built in the sand.

Have the children read the story silently.

Ask questions similar to these:

"Will Jan have fun?"

"What will she do in the sand?"

"What do you think she is building?"

"Will the water wash it away?"

Have the children find the rhyming words in the story. Have them find the short /i/ words.

Page 15: Activity Page

CONCEPT: rhyming words

TEACHER GOALS: To teach the children
To identify the sound of short *i* in words;
To write rhyming words for the endings *im, iss, id,* and *ig;* and
To read the short *i* words they have written.

MATERIALS NEEDED: alphabet cards

TEACHING PAGE 15:

Have the children form the ending *im* on their desks with alphabet cards. Have the children put the letter *h* in front of the ending and sound out the word. Repeat with the letters *d, r, K, J,* and T.

Read the directions with the children. Have the children read the *im* ending and trace the word *dim* and read it. Have the children write two more words on the lines and read them.

Have the children read the *iss* ending and trace *this.* Have them read the word and call their attention to the fact that the word *this* rhymes with the *iss* ending even though it has only one *s.* Have them trace the word *hiss* and read it.

Note: Always be sure the children know the meanings of all the words they write. Have the children give the meanings of the words after they read them or use them in a sentence.

The teacher should explain any they do not know.

Follow the same procedure for the *id* and *ig* endings.

Read the question and direction at the bottom of the page with the children. Have them write the four endings at the top of the folded writing tablet sheet (two on each side) and write more rhyming words.

Write rhyming words.

____ im   ____ iss

dim   this

hiss

____ id   ____ ig

bid   big

Can you think of more words?

Write them in your LIFEPAC Writing Tablet.

page 15 (fifteen)

Write the four endings on the board and have the children read words from their lists. Write the words under the proper ending and have the children correct and add to their lists. Have the children read the lists on the board several times.

ACTIVITY:

Anytime you have four or five minutes available, have the children make words on their desks with their alphabet cards. Have them make spelling words, rhyming words, words with the same beginning or ending sound, words with capital letters, names, and sight words or have them add the *s, ed,* or *ing* endings to the same words. If you have the children make extra cards for the vowels and letters like *t, r,* and *s,* they will be able to spell more words.

Page 16: Learning about Nine and Ten

CONCEPTS: number words nine and ten, color words, following directions

TEACHER GOALS: To teach the children
To understand and read the number words nine and ten,
To understand ordinal numbers first through tenth,
To read the color words, and
To read and follow the directions.

VOCABULARY: nine, ten

MATERIALS NEEDED: crayons, number-word flash cards, color charts, number charts

TEACHING PAGE 16:

Make flash cards for the number words *nine* and *ten.*

Go through the flash cards for the first eight numbers several times. Hold up the card for *nine* and ask what number comes after *eight.* Put it with the other cards and go through them at least twice.

Hold up the card for *ten* and ask what number comes after *nine.* Put it with the others and go through the cards several times.

Read the title with the children. Have them count the dots, read the number, and the number words. Ask which number is *one* less than *ten, one* more than *nine.*

Ask a child to read the direction. Tell the children to read the phrase in each box carefully and to do exactly what it says. Help only if needed. Be sure the children have individual color and number charts available. Check by having the children tell what they have in each box. The teacher also should check the page and have the children correct any mistakes.

LEARNING ABOUT NINE AND TEN

You can say **9** and **10**.
Now you can read
the words for **9 -nine**
and **10 -ten**.

Draw and color.

●●●●● **nine** ●●●●● **ten**
●●●● ●●●●●

nine red hats
ten blue caps
seven black pigs
nine yellow tops
ten purple mops

page 16 (sixteen)

ACTIVITY:

After the children have corrected the page, give these directions. Remind the children to listen carefully.

1. Put a black X on the first, second, third, and fourth hats.
2. Draw a red circle around the eighth, ninth, and tenth caps.
3. Put an orange box around the fifth pig and the next-to-last pig.
4. Put a blue X over the sixth and seventh tops.
5. Put a yellow circle around all of the mops except the ninth and tenth.

The teacher should correct this exercise.

Page 17: Listen and Do

CONCEPTS: listening, following directions, ordinal numbers

TEACHER GOALS: To teach the children

To listen and follow oral directions given once, and

To understand and use the ordinal numbers first through tenth.

MATERIALS NEEDED: crayons

TEACHING PAGE 17:

Draw ten circles on the board and have the children count them and give the ordinal number for each.

Read the title and directions with the children. Tell them to listen carefully and to do exactly as you say. Have them put their fingers on the numbers at the left to keep their places on the page.

Have the children put their green, yellow, brown, orange, black, purple, blue, and red crayons near their paper for this page.

1. Draw a green circle around the ninth tree.
2. Draw a yellow circle around the seventh flower.
3. Draw a brown circle around the sixth rabbit.
4. Draw an orange circle around the third cat.
5. Draw a purple circle around the fifth doll.
6. Draw a blue circle around the eighth cup.
7. Draw a red circle around the fourth Bible.

The teacher should check this page.

ACTIVITY:

Do the page again using the following directions:

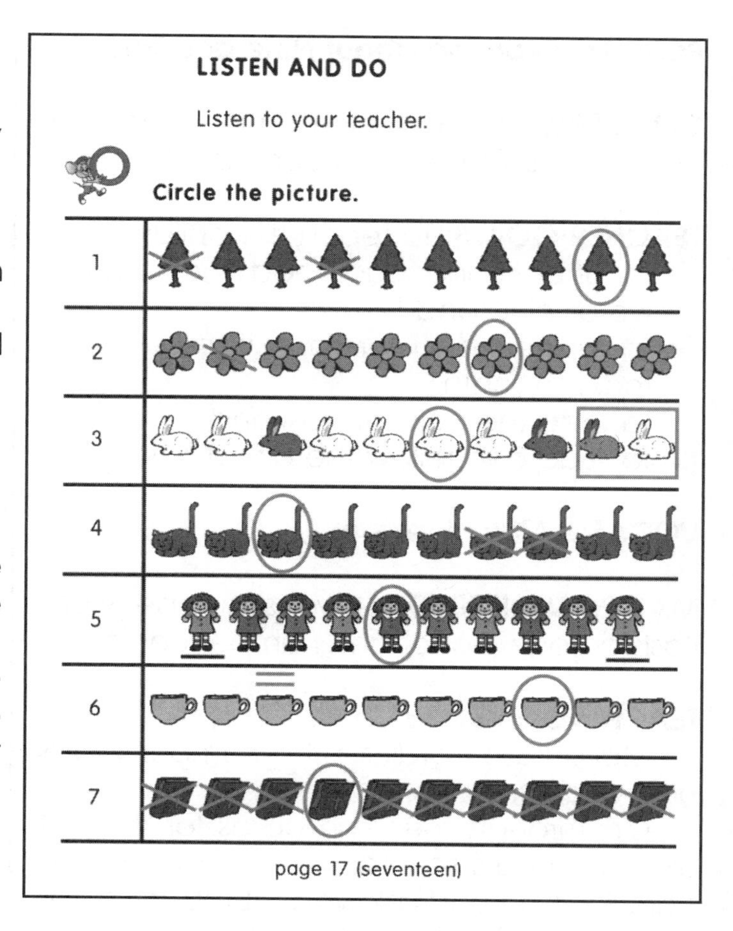

1. Put a blue X on the first and fourth trees.
2. Put a red line over the second flower.
3. Put a purple box around the ninth and tenth rabbits.
4. Put a blue X over the seventh and eighth cats.
5. Put a black line under the first and last dolls.
6. Put two brown lines over the third cup.
7. Put X's on all the Bibles except the fourth.

The teacher should check this page. Go over the page individually with the children who are making mistakes to find out what they do not understand. Reteach the skills individually or in small groups.

Page 18: Rhyming

CONCEPTS: rhyming words, sound of short *o, i, e*

TEACHER GOALS: To teach the children
To write rhyming words with the endings *ob* and *ox,* and
To match rhyming words with the sound of short *o* and short *i.*

MATERIALS NEEDED: Worksheet 7

TEACHING PAGE 18:

Review the meaning of rhyming words.

Read the first direction with the children. Read the two endings and have the children give two or three words that rhyme with each one. Let the children write the rhyming words on the lines.

Prepare the sheet of writing tablet paper with the endings at the top. Have the children write more rhyming words while you correct this page.

Write the endings on the board and have the children give words from their lists. Write them under the proper ending. Have the children add to and correct their lists from the lists on the board. Have the children read the lists several times.

Read the last direction with the children. Have them trace the line and read the two words.

Have the children draw the lines between the pairs of rhyming words. Read the words.

ACTIVITIES:

1. Do Worksheet 7.

Read the directions on the page with the children. Have them write rhyming words.

Check by writing the same words and endings on the board and by having the children give the rhyming words for you to write. The children should correct and add to their lists.

Write rhyming words.

____ob　　　　____ox

Can you think of more words?

Write them in your LIFEPAC Writing Tablet.

Match the rhyming words.

mops　　hot

not　　tops

sobs　　digs

pigs　　cobs

page 18 (eighteen)

The starred exercise at the bottom of the page is more difficult and some children may need help.

The teacher should collect the worksheets and writing tablet sheets and correct them. Have children correct any mistakes.

2. Dictate five *ob* words and *ox, fox,* and *box* and have the children write them on a sheet of writing tablet paper. Correct the papers and have the children write their misspelled words five times on the back of the paper.

Write rhyming words.

cog jog

Ron

loll

Tom

___op

___ock

H **Write a word that rhymes with stocking.**

Language Arts 103
Worksheet 7
with page 18

Teacher check ____________
Initial Date

Page 19: The Girls' Dolls

CONCEPTS: reading, possessives, plurals, subject-verb agreement, retelling a story

TEACHER GOALS: To teach the children
- To read the story,
- To understand the meanings of the possessives,
- To tell whether the subject and verb in a sentence agree,
- To retell the story in their own words,
- To note and recall details of the story,
- To make inferences from the story,
- To predict what might happen next in the story, and
- To tell which words in the story are plurals.

VOCABULARY: possessives, were

TEACHING PAGE 19:

Point to a child's shirt or sweater and ask the class to tell whose it is. Do this several times, then tell the children that words which tell that something belongs to someone are called *possessives*. Give a few examples:

The cat that belongs to Mary is Mary's cat. *Mary's* is the *possessive*.

The dog that belongs to John is his dog. *His* is the *possessive*.

Have the children give more examples.

Write a list of *possessives* on the board and have the children use them in sentences. Use several names, such as John's, Tim's, or Mary's and also the possessive pronouns, such as his, her, our, my, their, and your.

Do not distinguish between *possessive* nouns and *possessive* pronouns at this level.

Read the title and sentence at the top of the page with the children. Ask the children to tell what a *plural* is and what a *possessive* is.

Read the title of the story. Read the story with the children. Have them follow along from left to right with their fingers as they read with you.

You will learn about possessives and plurals.

THE GIRLS' DOLLS

Molly and Polly were playing with **their** dolls.

Polly's doll had yellow hair.
Her dress was blue.

Molly's doll had brown hair.
Her dress was green.
Both **dolls'** shoes were black.

The girls were in **Molly's** room.
Next time they would go
to **Polly's** house.
The girls liked to play
with **their** dolls.

page 19 (nineteen)

Ask the children to tell what the story is about. Ask them to tell about Polly's doll and about Molly's doll. Ask what was the same about both dolls (black shoes). Ask where the girls were playing and where they would play next time.

Ask the children if they can tell what time of day it is or what the weather might be like. Have them tell why they think so.

Have the children tell what they think might happen next.

Read the sentences using *was* and *were*. Change the *was* to *were* and the *were* to *was* and have the children tell which sounds better and why. Read each sentence and have the children tell which word is the *possessive* or *possessive* pronoun; who the *possessive* pronoun refers to; and what it is that belongs to the person or persons.

Ask the children to tell which words in the story are *plurals*.

ACTIVITIES:

1. Have several children retell the story in their own words.
2. Have the children write a sentence in their LIFEPAC Tablets for each of the *possessives* on the board.
3. Write the titles *My Doll* and *My Truck* on the board and have the children choose one and write a paragraph about it. Tell them to use as many *possessives* in their sentences as they can. Remind them that all the sentences in the paragraph must be about the title. Correct the children's work and have them recopy it. Let them draw a picture about their stories and read their stories to the class.
4. Read stories or poems about children and friends or about toys.

TEACHING READING:

Write the word "bug" on the board. Ask them to tell you what the word bug means. (accept all possible answers - insect, bother, VW bug, flu, etc.) Tell them, today we are interested in the bug that means insect. Have students help you make a list of insects.

Ask students what they could do if they found a bug and they didn't know what it was. (book, library, computer). What would you need to know? (clues —what it looks like) Tell students they'll read a story about a bug Katy discovers.

Read the story "The New Little Bug" together and then answer the following questions:

"What do Katy and Joey like to do?" (hunt for bugs)

"Where do they look?" (sidewalk cracks, grass)

"Where did Katy find the new little bug?" (on a twig)

"What did she do with the bug?" (took it to show Joey)

"What did Joey suggest they do?" (look it up in a book)

"Why did Katy say they would have to remember what it looked like?" (the wind blew it away)

Find the words with beginning blends (gr, sm, bl, sw, fl, tw).

Find the compound words (sidewalk, everywhere).

ACTIVITY:

Verbally give students the clues from the story and have them draw the bug Katy found. Take the students on a bug hunt. Give them magnifying glasses if possible. Tell them this is observation activity only, and not to capture any insects. Share nonfiction books on insects. Have students choose an insect and do a mini report. Teach the characteristics of insects: (3 body parts, 6 legs, antennae). Have students create an imaginary insect using the correct characteristics. Write a story: "If I had a bug...." Find poems about insects to read and learn.

Challenge Question: Are spiders insects? (no) Discuss why not.

Page 20: Possessives

CONCEPTS: possessives, apostrophe

TEACHER GOALS: To teach the children
To understand and use possessives, and
To understand the use of the apostrophe.

VOCABULARY: phrases

MATERIALS NEEDED: Worksheet 8

TEACHING PAGE 20:

Read the sentence with the children. Have them point to the first two pictures in the top section and read the phrases. Have the children tell which word is the possessive. Ask them how they can tell that it is a possessive. Then have the children tell what belongs to that person.

Have the children look at the next two pictures and read the phrases. Tell the children that dolls' means more than one doll has dresses and shoes. Write the word dolls' on the board. Call attention to the 's.

Have the children look at the pictures of the room and the house, read the phrases and tell what they mean. Have the children read the next four phrases.

Have the children look at the last four pictures and read the phrases. Call attention to the possessive pronouns.

Have the children use each phrase in a sentence.

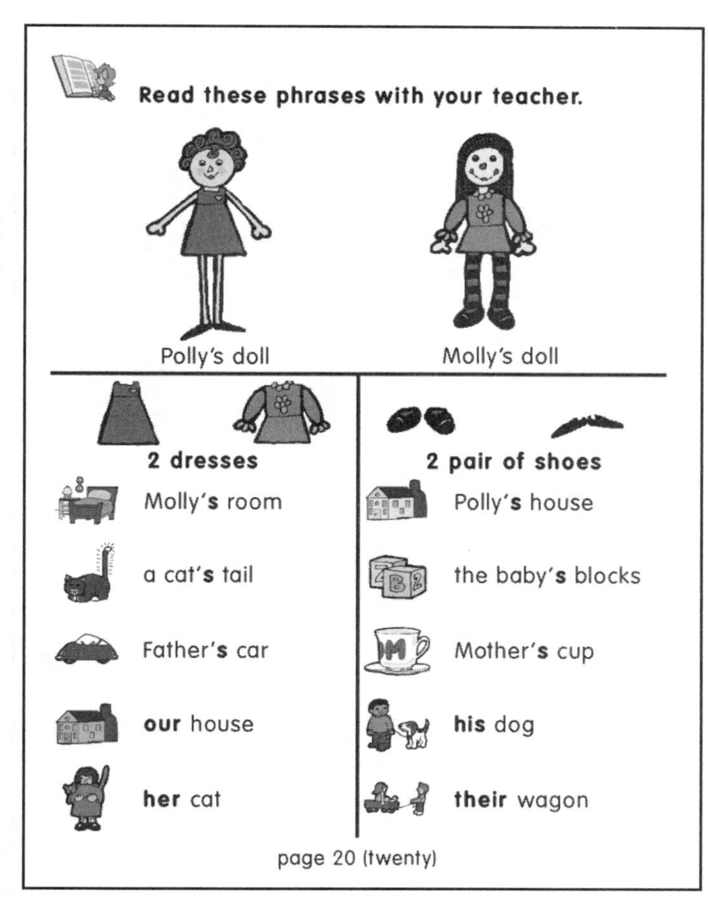

ACTIVITIES:

Do Worksheet 8.

Read the direction with the children and ask what the 's means. Tell the children to look at the picture in the first box and read the phrase. Ask what the phrase means. Have them write the 's.

Do the same with the other three boxes.

Read the direction with the children. Have the children read each sentence silently first, then aloud. Help them sound out words if necessary. Ask the children to identify the possessive pronoun. Ask the children to tell what kind of sentence they are reading. Ask if the possessive pronoun refers to a boy or a girl. Ask which pronouns are used for either a boy or a girl. Call attention to the children's use of possessive nouns and possessive pronouns in their daily conversation and discussions.

Name ______________

Put in the 's.

 Tom 's rod	 Bob 's dog
 Tim 's pig	 Kim 's cat

Read the sentences.

This is **my** house.
Is this **your** ball.
What is **his** name?
That is **her** mother.
Our car is blue.

Language Arts 103
Worksheet 8
with page 20

Teacher check ______________
Initial Date

Page 21: Soft c

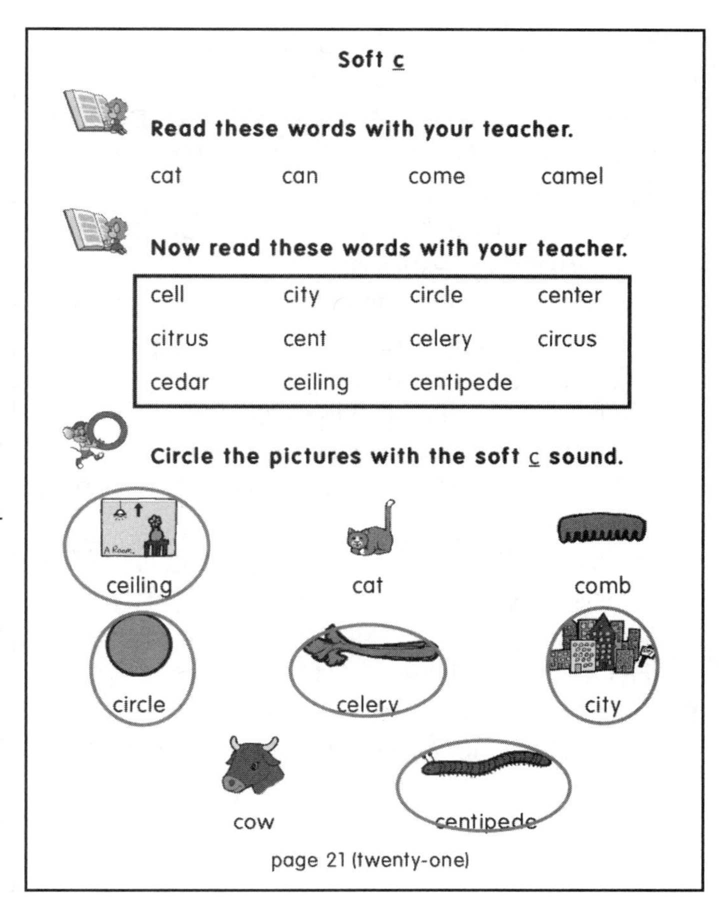

Soft c

Read these words with your teacher.

cat can come camel

Now read these words with your teacher.

cell	city	circle	center
citrus	cent	celery	circus
cedar	ceiling	centipede	

Circle the pictures with the soft c sound.

page 21 (twenty-one)

CONCEPT: sound of *c* as in city (soft *c*)

TEACHER GOAL: To teach the children
To recognize the sound of c as in city (soft *c*).

MATERIALS NEEDED: Worksheet 9

TEACHING PAGE 21:

Read the title and tell the children that the letter *c* has two sounds. One sound they already know, the /*k*/ sound of *c* in *cat* and *can*. This sound is called the hard *c*. The other sound is like the *c* in *city* or *cent*. This sound is called the soft *c* because it sounds like the /s/ sound.

The letter *c* has two sounds. When the letter *c* is followed by the letters *e, i,* or *y*, it has the soft sound of *s*.

Read the hard *c* words and emphasize the /*k*/ sound. Ask the children if the sound is hard or soft.

Read the soft *c* words and emphasize the /s/ sound. Ask the children if the sound is hard or soft.

Read the final direction with the children. Have the children name the first picture and tell if the *c* is hard or soft.

Work through the entire exercise with the children. Have the children name all the pictures again, listening for the /s/ sound.

ACTIVITY:

Do Worksheet 9.

Since this worksheet is more difficult, you may wish to work through the entire exercise with the children.

Note: Do not expect the children to master the concept of soft *c* at this time. It is introduced here because children should know about it when they come upon it in their reading. Call attention to the soft *c* sound whenever it occurs.

Read the direction with the children. Ask the children to name the first picture (celery). Ask what sound they hear. Ask which letter follows the *c*. Remind them about the rule for soft *c*. Tell them celery begins with a *c* that sounds like an s. This *c* is called a soft *c*.

Do the page with the children the same way. Name all the pictures again and have the children listen for the sound of the *c* (celery, cow, coat, city, cat, comb, centipede, ceiling). Have them circle the soft *c* pictures in the top section. In the bottom section have the children name the picture, then write c if the picture begins with a *c* and *s* if the picture begins with an *s* (cent, sock, centipede, seal, seven, cereal). Do this section with the children.

TEACHING READING:

Read the story "Pets" in Reader 2.

Present the words *black* and *tan*. Have the children find some things in the room that show the colors, black and tan. Write the words on the board.

Have the children look at the picture and tell what is happening. Have several children tell about their pets.

Have the children read the story silently.

Ask these questions:

"What kind of pets does the girl have?"

"What color is the cat?"

"What color is the dog?"

"What does the girl like to do?"

"What do the animals do?"

"Does the girl think it is fun to have a pet?"

"Do you think it is fun to have a pet?"

"When would it not be fun to have a pet?"

Have the children find the color words in the story. Have them find the short /e/ words. Have them find the short /u/ words.

Name ______________

Circle the pictures with the soft c sound.

Write c or s.

c s c

s s c

Language Arts 103
Worksheet 9
with page 21

Teacher check ______________
Initial Date

Page 22: Plurals

CONCEPTS: plurals, number words

TEACHER GOALS: To teach the children
To understand that a plural means more than one,
To make plurals by adding *s* to a noun, and
To read and understand the number words one to ten.

MATERIALS NEEDED: Worksheet 10

TEACHING PAGE 22:

Read the title with the children and ask what a plural is.

Read the directions with the children. Tell the children to look at the first box. Read the phrases with them. Ask a child to tell how the plural was made. Do the same with the second box (pins).

Tell the children to look at the things in the boxes carefully, read the phrases, and write an *s* in each box on the lines. Read all the phrases on the page aloud.

ACTIVITIES:

1. Do Worksheet 10.

Read the directions with the children or have a child read them.

Tell the children to look at the picture in the first box, count the pins, and read the phrase. Have them trace the letters and read the phrase again.

Tell the children to look at the picture in the next box and count the caps. Tell them to read the word and tell what word they should write on the lines. Have the children spell the word, then write it. Put the word on the board for the children to check.

2. Call attention to plurals used by the children in their daily speech and discussions.

3. Make a set of folding cards for the plurals that the children use most. Write the singular word on one side of the card.

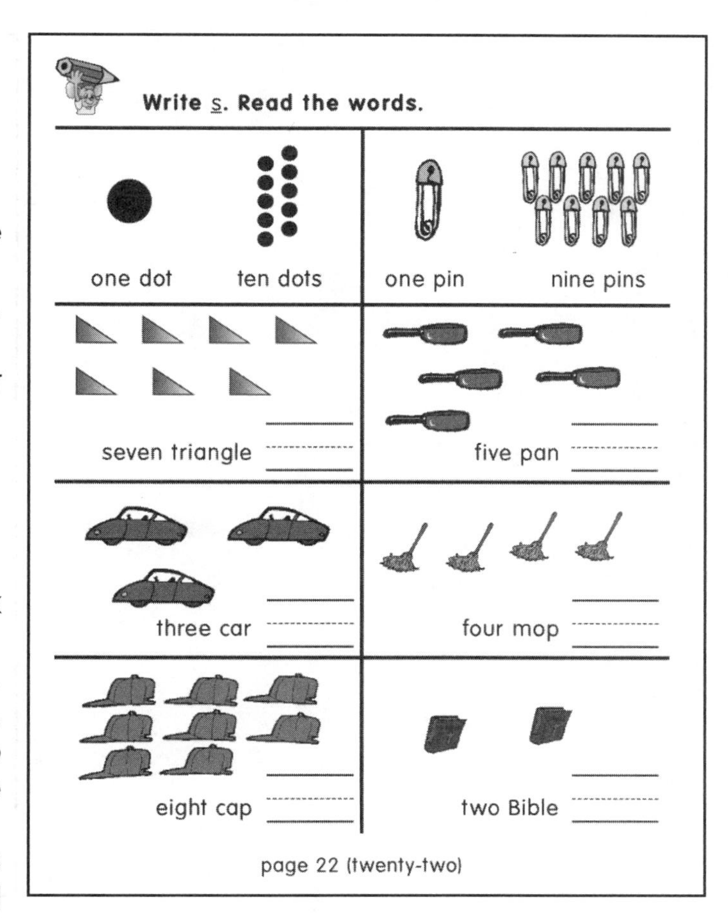

Write the plural ending on the other side of the card so that it is at the end of the word when folded.

Children may work with these cards alone or in pairs.

Name ______________

Write the words. Read the words.

six pins

five caps

four tops

three pigs

seven twigs

eight clocks

Language Arts 103
Worksheet 10
with page 22

Teacher check ______________
Initial Date

SELF TEST 2

CONCEPTS: possessives, rhyming words, soft /c/ sound, plurals, following directions

TEACHER GOAL: To teach the children
To check their own progress periodically.

TEACHING PAGE 23:

Read the title and ask the children what it means.

Read the directions for all the sections with the children. Be sure they understand what they are to do. Name the pictures (city, centipede, cow). Tell the children to color 3 circles in the last section.

Let them do the page independently.

Check as soon as possible and go over the page with the child so that he can see what he did well and where he needs extra help.

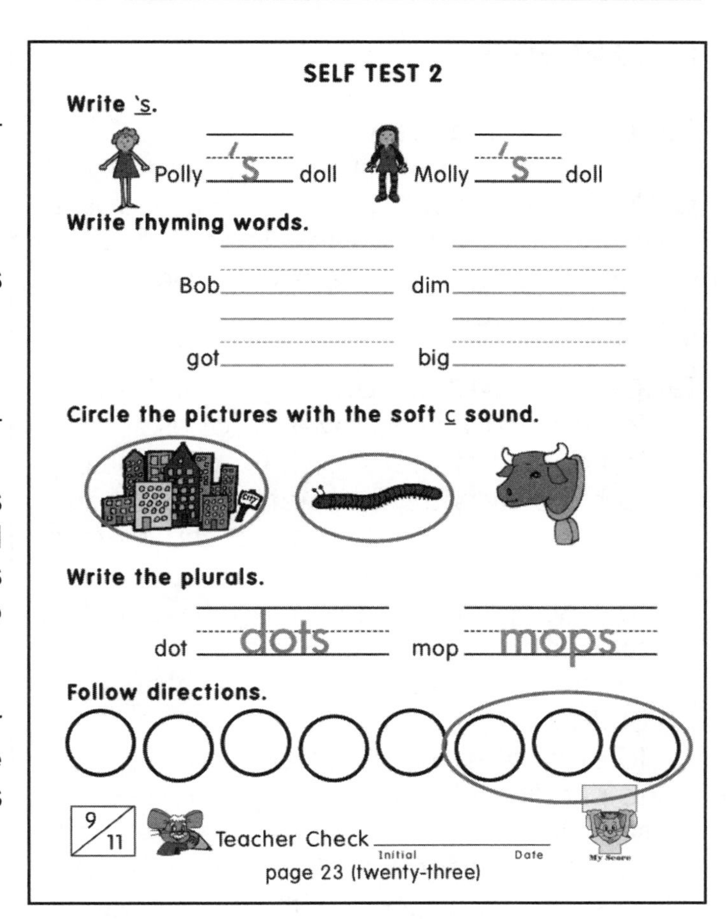

SELF TEST 2

Write 's.

Polly 's doll   Molly 's doll

Write rhyming words.

Bob ________ dim ________

got ________ big ________

Circle the pictures with the soft c sound.

Write the plurals.

dot dots   mop mops

Follow directions.

9/11   Teacher Check ________ Initial Date

page 23 (twenty-three)

ACTIVITIES:

1. Give individual help on items missed.
2. If several children miss the same things, reteach the skill (in small groups, if possible).

SPELLING WORDS:

her
his
cell
one
two

III. PART THREE

Page 24: Tell the Story

CONCEPTS: God's love for His people, telling a story, main idea, making judgments, making inferences, predicting outcomes, speaking in a group

TEACHER GOALS: To teach the children
To know that God loves all of us,
To know that the Bible is God's Word,
To tell a story from a picture,
To identify the main idea of a picture or story,
To choose the right thing to do in a situation,
To make inferences from stories or pictures,
To choose rhyming words,
To predict what might happen next in a situation,
To retell a story in their own words, and
To speak in a group with confidence.

BIBLE REFERENCES: Genesis chapters 7 through 9; Daniel chapter 6; Luke 2:1 through 20

MATERIALS NEEDED: Bible or children's Bible story book, Worksheet 11

TEACHING PAGE 24:

Read the title and sentence at the top of the page with the children. Tell them on this page they will learn to use good sentences to tell stories.

Read the title. Tell the children to look at the first picture and tell what is happening. Ask the children to tell what the Bible is (God's Word). Ask the children to tell all the places where they can hear the Bible being read (home, school, Sunday school, church, Bible camp, vacation Bible school).

Ask where they think this family is. How can they tell? Can they tell what time of day it is? What might happen next? Ask what story the father might be reading.

III. PART THREE

TELL THE STORY

Tell a story about each picture.

page 24 (twenty-four)

Tell the children to look at the other pictures and think about the stories. Have the children choose one of the stories and tell it to the class. Discuss the stories after each has been told once and bring out any parts that the children left out. Have the children tell how God showed His love for His people.

Before the children begin telling stories, go through the rules for telling stories (see Teacher Notes for page 20 of LIFEPAC 102).

Give every child a chance to tell a story either in the large group or in a small group at a later time.

(During the discussions ask questions similar to the following ones:)

"Why did God send Jesus to earth?"
"Why was He born in a stable?"
"Why was He not born in a hospital?"
"Why was Daniel put into the lions' den?"
"Why did the lions not hurt him?"

"What did the people think about Noah when he began building the ark?"
"Why could they not go on the ark?"
"How do you think the animals got along on the ark?"
"What was the meaning of the rainbow?"

ACTIVITIES:

1. Read the stories in the pictures from the Bible.
2. Let children tell their favorite Bible stories.
3. Do Worksheet 11.

Ask the children to give you words that rhyme with *will* and *wish.*

Read the first direction with the children as they follow along from left to right.

Have the children read the ending *-ill.* Have them trace the word *bill* and read it. Have them write two more rhyming words on the lines. Do the same for the *-ish* endIng.

Read the question and direction with the children and have them prepare the folded sheet of writing tablet paper with the ending *-ill* and *-ish* written at the top. Put it aside until the children finish the matching exercise.

Read the matching direction and have the children read the first two columns of words. Help them sound out if necessary. Have them trace the line between *sit* and *fit* and read the words. Let them finish the exercise and then read the pairs of rhyming words.

Do the same for the other exercise. Check the page while the children are writing the rhyming words on the sheet they prepared earlier.

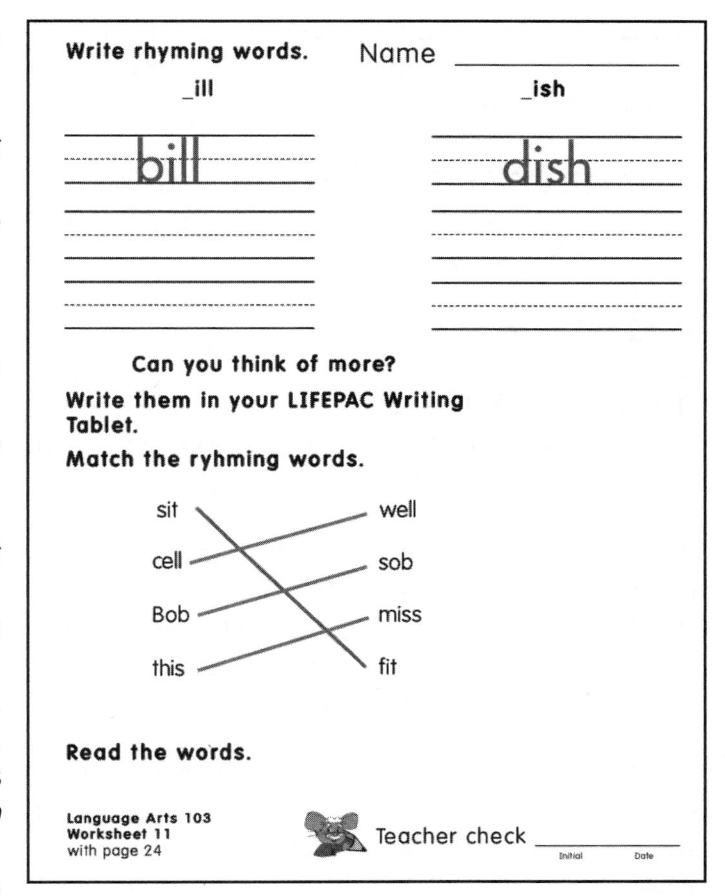

Page 25: Compound Words

CONCEPT: compound words

TEACHER GOAL: To teach the children
To understand, use, and write compound words.

VOCABULARY: compound

TEACHING PAGE 25:

This page and the next should be done in the same class period.

Read the title and the sentences with the children. Tell the children that on this page they will be putting two small words together to get a longer word. This longer word is called a compound word. Compound means having more than one part.

Read through each illustration and talk about it. Help the children to understand that sometimes the words you make get their meaning from the words you put together, a *fireman* is a man who puts out fires. Sometimes words may be harder to figure out, such as in *butterfly* or *toenail.*

Read the question at the bottom of the page with the children. Have the children name the pictures and write the words on the lines. Have them read the compound words.

Go directly to the next lesson.

COMPOUND WORDS

Some words have
more than one word in them.

Put <u>two</u> words together to get <u>one</u> word.

foot + ball = football

fire + man = fireman

dog + house = doghouse

Can you write these words?

cow + boy = cowboy

basket + ball = basketball

page 25 (twenty-five)

Page 26: Compound Words

CONCEPT: compound words

TEACHER GOAL: To teach the children
To understand, use, and write compound words.

MATERIALS NEEDED: Worksheets 12 and 13, crayons

TEACHING PAGE 26

Use this page with the previous page.

Read the direction at the top of the page with the children. Have the children name the pictures, read the compound word, and write it on the lines.

When they finish writing the words, ask them to tell what the words mean and why they think those words were put together.

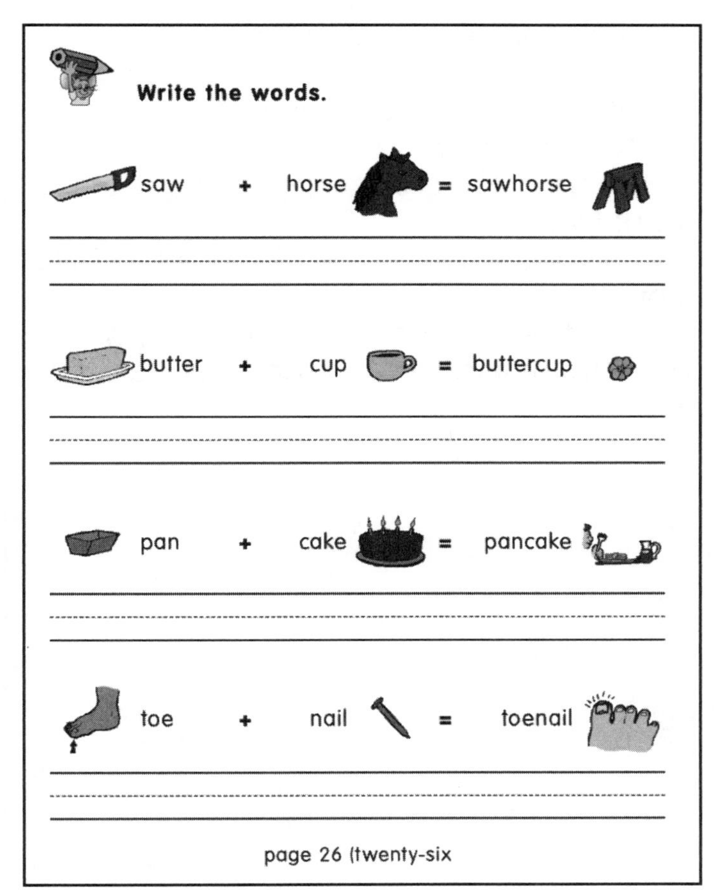

ACTIVITIES:

1. Do Worksheet 12.

Have the children read the direction.

Tell the children to look at the pictures and read the word under each. Have them look at the last picture and read the compound word. Ask them to tell what they know about cowboys.

Check by having the children read the pictures and words and by having them write them on the lines. Write the compound words on the board.

The teacher should collect the papers and check them. Have the children correct any mistakes.

2. Do Worksheet 13 .

This worksheet is more difficult. Read the directions with the children. Tell them to look at the pictures, read the words, and put them together to get a compound word. Have them write the compound word on the lines.

Work through each example with the children. Write the compound words on the board.

The teacher should collect the papers and check this page.

3. Have the children use the compound words in sentences.

4. Begin a compound word chart. Put the words from this page and the previous page 25, Worksheet 12 and 13, and any other compounds the children know, on the chart.

TEACHING READING:

Read the story "The Cowboy" in *Reader 2.*

Present the compound words, *cowboy, sawhorse,* and *Buttercup.* Write them on the board and have the children read them.

Have the children look at the picture and tell what is happening. Have them read the title.

Have the children tell about a time when they pretended to be a cowboy or cowgirl.

Have the children read the story silently.

Ask these questions:

"What is Jim pretending to be?"
"What is he riding?"
"What is his horse's name?"
"What is Jim's wish?"
"When Jim grows up, what does he want to do?"
"What sound word is at the end of the story?"

Let the children "yip" like cowboys. Have them find all of the compound words in the story.

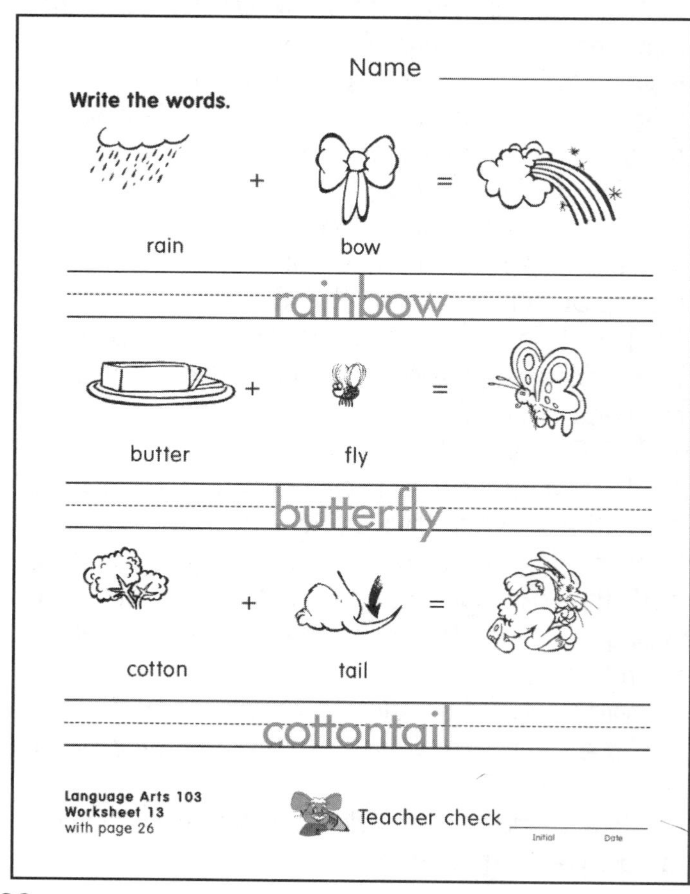

Page 27: Activity Page

CONCEPT: syllables

TEACHER GOALS: To teach the children
To hear the parts of a word, and
To understand that the parts of a word are called syllables.

VOCABULARY: syllable

MATERIALS NEEDED: 3″ x 5″ cards with 1, 2, and 3 on them (one set for each child), Worksheet 14

TEACHING PAGE 27:

Prepare the sets of number cards.

Tell the children to listen carefully, then to say the word *the*. Ask the children to tell how many parts they heard. Say the following words and have the children tell how many parts they hear in each one: *go, candy, jump, happy.*

Give each child a set of number cards and tell them to hold up the number that tells how many parts each word has. Tell the children that the word parts are called *syllables*. Use the word so that children become familiar with it.

Tell them that there are as many syllables in a word as the number of vowels that you can hear.

Read these words. Pause slightly between syllables.

birth day	house	cat
white	lad der	walk ing
dif fer ence	bird	bas ket
with	hap pen ing	moth er
child	won der ful	tell

If a child holds up the wrong number, say the word again and have the child repeat it, and hold up the right number card.

Read the list of words again and have the children clap once for each syllable as they repeat the word after you.

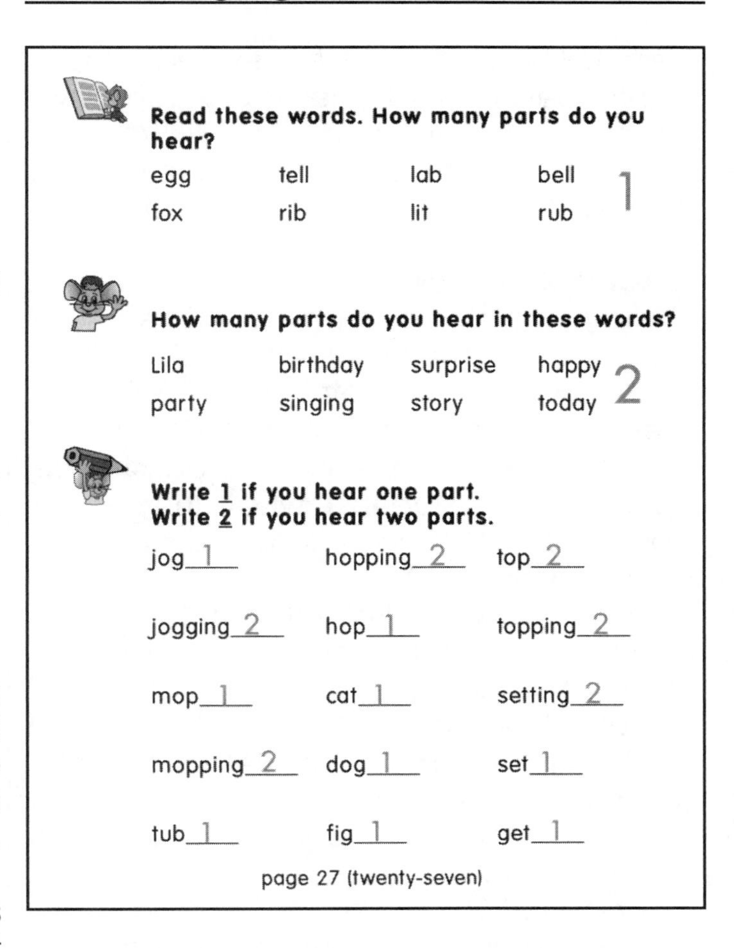
Read these words. How many parts do you hear?

egg	tell	lab	bell	1
fox	rib	lit	rub	

How many parts do you hear in these words?

Lila	birthday	surprise	happy	2
party	singing	story	today	

Write 1 if you hear one part.
Write 2 if you hear two parts.

jog 1	hopping 2	top 2
jogging 2	hop 1	topping 2
mop 1	cat 1	setting 2
mopping 2	dog 1	set 1
tub 1	fig 1	get 1

page 27 (twenty-seven)

Read the direction and question at the top of the page. Have the children read each word and tell how many parts each word has.

Read the next question. Have the children read each word in the list and tell how many parts each word has. Read each word again and clap for the number of syllables in it.

Read the directions in the middle of the page. Do the words together.

ACTIVITIES:

Do Worksheet 14.

Have the children read the directions at the top of the page.

Do the first row of words together. Have the children say the word, then tell how many parts they hear in it. Have them write the number on the line. Read the directions for the next exercise. Read each of the words with the children and have them tell how many parts they hear. Pause slightly between syllables if children have trouble hearing the parts.

Have the children clap the syllables as they say the words in the last exercise.

TEACHING READING:

Have students form a circle. Do movement activities with them. Arms flap, bodies twist, twirl and other ideas. Tell them they are a flying animal....but not a bird. Can you guess? If they guess a bat, they're correct! Ask students what they know about bats. List answers on the board or chart paper.

Read the story "Betty the Bat" together and then answer the following questions:

"What is the bat's name?" (Betty)

"Who is telling the story?" (I)

"What are some things Betty can do?" (flip, flap, twist, twirl, fly)

Do you think bats can really do this?" (answers will vary - yes)

Find short vowel words.

Find words with beginning and ending blends (flap, wings, flip, twist, twirl, fly, round)

ACTIVITY:

Provide nonfiction books about bats. Do mini individual or group reports about bats. Do movement activities again, only this time think about being a bat. Make a list of all the words that rhyme with bat. Write poems using the rhyming words. Make bat puppets out of black construction paper and craft sticks. Write a creative story about other things Betty the Bat likes to do.

Name ____________

Write 1 if you hear one part.
Write 2 if you hear two parts.

him 1	the 1	running 2
wanted 2	singing 2	nod 1
cab 1	birthday 2	Sunday 2
willing 2	Bible 2	tug 1

Read these words. How many parts do you hear?

minister 3	contraction 3
nursery 3	banana 3
dictionary 4	apostrophe 4

How many parts in these words?

sentences 3	animal 3
together 3	another 3
butterfy 3	invitation 4

Language Arts 103
Worksheet 14
with page 27

Teacher check ____________
Initial Date

Page 28: Following Directions

CONCEPTS: listening, following directions, length, position words, ordinal numbers

TEACHER GOALS: To teach the children
To listen and follow longer and more difficult oral directions given only once,
To understand shortest and longest,
To understand left, right, back, beside, over, under, in front of, in, out, on, off, full, half-full, empty, and
To understand the ordinal numbers first through tenth.

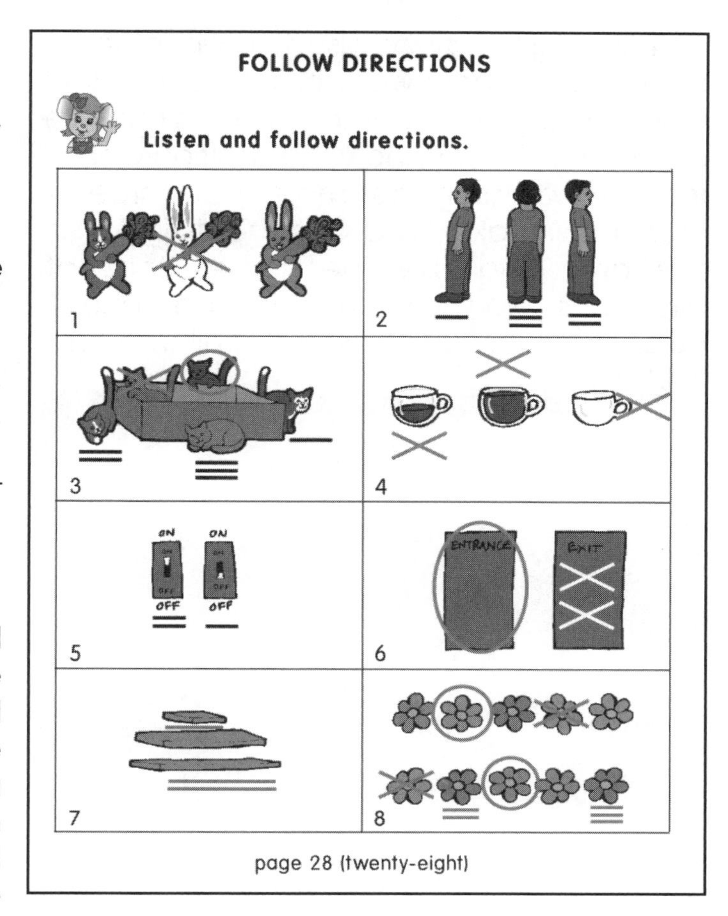

TEACHING PAGE 28:

Read the direction with the children. Tell them to listen carefully because the directions you read will be longer and because they will be doing two or three things in each box. Remind them that you will read the directions only once for each box. Wait until everyone is quiet and listening before reading any of the directions. Have the children put their fingers on the numbers in the corners of the boxes so they are sure they are in the right box.

Read the directions slowly and emphasize the underlined words slightly. Pause between the instructions within a sentence.

1. Put an X on the rabbit with the longest ears and circle the rabbit with the shortest ears.
2. Draw one line under the boy facing left, two lines under the boy facing right, and three lines under the boy with his back to us.
3. a. Put an X on the kitten that wants to get out of the box and a circle around the kitten that wants to get in the box.

   b. Draw one line under the kitten beside the box on the right, two lines under the kitten beside the box on the left, and three lines under the kitten in front of the box.
4. Put an X over the full cup, put an X under the cup that is half-full, and put an X beside the empty cup.
5. Put one line under the switch that is off and two lines under the switch that is on.
6. Draw a circle around the door that would let you come into a building and put two X's on the door that would let you go out of a building.
7. Draw two lines under the longest board and one line under the shortest board.
8. a. Circle the second flower in the top row and the third flower in the bottom row.

   b. Put an X on the fourth flower in the top row and the first flower in the bottom row.

   c. Counting all the flowers, put two lines under the seventh flower and three lines under the tenth flower.

This page may be used as an informal check to see how well children can follow longer and more complicated directions and how well they know the position words. If several children miss more than three or four items, make up a worksheet similar to this one and use the same kinds of directions. Work in small groups and check each box as soon as the children are finished.

Page 29: Soft g

CONCEPT: sound of *g* as in giant (soft *g*)

TEACHER GOAL: To teach the children
To recognize the sound of *g* as in giant (soft *g*).

MATERIALS NEEDED: Worksheet 15, crayons

TEACHING PAGE 29:

Read the title and tell the children that the letter *g* also has two sounds. The sound of *g* as in *go* they already know. That sound is called the hard *g*. The other sound of *g* is called the soft *g* and words like *giant, giraffe,* and *ginger* begin with it. It is the same as the /j/ sound.

When *g* is followed by *e, i,* or *y, g* often has the soft sound of *j*.

Read the hard *g* words and emphasize the /g/ sound. Ask if this sound is hard or soft.

Read the soft *g* words and emphasize the /j/ sound. Ask if this sound is hard or soft. Ask where the sound is in the word.

Read the final direction with the children. Have the children name the first picture and tell if the */g/* sound is soft or hard. Have them trace the circle.

Work through the entire exercise with the children. Have the children name all the pictures again, listening for the soft */g/* sound.

ACTIVITY:

Do Worksheet 15.

Since this worksheet is more difficult, you may wish to work through the entire exercise with the children.

Note: Do not expect children to master the concept of soft *g* at this time. It is introduced here for children who come upon it in their reading and should know about it. Call attention to the soft *g* sound whenever it occurs.

Soft G.

Read these words with your teacher.

go got God give girl

Now read these words with you teacher.

giraffe	general	gym
gingerbread	giant	Gerald
change	Genesis	gem

Circle the pictures with the soft g sound.

page 29 (twenty-nine)

Read the direction with the children. Have the children point to the first picture. Tell them the picture is of a *general*.

Write it on the board and point out to the children that it begins with the letter *g* but it has the /j/ sound. This sound is called the soft *g*.

Say the name of each of the other pictures and have the children listen for the sound of *g*. Ask them to tell whether they hear the soft or hard /g/ sound. Emphasize the /g/ sound slightly as you say the words (general, gem, gingerbread, giraffe, goat, glass).

Read the direction for the bottom section with the children. Have the children give the name of the picture and tell whether it should begin with a *g* or *j*. If they are not sure, write the names of the pictures on the board (general, jet, gem, jungle, jar, giraffe). Check by having the children tell which letter they put under each picture.

Since the children are only being introduced to the concept of the soft /g/ sound, do not expect them to master it. Call attention to the sound as it comes up in the children's reading or writing.

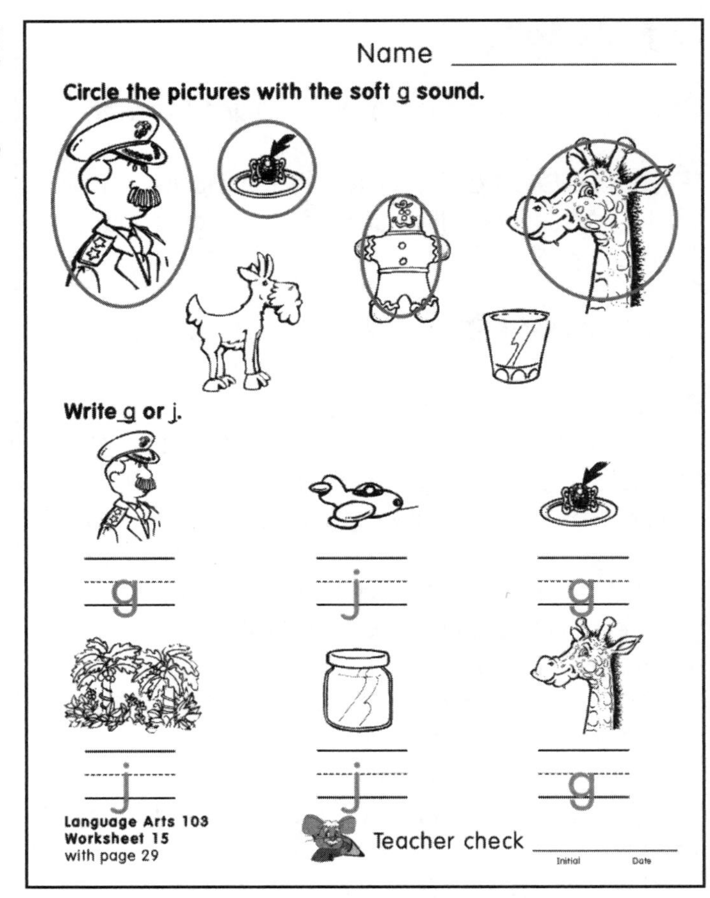

Name ______________

Circle the pictures with the soft g sound.

Write g or j.

g j g

j j g

Language Arts 103
Worksheet 15
with page 29

Teacher check ______________
Initial Date

Page 30: More Plurals

CONCEPTS: plurals, number words

TEACHER GOALS: To teach the children
To understand, read, and write plurals made by adding *s* or *es* to a noun and
To read and understand the number words *one* to *nine.*

MATERIALS NEEDED: Worksheet 16

TEACHING PAGE 30:

Read the title with the children. Ask what a plural is.

Have the children read the directions at the top of the page.

Tell the children to look at the pictures in the first box and read the phrases. Ask how the plural is different (*es* instead of *s*). Explain that words that end in letters such as *s, x, sh,* or *ch* must have the *es* ending for plurals because it is much easier to say. Let them try to say *foxs* or *wishs* to show them what you mean. Then have them say *foxes* and *wishes* and listen to the difference.

Look at the pictures and read the phrases in the next box. Have the children tell which ending is used to make the plural of glass.

Let the children finish the page by themselves. Check by having the children read the phrases and spell the plurals.

ACTIVITY:

Do Worksheet 16.

Read the directions with the children. Do the first two boxes together. Look at the pictures, read the phrases, and write the letters.

Have the children match the words and pictures in the second section.

MORE PLURALS

Now you will learn more plurals.

Write the letters. Read the words.

one fox two fox**es**	one glass three glass**es**
six box e s	two bus e s
three church e s	nine block s

page 30 (thirty)

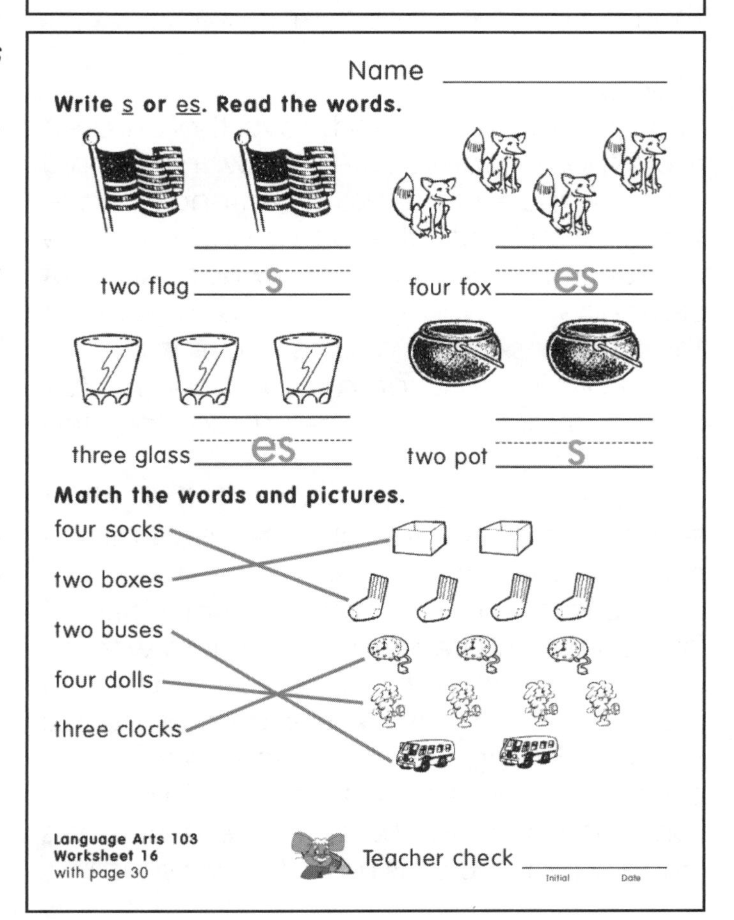

Name ______

Write s or es. Read the words.

two flag s

four fox es

three glass es

two pot s

Match the words and pictures.

four socks

two boxes

two buses

four dolls

three clocks

Language Arts 103
Worksheet 16
with page 30

Teacher check ______
Initial Date

Page 31: Sentences

CONCEPTS: sentences, capital letters, punctuation marks, subject-verb

TEACHER GOALS: To teach the children

To recognize, read, and write sentences,

To tell that the first word in a sentence and all names must begin with capital letters,

To tell that a statement is a kind of sentence and that it has a period at the end,

To rearrange words to make a sentence, and

To tell whether the subject of a sentence agrees with its verb.

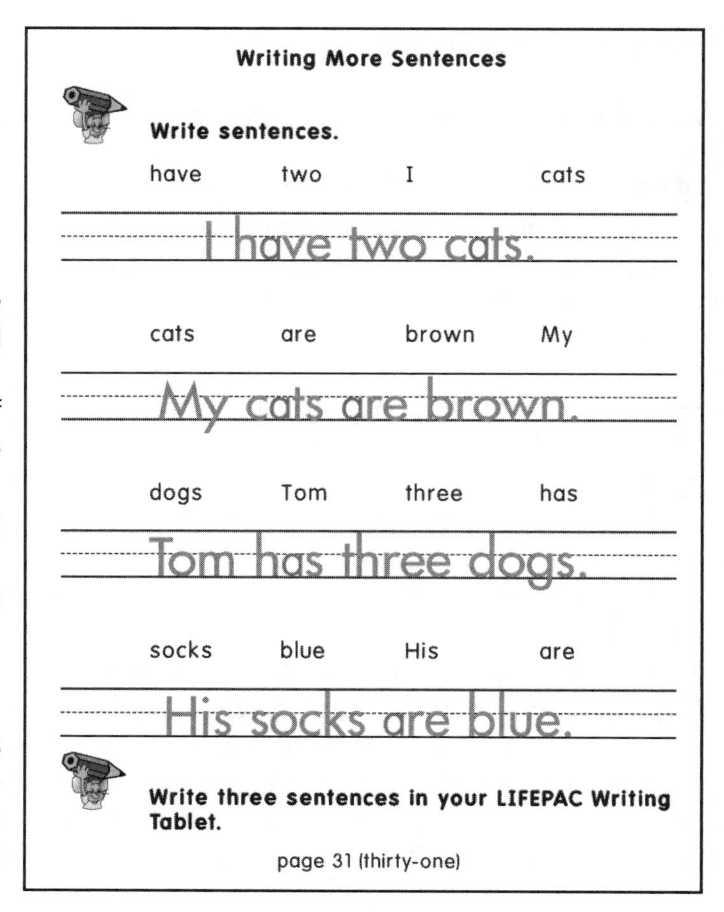

TEACHING PAGE 31:

Have the children name the three kinds of sentences and tell what the punctuation mark is for each. Have them give several examples of each. Remind them to use the proper expression.

Read the title and direction with the children.

Read the words and have the children read them after you. Ask how they could be rearranged to make a sentence. Have the children write the words and read the sentence. Ask children what kind of sentence it is and what kind of mark is at the end. Ask why the *I* is a capital letter (first word in sentence and pronoun *I*). Ask how a question could be made from the same words.

Do the same for each of the other sentences. Have the children read all the sentences again.

The last sentence is a little more difficult and some children may need help with it.

Change either the subject or the verb in the sentence and ask the children to tell what is wrong with the sentence. The children should recognize by now that plural subjects have *are, have,* or *were* as verbs and singular subjects have *is, has,* or *was.*

Example: I *has* two cats. or I *have* two cats.

My *cat* are brown. or My *cats* are brown.

Read the last direction with the children. Tell them they may write any kind of sentences they wish. The teacher should check the page and have the children recopy sentences if words are misspelled or the writing is not done well.

ACTIVITY:

Write two titles on the board and let the children choose one and write a short story about it. Have the children write at least four or five sentences and remind them that all of the sentences must tell something about the title. Check the stories and have the children correct and recopy. Have them draw and color or paint a picture to go with their story. Take class time for the children to read their stories to the rest of the class.

Suggested titles: My Cat, My Dog, My Best Toy, My Mother (or Father)

TEACHING READING:

Provide a variety of musical instruments (or pictures). Do not include a piano, yet. Discuss what each looks like —list descriptive characteristics on the board. Then write the words "black and white". Ask students what musical instrument you're thinking about. (piano). Ask how many students have played the piano or take lessons. Ask them what words might describe how a piano sounds. List answers. Read the story "Black and White Keys" together then ask the following questions:

"What is black and white?" (the keys)

"Are they keys like you use with a lock?" (no)

Describe how they are different. (except any reasonable explanations)

"What other clues tell you this is a piano?" (sit, look at the black and white keys, go up & down, make a sound, make a song)

Have students find words with beginning and ending blends (black, long, plink, plunk, sound, song)

ACTIVITY:

If you have a piano or keyboard, play some songs for a sing-a-long. Give students an opportunity to make a "lovely sound" on the piano. Play musical tapes which feature the piano music. Share stories about famous composers: i.e., Beethoven, Mozart, Bach, etc. Ask students how many are interested in learning to play a musical instrument. Make a graph showing their interests. Paint pictures listening to different kinds of music - soft, loud, fast.

SELF TEST 3

CONCEPTS: plurals, syllables, sentences, subject-verb agreement, punctuation marks, compound words, and soft /g/ sound

TEACHER GOAL: To teach the children
To check their own progress periodically.

TEACHING PAGE 32:
Read the title and ask the children what it means.
Read all the directions on the page and be sure the children understand what they are to do.
Have the children complete the page independently. Check the page as soon as possible and go over it with the children so that they can see where they did well and where they need extra work. (gem, gingerbread, gate)

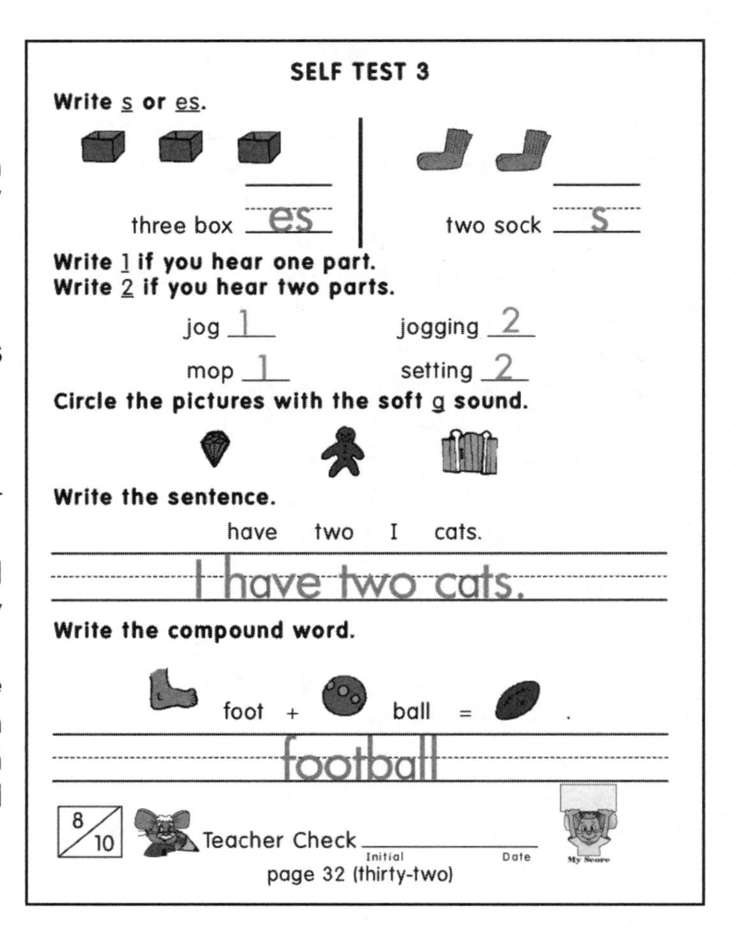

ACTIVITIES:
1. Give individual help on items missed.
2. If several children miss the same things, reteach the skill (in a small group, if possible).

SPELLING WORDS:

gem
gym
three
cat
dog

LIFEPAC TEST AND ALTERNATE TEST 103

CONCEPTS: consonant digraphs, contractions, rhyming words, soft /c/ sound, soft /g/ sound, plurals, and sentences

TEACHER GOAL: To teach the children to check their own progress periodically.

MATERIALS NEEDED: crayons

TEACHING the LIFEPAC TEST:

Administer this test in at least two sessions.

Read all the directions on each page as the children prepare to do it. Be sure they understand everything they are to do. Let them finish the page independently.

Give no help except with directions.

Go over each page with the child as soon as possible after you check it so that he can see where he did well and what needs more work.

Evaluate the tests and review areas where the children do poorly. Review the pages and activities that stress the concepts tested. (chain, chair, check, chimney, thread, shoe, shirt, shell, sheep, whale)

Listen and do: Put a red circle around the fifth cat in the first row, put a blue line over the third cat in the second row. Counting all the cats, color the eighth cat green. (thread, three, chain, thirty, thumb, whiskers, whistle, whale, shell, wheel) (celery, comb, circle, goat, giant, giraffe)

If necessary, when the children have reviewed sufficiently, administer the Alternate LIFEPAC Test. Follow the same procedure used for the LIFEPAC Test.

ALTERNATE TEST:

(thread, wheel, check, sheep)

Listen and do: Color the second whale in the first row brown, color the fifth whale in the second row orange. Counting all the whales, put a green line under the seventh

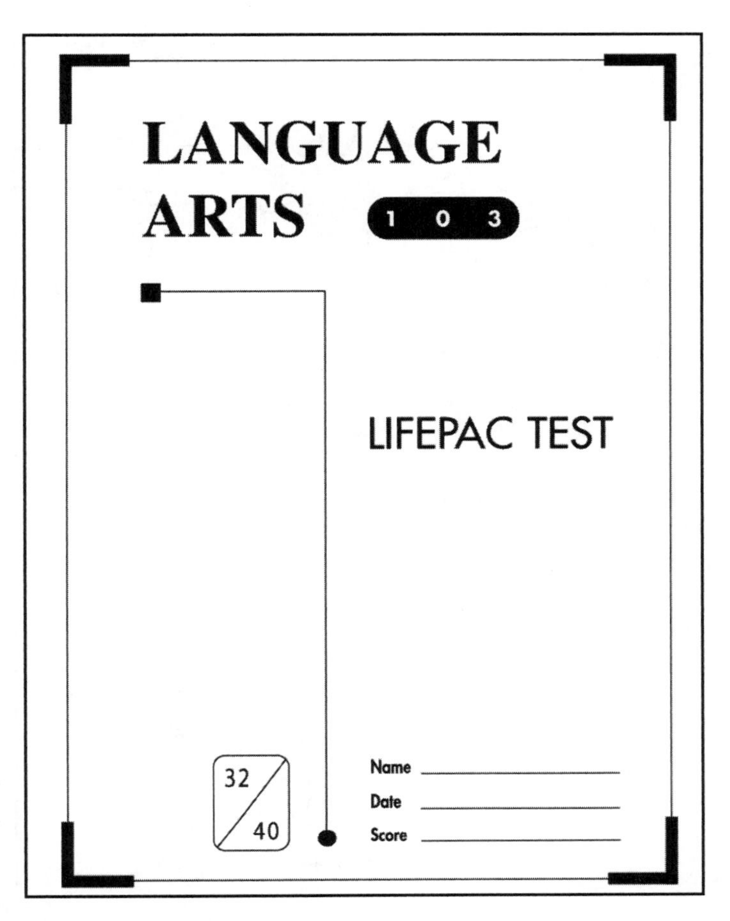

whale. (gate, giant, gem, circle, ceiling, comb)

SPELLING WORDS:

LIFEPAC words	Alternate words
thick	his
whip	her
shell	cell
chuck	gym
her	cat
cell	thick
one	that
two	whip
three	shell
gem	chuck

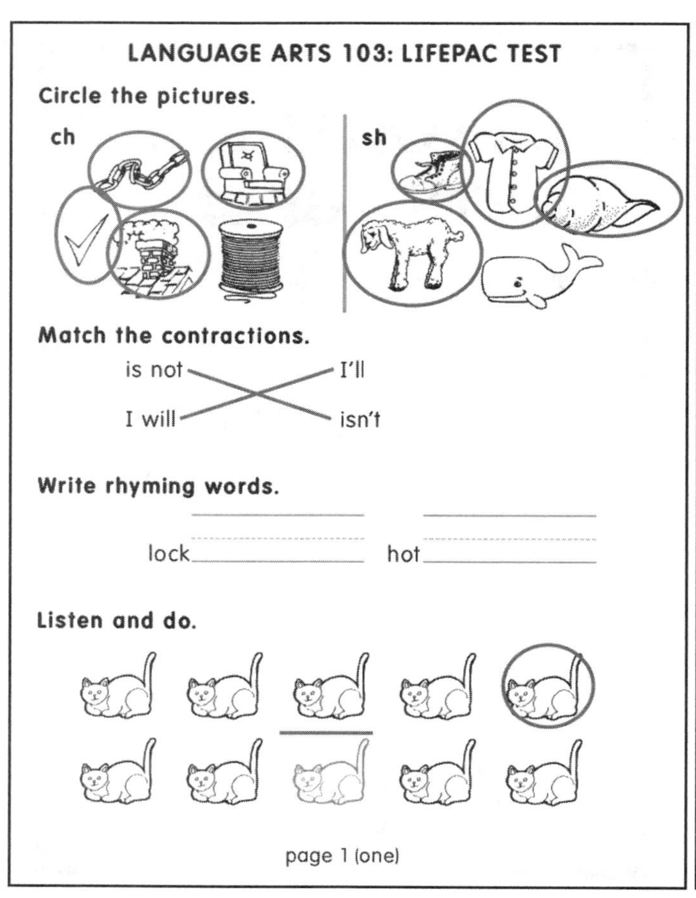

LANGUAGE ARTS 103: LIFEPAC TEST

Circle the pictures.

ch

sh

Match the contractions.

is not — isn't

I will — I'll

Write rhyming words.

lock ____ hot ____

Listen and do.

page 1 (one)

Circle the pictures.

th

wh

Circle the pictures with the soft c sound.

Circle the pictures with the soft g sound.

Write s or es.

two clock s

four pot s

two cot s

three glass es

page 2 (two)

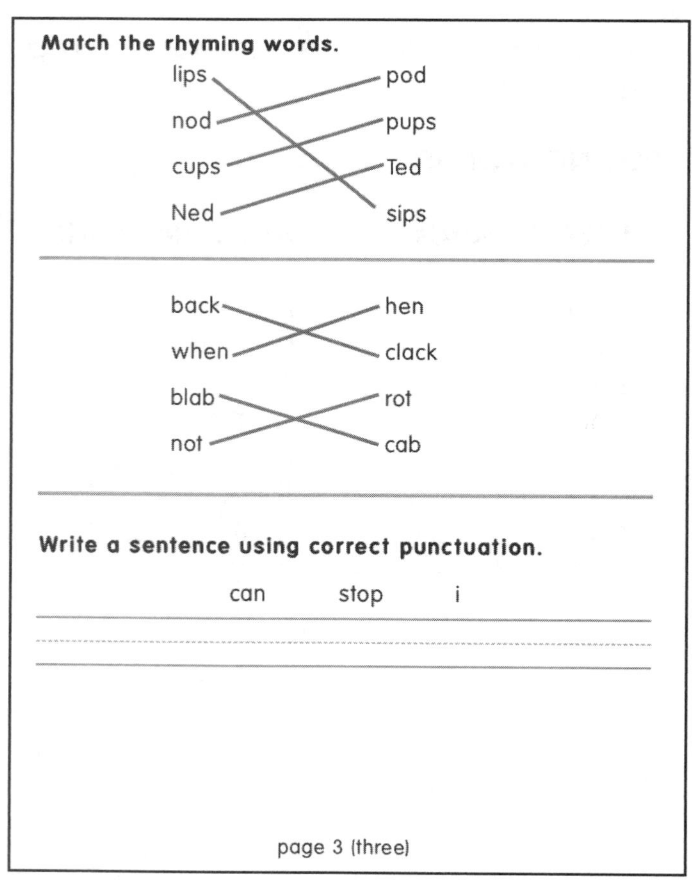

Match the rhyming words.

lips — sips

nod — pod

cups — pups

Ned — Ted

back — clack

when — hen

blab — cab

not — rot

Write a sentence using correct punctuation.

can stop i

page 3 (three)

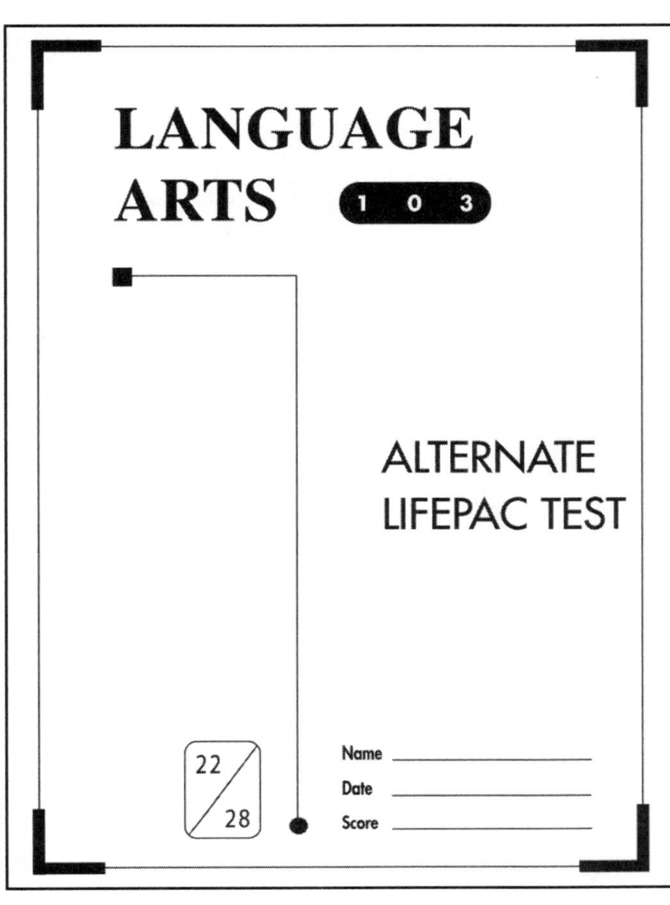
LANGUAGE ARTS 1 0 3

ALTERNATE LIFEPAC TEST

22/28

Name ____________

Date ____________

Score ____________

LANGUAGE ARTS 103
ALTERNATE LIFEPAC TEST

Write the letters ch, sh, wh, or th.

th

wh

ch

sh

Match the contractions.

I am — I'm

do not — don't

Write rhyming words.

bob ____________ box ____________

Listen and do.

page 1 (one)

Circle the pictures with the soft g sound.

Circle the pictures that begin with the soft c sound.

Write s or es.

three dot s

four top s

two doll s

two fox es

page 2 (two)

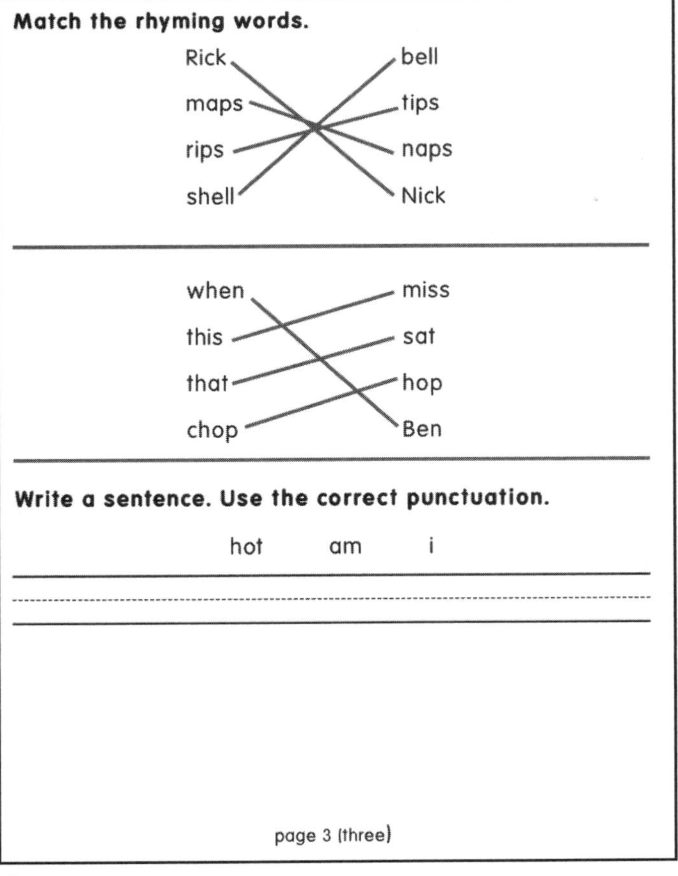
Match the rhyming words.

Rick — Nick

maps — naps

rips — tips

shell — bell

when — Ben

this — miss

that — sat

chop — hop

Write a sentence. Use the correct punctuation.

hot am i

page 3 (three)

Page 1: FUN WITH WORDS

CONCEPTS: purpose of LIFEPAC, child's objectives

TEACHER GOALS: To teach the children
To know what kinds of things they will learn about in Language Arts LIFEPAC 104,
To know what an objective is, and
To tell the main things they will be learning in this LIFEPAC.

TEACHING PAGE 1:

Read the title and the paragraphs with the children. Have them follow along from left to right with their fingers under the sentence being read and repeat after you. Talk about each paragraph.

Ask if anyone remembers what objectives are. If no one does, remind them that an objective is something they decide they want to do or must do. Remind them also that once they decide what must be done, their job is to do their very best to get it done. So in this case it will be their job to do their best to learn everything in the list of objectives.

Read the list and discuss each one.

Have the children write their names on the lines.

ACTIVITY:

Children who are still having trouble writing their names or any of the letters in their names should be given individual help. Write the child's name or letters from his name on the first line of a sheet of writing tablet paper. Show the child again how to form the letters, then let him practice them.

FUN WITH WORDS

In this LIFEPAC
you will learn more
about words and sentences.

You will learn
about consonant blends, silent letters,
and correct verb forms.

1. I will learn about rhyming.
2. I will learn about letter blends.
3. I will spell and write words.
4. I will learn about sequencing.
5. I will learn about subject-verb agreement.
6. I will learn about cardinal and ordinal numbers.

Write your name.

page 1 (one)

I.PART ONE

Page 2: Listen and Find

CONCEPTS: listening and following directions, classifying into groups, subject-verb agreement, verb forms, plurals, ordinal numbers *first* through *sixth,* positions

TEACHER GOALS: To teach the children

To listen and follow directions given only once,

To classify animals into groups according to descriptions (four legs, scales, etc.),

To recognize and use correct subject-verb agreement in a sentence,

To recognize and use correct verb forms in a sentence,

To identify plurals made by adding *s,*

To understand the ordinal numbers *first* through *sixth,* and

To understand the meanings of the position words *up, in, under, behind, left,* and *right.*

I. PART ONE

LISTEN AND FIND

Listen to your teacher.
Listen to the story.

Listen and follow directions.

1 2 3 4

1 2 3

page 2 (two)

VOCABULARY: first, second, third, fourth, fifth, sixth

MATERIALS NEEDED: crayons, color chart

TEACHING PAGE 2:

Put a diagram like this one on the board.

○ ① ② ③ ④ ⑤ ⑥

first second third fourth fifth sixth

Next, write the same diagram in the opposite direction. Thirdly, write the same diagram up and down with the large circle on top. Fourthly, write the same diagram up and down with the large balloon on the bottom. Finally, write the diagram diagonally across the board with the large balloon on the right.

Tell the children that how you count from first to last depends on which way the line is going. Tell the children to imagine that the large circle is a mother animal and that the small circles are her babies lined up in single file behind her. Then write the numbers from *1* to *6* on the circles, starting with number *1* on the first circle after the large circle. Have the children read the numbers. Then write the ordinal numbers from *first* to *sixth* under the circles. Leave the diagram on the board until the children finish the page.

Note: This diagram could be put on a large sheet of tagboard to be used again when the children are working with the ordinal numbers. The ordinals seventh through tenth may be added as they are taught.

Read the title and the direction with the children. Tell them to look at the picture and then to listen carefully as you read some things for them to do. Tell them you will read the direction only once and then they are to mark the picture.

Read these directions:

It is a warm summer day. The animals are out in the forest. Some of them are looking for food, some are playing, and some are resting.

1. Put a blue X on the animal *behind* the tree.
2. Put a yellow circle around the animal *up in* the tree.
3. Put a red circle around the baby quail on the *left* side of its mother. Put a brown X on the baby quail on the *right* side of its mother.
4. Put a green X on one of the animals that is *in* something. (baby birds in the nest)
5. Put an orange line *behind* the *fourth baby* skunk.
6. Put a black line *under* the *second baby* turtle.
7. Write the number of each baby skunk right above it.
8. Write the number of each baby turtle right above it.

Read each direction again and have the children tell which animal they marked or which way they counted. Have children correct their mistakes, if any.

Have the children name the animals in the picture that have two feet, that have a shell, that have fur or hair, that have feathers, that can run fast, and that can climb trees.

After the children name the animals in the picture that fit each category, ask them to name other animals that would fit.

Give the name of one of the animals in the picture and ask the children to give the plural. You may have to tell the children that *deer* and *quail* may mean one or many.

If necessary, review the position words before you begin (up/down, left/right, before/behind, etc.).

Tell the children that we use the word *is* when we refer to only one thing. We use the word *are* when we refer to more than one (also has/have, go/goes, was/were, etc.).

Make up sentences about the animals in the picture and have the children tell which sentence has the correct verb form or subject-verb agreement.

Examples: The mother robin *feed* or *feeds* her babies. Baby skunks *has or have* a white stripe. The *turtle* or *turtles* are following their mother. The baby bear *climb* or *climbed* up the tree. *Turtle* or *turtles* have shells.

ACTIVITIES:

1. Have the children use the following words in sentences:

come/came	choose/chose
run/ran	break/broke
know/knew	eat/ate
do/did	fall/fell
bring/brought	drink/drank
take/took	go/went

2. Make a note of the children who use the wrong verb form in their daily speech and give them extra help. Have them choose between the correct form and the incorrect form in sentences or use the form in a sentence.

TEACHING READING:

Write hippopotamus and crocodile on the board. Have students learn the words in a fun way with chants: Hip, hip, hippo, hip, hip, hippopotamus! Croc, croc, croco, croc, croc, crocodile! Divide the class — one side doing hippopotamus; the other crocodile.

Tell students they're going to read a story called The Big Problem.

Ask them what sort of big problem a hippopotamus or crocodile might have.

List their answers.

Read the story "A Big Problem" together and then answer the following questions:

"Who has the problem?" (Mrs. Hippopotamus)

"What is her problem?" (water is gone from her "tub", she needs to take a bath)

"Who does she ask for help?" (Mr. Crocodile)

"Does he help her?" (no)

"How do you know?" (he says "mud is fine with me")

"What do you think Mrs. Hippopotamus will do now?" (answers will vary)

"What do you think Mr. Crocodile will do now?" (answers will vary)

Find rhyming words (dud-mud, see-me, hippopotamus-fuss) Add to each group.

Find short vowel sounds — even the big ones!

ACTIVITY:

Make a class book! Continue the story with other characters for Mrs. Hippopotamus to ask. (Keep in mind where hippos live.) Have students each pick a character (elephant, bird, tiger, lion, zebra, etc.) and write what Mrs. Hippopotamus and the new character say to each other. The problem is she still needs a bath but nobody helps. Then, as a class choose one animal/character that WILL help and write the ending together. Have students illustrate a page to go with their writing. Bind pages together to make a class book. Have students design a new tub for Mrs. Hippopotamus so she doesn't have this problem in the future.

Draw a picture of Mr. Crocodile enjoying himself in the mud.

Challenge: How many 3-4 letter words can you make from the letters in Hippopotamus? (examples: hip, hop, hot, hat, mat, pop, top, must, hut, tip, past, post, pat, tap, ...)

Page 3: Consonant Blends

CONCEPT: consonant blends

TEACHER GOAL: To teach the children
To identify pictures and words beginning
with the consonant blends *bl, cl,* and *fl.*

MATERIALS NEEDED: tagboard flash cards for *bl, cl,* and *fl,* crayons

TEACHING PAGE 3:

Make flash cards for the consonant blends *bl, cl,* and *fl.*

Hold up the flash cards for *b* and *l* and ask for the names and sounds of the letters. Put the two cards together and tell the children that when the two letters are together in a word they are called a blend, or a consonant blend. Say the sound of *bl* and have the children repeat it several times.

Do the same with *cl* and *fl.* Go through the flash cards for the three blends several times and have the children give the names of the letters and the sounds.

Read the direction with the children or have a child read it.

Have the children name the pictures in this section and circle the ones that begin with *bl.* Check by having the children tell which pictures they circled (grapes, blanket, blocks, blade, blouse).

Follow the same procedure with *cl* and *fl.* Have children name the pictures in each section before they circle. Be sure they know the meaning of each word.

cl_____

(clown, glass, clover, cloud, club, clock)

fl______

(flower, flag, floor, blanket, flipper, flashlight)

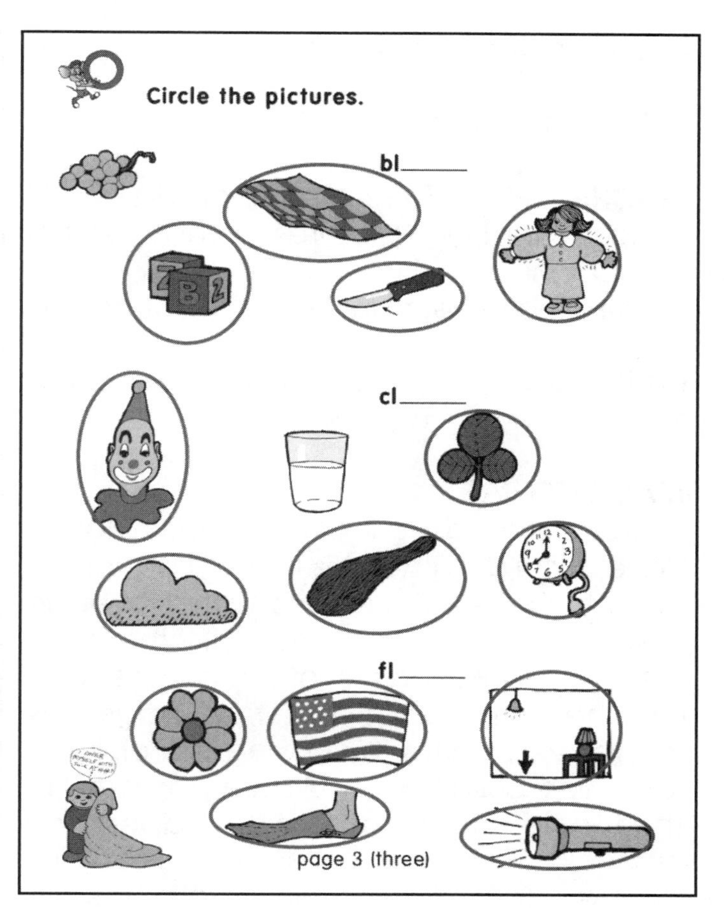

Page 4: Consonant Blends

CONCEPT: consonant blends

TEACHER GOAL: To teach the children
To identify pictures and words beginning
with the consonant blends *bl, cl,* and *fl.*

MATERIALS NEEDED: tagboard flash cards for *bl, cl,* and *fl,* crayons

TEACHING PAGE 4:
Read the direction with the children. Have a child tell what is in the first picture. Ask which blend it begins with. Have the children say the word and write the *cl* on the lines. Name the rest of the pictures and let the children finish the page by themselves. Check by having the children tell which blend each picture begins with. The teacher should collect the papers and recheck. Have the children correct any mistakes (cliff, flute, blowing, clippers, fly, blanket, blimp, closet, clapping, flame, blindfold, snowflake).

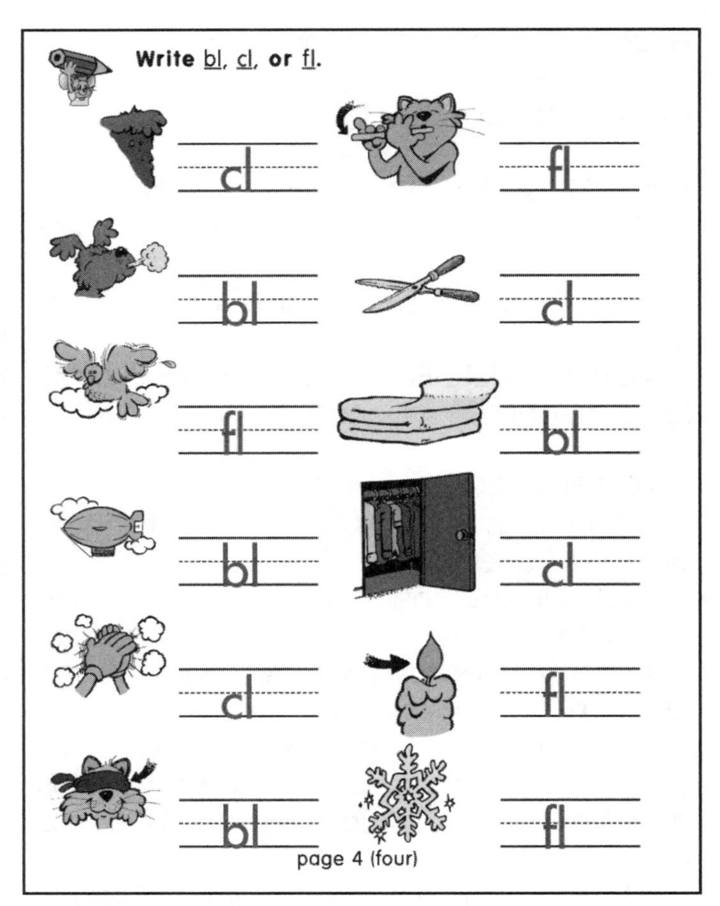

ACTIVITIES:
1. Use a picture card collection for children who have a difficult time with blends. Have the children sort out the picture cards that begin with the three blends.

Page 5: Consonant Blends

CONCEPT: consonant blends

TEACHER GOAL: To teach the children

To identify pictures and words beginning with the consonant blends *gl, pl,* and *sl.*

MATERIALS NEEDED: alphabet cards, tagboard for flash cards (*gl, pl, sl,*) Worksheet 1, scissors, paste, crayons

TEACHING PAGE 5:

Make flash cards for the consonant blends *gl, pl,* and *sl.*

Hold up the flash cards for *g* and *l* and ask for the names and sounds of the letters. Put the two cards together and ask if anyone remembers what we call it when we put the two letters together. If no one remembers blend or consonant blend, tell them. Say the sound of *gl* and have the children repeat it several times. Ask the children if they can give words that begin with the sound of *gl.*

Do the same with *pl* and *sl.*

Go through the flash cards for the three blends several times and have the children name the letters and give the sounds. Add these blends to the blends from earlier pages and go through all six blends several times.

Have the children read the direction and the three blends at the top of the page. Name the first picture (glue) and ask how it begins. Have the children circle it. Name the rest of the pictures in the first section and have the children circle all those beginning with *gl.* Check by having the children name what they circled (clock, globe, gloves, glass).

Follow the same procedure for *pl* and *st.*

pl______

(plane, blanket, plant, plate, pliers).

sl______

(sleeve, sled, clam, slice of bread, slide).

Be sure the children know the meaning of every word.

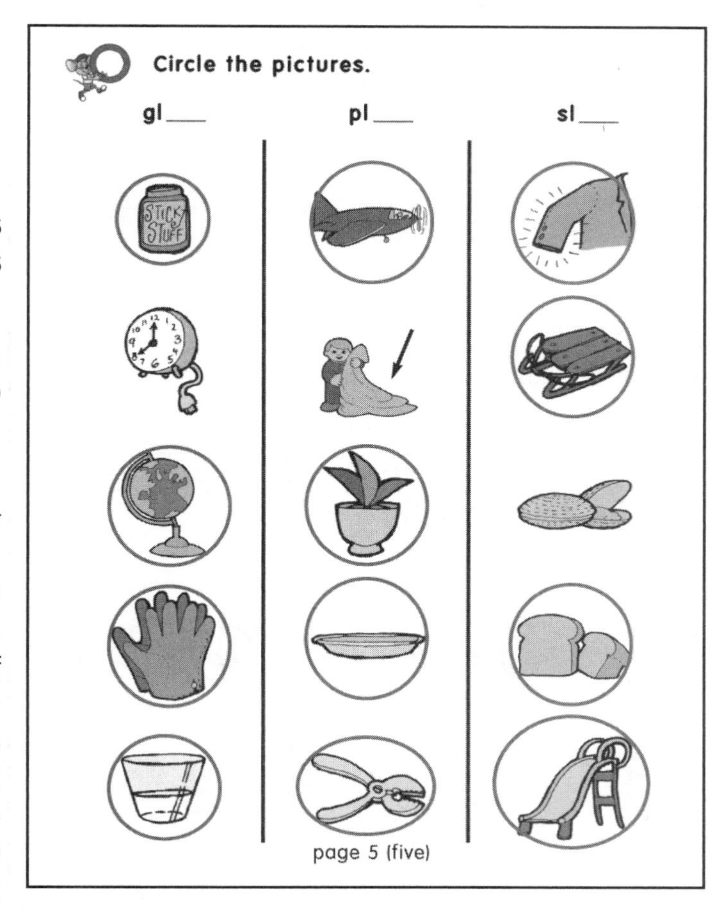

ACTIVITIES:

1. Do Worksheet 1.

Read the direction with the children.

Have them cut along the heavy black line and cut the consonant blends apart. Remind them to cut only on the lines. Have the children paste the consonant blend under the picture beginning with that blend. Have the children name all the pictures before they begin pasting(sling, glass, plums, glove, slippers, sleep, plow, globe, plank, slide, plaid, glasses).

Collect the papers and check. Have the children correct any mistakes.

2. Have the children sort out the picture cards that begin with these three blends.

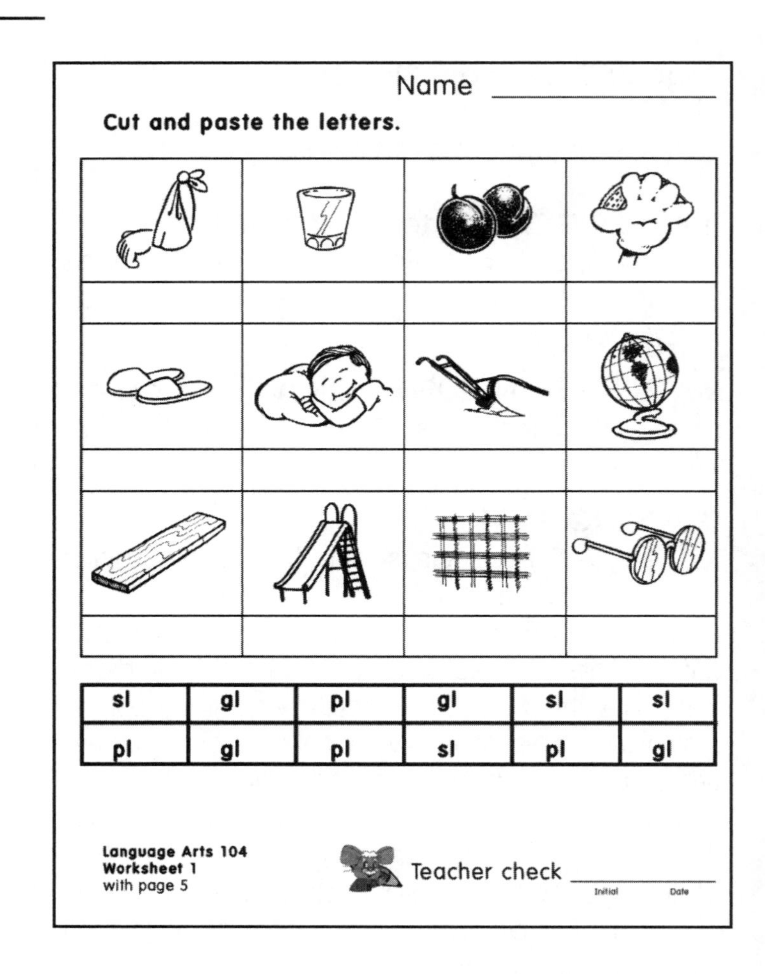

Name ______________

Cut and paste the letters.

sl	gl	pl	gl	sl	sl
pl	gl	pl	sl	pl	gl

Language Arts 104
Worksheet 1
with page 5

Teacher check ______________
Initial Date

Page 6: Consonant Blends

CONCEPT: consonant blends

TEACHER GOAL: To teach the children
To identify and write the consonant blends *bl, cl, gl, pl, fl,* and *sl* at the beginning of pictures and words.

MATERIALS NEEDED: flash cards for blends, drawing paper, paste or glue

TEACHING PAGE 6:

Go through the flash cards for the blends several times. Have the children give the names of the letters and a word that begins with that blend. *(example: bl* blue).

Have the children read the direction at the top of the page and the blends. Have them name all the pictures on the page and let the children complete the page independently. Check by having the children name the picture and tell which blend they wrote on the lines (blanket, gloves, plate, flame, clock, slippers, cloud, slide, blocks).

Work through the page with those who need help. Have them say the words several times, listening for the beginning sounds before they write the letters on the lines.

ACTIVITY:

Have the children start a consonant blends dictionary. Write each of the blends at the top of a sheet of drawing paper. As the children use words beginning with the blends in their reading or writing, have them write them on a strip of writing tablet paper and paste them on the sheet of drawing paper. The children could draw pictures or cut them from magazines to illustrate the words. Those words that cannot be illustrated with pictures could be used in a sentence. A sheet or sheets may be added to the book for each blend as children learn them. Children can use the book for help in spelling when they are writing sentences and stories. Put the book together with string, yarn, or brass fasteners. If you use tag board it will last longer. Decorate the cover any way you wish.

Page 7: Rhyming

CONCEPTS: rhyming words, sound of short *o, i, e*

TEACHER GOALS: To teach the children
To write rhyming words with the endings *oss* and *og,* and
To match rhyming words with short /o/, short /i/, and short /e/ sounds.

VOCABULARY: LIFEPAC

TEACHING PAGE 7:

Ask the children to tell what rhyming words are.

Read the first direction with the children. Read the two endings and have the children give two or three words that rhyme with each one. Let the children write the rhyming words on the lines.

Prepare the sheet of writing tablet paper with the endings at the top. Have the children write more rhyming words while you correct this page.

Write the endings on the board ond have the children give words from their lists. Write them under the proper ending. Have the children add to and correct their lists from the lists on the board. Have the children read the lists several times.

Read the last direction with the children. Have them trace the line and read the two words.

Have the children draw the lines between the pairs of rhyming words. Read the words.

ACTVITIES:

Dictate five *oss* words and *fog, hog,* and *log* and have the children write them on a sheet of writing tablet paper. Correct the papers and have the children write their misspelled words five times on the back of the paper.

TEACHING READING:

Read the story "The Pup and the Box" in *Reader 2.*

Write rhyming words.

_____ **oss** _____ **og**

Can you think of more words?

Write them in your LIFEPAC Writing Tablet.

Match the rhyming words.

blocks	tops
mops	hot
not	clocks
sobs	digs
beds	cobs
pigs	sleds

page 7 (seven)

Present the word *jump.* Write it on the board and have the children show you what it means.

Have the children think of a time when they have been so surprised by something that they jumped!

Present the word *jack-in-the-box.* Have the children tell you what a *jack-in-the-box* looks like and how it works.

Read the story with the children.

Ask these questions:

"What does the pup have?"

"What size is the box?"

"Is the box open or shut?"

"What will the pup do to the box?"

"What will happen to the lid?"

"What will jump out of the box?"

"Will the pup be surprised?"

"What do you think the pup will do when the small man jumps up?"

Have the children find the words that have the short /o/ sound. Write them on the board.

Page 8: Following Directions

CONCEPTS: listening, following directions, ordinal numbers, colors, shapes

TEACHER GOALS: To teach the children
To listen and follow oral directions given only once,
To identify ordinal numbers through tenth,
To identify colors, and
To identify the basic shapes.

VOCABULARY: seventh, eighth, ninth, tenth

MATERIALS NEEDED: crayons, number charts, color charts

TEACHING PAGE 8:

Draw ten circles on the board and have the children go up and point to the appropriate circle:
third from the left;
first on the right;
seventh from the left;
fifth from the right; and so on.

Have a child point to and give the ordinal number for each circle from the left and another child do the same from the right.

Read the title and direction at the top of the page with the children. Have them put their fingers on the numbers to keep their places as you read the following directions only once. Tell children to listen carefully and do exactly as you say. Have color charts where children can see them.

Have the children take out the crayons needed before they begin, so that they may concentrate on the directions.

1. Color the third circle blue. Put a blue X on the fifth circle.
2. Put a black circle around the ninth square. Color the fourth square green .
3. Put a brown X on the first and last triangles. Color the tenth triangle red.

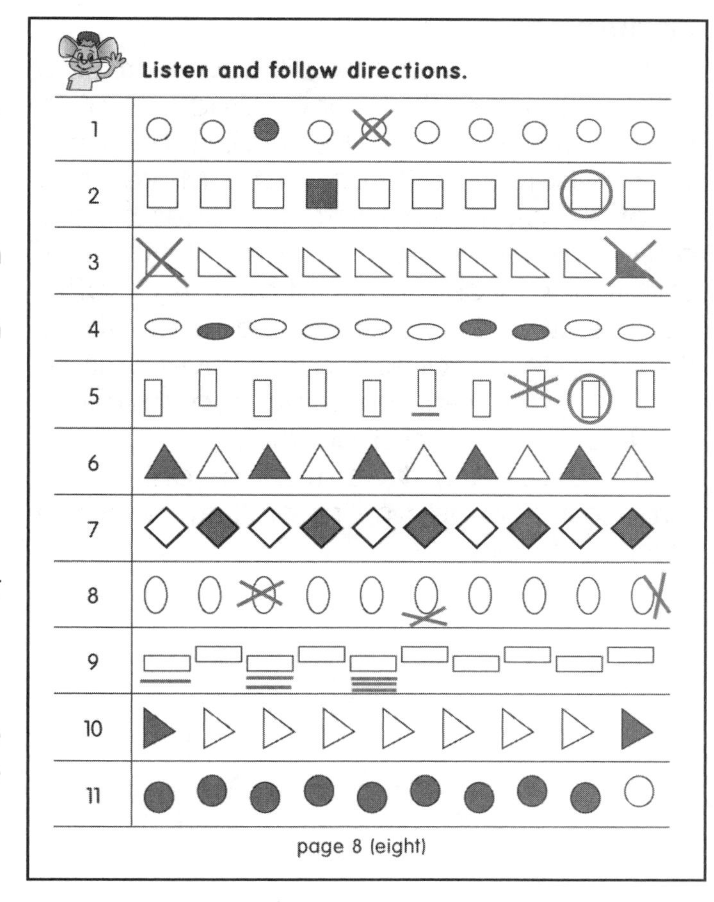

4. Color the second oval black, the seventh oval yellow, and the eighth oval purple.
5. Draw a blue line under the sixth rectangle, put a blue X on the eighth rectangle, and put a blue circle around the next to the last rectangle.
6. Color the first, third, fifth, seventh, and ninth triangles brown.
7. Color the second, fourth, sixth, eighth, and tenth diamonds orange .
8. Put a red X on the third oval, under the sixth oval, and beside the tenth oval.
9. Put one green line under the first rectangle, two green lines under the third, and three green lines under the fifth rectangle.
10. Color the first and last triangles red.
11. Color all the circles green except the last one.

The teacher should check this page.

ACTIVITY:

For children who are still having trouble following more than one direction at a time, make up a worksheet using the same shapes but in a different order. Make up a list of directions similar to the ones on this page and give them to a small group of children. Check the children's work after each row so the children can see where they made mistakes. Do this several times until the children have learned to follow more complicated directions.

If necessary, begin with only one direction and add more as they become more capable.

Page 9: Activity Page

CONCEPTS: ordinal numbers, numerals, and number words

TEACHER GOALS: To teach the children

To practice ordinal numbers through tenth, and

To teach number symbols as numerals.

VOCABULARY: numerals

MATERIALS NEEDED: word cards *one* through *ten* and *first* through *tenth*, number cards *1* through *10*, Worksheet 2 (two copies needed per student).

TEACHING PAGE 9:

Go through the flash cards for the numerals once or twice.

Note: Even though we call them *numbers* in everyday speech, children should learn that the correct name for the number symbols is *numerals*.

Go through the flash cards for the number words once or twice and have the children match them with the numeral cards. Put the flash cards for the *ordinal number words* on the ledge of the chalkboard or on a table and see how many of the children can match them with the numeral and with the number word cards.

Have a child read the direction at the top of the page. Have the children count the rabbits first by reading the numerals, then by reading the number words, and finally by reading the ordinal number words.

Point out the ordinals that are easy to remember because they are almost the same as the number words (fourth, sixth, seventh, eighth, ninth, tenth). Point out those that are different (first, second, third, fifth).

Match the *1, one,* and *first* by having the children trace the dotted lines and read the numeral and words. Let them finish the page by themselves. The teacher should check this page.

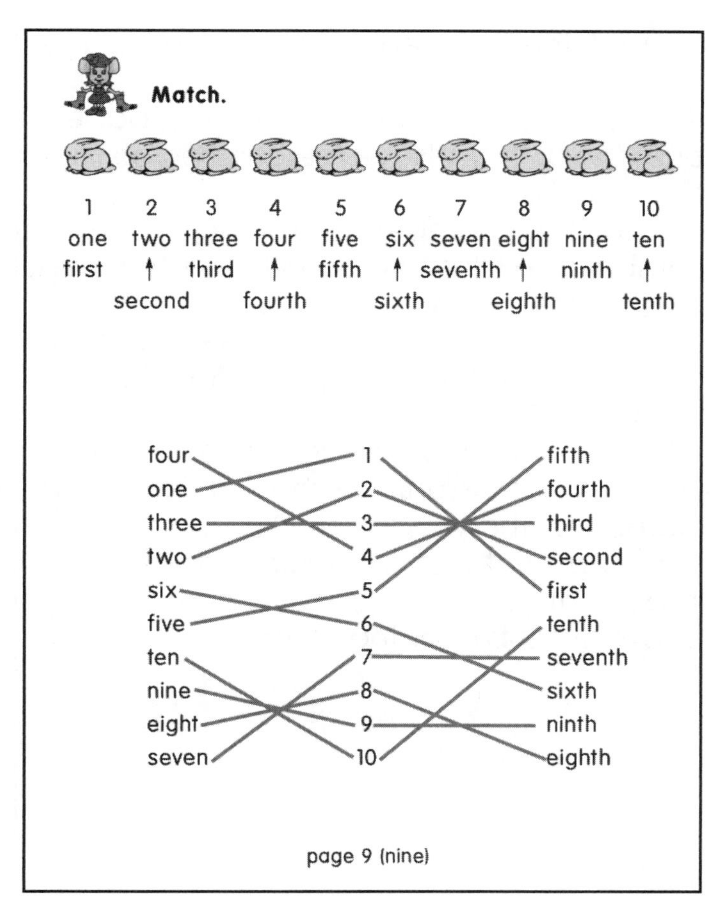

ACTIVITIES:

1. Do Worksheet 2.

Have the children tell how many cars and trucks are in the row and which direction they are facing.

Have the children write the numerals under the pictures and read them.

Have the children read the number words and the ordinal number words. Give several numbers out of order and have the children read the number word and the ordinal number word .

Example: 5—-five—fifth.

Read the direction and have the children find the vehicle pictured in the row at the top. Have them write the ordinal number words in the spaces.

Do the entire page with the children. Point out the differences in the cars—some are hard to see.

Give each child a second copy of Worksheet 2. Read the direction again and let the children complete the page independently.

The teacher should collect the papers and check them. Have the children correct any mistakes.

Use the number word and ordinal number word flash cards with children who need more practice.

2. Go through the three sets of flash cards often when you have a few minutes between classes.

3. Work with the children in small groups with flash cards until all the children have learned all the words.

4. Read stories in which numbers are important and have several counting books available for the children.

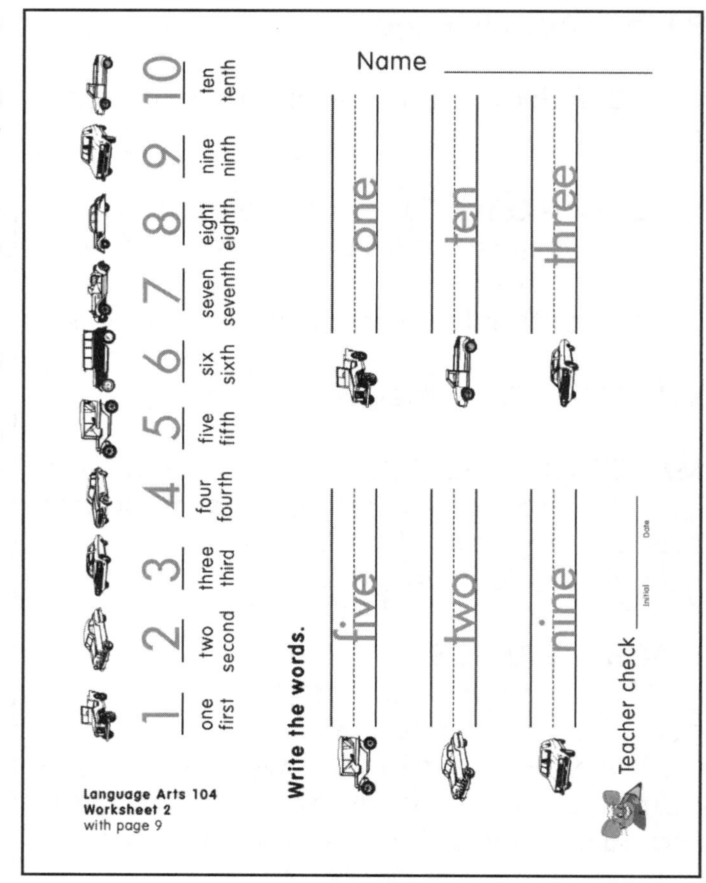

Language Arts 104
Worksheet 2
with page 9

Name ______

1 one first
2 two second
3 three third
4 four fourth
5 five fifth
6 six sixth
7 seven seventh
8 eight eighth
9 nine ninth
10 ten tenth

Write the words.

five
one
two
ten
nine
three

Teacher check ______ Initial Date

Page 10: Consonant Blends

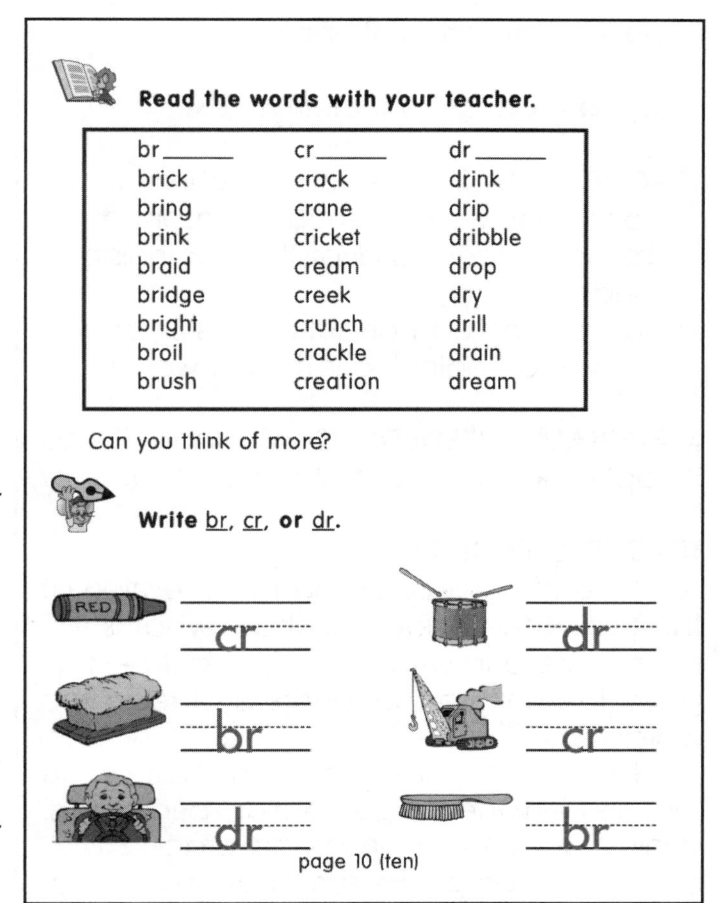

Read the words with your teacher.

br___	cr___	dr___
brick	crack	drink
bring	crane	drip
brink	cricket	dribble
braid	cream	drop
bridge	creek	dry
bright	crunch	drill
broil	crackle	drain
brush	creation	dream

Can you think of more?

Write br, cr, or dr.

cr dr

br cr

dr br

page 10 (ten)

CONCEPT: consonant blends

TEACHER GOALS: To teach the children
To identify words with the consonant blends *br, cr,* and *dr* at the beginning, and
To write the consonant blends *br, cr,* and *dr* as the beginning letters of words.

MATERIALS NEEDED: Consonant Blend Scrapbook, consonant blend card *br, cr, dr*

TEACHING PAGE 10:

Read the sentence at the top of the page with the children. Read the consonant blends.

Note: When saying the blend sounds, keep them as short as possible. Try not to say *ber* or *bru* for *br* as this distorts the word. Sometimes it may be best to say *b r* (naming the sounds) as in *bring.*

Read each word in each list and have the children say it after you. Tell them to listen for the beginning sound and to tell which two letters are at the beginning of each word. Have the children give more words if they can.

Have the children read the last direction. Have them name the pictures then write the blend. Check by having the children read the letters they wrote on the lines for each picture (crayon, drum, bread, crane, driving, brush).

Hold up the flash cards for *br, cr,* and *dr* and have the children give words that begin with those blends.

ACTIVITIES:

Add pages to the Consonant Blend Scrapbook begun with LA 104. Have the children paste pictures they cut from magazines on the pages. Words that cannot be pictured may be used in sentences and written on one section of the page.

Page 11: Consonant Blends

CONCEPT: consonant blends

TEACHER GOALS: To teach the children

To identify words with the consonant blends *br, cr,* and *dr* at the beginning and

To write the consonant blends *br, cr,* and *dr* as the beginning letters of words.

MATERIALS NEEDED: Consonant Blend Scrapbook, consonant blend card *cr, br, dr*

TEACHING PAGE 11:

Have the children read the direction at the top of the page. Ask them what is the first picture and with which blend it begins. Have them write the letters and read the word.

Have the children name the rest of the pictures on the page (braids, bricks, drill, drink, crackers, crayon, bread, crack, crawl, brain, drain, drop). Be sure they know what each one is. Tell them to say the words and listen for the beginning sounds, then to write the beginning sounds on the lines.

Check by having the children read the word and tell which blend they wrote on the lines. The teacher should check the papers and have the children correct any mistakes.

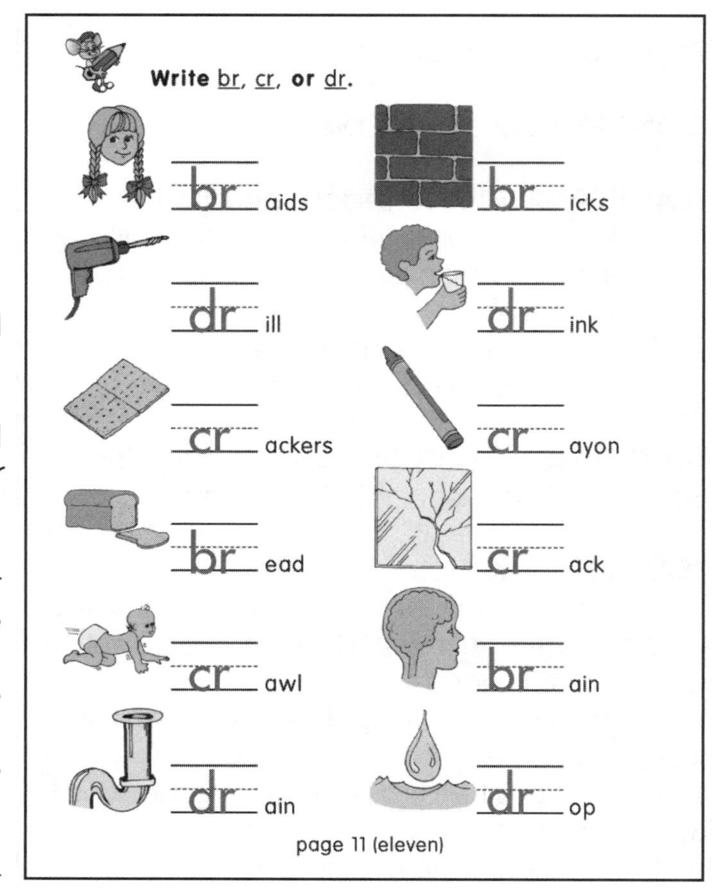

Page 12: Consonant Blends

CONCEPT: consonant blends

TEACHER GOAL: To teach the children
To identify and write the consonant blends *fr* and *gr* at the beginning of words.

MATERIALS NEEDED: *fr* and *gr* flash cards, Consonant Blend Scrapbook

TEACHING PAGE 12:

Read the sentence at the top of the page with the children. Read the consonant blends. Read each word in each list and have the children say it after you. Tell them to listen for the sounds at the beginning of the word and to tell which two letters make those sounds. Have the children think of more words.

Have a child read the next direction. Have the children name the picture, write the blend on the lines, and read the word. Check by having the children read the word and tell which letters they wrote on the lines (freckles, frog, grass, fringe, frame, grapes).

ACTIVITIES:

1. Make pages for the Consonant Blend Scrapbook. Have the children find pictures beginning with the blends and paste them on the pages. Words that cannot be pictured may be written in one section of the page and used in sentences.
2. Hold up the flash cards for *fr* and *gr* and have the children give words beginning with each.

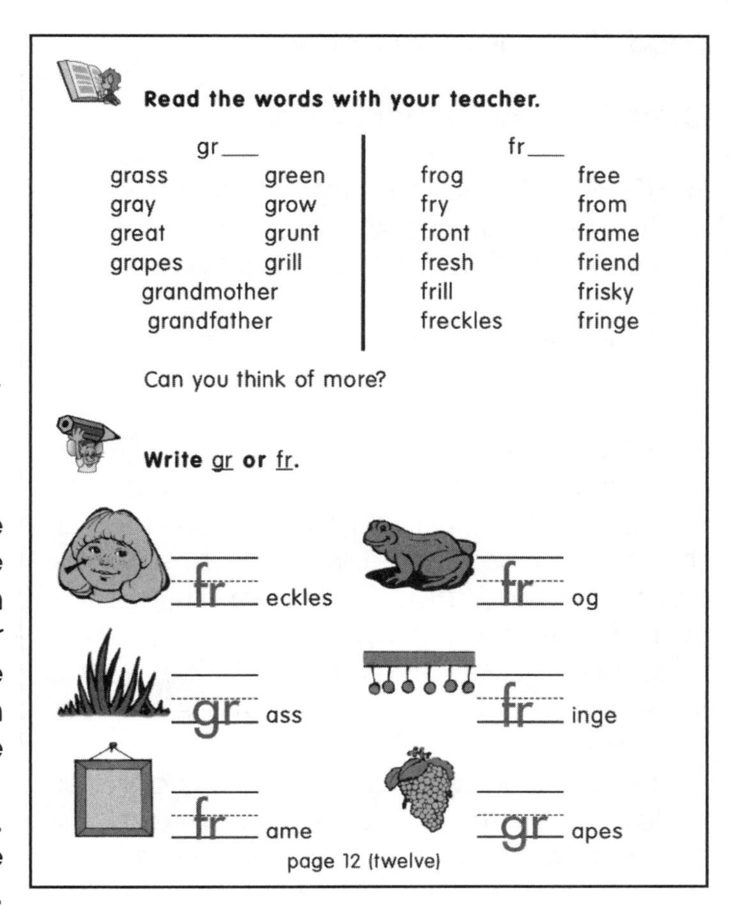

Read the words with your teacher.

gr___		fr___	
grass	green	frog	free
gray	grow	fry	from
great	grunt	front	frame
grapes	grill	fresh	friend
grandmother		frill	frisky
grandfather		freckles	fringe

Can you think of more?

Write gr or fr.

fr eckles fr og
gr ass fr inge
fr ame gr apes

page 12 (twelve)

Page 13: Consonant Blends

CONCEPT: consonant blends

TEACHER GOALS: To teach the children
To identify words with the consonant blends *fr, gr, pr,* or *tr* at the beginning, and
To write the consonant blends as the beginning letters of words.

TEACHING PAGE 13:

Read the direction at the top of the page with the children. Have them look at the first consonant blend and say the names of the letters. Ask them to give the sounds of the letters separately, then together. Have them repeat the sound several times but do not let them exaggerate it.

Read each word and have the children repeat it. When you have gone through all the words, say one of the words and have the children name the two letters at the beginning. Do this several times. Do the same for the next consonant blend.

Have the children read the next direction. Have them name the pictures and write the blend on the lines. Check by having the children tell the two letters they wrote for each picture. Have them read the words again (prunes, frame, tree, tray, grapes, praying).

ACTIVITIES:

Give the children many opportunities to identify consonant blends. Use words from their reading, writing, or daily conversation, and ask them to name the two beginning letters.

TEACHING READING:

Read the story "Pigs" in Reader 2.

Present the words *cob, grab, slip, trip* and *grip.* Write them on the board and have the children read them. Tell the meaning of each word.

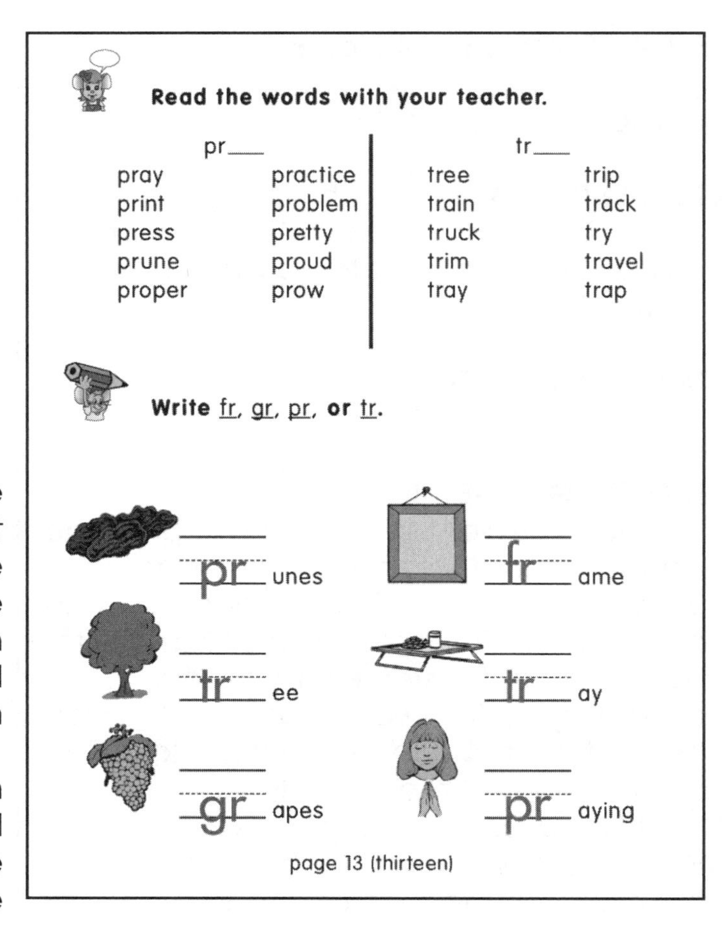

Read the words with your teacher.

pr___		tr___	
pray	practice	tree	trip
print	problem	train	track
press	pretty	truck	try
prune	proud	trim	travel
proper	prow	tray	trap

Write fr, gr, pr, or tr.

pr unes

fr ame

tr ee

tr ay

gr apes

pr aying

page 13 (thirteen)

Have the children look at the picture. Talk about the pigs and what they might be
doing.

Have the children read the story silently.

Ask questions similar to these:

"Where are the pigs?"

"What are they standing and sitting in?"

"What are the pigs after?"

"Will the pigs get the cobs?"

"What will they do with the cobs?"

Have the children find the *gr, tr,* and *sl* words. Write them on the board.

Page 14: Consonant Blends

CONCEPT: consonant blends

TEACHER GOALS: To teach the children
To identify words with the consonant blends *fr, gr, pr,* or *tr* at the beginning, and
To write the consonant blends as the beginning letters of words.

MATERIALS NEEDED: Worksheet 3

TEACHING PAGE 14:
Have the children read the direction at the top of the page and the consonant blends.
Have the teacher name the pictures and let the students tell which blend is at the beginning. When they have done the whole page, tell them to say the name of the picture and to write the blend on the lines. Let them finish the page.
Check by having the children name the picture and tell which blend they wrote on the lines (frame, problem, grass, tree, pressing, grill, train, praying, track, grandfather, trap, prunes).
Have them give other words beginning with each of the blends.

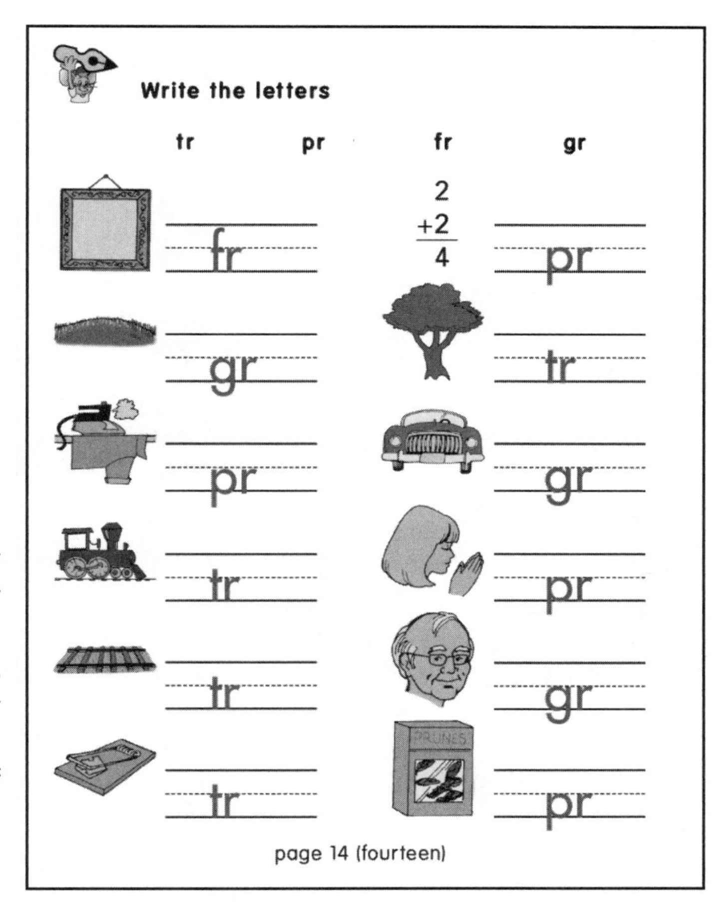

ACTIVITIES:
1. Dictate the following words and have the children write them on a sheet of writing tablet paper.

tree	pray
truck	print
trap	prim
trim	prick
trip	prop

Collect the papers and check them. Have the children write misspelled words five times on the back of their paper. Be sure they know the meanings of the words and can use them in sentences.

2. Do Worksheet 3.
Have the children read the direction at the top of the page. Tell the children to look at the pictures, to say the name of the picture, then to circle the beginning letters. Do the first box together.
Check by having children name the picture and tell which letters they circled. The teacher also should check this page to see which children may still need help on consonant blends (clam, tree, glasses, frog, plow, crow, praying, sled, blister, bread, plug, truck, slide, flag, broom, grapes, drum, blouse, grass, tray).
3. Children who need help should work with the charts for the letters or with the Consonant Blends Scrapbook.

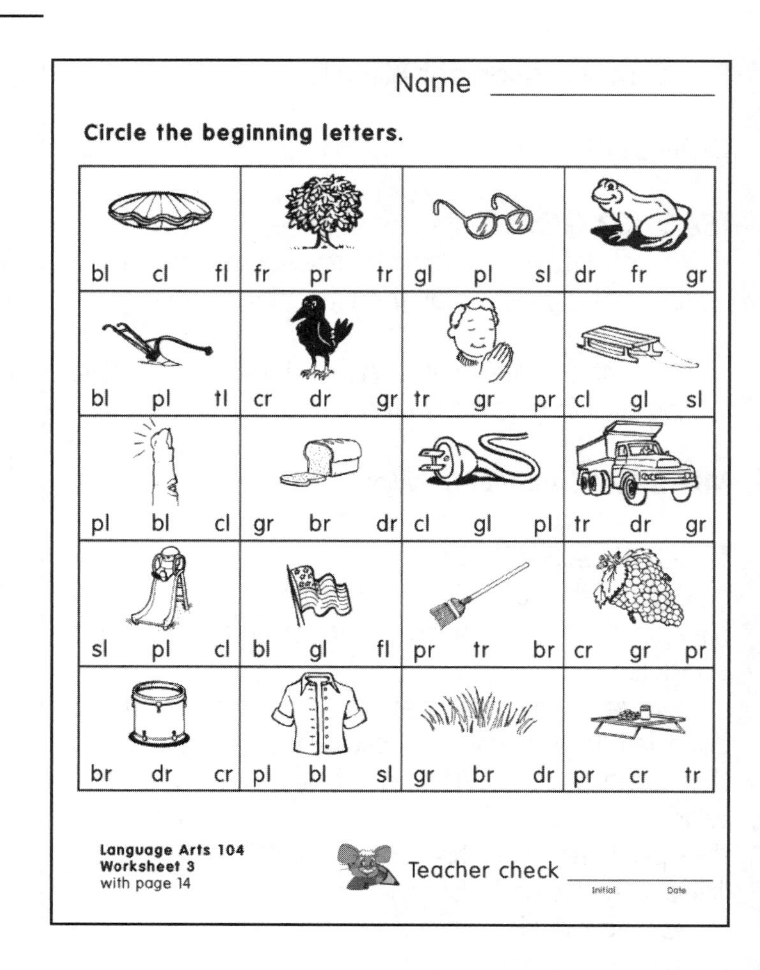

Name ____________

Circle the beginning letters.

bl cl fl	fr pr tr	gl pl sl	dr fr gr
bl pl tl	cr dr gr	tr gr pr	cl gl sl
pl bl cl	gr br dr	cl gl pl	tr dr gr
sl pl cl	bl gl fl	pr tr br	cr gr pr
br dr cr	pl bl sl	gr br dr	pr cr tr

Language Arts 104
Worksheet 3
with page 14

Teacher check ____________
Initial Date

SELF TEST 1

CONCEPTS: letter blends, ordinal numbers, cardinal numbers, consonant blends, and oral directions

TEACHER GOAL: To teach the children
To check their own progress periodically.

TEACHING PAGE 15:

Ask the children to tell what a Self Test is.

Read all the directions on the page with the children. Be sure they understand what they are to do. Name the pictures (flag, clock, sled, brush, tree, frame). Have the children circle the third bunny and draw a line over the next to the last bunny. Let the children finish the page.

Check the page as soon as possible and go over it with each child so he can see where he did well and where he needs extra help.

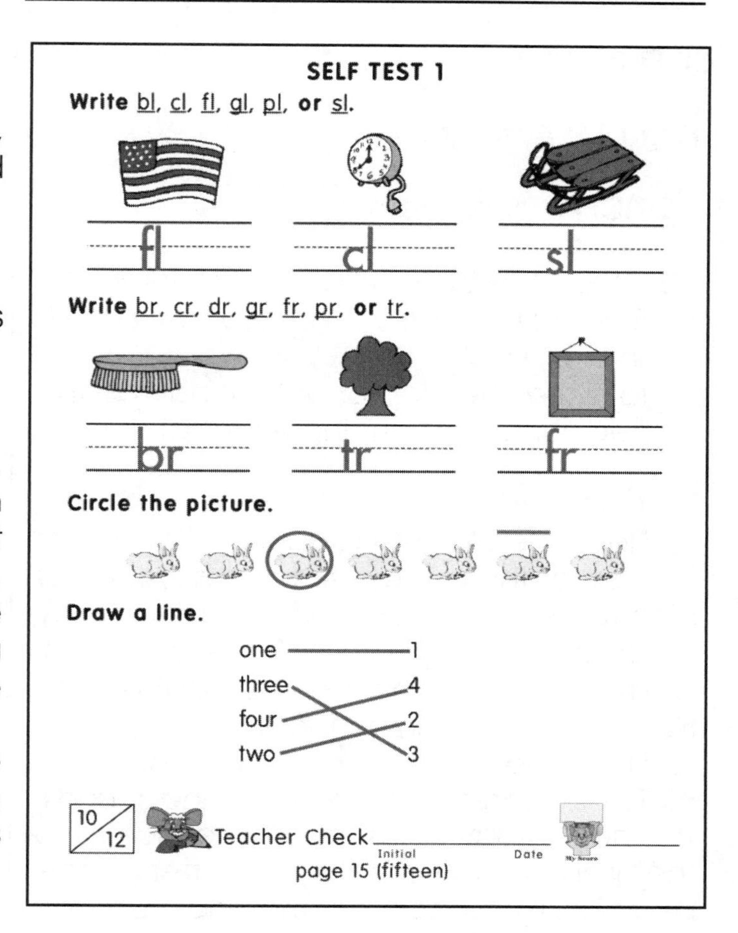

ACTIVITIES:

1. Give individual help on items missed.
2. If several children miss the same things, reteach the skills (in small groups, if possible).

SPELLING WORDS:

block
cluck
flag
glad
plan
grass
grip
frog
press
trim

II. PART TWO

Page 16: Activity Page

CONCEPT: consonant blends

TEACHER GOALS: To teach the children
To identify words with consonant blends *sn* or *st, and*
To write the consonant blends as the beginning and ending letters of words.

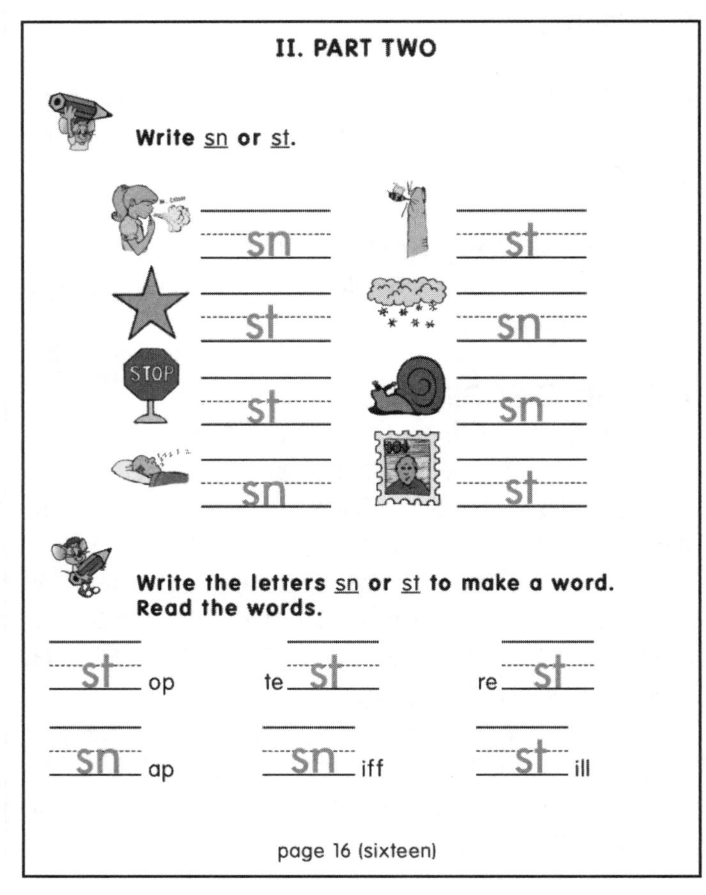
II. PART TWO

Write sn or st.

sn st
st sn
st sn
sn st

Write the letters sn or st to make a word. Read the words.

st op te st re st
sn ap sn iff st ill

page 16 (sixteen)

TEACHING PAGE 16:

Have the children read the direction at the top of the page. Ask what is in the first picture (sneeze), and what sounds they hear at the beginning of the word. Ask what letters they should write on the lines. Have them write *sn* on the line.

Have the children name the rest of the pictures, listening for the beginning sounds. Tell them to say the name of the picture to themselves and write the two letters at the beginning of each on the lines. Let the children finish the exercise by themselves.

Check by having the children name the picture and tell which letters they wrote on the lines (sneeze, sting, star, snow, stop, snail, snore, stamp).

Have the children read the second direction and sentence. Tell the children to read the part of the word that is there, then to write *sn* or *st* in the space to make a word. Do the first one together. Have the children read the direction and word endings in the middle of the page and the sentence at the bottom. Have the children give several rhyming words for each pair of endings.

Have the children do the page by themselves and write more rhyming words on the sheet of writing tablet paper. Give help if needed .

Check the first exercise by writing the correct words on the board. Have the children check their own papers and correct any mistakes. Have the children read all the words.

TEACHING READING:

Read the story "Fish, Fish, Fish" in *Reader 2.*

Have the children look at the picture and tell what is happening. Let them share their fishing experiences. Have a child read the title. Ask a child to tell what the story will be about and how they know before they read the story. (The title should be the main idea of the story.)

Let the children read the story silently.

Ask questions similar to these:

"What is the story about?"

"Who will catch fish?"

"What will they do with them?"

"When will they go fishing?"

"How many exclamations are there in the story?" Have a child read the sentence.

"What is the punctuation mark at the end of the exclamation?"

"Will the sun get hot?"

"Will the boys stop?"

"Do they like to fish?"

Have a child read the story again and find all the short vowel words. Read a sentence at a time and have children tell which words they found.

Have the children tell which word has the sound of *st* .

ACTIVITIES:

1. Make a large wall mural on wrapping paper or sheets of newsprint. Draw and color or paint brightly colored fish and other underwater plants and animals.

2. Read stories about fishing and articles about fish from science books, encyclopedias, or sports magazines.

Page 17: Activity Page

CONCEPT: consonant blends

TEACHER GOAL: To teach the children
To identify words with consonant blends *sk, sp, str, scr, spr.*

MATERIALS NEEDED: Worksheet 4

TEACHING PAGE 17:

Have the children read the direction at the top of the page. Ask a child to tell what is in the first picture and with which blend it begins. Have the children write the *sp* on the line. (spoon)

Have the children name the rest of the pictures and write the blend with which each begins (skates, spool, skirt, spot, skis).

Check by having the children name the picture and tell which blend they wrote on the lines.

Have the children read the next direction and the letter clusters. Have the children sound out and read the lists of words. Have them tell the meaning of each word or use it in a sentence.

ACTIVITIES:

Do Worksheet 4.

Have a child read the next direction. Ask what the picture in the first box is (desk). Ask where they hear the */sk/* sound. Have them circle the—*sk* to show that it is an ending sound.

Have the children name the rest of the pictures (desk, nest, spool, moth, fish, catcher, basket, blister, wasp, mother, ship, chain).

Ask the children to give the sounds for *th, sh, sp, ch,* and *tch.* Tell them to listen carefully for the sound at the bottom of the box as they say the name of the picture. Tell them to circle the sound in the right place. Check by having the children name the picture and tell where they heard the sound. The teacher should recheck this page and have the children correct any mistakes.

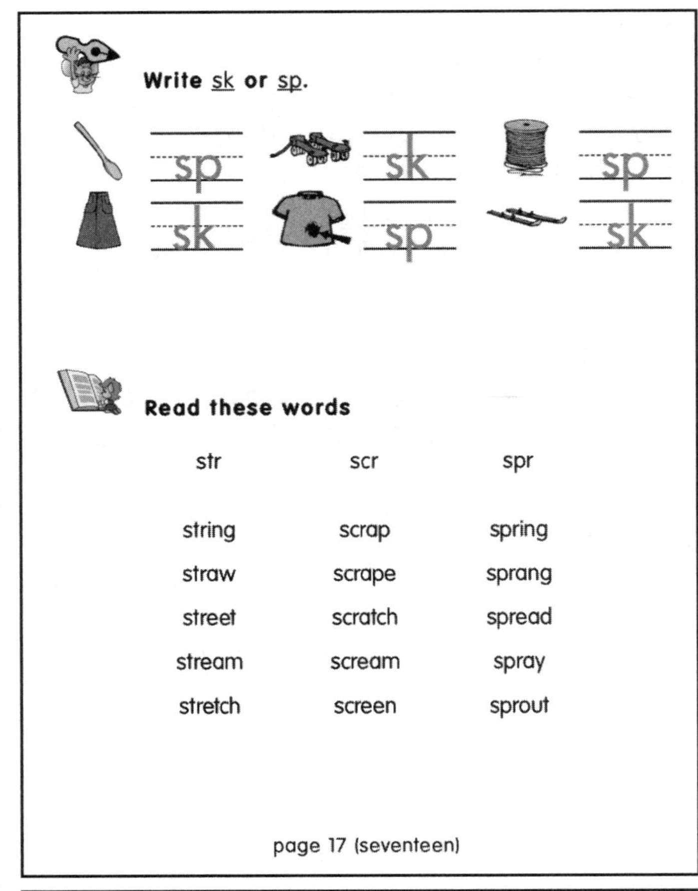

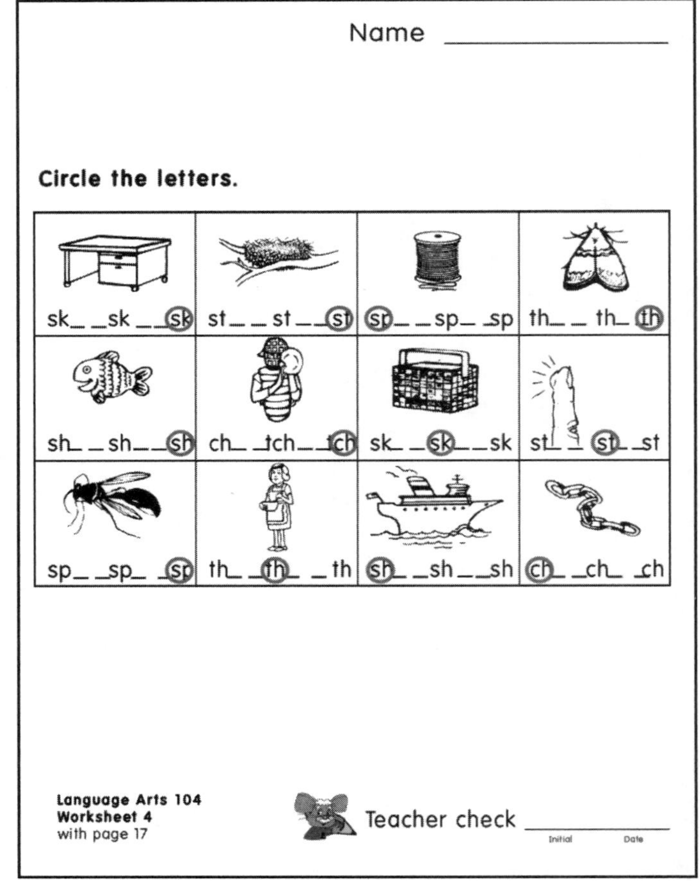

Page 18: Activity Page

CONCEPT: consonant blends

TEACHER GOALS: To teach the children

To identify words used with the sounds of *nd, nt, ng, nk,* and

To write *nd, nt, ng, nk* as the ending letters of words

TEACHING PAGE 18:

Have the children read the direction at the top of the page. Have the children name the letters in each blend and say the sound of each. Tell them that these blends are never found at the beginning of words, only in the middle or at the end. Remind the children that the *nk* and *ng* sounds are made in the nose and have a very different sound. Have them say *sing* and *sink* and listen for the sound at the end of each *(nk* should sound like *ngk).*

Read each word in each list and have the children repeat it after you. Then have them read each list and listen for the ending sound.

Have the children read the next directions. Have them write the endings and read the pairs of words.

Do the same for *nk* and *ng.*

ACTIVITY:

Dictate the following words and have the children write them on a sheet of writing tablet paper. Collect the papers. Correct them by drawing a line through each misspelled word and writing the correct word on the line behind it. Have the children write each word they misspelled five times on the back of the paper (hand, bend, bunk, sing, hang, pant).

TEACHING READING:

Read the story "Ann and the Fish" in *Reader 2.*

Present the words *still, grab* and *string.* Ask the children to give the meaning of the words.

Read these words.

__nd	__nt	__ng	__nk
hand	bent	sing	sink
send	pint	bang	bank
find	pant	rung	bunk
sound	punt	wrong	honk

Write nd and nt. Read the words.

be__nd__ se__nd__ spe__nd__

be__nt__ se__nt__ spe__nt__

Write nk and ng. Read the words.

ba__nk__ sa__nk__ thi__nk__

ba__ng__ sa__ng__ thi__ng__

page 18 (eighteen)

Have the children look at the picture and tell what is happening. Have them read the title of the story. Have the children read the story silently.

Let two or three children tell the story in their own words.

Ask these questions:

"Who will fish with Ann?"

"Why does Ann sit still?"

"What will grab the string on her fishing pole?"

"Why will Ann jump?"

"Why will Ann hop and tug?"

"What will Ann catch?"

Have the children find the *ng* word in the story. Have them find the *st* and *str* words.

ACTIVITY:

Let the children work out a playlet for the story. Let several groups play the story.

Page 19: Activity Page

CONCEPTS: silent consonants; *ph* and *gh* as the sound of *f*

Teacher Goals: To teach the children
To know about silent letters,
To learn that *ph* and *gh* sometimes have the sound of *f.*

MATERIALS NEEDED: magazines or newspapers

TEACHING PAGE 19:

Have the children read the direction and question at the top of the page. Read each word and have the children repeat it after you. Have them tell which letter is silent. Be sure the children understand that the letters must be put in when they write the words, even though they do not hear them.

Have the children tell the meaning of each word or use it in a sentence.

Have the next set of directions read by the children. Read each word and have the children listen for the sound of *f* Have them tell which letters make the sound.

This page is only an introduction. Do not expect the children to master the spelling or pronunciation of all these words.

ACTIVITY:

Have the children find words with silent letters or with the sound of *f* in newspapers or magazines.

Read the words.
Which letters are silent?

lam**b**	com**b**	ta**l**k	fo**l**k
lim**b**	tom**b**	wa**l**k	ha**l**f
gnash	**g**nu	li**gh**t	thou**gh**
gnat	si**g**n	ni**gh**t	thou**gh**t
knife	**k**nock	lis**t**en	of**t**en
know	**k**nee	fas**t**en	whis**t**le

Do you know what each word means?

Read these words. Listen for the ph and gh with the sound of f.

tele**ph**one	**ph**rase	lau**gh**
ele**ph**ant	**ph**onics	tou**gh**
phonogra**ph**	**ph**ysical	rou**gh**
photogra**ph**	**Ph**araoh	trou**gh**

page 19 (nineteen)

Page 20: Real or Make-Believe

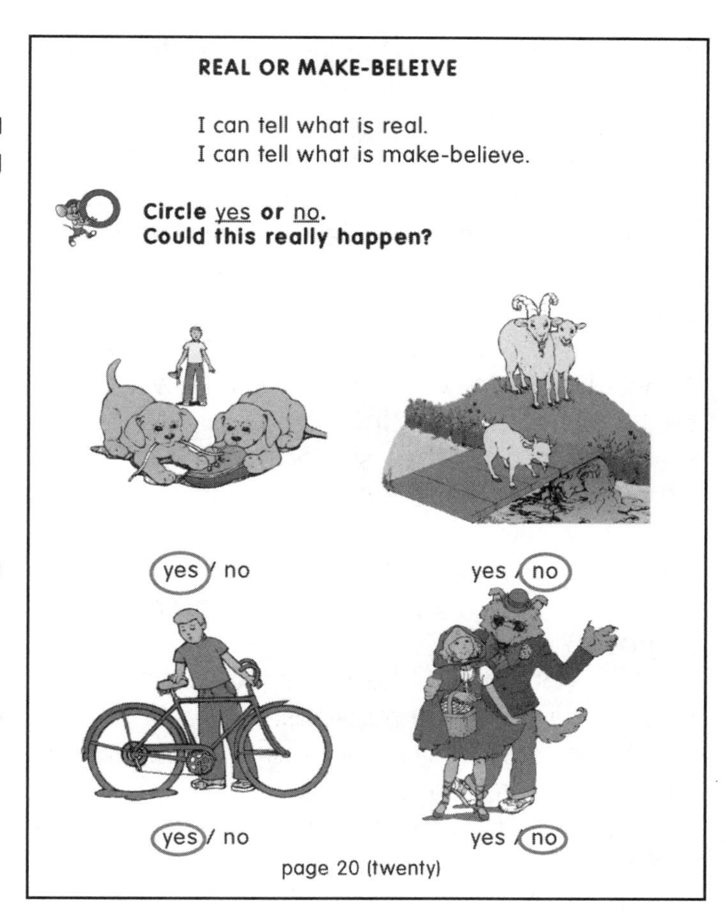

CONCEPTS: real or make-believe, telling a story, making inferences, predicting outcomes, speaking in a group

TEACHER GOALS: To teach the children
- To tell whether a picture shows a real situation or a make-believe one,
- To tell a story from a picture,
- To tell the main idea of the story or picture,
- To note and recall details of a story,
- To make inferences from a picture,
- To predict what might happen next in a situation, and
- To speak in a group with confidence.

MATERIALS NEEDED: storytelling rules (see TN for LAN 102, page 20)

VOCABULARY: make-believe

TEACHING PAGE 20:

Read the title, sentences, and the direction with the children.

Have the children look at the first picture and tell what is happening. Have them circle the *yes*.

Tell the children to look at the other three pictures carefully and to circle the *yes* if the picture shows something that could really happen or the *no* if it is a make-believe situation.

Have the children tell which word they circled and why. Ask what they think happened before what they see in the picture; what might happen next; what time of day or year it is and how they know; how the people feel; whether they would feel the same way; whether something could have been done so this would not have happened; what would be the right thing to do; and so on.

ACTIVITIES:

1. Have the children choose a story and tell it to the class. Before they begin, go through the rules for telling stories they learned earlier in the year.
2. Read stories about real children doing real things.
3. Read stories, such as fairy tales, that are obviously make-believe. Ask the children why the stories are not real.

TEACHING READING:

Give each student a cut-out pattern of a lamb and 2-3 cotton balls. Have them cut out the lamb and glue on the cotton balls. Create a pasture with a large green paper and staple or tape each lamb to the "pasture". Ask students who takes care of the lambs. If they don't know, tell them about shepherds and the job they have. Ask them why lambs might need a shepherd. (dangers —wolves, lost, etc.) Ask students if they have any stories about a time when they got lost. Ask: How did you feel? What did you do? Who found you? etc.

Read the story "Little Lamb" together and then ask the following questions:

"Who is this story about?" (Little Lamb)

"Why did the shepherd tell Little Lamb to stay inside the white fence?" (dangers)

"Why didn't Little Lamb listen?" (couldn't be that bad, same old grassy field)

"What happened when the Shepherd saw Little Lamb was missing? (he watched by the fence, he didn't rest)

"When did the shepherd hear Little Lamb?" (just before the sun came up)

"How did the shepherd feel when he saw Little Lamb?" (glad)

"How do you know?" (he gave her a big hug)

"Do you think Little Lamb will wander off again?" (no) Give reasons.

"Who does the Shepherd remind you of?" (Jesus) Give reasons.

Find words with silent letters: mb, kn, gh (lamb, knew, high, night)

Find the contractions: (couldn't, didn't)

ACTIVITY:

Share the story about the Good Shepherd in the Bible (John 10) (appropriate level). Write on the board: "I am the Good Shepherd. I know My sheep, and My sheep know Me." Have students copy this in their best handwriting. Discuss what Jesus meant by these words.

Have students draw a picture of Jesus as the Good Shepherd. Have students share ways Jesus takes care of them. Have students write a letter to Little Lamb telling him why he should listen to the Good Shepherd.

Sing the song: "Jesus Loves Me".

Page 21: Activity Page

CONCEPT: short *u*

TEACHER GOALS: To teach the children
To identify the short /*u*/ sound in words, and
To read words with the short /*u*/ sound.

TEACHING PAGE 21:

Say a short *u* word and ask the children to give a rhyming word.

Read the direction at the top of the page with the children.

Read both lists of words. Ask which word rhymes with *cub* and have the children trace the line. Let the children match the rest of the rhyming words and read them.

Read the next set of directions or have a child read them. Read the endings and have the children trace and read the dotted words. Let the children finish the page by themselves.

Prepare a sheet of writing tablet paper by folding it in half. Have the children write two of the endings on each side of the folded paper and write rhyming words.

Check the rhyming words by writing the endings on the board and having the children read words from their lists for you to write under the proper ending. The children should correct spellings and add words to their lists from those on the board. Read all the lists again.

The teacher should check both this page and the tablet page.

ACTIVITIES:

1. Dictate three words from each list and have the children write them on a sheet of writing tablet paper. Correct the children's papers and have them write each misspelled words five times on the back of their paper.
2. Have the children make the endings *um, un, ub,* or *ud* on their desks with their alphabet cards one at a time. Give a word and have the children put the beginning letter in front of the ending. Have them read the word before you give the next word.

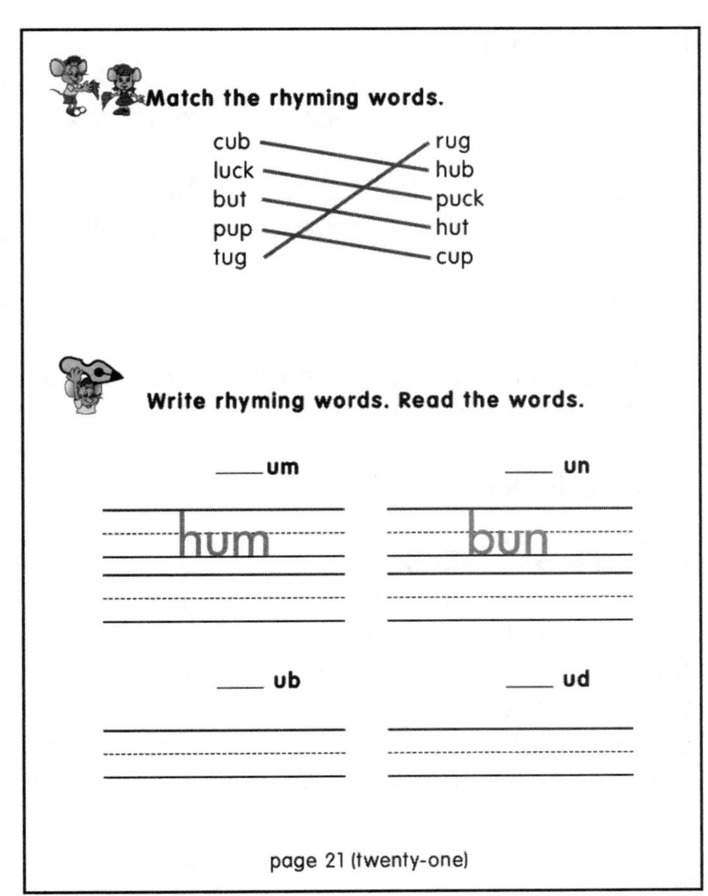

Page 22: Short u

CONCEPTS: sound of short *u,* rhyming words

TEACHER GOALS: To teach the children
To write and read rhyming words with endings *ump, uck, up, us,* and *uss,*
To identify the short /u/ sound in the words, and
To identify words in which the *o* has the sound of short *u.*

VOCABULARY: tablet

TEACHING PAGE 22:

Have the children read the direction at the top of the page. Say each ending in turn and have the children give two or three words that rhyme with it. Have the children fold a sheet of writing tablet paper and write the endings on it so that it will be ready to use.

Read the direction at the middle of the page and have the children repeat it. Have them look at the words and listen for the short /u/ sound as you read the words again.

Talk about the last sentence. Let the children tell how they know that Jesus loves them.

Let the children write the rhyming words on the lines at the top of the page and complete the sheet of writing tablet paper that they prepared earlier.

Check by having the children read words from their lists for you to put under the endings you have written on the board. Read all the lists several times. The teacher should check these pages.

Write rhyming words. Read the words.

___ump   ___uck

___up   ___us   ___uss

Write more words in your LIFEPAC Tablet.

In some words the o has the short u sound.

love	dove
other	glove
brother	shovel

Can you think of more?

Read the sentence. Write it in your Tablet.

We **love** each **other** because Jesus **loves** us.

page 22 (twenty-two)

ACTIVITIES:

1. Have the children make the short *u* endings *ump, uck, up,* and *us* or *uss* on their desk one at a time with alphabet cards. Give words such as *jump, bump, lump,* and have the children put the beginning letter in front of the ending. Have them read the word before you give the next one.

2. Dictate the following words and have the children write them on a sheet of writing tablet paper. Correct the papers and have the children write any misspelled words five times on the back of their paper.

jump	cluck
bump	bus
hump	fuss
cup	Jesus
duck	love

3. Read and discuss stories about Jesus' love for little children.

TEACHING READING:

2. Read the story "Glad Tammy" in *Reader*

Present the words, *she* and *shoes.* Write them on the board. Have the children use them in a sentence.

Have the children read the story silently. *Ask these questions:*

"Who is glad?"
"What will Tammy do?"
"Why is Tammy glad?"
"Who will Tammy thank?"

Have the children find the *gl* word in the story. Have them find the *cl* word in the story. Write these words on the board. Have them find the *ump* word. Have them find the *th* word that appears two times in the story. Point out the *nk* at the end of thank.

ACTIVITY:

Have the children think of the things for which they are thankful. Write these on the board. Encourage them to think of the things they may take for granted, such as food, clothes, or a bed. Have several children pray a prayer of thanksgiving for the things God has provided. Remind the children that God has provided someone to care for them at home, whether it be a mom and dad, grandparents, or someone else. Include these people in your prayer of thanksgiving.

Page 23: Sentences

CONCEPTS: sentences, subject-verb agreement, plurals

TEACHER GOALS: To teach the children
To tell which sentences are statements, and
To tell if a subject is singular or plural and whether the verb agrees with it.

TEACHING PAGE 23:

Ask the children to name the three kinds of sentences and tell what punctuation mark is at the end of each one. Ask how the first word of a sentence must begin. Have the children give examples of statements, questions, and exclamations. Have them use good expression.

Ask the children to tell what a plural is and to give some examples.

Read the title and directions with the children.

Tell the children to listen to the sentences carefully as they read them and decide which sentence sounds better. Ask them what kind of sentence each one is.

Ask the children to tell which words have the short /u/ sound in them, and which words are plurals.

Do the first two sets with children, then let them complete the page by themselves. Help if needed.

Check by having the children read the sentence they underlined.

Go directly to the next page.

WHICH SOUNDS BETTER?

I can tell which words sound better.

Read the sentences.
Draw a line under the one that sounds better.

A buck can **jumps**.
A buck can **jump**.

This duck **is** white.
This duck **are** white.

The trucks **is** stuck.
The trucks **are** stuck.

I **have** two mugs.
I **has** two mugs.

Here **come** the bus.
Here **comes** the bus.

page 23 (twenty-three)

TEACHING READING:

If possible, play circus music. Survey students to see how many have been to the circus. Have them tell about their favorite part of the circus. List everything they can tell about it. Give students paper, crayons and scissors. Have them each choose something different from the list of circus animals and events. Have them draw, color and cut out their work. Combine their work on a board to make the classroom circus. Tell students they're going to read a story about a boy who was excited to go to the circus. Tell them to listen carefully to find out his favorite thing about the circus.

Read the story "Cotton Candy" together then answer the following questions:

"What is the boy's name?" (Alex)

"Has he ever been to the circus?" (yes)

"How do you know?" (it says he went last summer, he couldn't wait to see it again)

"Why was Alex so excited about going to the circus?" (he liked cotton candy)

"Did he get cotton candy right away?" (no)

"What are some of the things he saw first?" (big tent, acrobats, dancing dogs)

"Who went to the circus with Alex?" (his family — parents and sister)

"What did Alex and his sister get?" (balloons)

"How did Alex act when he had to wait for cotton candy?" angry silly patient sad

"How much did the cotton candy cost?" (10 cents)

"What do you think Alex would've done if he didn't have the ten cents?" (answers will vary)

"Do you think Alex will want to go to the circus next year?" (yes)

Share responses that tell why. Find words that have the sounds of c. c /k/ and c /s/ (circus, excited, nice, dance, cents; cotton candy, couldn't, can, clowns, pocket, came, acts, smack, acrobats)

ACTIVITY:

Create a class circus! Brainstorm acts students could do to entertain the others. Put students in small groups to perform their acts. Pop popcorn! Make clown masks. Make posters advertising the circus.

Page 24: Activity Page

CONCEPTS: sentences, subject-verb agreement, plurals, paragraphs

TEACHER GOALS: To teach the children
To tell what kind of sentence,
To tell what words are plurals, and
To tell if the subject and verb agree.

VOCABULARY: copy

TEACHING PAGE 24:

This should be done in the same class period as the previous page.

Read the directions with the children. Have the children read each sentence including the two words under each line. Have them circle the word that makes sense in the sentence and copy it on the line. Have them read the sentence again to be sure they have chosen the right word. Have them tell which word they chose and have them spell the word. The teacher should check this page.

Read the direction at the bottom of the page with the children. Tell them something about a duck. Ask if anyone can remember what several sentences about the same thing is called. Someone should remember that it is called a paragraph. Ask the children to tell what they must remember when writing sentences.

Collect the papers, check them, and have the children recopy the paragraph if they have misspelled more than one or two words, if the letters are poorly made, or if the paper is messy.

ACTIVITIES:

Have the children draw a picture to go with their paragraph about a duck. The children may show their picture and read their paragraphs to the class.

Note: Always take time as soon as possible after the children finish their writing to let them read it to the class. This helps them learn to stand in front of a group and speak. It will also encourage them to be more creative in their writing and drawing because they know they will be sharing it with their classmates.

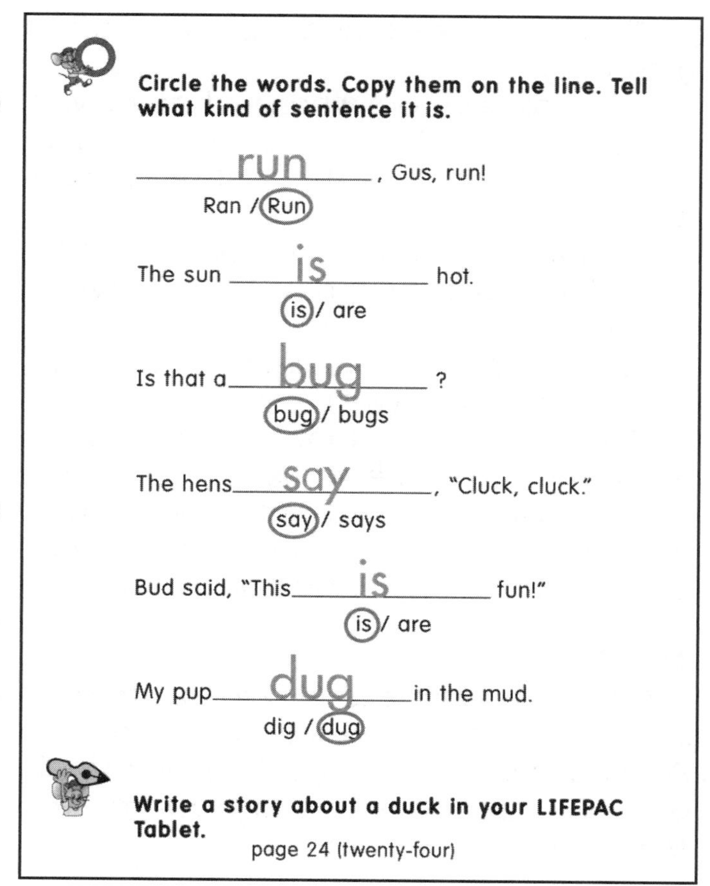
Circle the words. Copy them on the line. Tell what kind of sentence it is.

run, Gus, run!
Ran / (Run)

The sun is hot.
(is) / are

Is that a bug?
(bug) / bugs

The hens say, "Cluck, cluck."
(say) / says

Bud said, "This is fun!"
(is) / are

My pup dug in the mud.
dig / (dug)

Write a story about a duck in your LIFEPAC Tablet.

page 24 (twenty-four)

TEACHING READING:

Ask students to share times when someone has played a trick on them. Some tricks are meant to be in fun, but are there tricks that can be harmful? Discuss feelings and outcomes – trust.

Read the story "The Last Trick" then answer the following questions:

Why were Jack's brothers mad at him? (he played too many tricks)

What did Jed and Jim think Jack needed when he called them? (help)

How many times did Jack call for help altogether? (three)

What happened to Jack the third time? (he was stuck in the tree)

Was it a trick this time? (no)

How do you know? (he was afraid, he was sad, he knew they didn't trust him)

Who finally came to help him? (his Uncle Mick)

Why did Uncle Mick help Jack? (he told him it wasn't a trick, he learned his lesson)

Find words with short vowels.

Find words with silent letters (laughed, know, knew, highest, climbed)

Find words with beginning blends (brothers, trick, smaller, climbed, branch, played, trust, stuck)

ACTIVITY:

Teach the children some activities which require TRUST such as leading a blindfolded buddy from one place to another. Write the word TRUSTWORTHY on the board. Explain what it means and how important it is for each of them to say and do things so others will trust them. Discuss this in terms of what God expects from each of us. Have students copy Ps. 37:3 "Trust in the Lord and do good." Have students draw a picture to go with the verse. Share the fable about the Boy Who Cried Wolf.

Page 25: Sequence

CONCEPTS: sequence, real or make-believe, telling a story

TEACHER GOALS: To teach the children
To put the parts of a story into proper sequence,
To tell which stories could really happen and which are make-believe,
To tell a story from pictures,
To make inferences about the stories, and
To predict what might happen next in the stories.

MATERIALS NEEDED: pencils, storytelling rules, Worksheets 5 and 6

TEACHING PAGE 25:

Read the title and directions with the children, or have a child read them. Have the children point to the numerals and the ordinal number words and read them.

Tell the children to look at the three pictures carefully, then to number them in the order in which they happened. Have someone recite the nursery rhyme for the second group of pictures. Let the children complete the page, then check it. (Row 1: 2, 1, 3 Row 2: 3, 2, 1, Row 3: 1, 3, 2)

Ask questions such as these about each series of pictures:

"Could this really happen?"

"What do you think happened just before this?"

"What time of day is it? What year? How can you tell?"

"Have you ever done anything like this?"

"How do the people feel? Would you feel that way?"

"What do you think will happen next?"

"What could have happened instead of what picture three shows?"

"What is the weather like? How do you know?"

Let the children choose a set of pictures to tell a story about. Review the rules for telling stories (stand straight, talk clearly, etc.).

ACTIVITIES:

1. Do Worksheet 5.

Have the children read the direction at the top of the page.

Tell them to look at the pictures carefully and to number them in the order they happened. Check by having the children tell which picture shows what happened first, second, and last. (Row 1: 1,3,2 Row 2: 2,1,3 Row 3: 1,2,3 Row 4: 3,1,2)

Have the children answer questions about the series of pictures such as these:

"What happened just before picture 1?"

"What might happen after picture 3?"

"What time of day is it? What year?"

"Is this something that could really happen or is it make believe?"

"Where is this taking place?" "What kind of weather do you think it is? How can you tell?"

Have the children choose a series of pictures and tell the story to the class. Remind them of the rules for telling stories before they begin.

2. Do Worksheet 6.

Have the children read the title and direction at the top of the page. Tell them to look at the pictures and to number them in the order they happened. Check by having the children tell which picture came first, next, and last. (Row 1: 2, 3, 1)

Have the children read the next direction. Tell them to read the letters and numbers, then to write them on the lines in order. The first one in each row is done for them. Be sure the alphabet chart and number line are where the children can see them if they need help. Write the letters and numbers on the board and have the children check their own papers. Have them correct any mistakes.

3. Have the children illustrate a story they have written or one they have heard or read. Have them divide a sheet of drawing paper into three parts and draw three important parts of the story on it. Remind the children that the first picture should come from the first part ot the story, the second from the middle part, and the third from the last part of the story. They may color or paint their pictures.

4 Read stories or rhymes that have a definite sequence of events such as "The Three Little Pigs" or "The Little Engine That Could".

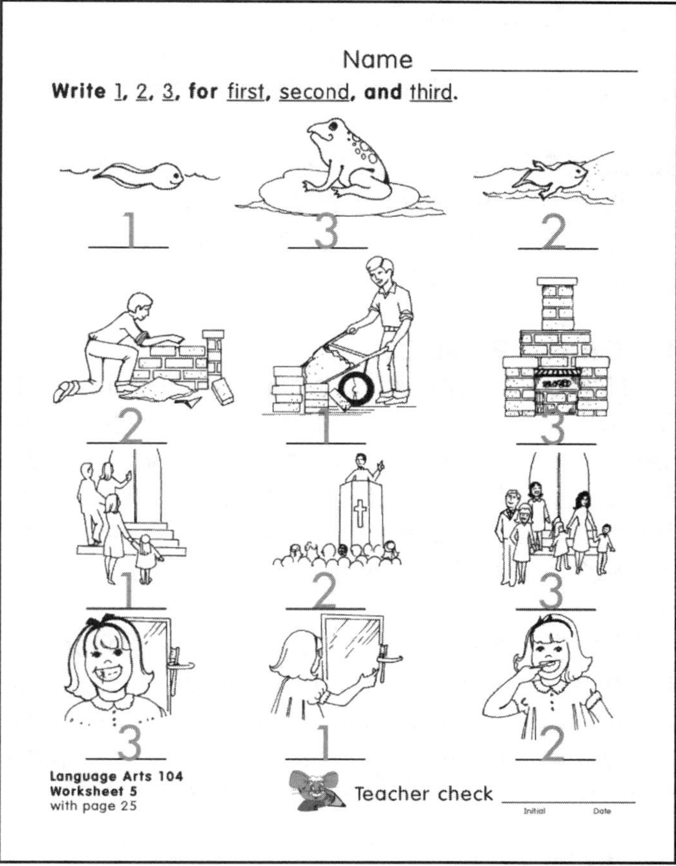
Name ______________

Write 1, 2, 3, for first, second, and third.

1 3 2

2 1 3

1 2 3

3 1 2

Language Arts 104
Worksheet 5
with page 25

Teacher check ______________
Initial Date

Name ______________

What Comes Next?

Write 1, 2, 3, for first, second, and third.

2 3 1

Put the letters and numbers in order.

d b e c f

b c d e f

w y z v x

v w x y z

6 9 5 8 7

5 6 7 8 9

11 13 12 14 10

10 11 12 13 14

Language Arts 104
Worksheet 6
with page 25

Teacher check ______________
Initial Date

Page 26: Activity Page

CONCEPTS: sentences, plurals, verbs

TEACHER GOALS: To teach the children
To identify plural words,
To tell what kind of sentence, and
To identify verbs.

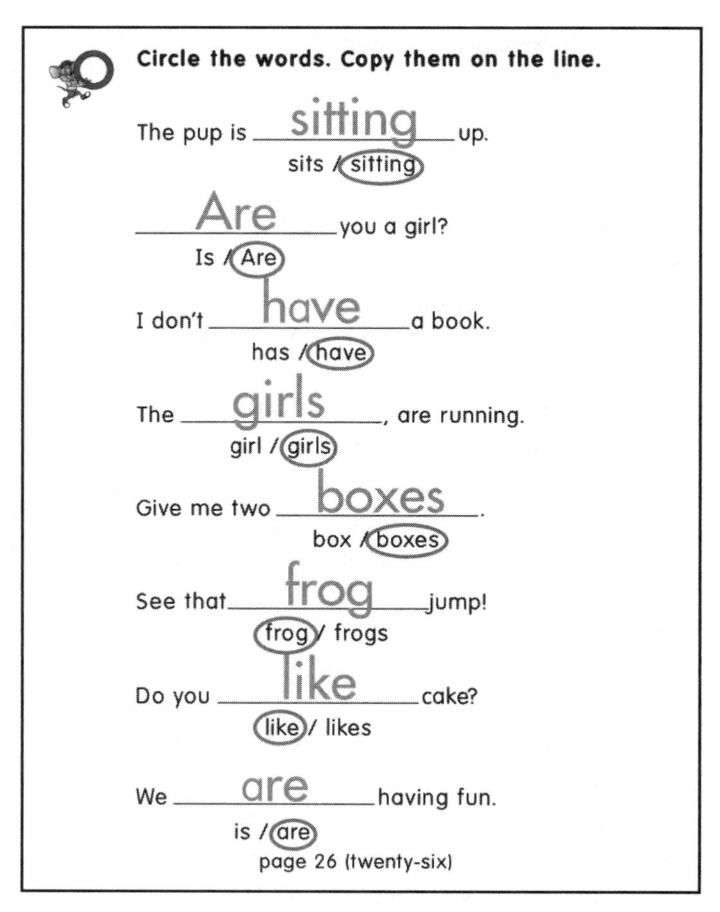

TEACHING PAGE 26:

Have the children read the direction at the top of the page. Tell them to read each sentence carefully, including the two words under the line. Tell them to circle the word that makes sense in the sentence and sounds right. Have them copy the word on the line.

Do the first sentence with the children, then let them complete the page by themselves. Check by having the children read the sentences with the right words. Children should correct any mistakes.

ACTIVITIES:

1. Have the children identify all the plurals in the sentences.
2. Have the children tell what kind of sentence each one is and what the punctuation mark is called.
3. Write a list of verbs on the board and have children use them in sentences. Examples:

run	ran
was	were
know	knew
sit	sat
jump	jumped
stand	stood

TEACHING READING:

Ask students if they have ever done something to earn money. Share stories. Together make a list of all the possible (age appropriate) ways they could earn money. Put Stan and Stella's names on the board. Have students tell you what their names have in common. (st) Tell them they're going to read a story about Stan and Stella. It's summer and they have a plan.... Ask: "What do you think their plan is?"

Read the story "The Lemonade Stand" together, then answer the following questions:

"What is Stan and Stella's plan?" (lemonade stand)

"Who do they tell?" (Mom)

"What does Mom suggest they do?" (make a list, look around the house so they don't spend too much money)

"What is the first thing they find?" (jug)

"How did they make lemonade stand building?" (they cut holes in a brown box)

"Why did they need holes?" (windows)

"Did they find everything they needed at home?" (no, they had to buy lemonade)

"What happened after everything was ready?" (no one came)

"Why?" (they forgot something)

"Can you tell me what they forgot?"..Listen again to the clues from the story. (a sign)

"How do Stan and Stella feel at the end of the story?" (excited)

"How can you tell?" (Here comes....!)

Find more words with s blends (spend, stand, scrub, store) Find words with r and l blends (plan, brown, crayons, front) Find all the contractions (that's, we'll, don't)

ACTIVITY:

Think of a class project to earn money. (i.e., bake sale) List all the things that would be needed. Make a plan to carry out the activity. Have students write a story about what Stan and Stella did with the money they earned. Have lemonade ready to make. Demonstrate with student help and enjoy a drink for all! Have students do a watercolor still life painting of fruit – lemons, limes, oranges and others.

SELF TEST 2

CONCEPTS: consonant blends, silent letters, *ph* and *gh* as the /*f*/ sound, subject-verb agreement

TEACHER GOAL: To teach the children

To check their own progress periodically.

TEACHING PAGE 27:

Read the title with the children. Have them tell what it means.

Read all the directions on the page and be sure the children understand what they are to do. Let the children do the page independently. (snow, stool, skates, spoon, hand, plant, sink, sing) (silent letters: b, g, k)

Check the page and go over it with the child as soon as possible so he can tell where he did well and where he needs to have extra work.

SELF TEST 2

Circle the letters.

sn sp st	sk sn st	st sk sp	sp sn sk
nd nt ng	ng nt nd	nd nt nk	ng nk nd

Circle the silent letters.

lamb sign knee

Circle the f sound.

laugh telephone tough

Circle the word.

My puppy ______ black.
is / are

The ______ are big.
truck / trucks

EACH ANSWER, 1 POINT

13/16

Teacher Check ______
Initial Date

page 27 (twenty-seven)

ACTIVITIES:

1. Give individual help on items missed.
2. If several children miss the same things, reteach the skills (in small groups, if possible).

SPELLING WORDS:

snap
stop
skip
spin
scrap
hand
plant
sing
lamb
comb

III. PART THREE

Page 28: Contents Page

CONCEPT: contents page

TEACHER GOALS: To teach the children
To tell what a contents page is for, and
To tell where a contents page is found in a book .

VOCABULARY: contents

TEACHING PAGE 28:

Read the title and sentence at the top of the page with the children.

Ask the children if they have seen a page like this before. Where? If no one knows, tell them to turn to the beginning of their LIFEPAC and find it. Read the titles of some of the pages they have already done and have them find those pages.

Turn back to the sample contents page and have the children look at the box. Have them find the same titles and page numbers. Have them find the title that tells what they will do after PART ONE.

Read the sentences at the bottom of the page and talk about them.

Have the children take out several LIFEPACs and find the contents page in each. Give a page number for PART ONE, TWO, or THREE and ask what they will find in that part.

ACTIVITY:

Whenever you begin a new LIFEPAC, take a few minutes to go over the contents page to see what is in the book.

III. PART THREE

You will learn about a contents page and write more sentences and stories.

CONTENTS

CONTENTS PAGE

The contents page tells you what you will find in a book.

It tells you on which page you will find each part of the book.

page 28 (twenty-eight)

Page 29: Tell the Story

CONCEPTS: telling a story, story of Moses, sequence, real or make-believe

TEACHER GOALS: To teach the children
- To tell a story from pictures,
- To tell who Moses was,
- To put the pictures in their proper sequence,
- To tell if the story is real or make believe,
- To tell the main idea of the sequence of pictures, and
- To recall details of the stories.

BIBLE REFERENCES: Exodus 1:8 through 2:10; 13:17 through 14:31; 19:16 through 20:22

MATERIALS NEEDED: Bible, copy of Ten Commandments

TEACHING PAGE 29:

Read the title with the children. Tell them that on this page they will tell the story of someone they have heard about in Sunday School or church. Ask if anyone can tell who it is (Moses).

Have the children look at the first picture and tell what is happening. Tell the children that the story the children are reading from the Bible is told in the three pictures. Ask if this story will be one that really happened or a make-believe one. How do they know?

If the children can tell who was in the pictures, have them tell what is happening in each of the pictures. Ask questions or give clues as they tell the stories if they forget important details.

(If the children have not heard the story of Moses, read it to them from the Bible or a good Bible story book. Then let them retell the story from the pictures.)

Read the story of Moses from the Bible and encourage the children to talk about it. Ask if they know any of the Ten Commandments. Read them and talk about each one. Have the children tell what they mean in their lives.

Read other parts of the story of Moses at other times so the children will understand everything he did for his people.

TEACHING READING:

Read the story "I Talk to God" in *Reader 2*.

Have the children look at the picture and tell what is happening. Have them talk about their bedtime routines.

Have the children read the story silently.

Ask questions similar to these:

"Who is the little boy talking to?"

"Who will he ask God to help?"

"Do Moms and Dads need God's help?"

"Do boys and girls need God's help?"

"Does God hear our prayers?"

"Will God help the boy and his family?"

Have the children talk about times when they have prayed and God has answered prayer.

Have the children find the blends at the end of words. Have them find *sk*, *lk*, and *lp* words. Write these words on the board.

ACTIVITY:

Begin a prayer journal with your children. Write their prayer requests in a notebook. Write the date of the request and the date that it is answered. Tell the children that sometimes our prayers are not always answered right away. We must be patient and wait for God's timing.

Page 30: Activity Page

MATERIALS NEEDED: Worksheet 7

CONCEPT: classifying

TEACHER GOAL: To teach the children
To identify things that are alike.

MATERIALS NEEDED: Worksheet 7, picture cards

TEACHING PAGE 30:

Have the children read the direction at the top of the page.

Tell the children to look at the pictures in the first box and name them (crackers, crayon, grapes, crane). Ask the children to tell how three of the pictures are alike (begin with *cr)* and how the one is different (begins with *gr*). Have them circle the three that are alike. Say the names of the pictures again.

Let the children complete the page carefully, and to read the words carefully before they circle the ones that are alike.

(frog, bridge, brick, brush)— *br*
(drum, crane, drink, driving)—*dr*
(frame, freckles, frog, bridge)—*fr*
(grandmother, grapes, grass)—*gr*
(one, three, blue, two)—*numbers*
(red, one, blue, yellow)—*colors*

Check by having the children name the picture or read the words and tell how the three are alike and the one is different.

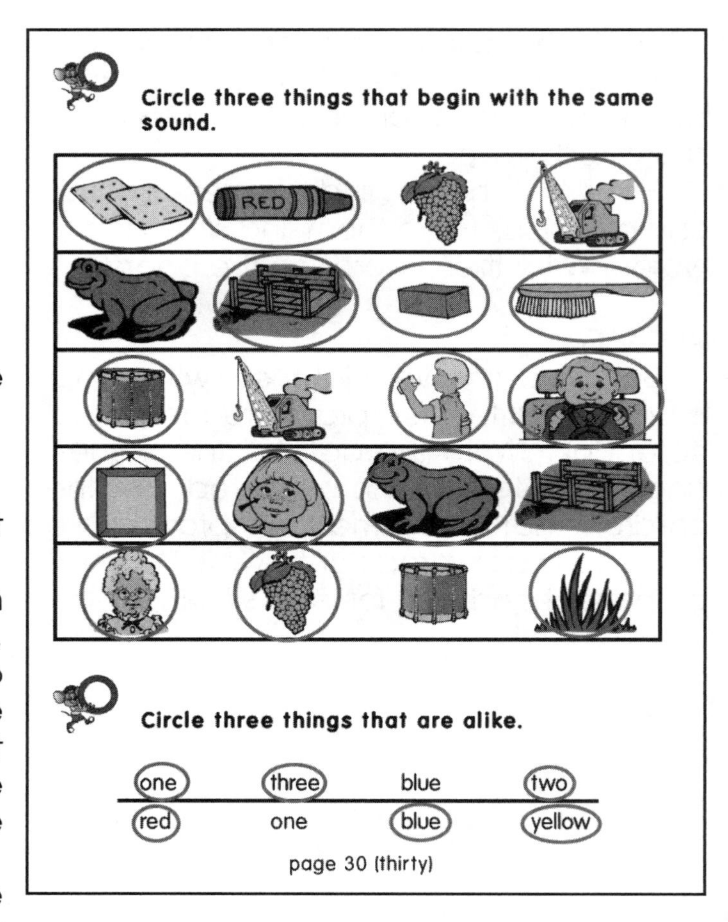

ACTIVITIES:

1. Do Worksheet 7.

Have the children read the direction at the top of the page. Tell them to look at the pictures and words and find three that are alike in some way. They should look for the same kinds of things, rhyming parts, or beginning or middle sounds.

Let the children do the page by themselves. Check by having the children tell which three things they circled and how they are alike. Have them tell why the fourth thing is not like the others.

2. Use a picture card collection for children who have a difficult time telling how things are alike. Give them a stack of cards and ask them to find all the things that have wheels, are fruits or vegetables, are used for cleaning, are kinds of clothing, and so on.

Then have them find things that are alike in a less obvious way, such as things to wear on the feet or on the head, green vegetables or vegetables that grow under the ground or above the ground, ways to tell time, ways to cook food, machines used in the kitchen, machines used in the garage, and so on.

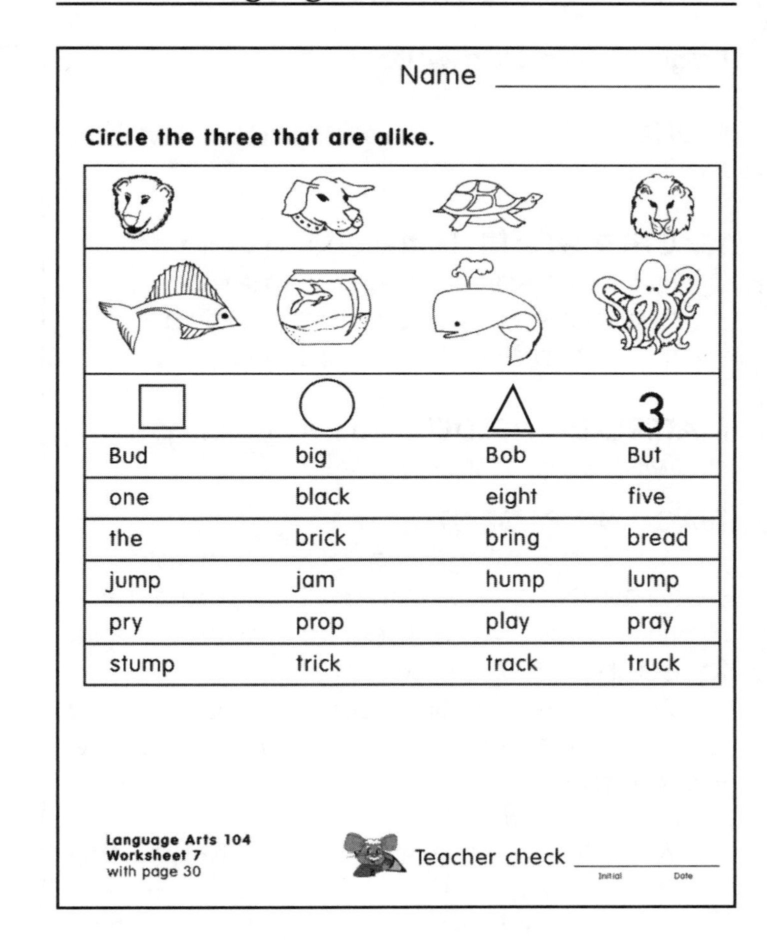

Name ____________

Circle the three that are alike.

Bud	big	Bob	But
one	black	eight	five
the	brick	bring	bread
jump	jam	hump	lump
pry	prop	play	pray
stump	trick	track	truck

Language Arts 104
Worksheet 7
with page 30

Teacher check ____________ Initial Date

Page 31: We Can Write

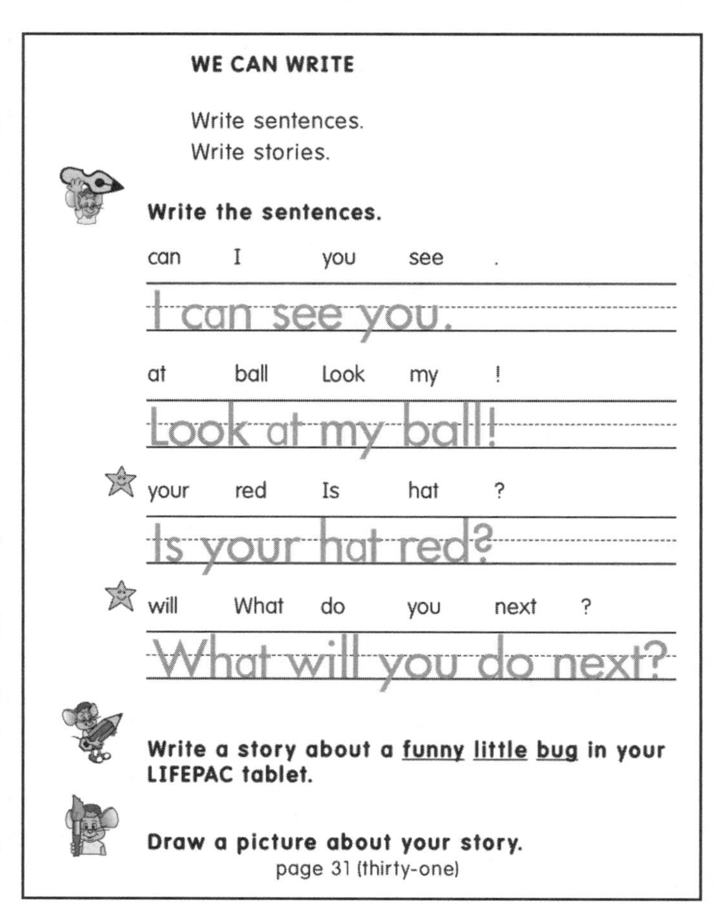
WE CAN WRITE

Write sentences.
Write stories.

Write the sentences.

can I you see .

I can see you.

at ball Look my !

Look at my ball!

your red Is hat ?

Is your hat red?

will What do you next ?

What will you do next?

Write a story about a funny little bug in your LIFEPAC tablet.

Draw a picture about your story.

page 31 (thirty-one)

CONCEPTS: writing sentences, writing stories.

TEACHER GOALS: To teach the children
To identify and write statements, questions, and exclamations, and
To write a two-paragraph story.

MATERIALS NEEDED: crayons or paints, drawing paper, Worksheet 8

TEACHING PAGE 31:

Ask the children to give examples of statements, questions, and exclamations. Have a child write the punctuation mark for each on the board .

Write these words on the board and have the children tell you how to arrange them into a sentence.

dog Is my this ?

Write the sentence and have the children read it.

Tell the children this type of sentence unscrambling is what they will be doing on this page. Have them read the title and the first direction.

Some children can write the sentences by themselves. Tell them to read the words carefully. Tell them to write the words on the lines in a sentence. Remind them that the first word in a sentence must begin with a capital letter.

Help those children who need help. The starred sentences are more difficult and should be done with the teacher.

Write the sentences on the board and have the children check their sentences and correct them if necessary. The teacher should also correct them and have the children recopy them if any mistakes were made.

Read the next directions with the children. Tell the children to write at least two paragraphs, or more if they have time. Remind them that the sentences in each paragraph should be about the same thing, and, the entire story must be about the funny little bug. Have the children write a title for their story.

Tell the children to write neatly, to space their words well, and to make their letters correctly. Have them keep a sheet of writing tablet paper on their desks for you to write words on that they cannot spell.

Have the children draw and color or paint a picture to go with their story.

Take enough class time for each child to be able to show his picture and read his story to the class. This sharing time is just as important as writing the story.

ACTIVITIES:

1. Do Worksheet 8.

Have the children read the direction at the top of the page. Have them read the words in the first row and arrange them into a sentence. Write the words on the board in the order the children give them and let them copy them on the lines.

Let the children finish the page by themselves. Give help only if needed. Tell them to read all the words carefully before starting to write, to write neatly, and to space the words well.

Check by writing the sentences on the board as the children give them. Children may correct their papers from the board. The teacher should collect the papers and recheck them. Have the children copy the corrected sentences on a sheet of writing tablet paper.

Have several children read the entire story.

Have the children draw and color or paint a picture of the story. Tell them to write a title for the story on the top edge of their picture. Give each child a chance to read the story and show his picture .

2. Read stories about insects and factual books about insects.

TEACHING READING:

Give students a half sheet of lavender construction paper and an oval pattern. Have them trace and cut out the oval. Fold the oval in half. Give them 8 strips of the same colored paper and have them glue them onto the bottom half of the oval. Instruct them to make eyes and a mouth on the top part. Ask students what animal they have just made. (Octopus) Ask them what they know about this animal. Write squid on the board. Ask students if what they know about squids. (Be prepared with books or other informative sources) Chart information.

Ask students if they have ever asked for help and the person they asked said "No". Take a little time to share experiences. Tell them they're going to read a story about a squid named Skippy and his friend Oscar.

Read the story "Stuck Again" together, then answer the following questions:

"What is Skippy's problem?" (he's stuck again)

"Where is he stuck?" (in the middle of a thick clump of seaweed)

Name ______________

Write the sentence.

is dog This my.

This

black is dog My.

run He can fast!

I my dog like.

you dog Do a have?

Read the story.
Draw a picture about the story.

Language Arts 104
Worksheet 8
with page 31

Teacher check ______________
Initial Date

"Who does he ask for help?" (Tim Tuna, Sherry Shark)

"Why can't Oscar help him this time?" (he doesn't see him, he's playing with his friends)

"Does the story tell us Oscar is an octopus?" (no)

"How do we know that he is?" (It says he has eight arms, he's in the sea)

"A little voice said, "Don't lose hope." "What does that mean?" (don't give up, ...)

"How did Oscar rescue Skippy?" (he blasted through the seaweed, strong arms)

"Do you think Oscar is a good friend?" (yes, he left his playtime to help Skippy)

"What was Skippy thinking about after he got rescued?" (the soft voice he heard)

"Who was it that spoke to him?" (the little seahorse)

"How do you think Oscar felt when he saw her slip away?" (answers may vary – good)

"How do you think the seahorse felt?" (glad, satisfied, happy, ...)

"What do you think Skippy will do if he ever sees or hears a friend who needs help?" (answers will vary)

"Do you think he should help Tim Tuna and Sherry Shark if they ever get into trouble?" (yes, Jesus would)

Find short vowel words.

Find s blends (stuck, Skippy, Squid, swish, swirl, stop, smiled, strong, swing)

Find words with th (thick, thought, thing, them, these, then, thank, that, they, thinking)

Find words with sh (ship, Sherry, shark, she, fish,) Find contractions (can't, don't, I'm)

ACTIVITY:

Give students a large piece of paper and have them glue their octopus onto it. Have them finish the picture adding details from the story and maybe some of their own. Read nonfiction books about the octopus, squid, shark and other marine animals. Give everyone two green streamers or ribbons and have them do movement to music. Have students write a story about the little seahorse. Where did she go?

Page 32: Activity Page

CONCEPTS: plurals, verbs, sentences

TEACHER GOALS: To teach the children
To identify the correct verb form,
To identify plural words, and
To tell what kind of sentences.

TEACHING PAGE 32:

Have the children read the directions at the top of the page. Have them read the three words at the top of each section.

Tell the children to read the sentences carefully, then to copy the correct word in the empty space. Remind them to read all three sentences before they begin writing words and to choose the word that sounds best in the sentence and makes good sense.

Check by having the children read the sentences with the correct words.

The teacher should check this page and have children correct any mistakes.

ACTIVITIES:

1. Correct the children when they use the wrong verb form in their daily speech *goed,* for *gone* or *gots* for *got* or *has,* for example.
2. Ask children to tell which sentence is correct using a correct and an incorrect verb form.

   Examples:

   He blowed out the candles. *or* He blew out the candles.

   He runned away. *or* He ran away.

   Mary jump down from the chair. *or* Mary jumped down from the chair.

   The children sit down. *or* The children sat down.
3. Ask the children to find the plurals on the page. Have them tell how the plurals were made and what they mean. Have them make plurals from singular subjects.
4. Have the children tell what kind of sentence each one on the page is and name the punctuation mark at the end.

Page 33: Activity Page

CONCEPT: sequence of events

TEACHER GOALS: To teach the children
To tell what happens next,
To identify the short /u/ sound, and
To identify subject-verb agreement.

TEACHING PAGE 33:

Have the children read the direction at the top of page.

Have them look at the pictures and tell what is happening in each. Have them tell which picture shows what happened first and trace the *1* under it. Have them tell what happened next and write a *2* under it and a *3* under what happened last.

Tell the children that the first group of sentences tells in words the same things they just saw in the pictures. Have the children read all three sentences. Ask them to read the sentence that tells what happened first, then trace the *1.* Ask them to read what happened next and write a *2* in the blank in front of the sentence. Have them read what happened last and write a *3* in the blank. Have them read all three sentences in order.

Have the children do the other two groups by themselves. Help those who need help with the reading. Check by having the children read the sentences in order. Have them correct their work If necessary.

ACTIVITIES:

1. Ask the children to tell what kind of sentence each one is. Have them turn a statement into a question or an exclamation, and tell what the punctuation mark would be.
2. Have the children find and circle all the words with the short /u/ sound. Have them read the words they circled.
3. Read one of the sentences but change the subject or the verb and ask the children if the sentence sounds right.

Write 1, 2, 3 **for** first, second, **and** third.

2 1 3

1 Tom is running.
3 Tom, Dan, and Jack are running.
2 Tom and Dan are running.

3 I can jump, run, and hop.
1 I can jump.
2 I can jump and run.

3 We ride on the bus to school.
2 We get on the bus.
1 Here comes the school bus.

page 33 (thirty-three)

Have them tell what the correct word should be.

TEACHING READING:

Read the story "The Gift" in *Reader 2.*

Have the children read the title. Have them look at the picture. Ask them what they think will happen in the story. Talk about shopping. Have several children tell about experiences they have had while shopping. Tell the children that this story is about buying a gift. Have the children tell about experiences they have had buying or receiving gifts.

Have the children read the story silently.

Ask these questions:

"Who is going to receive the gift Bob buys?"

"What color is the doll he sees?"

"What kind of boat does he see?"

"How will Bob decide what to buy?"

"Which toy do you think he will buy for Beth?"

"Is Bob a thoughtful brother?"

"Would you like to have a brother like Bob?"

Have the children find a color word in the story. Have them find a compound word. Have them find a word ending in *ft*. Write these words on the board.

ACTIVITY:

Make a pretend store for your children. Used toys and games would be helpful. Have several children "sell" the toys to the "customers". Have the children pretend they are buying gifts for their families.

SELF TEST 3

CONCEPTS: subject-verb agreement, verb forms, sequence

TEACHER GOAL: To teach the children
To check their own progress periodically.

TEACHING PAGE 34:
Have the children read the title and all the directions on the page. Be sure they know what they are to do in each section. Let the children complete the page by themselves.
Check the page as soon as possible and go over it with the child so he can see what he did well and where he will need more work (are, jump, boys) (2 ,1, 3).

SELF TEST 3

Circle the words.

Tom and Dan ________ running.
is / are

We can ________ up.
jump / jumps

The ________ are running.
boy / boys

Write the sentence.

at bat! Look that

Look at that bat!

Write 1, 2, 3 for first, second, and third.

2 Tom and Dan are running.

1 Tom is running.

3 Tom, Dan and Jack are running.

6/7 Teacher Check Initial Date My Score

page 34 (thirty-four)

ACTIVITIES:
1. Give the children individual help on the kinds of items they missed.
2. If several miss the same things, work with them in small groups.

SPELLING WORDS:

jump
bump
hump
talk
walk
help
task
phone
stand
band

LIFEPAC TEST AND ALTERNATE TEST 104

CONCEPTS: consonant blends, alike and different, subject-verb agreement, rhyming words, silent letters, *ph* and *gh* as the sound of *f*, sentence order, and ordinal numbers

TEACHER GOAL: To teach the children

To check their own progress periodically.

TEACHING the LIFEPAC TEST:

Administer the test to the class as a group. Ask to have directions read or read them to the class. In either case, be sure that the children clearly understand. Put examples on the board if it seems necessary. Give ample time for each activity to be completed before going on to the next. Name the pictures (globe, blocks, slide, frame, drum, bread) (sequence: 3, 2, 1). Oral directions: Have the children circle the second and third ovals in the last section of the test; then, color the next to the last oval pink.

Correct immediately and discuss with the child.

Review any concepts that have been missed.

Give those children who do not achieve the 80% score additional copies of the worksheets and a list of vocabulary words to study. A parent or a classroom helper should help in the review.

Review any concepts that have been missed.

When the child is ready, give the Alternate LIFEPAC Test. Use the same procedure as for the LIFEPAC Test. Name the pictures. (sled, plate, glasses, driving, crane, praying) (sequence: 3, 1, 2) Oral directions: Have the children circle the first and third triangles in the last section of the test; then, color the second from the last triangle green.

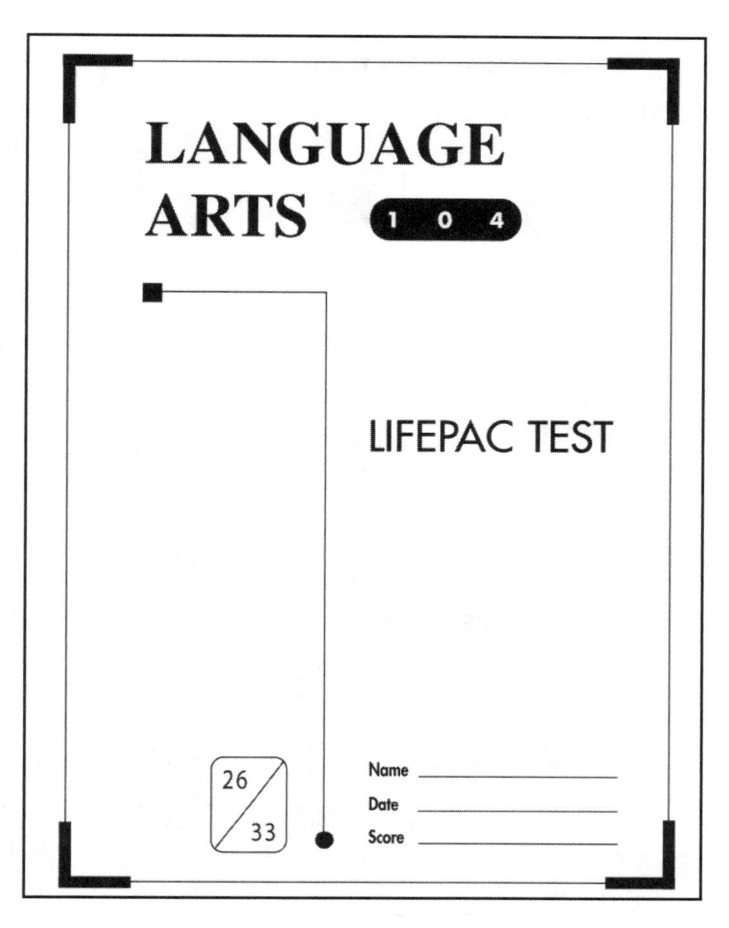

SPELLING WORDS:

LIFEPAC words	**Alternate words**
block	cluck
flag	glad
grass	plan
snap	spin
skip	hand
plant	sing
jump	lamb
talk	bump
help	walk
comb	task

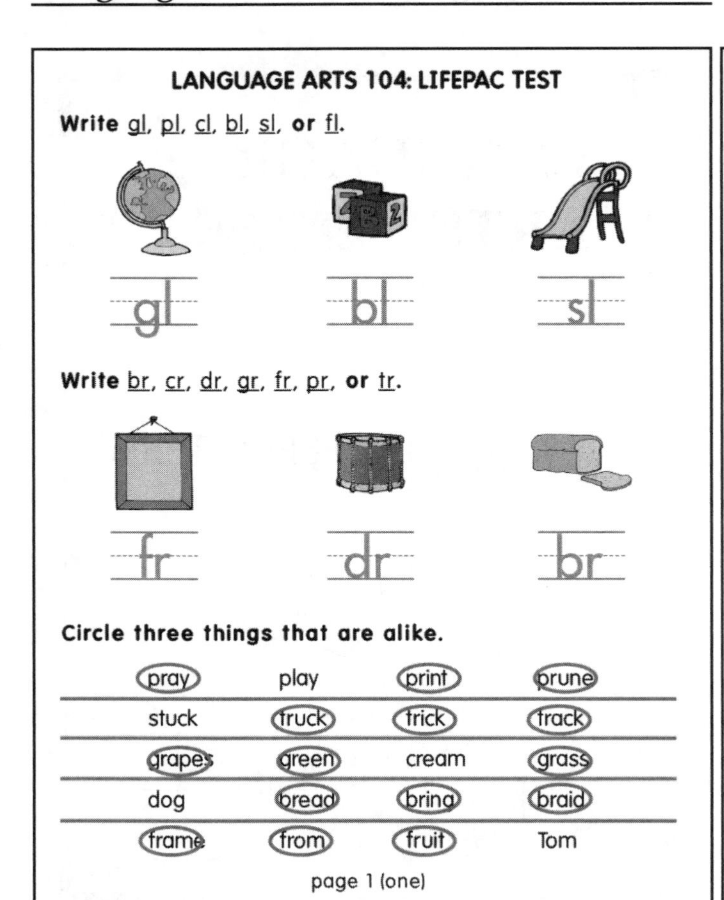

LANGUAGE ARTS 104: LIFEPAC TEST

Write gl, pl, cl, bl, sl, or fl.

gl bl sl

Write br, cr, dr, gr, fr, pr, or tr.

fr dr br

Circle three things that are alike.

(pray)	play	(print)	(prune)
stuck	(truck)	(trick)	(track)
(grapes)	(green)	cream	(grass)
dog	(bread)	(bring)	(braid)
(frame)	(from)	(fruit)	Tom

page 1 (one)

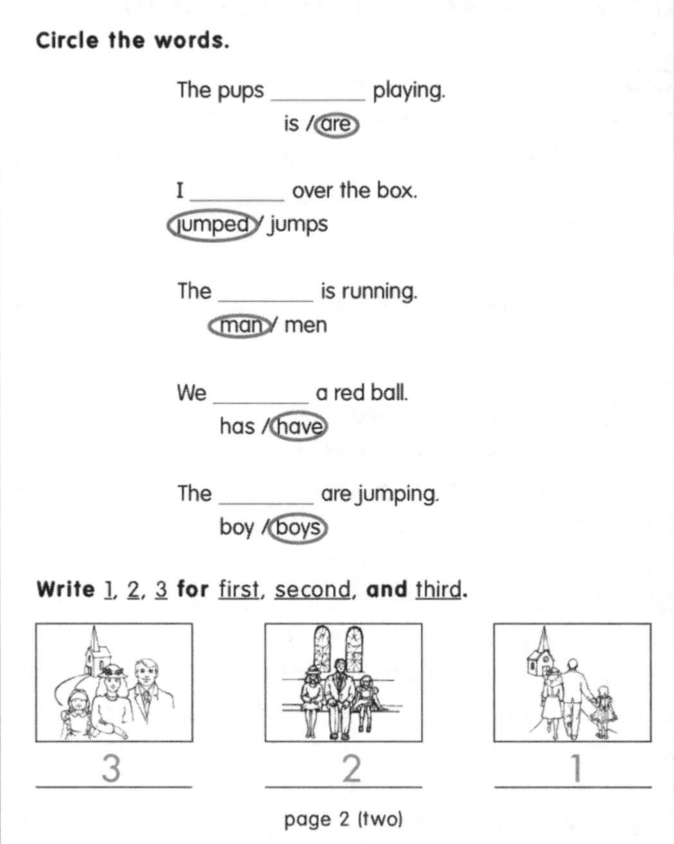

Circle the words.

The pups ________ playing.
is / (are)

I ________ over the box.
(jumped) / jumps

The ________ is running.
(man) / men

We ________ a red ball.
has / (have)

The ________ are jumping.
boy / (boys)

Write 1, 2, 3 for first, second, and third.

3 2 1

page 2 (two)

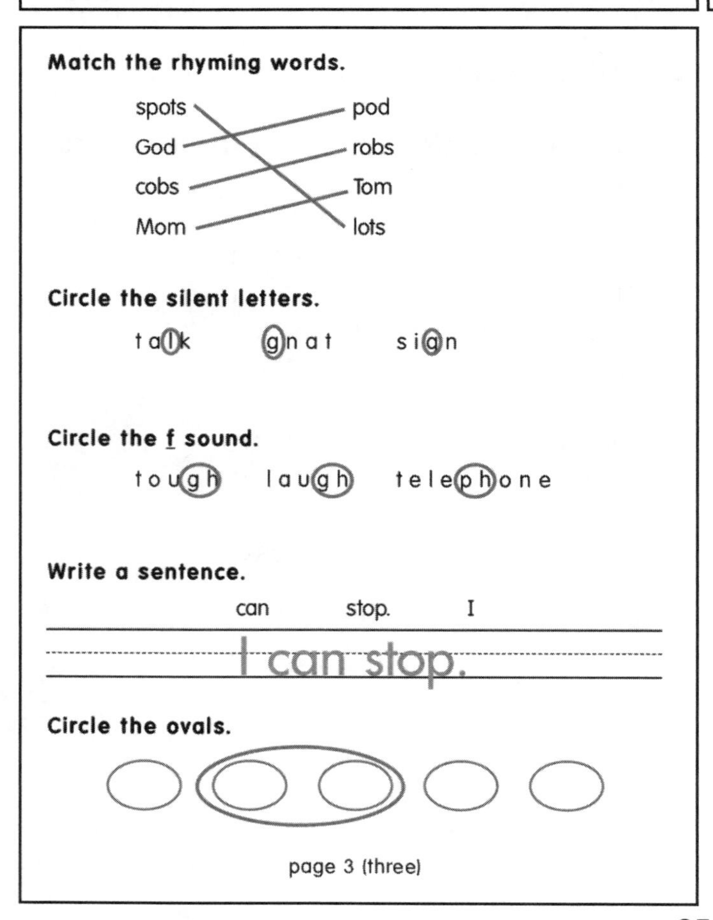

Match the rhyming words.

spots — lots
God — pod
cobs — robs
Mom — Tom

Circle the silent letters.

t a (l) k (g) n a t s i (g) n

Circle the f sound.

t o u (g h) l a u (g h) t e l e (p h) o n e

Write a sentence.

can stop. I

I can stop.

Circle the ovals.

page 3 (three)

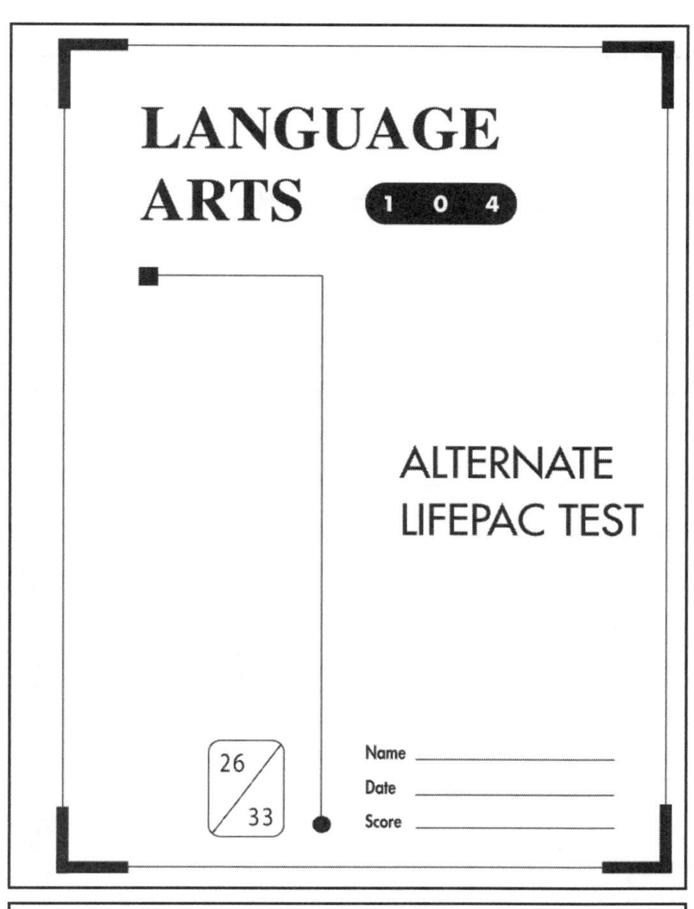

LANGUAGE ARTS 1 0 4

ALTERNATE LIFEPAC TEST

26 / 33

Name ______

Date ______

Score ______

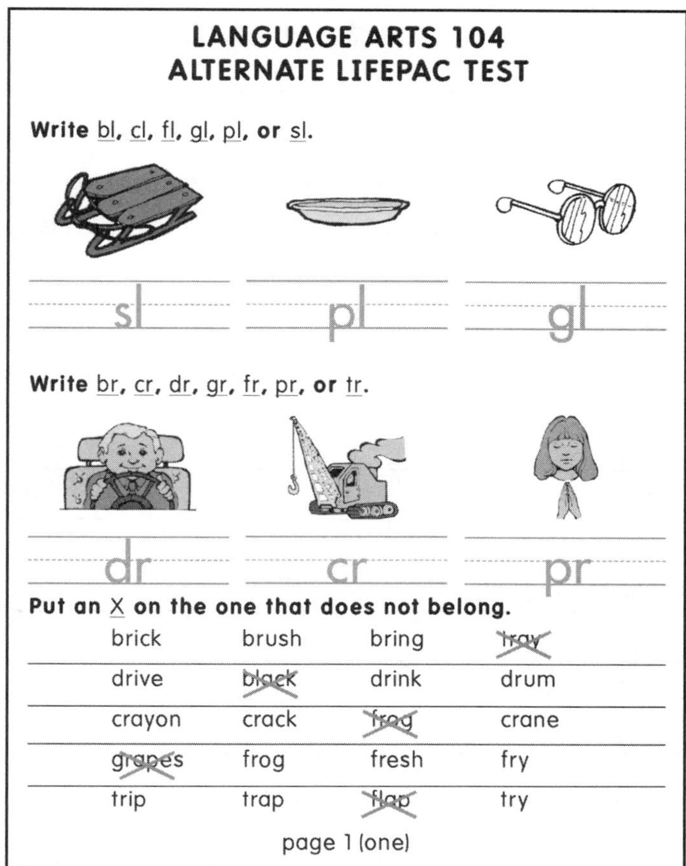

LANGUAGE ARTS 104
ALTERNATE LIFEPAC TEST

Write bl, cl, fl, gl, pl, or sl.

sl   pl   gl

Write br, cr, dr, gr, fr, pr, or tr.

dr   cr   pr

Put an X on the one that does not belong.

brick	brush	bring	~~tray~~
drive	~~black~~	drink	drum
crayon	crack	~~frog~~	crane
~~grapes~~	frog	fresh	fry
trip	trap	~~flap~~	try

page 1 (one)

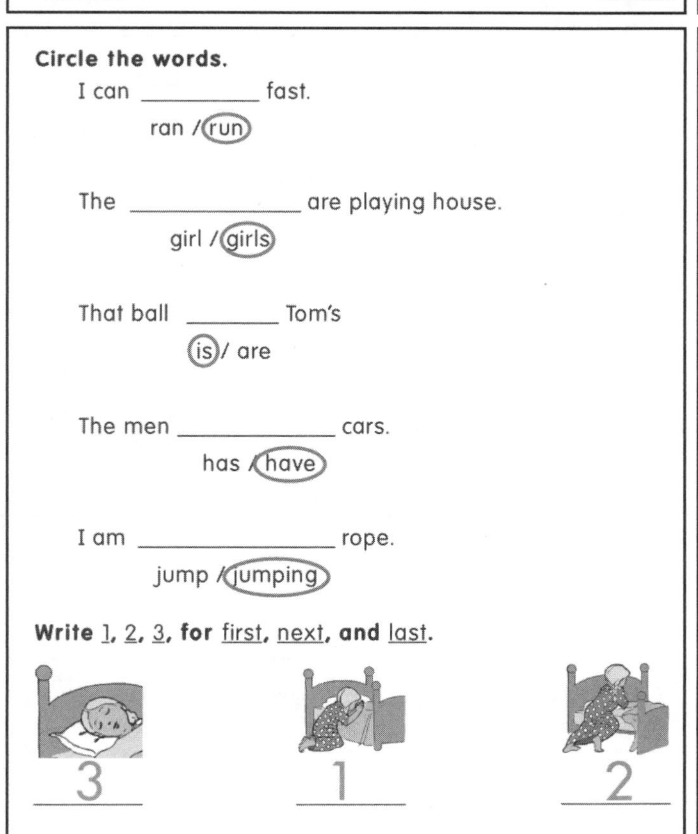

Circle the words.

I can ______ fast.
ran / (run)

The ______ are playing house.
girl / (girls)

That ball ______ Tom's
(is) / are

The men ______ cars.
has / (have)

I am ______ rope.
jump / (jumping)

Write 1, 2, 3, for first, next, and last.

3   1   2

page 2 (two)

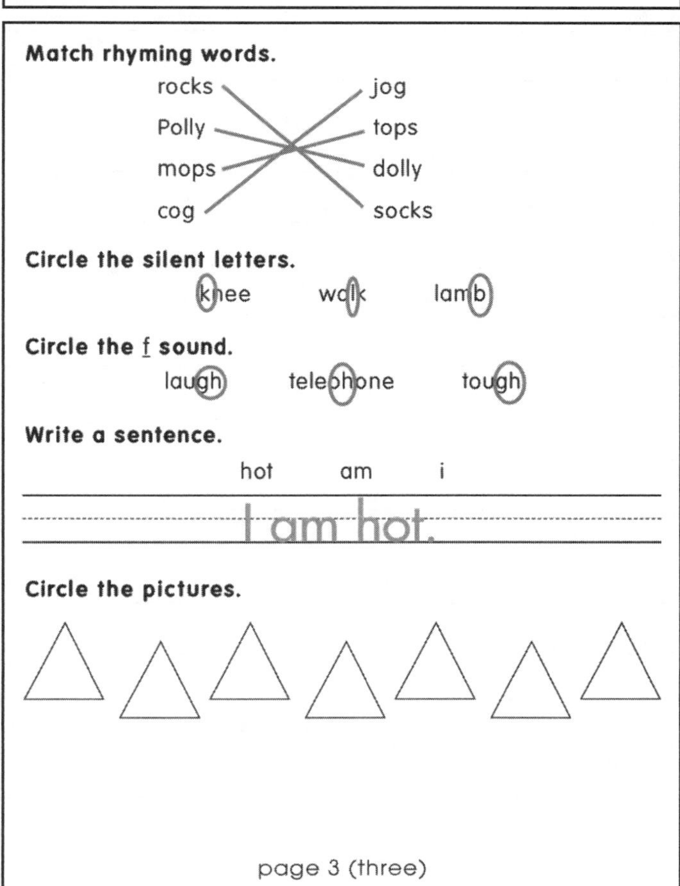

Match rhyming words.

rocks — socks
Polly — dolly
mops — tops
cog — jog

Circle the silent letters.

knee   walk   lamb

Circle the f sound.

laugh   telephone   tough

Write a sentence.

hot   am   i

I am hot.

Circle the pictures.

page 3 (three)

Page 1: Fun With Words

CONCEPTS: purpose of the LIFEPAC, children's objectives

TEACHER GOALS: To teach the children
To understand what will be taught in this LIFEPAC, and
To understand what will be expected of them in Language Arts LIFEPAC 105.

TEACHING PAGE 1:
Read the title and sentences at the top of the page with the children. Talk about each one so the children will know what they will be learning about in this LIFEPAC.
Ask the children to tell what objectives are. Read the list of objectives with them and talk about each one. The children should understand that these are the things they will be able to do when this LIFEPAC is finished.
Have the children write their names and ages on the lines.

FUN WITH WORDS

You can have fun reading, listening, and writing.

In this LIFEPAC
you will learn about words with long vowels.
You will learn to read stories.
You will learn to write good sentences.
You will learn to spell and write rhyming words.
You will learn to write paragraphs and stories.

Objectives

1. I can choose words with the sound of long a, e, i, o, u.
2. I can read and write good sentences.
3. I can learn about contractions and possessives.
4. I can write paragraphs and stories.
5. I can tell what will happen next.

My name is ______________________

I am _______ years old.

page 1 (one)

I. PART ONE

Page 2: Long a

CONCEPT: sound of long *a*

TEACHER GOALS: To teach the children
To identify pictures with the sound of long *a,* and
To tell what is happening in the picture.

VOCABULARY: long

MATERIALS NEEDED: *Aa* card, tagboard, *a* flash cards

TEACHING PAGE 2:

Point to the *Aa* card and ask children to tell what sound the *a* has (short sound). Tell the children they will be learning about another sound for *a* which is the long sound of *a* as in *cake* and *gave.* Read this list of words and have the children raise their hands when they hear the long /a/ sound.

tame	gate	set
bat	wait	frame
they	sat	whale
can	tail	beg

Read the title and sentences at the top of the page with the children and talk about them. Ask the children to tell what rhyming words are.

Read the direction with the children and tell them to look at the picture. Have the children find things with the long /a/ sound and circle them (plane, train, sailboat, nail, chain, name, Jane, tail, gate, pail, lake).

Check by having the children tell what they circled. If anything is missed, give clues until the children find it.

ACTIVITIES:

1. Make a chart for the long /a/ sound. Write Long *Aa* at the top of a sheet of tagboard and have the children paste pictures cut from old magazines and catalogs on it. The long /a/ sound can be at the beginning or in the middle. Words which cannot be pictured may be written in one section of the chart.

I. PART ONE

You will learn
many new words
with the long a sound.
You will write rhyming words and
contractions.

 **Circle the pictures with the long /a/ sound.**

page 2 (two)

2. Have the children name the pictures on the chart and listen for the long /a/ sound.

TEACHING READING:

Ask students about activities they do with their family. Ask if there are things they only do certain times of the year. List their responses and then give time to share a few experiences. Ask how many have gone camping with their family. Survey students to find out how many like and dislike camping. Have students tell you things that are necessary to take on a camping trip. List their responses. Tell students their going to read a story about Kelly. Tell them to listen carefully and to see if Kelly likes to go camping.

Read the story "Kelly's Daisies" then answer the following questions:

"When does Kelly's family go camping?" (Spring)

"Where do they go?" (Pine Lake)

"How long do they stay at Pine Lake?" (one week)

"Did Kelly like to go camping?" (yes)

"How do you know?" (she couldn't wait)

"What did she like to do?" (gather pine cones and look at wild flowers)

"What did she want to do?" (pick some daisies for her yellow vase at home)

"Did she pick them?" (no - she understood what her mother said)

"What did she do instead?" (painted a picture of the daisies)

"Do you think she did the right thing?" "Why"? (accept reasonable explanations)

"Why is she going to pack her paper and paints first this year?" (she wants to be ready to paint more pictures, she remembers last year's picture)

Have students:

Find long vowel words: (Pine, Lake, week, green, way, trees, okay, take, gave, cones, wild, sunshine, smile, daisies, home, vase, paper, paints, later, painting, white, made)

ACTIVITY:

Plan an imaginary camping trip. Decide on a place and then have students work in groups to list all the things they need. Then have them make a list of things they don't need, but would like to take. Make a chart showing the two lists. Decide which things are most important - they can't take everything! Have books on wild flowers to share.

Have students paint pictures of flowers as they might see them in the wild, garden or yard. Ask them if they learned a good rule from this story. Discuss. Tell them there are some national parks and forests which display this sign: TAKE NOTHING BUT PICTURES, LEAVE NOTHING BUT FOOTPRINTS. Have a discussion about what this motto means. Plant flowers or class garden. Make posters about taking care of parks and camping areas.

Page 3: Activity Page

CONCEPTS: long *a*, nonsense poems

TEACHER GOALS: To teach the children
To identify words with the long /a/ sound,
To learn about nonsense poems and limericks, and
To read and write nonsense poems

MATERIALS NEEDED: *Aa* card

TEACHING PAGE 3:

Read the sentence and the direction at the top of the page with the children. Tell the children to listen for the sound of long *a* in each word. Read the list of *ay* words, then read it a second time and have the children repeat each word after you. Ask which part of the word rhymes.

Do the same for each list of rhyming words. Call attention to the words *they* and *obey* that rhyme with the *ay* words but are spelled differently, to the word *wait* that is different from the *ate* words, and to the words *tale* and *whale* that are different from the *ail* words.

Have the children read the direction at the bottom of the page. Have them name the pictures and listen for the long /a/ sound (train, cat, cake, rain, chain, cup, pail, rabbit, box, fish, table, snake, whale, bee)

Tell them to circle all the pictures that have the sound of long *a*. Check by having the children tell which pictures they circled.

ACTIVITIES:

1. Cut pictures with the long /a/ sound from magazines and catalogs and paste on tagboard to add to the picture card collection.
2. Separate the short *a* and long *a* picture cards from the other letter cards, mix them together and have the children sort them into two groups again.

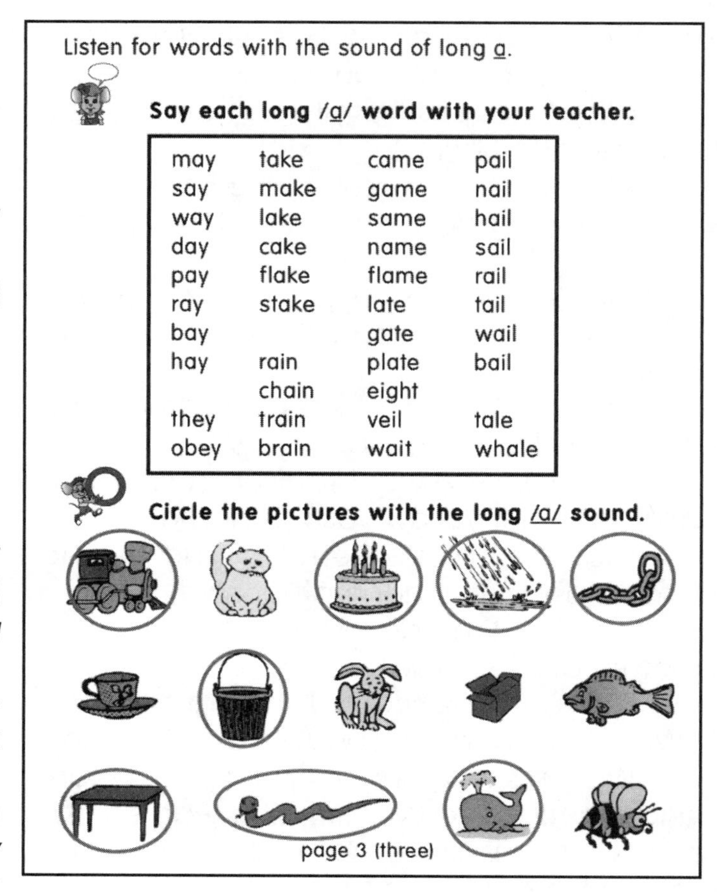

Listen for words with the sound of long a.

Say each long /a/ word with your teacher.

may	take	came	pail
say	make	game	nail
way	lake	same	hail
day	cake	name	sail
pay	flake	flame	rail
ray	stake	late	tail
bay		gate	wail
hay	rain	plate	bail
	chain	eight	
they	train	veil	tale
obey	brain	wait	whale

Circle the pictures with the long /a/ sound.

page 3 (three)

TEACHING READING:

Find "Nonsense Poem" in *Reader 3*.

Read the title to the children. Ask if anyone knows what nonsense is. Tell them they are going to listen to a poem that does not mean anything, but is just for fun. Tell them to listen for the rhyming words.

Read the poem. Ask what was funny about it. Ask if this could really happen. Have the children give the rhyming words and write them on the board. Have the children read the list.

Read the poem again and have the children read it with you.

Write a nonsense poem as a group. Have the children give ideas and rhyming words. Write the suggestions on the board and see which ones could be used. Often if you begin with a first line, the children will be able to finish the poem. You may prefer to write several two-line poems instead of one longer one.

Read nonsense poems and limericks.

Page 4: Rhymes

CONCEPTS: rhyming words, long *a*

TEACHER GOALS: To teach the children
To tell how rhyming words are alike, and
To learn to write words that rhyme using long *a*.

TEACHING PAGE 4:

Have the children read the direction at the top of the page and read the words under the pictures. Have them tell how the words are alike.

Read the next direction with the children and have them find all the rhyming words in the poem. Read the words and write in their tablets.

Read the next direction with the children. Tell them to think of more words that rhyme with *cake* and *lake* and to write them under the first ending.

Read *ate* and have the children give some words that rhyme. Tell them to write three words on the lines, then to write as many more as they can think of on a sheet of writing tablet paper.

Read the sentences at the bottom of the page. Children should be able to prepare their own sheet of paper with the endings written at the top.

ACTIVITIES:

1. Read poems in which every two or four lines rhyme.
2. Dictate five *ake* words and five *ate* words and have children write them on a sheet of writing tablet paper. Correct and have the children write misspelled words five times.

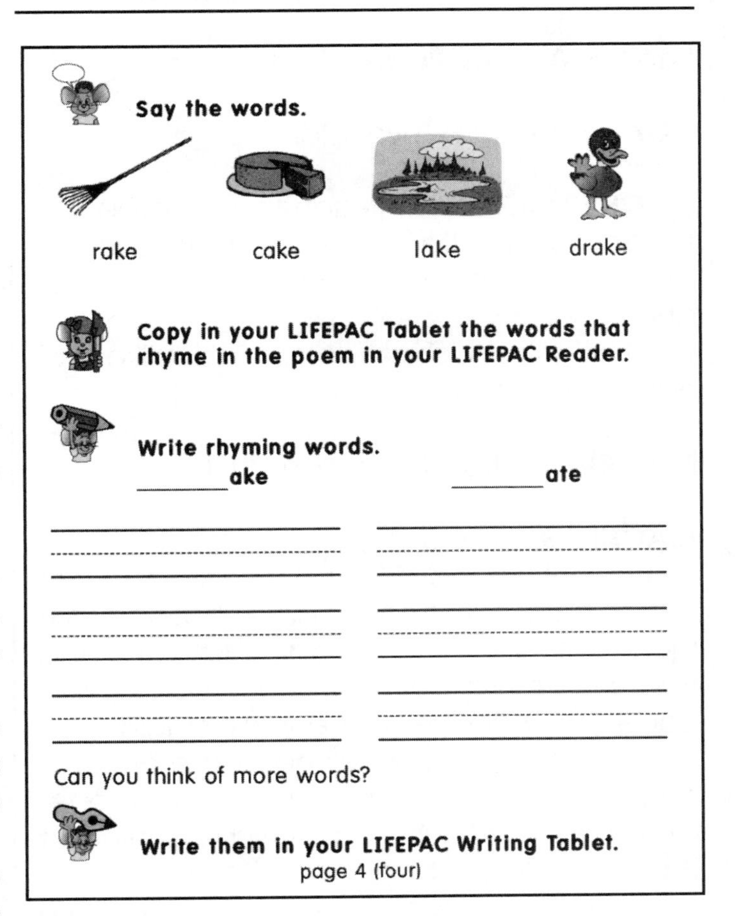

Page 5: Activity Page

CONCEPTS: homonyms, long *a*

TEACHER GOALS: To teach the children
To read and write words with long *a* in the middle and at the beginning of the word, and
To recognize words that sound alike but have different meanings.

MATERIALS NEEDED: Worksheet 1

TEACHING PAGE 5:

Have the children read the directions at the top of the page. Ask what the first picture is. Have them read the word and tell what the vowel should be. Have them trace the *a* and read the word again.

Have the children name all the pictures on the page, then write the *a* in each one. Call attention to the *a* at the beginning of the words at the bottom of the page.

Check by having the children read all the words.

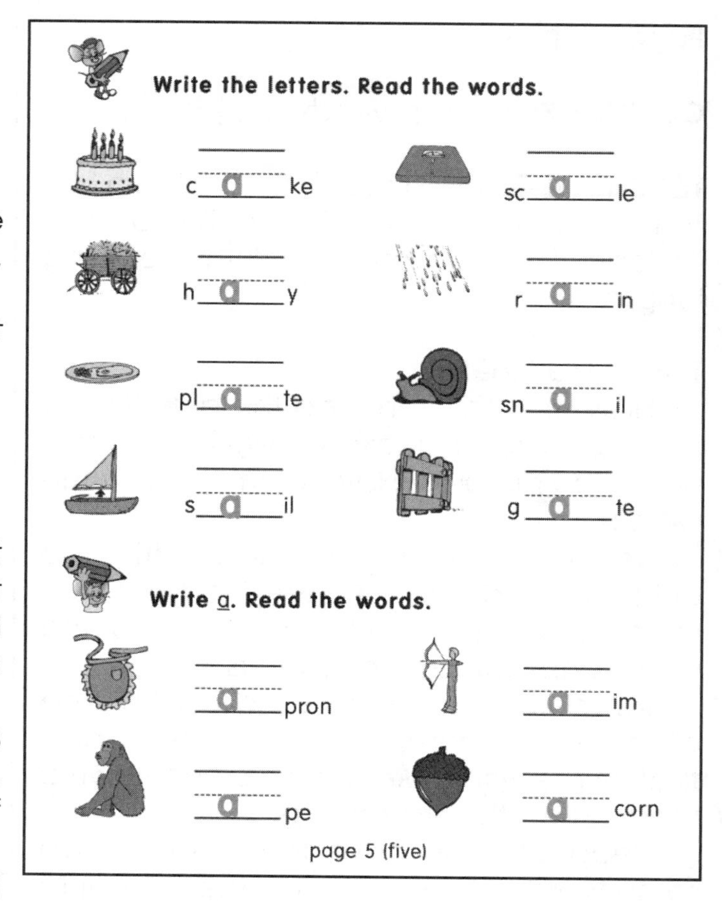
Write the letters. Read the words.

c a ke — sc a le
h a y — r a in
pl a te — sn a il
s a il — g a te

Write a. Read the words.

a pron — a im
a pe — a corn

page 5 (five)

ACTIVITIES:

1. Do Worksheet 1. Have the children read the direction at the top of the Worksheet.

Have them read the endings at the top of the page. Tell the children that the two endings sound the same, but are not spelled the same. Write the words *pane* and *pain* on the board. Tell the children the meanings of the words and say them. Have the children copy them on their papers. Do the same with the following list of words.

mane vane plane cane

main vain plain Cain

When the children have copied them on their papers, ask which one is the weather vane and have children spell the word. Ask for the horse's *mane*, for the one you fly in, for the one that helps you walk, and so on.

Have the children give more words. Write them on the board for children to copy on their worksheet. Talk about each one's meaning.

Have the children choose any six of the words on the page and write a sentence for each one on a sheet of writing tablet paper. Correct their papers and have children recopy corrected sentences.

2. Read poems or stories about games; read about games from a game book.

Name________________

Write words that rhyme.

-ane	**-ain**

mane

plane

cane

Language Arts 105
Worksheet 1
with page 5

Teacher check ______________
Initial Date

Page 6: The Bee

CONCEPTS: long *e*, rhyming words, main idea, retelling a story

TEACHER GOALS: To teach the children
To identify words with the sound of long *e*,
To identify the rhyming words in the poem,
To understand what a poem is,
To retell the story in their own words,
To tell the main idea of the poem,
To tell what might happen next, and
To make inferences from the poem and the picture.

MATERIALS NEEDED: tagboard, magazines or catalogs, paste or glue, scissors

TEACHING PAGE 6:

Read the title and sentence at the top of the page with the children.

Have the children look at the picture and tell what is happening. Ask the children if they remember this girl from a story in *Reader 1*. Does this girl like bees? Ask what they see in the picture that has the long /e/ sound (bee, feet, knees). Write these words on the board and have the children read them several times.

Read the poem with the children. Ask which words rhyme, which words tell the sound the bee makes, and which sentences are exclamations.

Ask the following questions:

"How did the girl know there was a bee near her?"

"Why was she afraid?"

"Is running the best thing to do?" (No, you should stand as still as possible to keep from frightening the bee into stinging.)

"What do you think will happen next?"

"Why do you think the bee might have come near the girl?" (The flower on her shirt might have attracted it.)

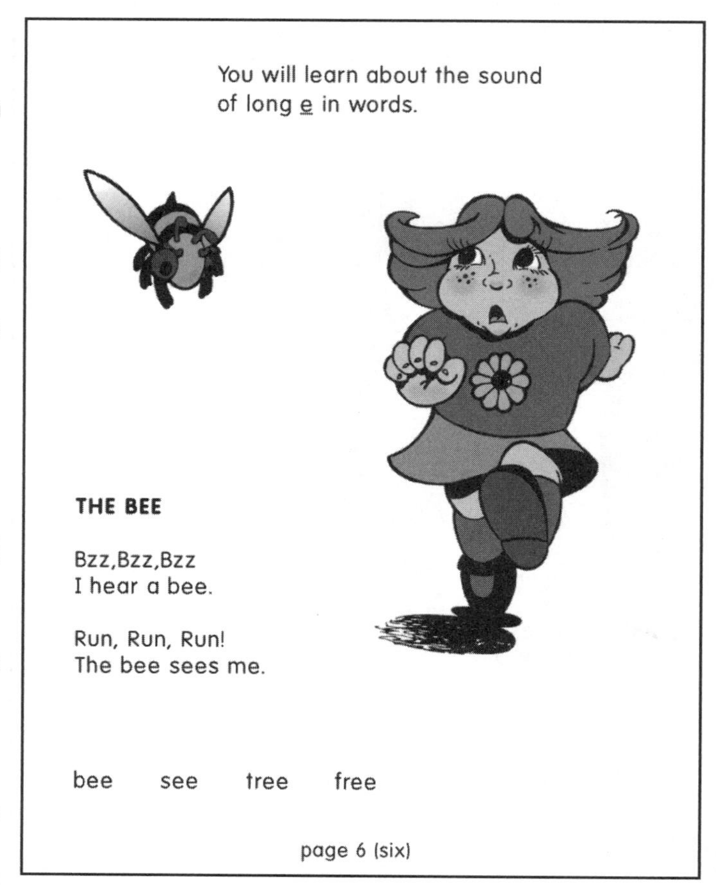

Have a child tell the story in his own words. Let several children tell what they think the ending might be.

ACTIVITIES:

1. Make a chart for the long /e/ sound. Cut pictures from magazines or catalogs and paste them on a sheet of tagboard. Print *Long Ee* at the top. Leave space to write words which cannot be pictured. Have the children use the chart in pairs or in small groups.

2. Read stories about bees, articles from encyclopedias, or sections on bees from science books.

TEACHING READING:

Ask students how many have seen or been in the snow. Together, create a list of things which can be done in the snow (snowballs, ski, etc). Create another list of things which can be done in the sunshine/warm weather. Show students a U.S. map and point out states which have lots of snow and others that don't (Florida, Ariz. etc). Explain to students that many people who live in the "snowy" states travel to warmer states during the winter. Ask them why these people want to spend the winters in the warmer states. (hard to shovel snow, very cold, icy roads, stay inside a lot, nothing to do...). Determine which category YOUR state falls into (snow or sunshine or combination). Tell the children the story they'll be reading is like a poem. It has rhyming lines.

Read the story "I Don't Know About Snow" together, then answer the following questions:

"Who is this story about?" (Grandpa Jones)

"Where does he live?" (Idaho)

"What months does he call home in the wintertime?" (his RV)

"How many days does he travel?" (2-3)

"Why doesn't Grandpa want to stay where it snows in the winter?" (hard to shovel the walk)

"What would he rather do?" (sit in the sunshine and talk)

"Do you think the person who's telling the story has ever been in snow?" (no)

"How do you know?" (last line..."I really wouldn't know")

Have students:

Find all the long vowel words: (Jones, Idaho, snow, owns, home, road, three, days, arrive, my, stay, play, sliding (slide), used, making (make), throw, sunshine, hope, old, really, know)

ACTIVITY:

Categorize the long vowel words by spelling or phonetic rule (ay, oa, ow, i_e, etc). Add new words to each column. Give students a large piece of light blue construction paper. Have them fold it in half. On one half they will make a picture of something fun to do in the snow, and the other side something fun to do in the sunshine. Brainstorm for rhyming words. Then write a poem about what Grandpa will do in the sunshine state during the winter. Make snowflakes. Read other stories that have a cold or snowy theme. Read stories about warmer climate places. Write a letter to Grandpa telling him you miss him during the summer. Tell him what you like to do.

Page 7: Activity Page

CONCEPTS: long *e*, *y* as long *e* or *i*, retelling a story

TEACHER GOALS: To teach the children
To identify words with the long *e* sound,
To tell the main idea of a story,
To recall details from a story, and
To tell what might happen next.

MATERIALS NEEDED: *Ee* card, Worksheet 2

TEACHING PAGE 7:

Show the *Ee* card and have the children listen for the long /e/ sound .

Read the sentence and direction at the top of the page with the children or have a child read them. Read the letters and ask the children to say the long /e/sound.

Have the children read each list of words. Ask the children to tell how the words are alike. Have them give the ending for each list.

Read the direction at the bottom of the page and have the children read the words, listening for the ending sound of long *e*. Tell them that in long words (those with two or more syllables) the *y* at the end has the long *e* sound . In short words (cry, by) the *y* at the end has the long /i/ sound.

Have the children read the lists several times and give more words that rhyme, or that end in *y*.

Listen for the sound of long e.

Read the long e words.

e		ee	
be	feed	eel	deep
he	need	feel	keep
me	seed	heel	sleep
we		peel	steep
	beef	wheel	
bee	reef		feet
see	seen		sheet
wee	peek	teen	street
tree	seek	green	
free	week	queen	freeze
thee	creek	between	sneeze

Listen for the long /e/ sound at the end of these words.

puppy	funny	happy	daddy
silly	baby	story	penny

page 7 (seven)

ACTIVITIES:

1. Have the children make the ending on their desks with alphabet cards. (Have the children make extra vowel cards so they can spell words with double vowels.) Read a word from the list and have the children put the beginning sound in front of the correct ending. Have them say the word and spell it before giving the next word.

2. Children who have trouble hearing the long /ē/ sound should work with another child or an aide with the *Ee* card.

3. Dictate the following words and have the children write them on a sheet of writing tablet paper (be, bee, he, see, me, wee, we, Lee, she, tree). (Use each word in a sentence so the children will know which spelling to use for words that sound the same.)

Collect the papers and correct them by drawing a line through the incorrect spelling and writing the correct spelling behind it. Have the children write the misspelled words five times each on the back of the paper.

TEACHING READING:

Find "The Tree Fort" in *Reader 3*. Point out the *y* with the long /e/ sound in *Tippy*.

Have a child read the title. Let the children read the story silently.

Ask these questions:

"What did Lee have?"

"Who was Lee, a boy or a girl?" "How did you know?"

"Who helped Lee?" "How do you think he helped?"

"What do Dad and Lee do in the tree fort?"

"What do you think they talk about?" (Bring out the idea that children should be able to talk to their parents about anything that is troubling them and share all their joys and successes with them because that is one of the reasons God gave them parents. Bring out that we, with our heavenly Father, should do this also.)

"Who is Tippy?"

"How do you know Tippy is not a cat?"

"What do you think will happen next?"

"How do you think Lee feels?"

"Could this story really have happened?" "How do you know?"

Have the children read the story aloud. Have them read the words with the long /e/ sound, words with short vowel sounds, and the pronouns. Have them tell the person or thing to which each pronoun refers.

ACTIVITIES:

1. Have the children share their experiences with tree houses, building things with their fathers, or doing other things with fathers and mothers.

Do Worksheet 2.

2. Have the children read the direction at the top of the page.

Have them read each word and give several rhyming words. Accept any words that rhyme even if they have different spellings (be, tree, tea). Have the children write one or two rhyming words on each line. Have the children read the words they write.

Have the children read the direction and the words in the middle of the page. Ask them to tell where they hear the long /e/ sound and which letter makes the sound. Have them read the words again.

Tell the children to read the sentences and write one of the words on the line. Tell

Name ____________

Write rhyming words.

see ____________

peal ____________

feet ____________

keep ____________

Write the words.

funny **puppy** **happy**

This story is funny.

My puppy is brown.

I am happy.

Language Arts 105
Worksheet 2
with page 7

Teacher check ____________
Initial Date

them to choose the word that makes sense in the sentence. Have the children read the sentences.

The teacher should check this page and have the children correct any mistakes.

Page 8: Activity Page

CONCEPTS: possession, writing a story

TEACHER GOALS: To teach the children
To identify words that show possession,
To write a story using paragraphs, and
To write sentences with the correct punctuation mark.

VOCABULARY: title

MATERIALS NEEDED: drawing paper, crayon or paints, construction paper

TEACHING PAGE 8:

Have the children read the direction at the top of the page. Have the children read the first sentence silently, then have one child read it aloud and tell which word should go on the line. Have them spell the word and tell what belongs to John.

Let the children finish the exercise by themselves. Check.

Have the children read the directions silently for writing the story, then aloud. Be sure they understand everything they are to do.

Write words the children need help in spelling on a sheet of writing tablet paper kept on each child's desk for that purpose.

Talk about the kinds of sentences they may write and the punctuation mark for each, what a good paragraph is, and what a good title is.

Have the children draw and color or paint a picture to go with their stories.

Take one or two class periods for the children to read their stories to the class. Go through the "Rules for Telling a Story"(LH 102, page 20) before they begin reading their stories.

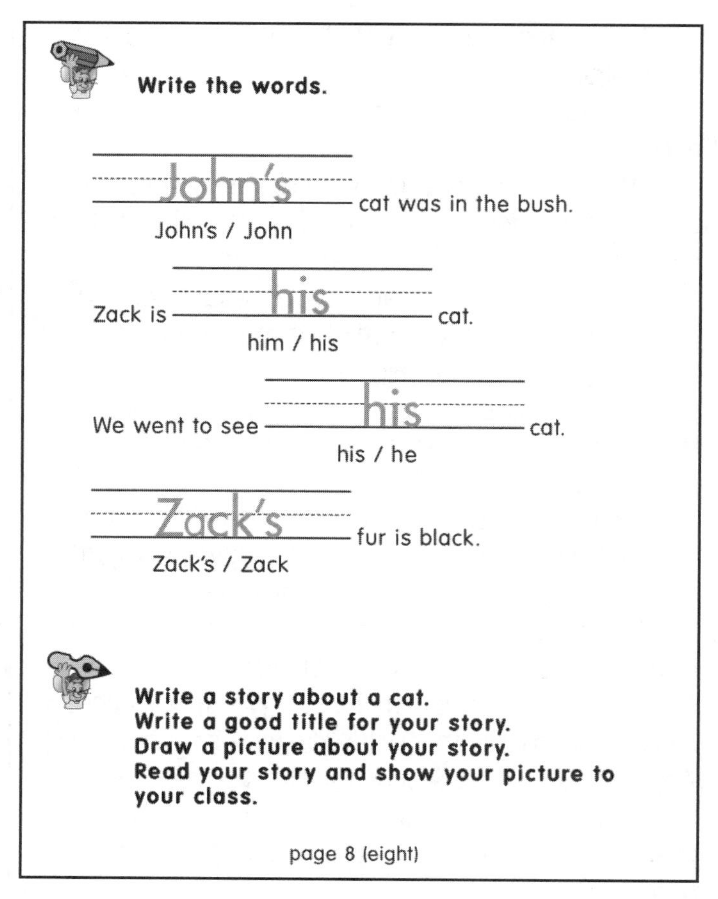

ACTIVITY:

Make a folder or booklet in which to keep the child's written work. Use tagboard or construction paper and let the child put his name on the cover and decorate it any way he wishes. He may also put a title on the cover. If the stories and other written work are dated as they are put in the folder, it will provide a good record of the child's writing and spelling progress in this LIFEPAC. The folders make it easy for the parents to see what the child is doing.

Page 9: Activity Page

CONCEPT: verb forms, subject-verb agreement

TEACHER GOALS: To teach the children
To listen to which verb sounds better, and
To understand that verbs must agree with subjects.

TEACHING PAGE 9:
Have the children read the direction at the top of the page. Read the first sentence and the two words under the lines with the children. Ask which word sounds better in the sentence. Have them circle the word *jump* and write it on the lines. (If you have the children circle the word first, then read the sentence over again before they write the word on the lines, they will make fewer mistakes.)

Let the children finish the page by themselves. Check by having the sentences read with the correct word. Ask the children to tell why that word sounded better. (All the subjects were singular).

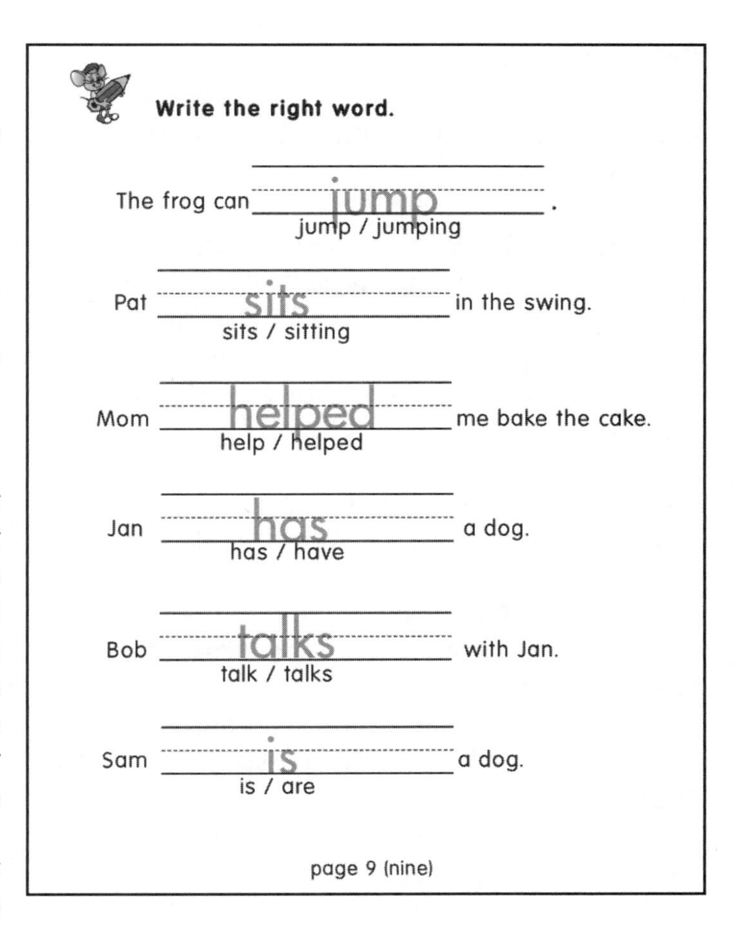

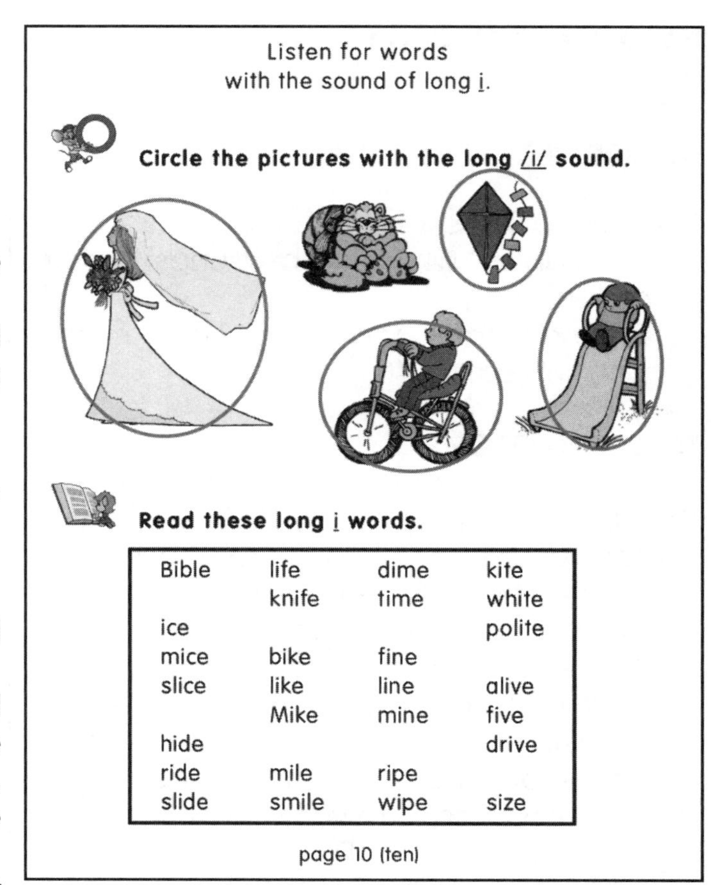

Listen for words
with the sound of long i.

Circle the pictures with the long /i/ sound.

Read these long i words.

Bible	life	dime	kite
	knife	time	white
ice			polite
mice	bike	fine	
slice	like	line	alive
	Mike	mine	five
hide			drive
ride	mile	ripe	
slide	smile	wipe	size

page 10 (ten)

Page 10: Long i

CONCEPTS: sound of long *i*, rhyming words

TEACHER GOALS: To teach the children

To read rhyming words that have the long /i/ sound and end in silent *e*, and

To recognize that the silent *e* at the end of the word gives the vowel the long sound.

MATERIALS NEEDED: Ii card, magazines, paste or glue, scissors, Worksheet 3

TEACHING PAGE 10:

Have the children read the title and sentence at the top of the page.

Have them read the first direction and name the pictures. Have them circle the pictures with the long /i/ sound (bride, cat, riding a bike, kite, sliding or slide). Have the children tell what they circled.

Have the children read the next direction.

Read each set of words, have the children repeat them after you and tell what the rhyming part of the words is. Have the children give other words that rhyme with each set.

Point out that in each word on this page the silent *e* makes the vowel have the long sound (or say its own name). Write several of the words on the board and have the children point to the silent *e*, then tell what the sound of the *i* is.

Have the children read all the words in the box again. Be sure they know the meaning of each word and can use each word in a sentence. Point out the silent *k* in the word *knife* and the soft sound of *c* in the *ice* words. Ask why Bible has a capital letter.

ACTIVITIES:

1. Do Worksheet 3.

Read the sentence at the top of the page with the children. Have them read the directions. Do the first set of words with the children. Have them read *bit,* then write the silent *e* and read the word *bite.* Have them read the words again.

Do the same with the words *kit* and *kite.*

Let the children finish the first section. Check by having the children read each set of words.

Do *cap* and *cape* together, then let the children do the other three sets. Check by having the children read each set of words.

Tell the children that for most words the silent *e* makes the vowel have the long sound, but that some words do not follow this rule.

Write the following words on the board and have the children read them (love, have, dove, give, some, come).

Have the children read the second direction, write the letter *i* in each word, then read the word. Check by having the child spell each word, say it, and use it in a sentence.

2. Make a chart for pictures and words with the long /i/ sound at the beginning, in the middle, and at the end. Write *Long Ii* at the top of the chart.

3. Dictate the following words and have the children write them on a sheet of writing tablet paper. Collect the papers and correct by drawing a line through the misspelled word and by writing it correctly. Have the children write each misspelled word five times on the back of the paper (time, size, dime, prize).

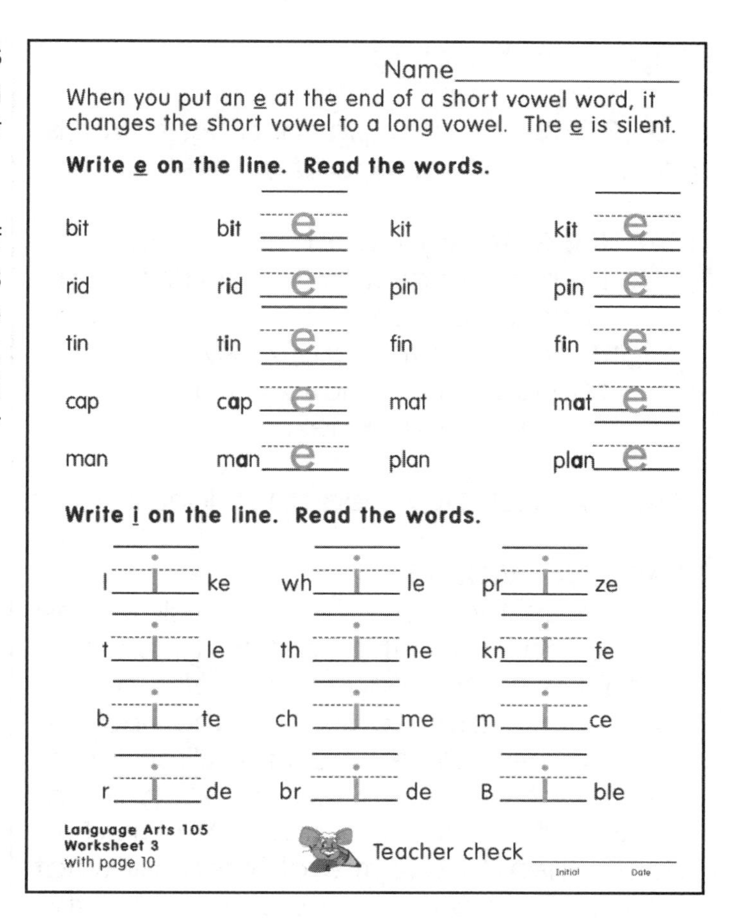

Name________________

When you put an e at the end of a short vowel word, it changes the short vowel to a long vowel. The e is silent.

Write e on the line. Read the words.

bit	bit e	kit	kit e
rid	rid e	pin	pin e
tin	tin e	fin	fin e
cap	cap e	mat	mat e
man	man e	plan	plan e

Write i on the line. Read the words.

l i ke	wh i le	pr i ze
t i le	th i ne	kn i fe
b i te	ch i me	m i ce
r i de	br i de	B i ble

Language Arts 105
Worksheet 3
with page 10

Teacher check ____________
Initial Date

Page 11: Activity Page

CONCEPTS: long *i, igh,* and *ight* words, contractions, sequence of events

TEACHER GOALS: To teach the children
To identify words with the long /*i*/ sound
To recognize words ending in *igh* and *ight* that have the long /*i*/ sound,
To recognize contractions, and
To tell what comes next.

MATERIALS NEEDED: *Ii* card, Worksheet 4,

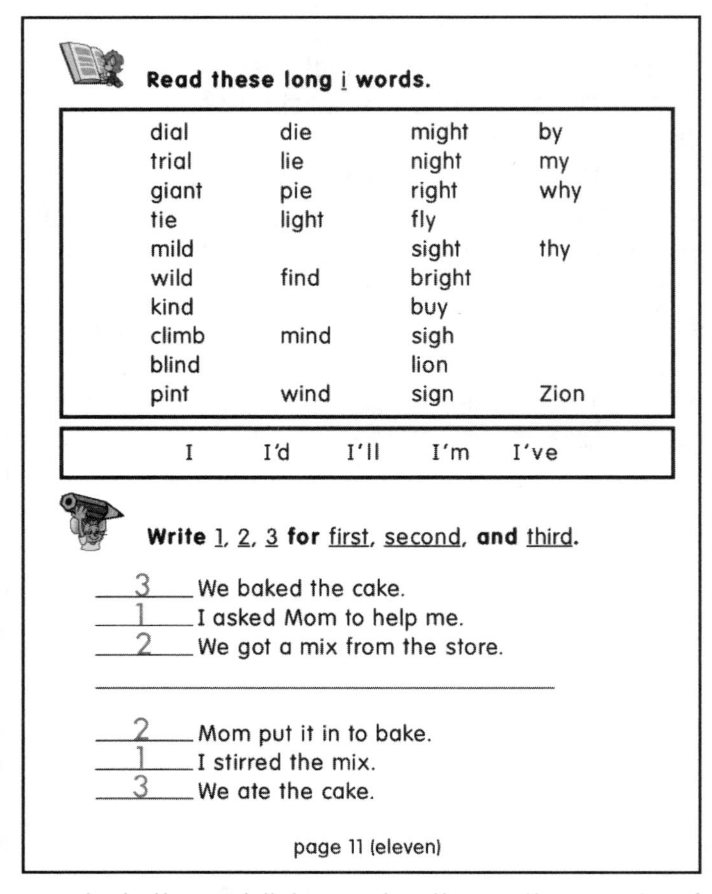

Read these long i words.

dial	die	might	by
trial	lie	night	my
giant	pie	right	why
tie	light	fly	
mild		sight	thy
wild	find	bright	
kind		buy	
climb	mind	sigh	
blind		lion	
pint	wind	sign	Zion

I I'd I'll I'm I've

Write 1, 2, 3 for first, second, and third.

__3__ We baked the cake.
__1__ I asked Mom to help me.
__2__ We got a mix from the store.

__2__ Mom put it in to bake.
__1__ I stirred the mix.
__3__ We ate the cake.

page 11 (eleven)

TEACHING PAGE 11:

Hold up the card for *i* and ask for the long sound. Have the children give words which have the long sound of *i* at the beginning, in the middle, or at the end.

Have the children read the direction at the top of the page. Read each set of words in the box and have the children repeat them. Have the children tell what the rhyming part of the words is. Ask the children to give the meaning of each word. Have the children give more words that rhyme with each group.

Point out the soft /*g*/ sound in giant, the silent *b* in *climb,* the silent *e* in the *ie* words, the silent *gh* in *sigh* and the *ight* words, the silent *g* in *sign,* and the silent *u* in *buy*. Point out that wind has two meanings and two pronunciations. Have the children read the words in the box again.

Have the children read the contractions and tell from which words each was formed. Have them use each one in a sentence.

Have the children read the next direction. Tell them to read all three sentences and to point to the one that happened first. Have a child read it. Have the children read the other two sentences and number them in order. Have the children read them. Have a child read all three sentences in order.

Let the children do the other set of sentences by themselves. Check by having the children read the sentences and tell which number they put in front of each. Have a child read all three sentences in order.

ACTIVITIES:

1. Do Worksheet 4.

Have the children read the directions at the top of the page. Tell them to write the letter *i* on the line in each word. Have them read the word. Let the children finish the exercise by themselves. Remind them that in every word the *i* will have the long sound. Check by having the child spell the word, then read it and use it in a sentence
.

Have the children read the direction for the next exercise.

Have them read the three words. Tell the children to read the sentences carefully, and to copy one of the words on the line to finish the sentence. Tell them to read the sentence over again to be sure the word they wrote makes sense in the sentence. Check by having a child read the sentence.

2. Dictate the following words and have the children write them on a sheet of writing tablet paper. Collect the papers and correct by drawing a line through the misspelled word and by writing the word correctly on the line behind it. Have the children write each misspelled word five times on the back of the paper (find, night, kind, right, wind, light).

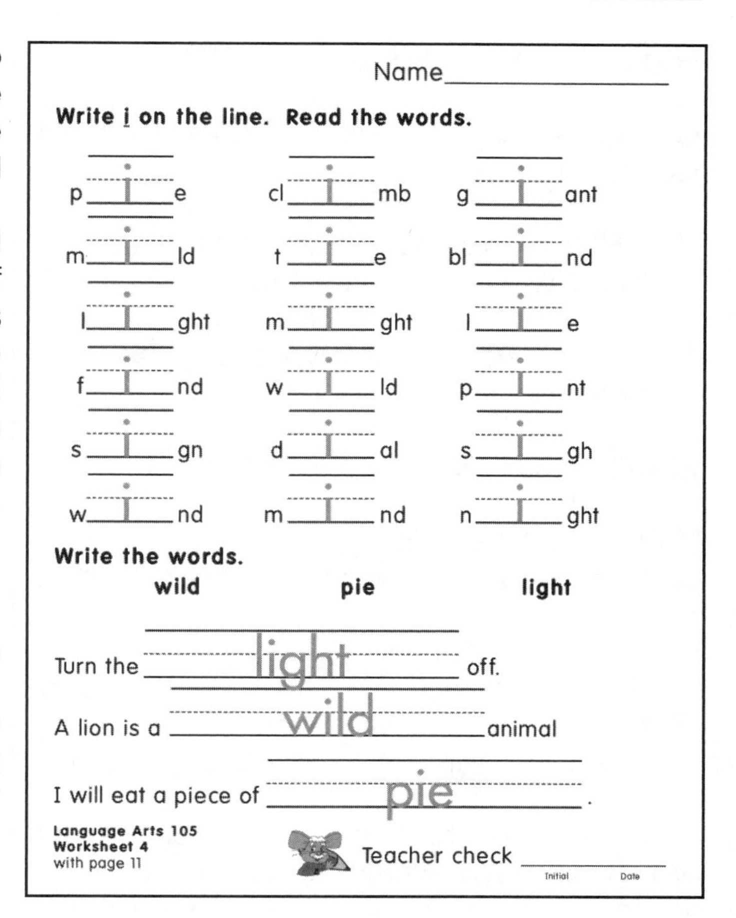

Name__________

Write i on the line. Read the words.

p i e	cl i mb	g i ant
m i ld	t i e	bl i nd
l i ght	m i ght	l i e
f i nd	w i ld	p i nt
s i gn	d i al	s i gh
w i nd	m i nd	n i ght

Write the words.

wild **pie** **light**

Turn the light off.

A lion is a wild animal.

I will eat a piece of pie.

Language Arts 105
Worksheet 4
with page 11

Teacher check __________
Initial Date

TEACHING READING:

Read the story "Mike's Light Bites" in *Reader 3.*

Tell the children to look at the picture and tell what is happening. Have them read the title and tell what *Light Bites* might be.

Ask these questions:

"What is the boy's name?"

"What is the name of the cereal he likes?"

What else does he like to eat for breakfast?"

"Who makes his breakfast?"

"Where did his mother buy the food?"

"When did his mother buy the food?"

"What do you like to eat for breakfast?"

Let several children share experiences they have had with fixing breakfast, for themselves or for others.

Have the children read the story aloud.

Have them find any long /i/ words in the story. Have the children look at the spellings of the long /i/ words.

Page 12: Activity Page

CONCEPTS: words that are alike, rhyming words with long *i*

TEACHER GOALS: To teach the children
To tell words that are alike,
To tell why they are alike, and
To write words that rhyme with the long /*i*/ sound.

MATERIALS NEEDED: alphabet cards

TEACHING PAGE 12:
Write these sets of words on the board in rows .

sit	stand	the	bend
my	four	cry	tie
the	then	three	she

Have the children read each set of words and tell which three are alike in some way. Remind them to look for beginnings, endings, or meanings (words could be alike in many ways). Have them tell why the fourth word is different:

first set: three ways to move; one *th* word

second set: three rhyming words with the long /*i*/ sound at the end; one number word

third set: three *th* words; one *sh* word

Have the children read the direction at the top of the page. Tell them to look at the words in each box carefully, read them several times if necessary, then choose the three that are alike in some way. Let the children do the exercise by themselves. Check by having the children read the words they chose, tell why they are alike, and tell how the fourth word is different.

Row 1: three words that tell what to do; one *wh* word

Row 2: three words beginning with *wh;* one with *th*

Row 3: three movement words; one for not moving

Row 4: three size words; one animal

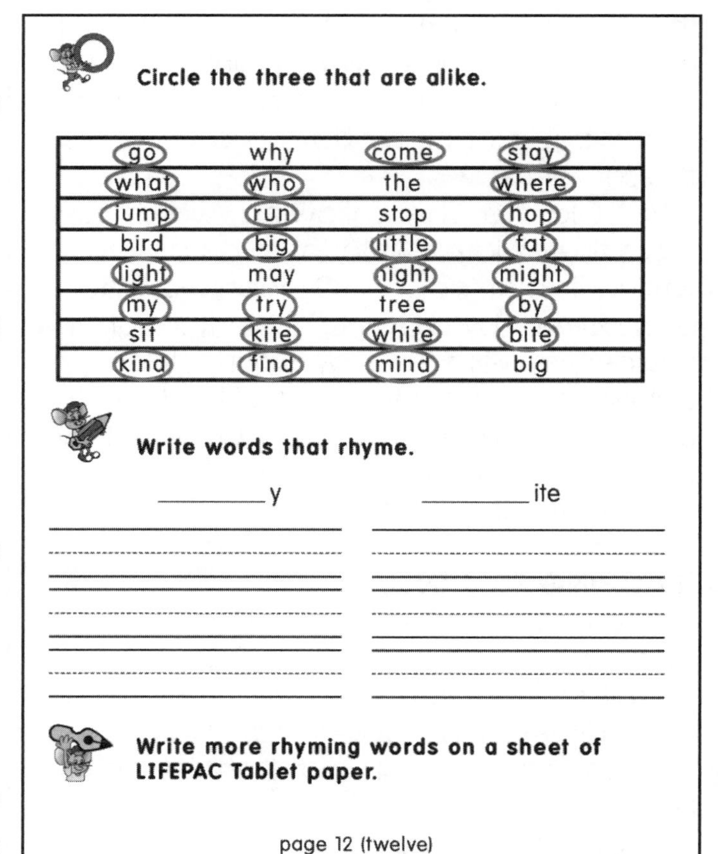
Circle the three that are alike.

go	why	come	stay
what	who	the	where
jump	run	stop	hop
bird	big	little	fat
light	may	night	might
my	try	tree	by
sit	kite	white	bite
kind	find	mind	big

Write words that rhyme.

________y ________ite

Write more rhyming words on a sheet of LIFEPAC Tablet paper.

page 12 (twelve)

Row 5: three *ight* words; one *ay* word

Row 6: three *y* ending words; one *ee* word

Row 7: three *ite* words; one *it* word

Row 8: three *ind* words; one *ig* word

Have the children read the next direction on the page. Have them read the word endings and give rhyming words for each. Have the children write one word for each on the lines and read them for you to write under the endings on the board. Remind them that the words do not have to be spelled the same at the end to rhyme, but they must sound alike. Write an *ie* word under the *y* ending, and an *ight* word under the *ite* ending to show them. Have them read the words and listen for the rhyming part.

Have the children finish writing the words on the lines, then prepare the sheet of writing tablet paper with the endings at the top of the folded sheet, and have them write more words on it.

Check by having the children give words from their lists for you to write on the board. They should tell you which ending to write the word under. Have the children add to and correct their lists. The teacher also should correct these papers. Have them read the lists from the board several times.

ACTIVITIES:

1. Have the children form the rhyming words on their desks with the alphabet cards as you say them. Have them read the word and spell it before you give them the next word. This exercise is a very good way for children to begin learning which words should be spelled with the *ight* ending and which ones with the *ite* ending. This principle also applies to the *y, uy,* and *ie* endings. Always give the meaning of the word you want them to spell or use it in a sentence. This exercise may be done many times during the day whenever you have five or ten extra minutes.

2. Dictate the following words and have the children write them on a sheet of writing tablet paper.

Use each one in a sentence.

by	night
my	bite
tie	kite
try	light
pie	white

Collect the papers and correct by drawing a line through the incorrect word and by writing the correct spelling behind it. Have the children write each misspelled word five times on the back of the paper.

TEACHING READING:

Provide materials for students to make a sail boat: colored and white paper. Have them attach a craft stick to the back to make it a movable object. Give them some time (play ocean music) to "sail" their boats. Ask how many have been on a boat (of any kind). Share stories. Ask: "If you could go on a boat, what would you like to see?" Share answers.

Write the homonyms tail and tale on the board. Discuss what each one means. Tell students they're going to read a story about two boys who go sailing with their friend, Captain Raymond.

Read the story "A Tale of a Tail" together, then ask the following questions:

"What are the boys' names?" (James and Clay)

"What time of year was it?" (summer)

"What did the boys bring with them?" (water bottles, lunch)

"Who brought a notebook?" (James)

"What was the sea like?" (calm)

"What did they hope to see?" (a whale)

"Why didn't James want to go back?" (they hadn't seen a whale yet)

"What words help describe the sounds they heard?" (swish, splash)

"What did the boys see?" (a large tail)

"Do you think it was a whale's tail?" (probably – it was large)

Have students:

Find long a words: (gray, today, James, Clay, Raymond, sailing, waiting, day, whales, raced, waves, late, maybe, bay tail, tale)

Find long i words: (sky, shining, bright, might, time, liked, dive, behind, smiled, I)

List contractions: (it's, we're, haven't)

ACTIVITY:

Share books on whales. Ask students what kind of whale they thought the boys had seen. Give the students a large piece of construction paper. Have them create a "sea scene" with details. They can add their sailboat to the scene by cutting a slit along the sea's surface and inserting the stick through the opening. Now they have a sailing sail boat! Ask students what energy powers a sailboat. (wind) Do some experiments with boats. Have students design boats at home and then bring them to school to determine which are the best floaters. Write stories about another adventure for James, Clay and Captain Raymond. Write a story or poem about the Whale's Tail.

SELF TEST 1

CONCEPTS: long a, long e, possessives, rhyming words

TEACHER GOAL: To teach the children
To check their own progress periodically.

TEACHING PAGE 13:
Read the directions on the page with the children. Be sure they understand everything they are to do. Name the pictures before they begin. (train, cake, rabbit, table, cup, cap, whale)
Let the children complete the entire page by themselves.
Check the page as soon as possible and go over it with the child. Point out what he did well and then show him where he will need extra help.

SELF TEST 1
Circle the pictures with the long /a/ sound.
Circle the long e words.
be set he pen me
Write the words.
That is my red balloon.
me / my
Here is Jack's hat.
Jack's / Jacks
Dave's bike is blue.
Daves / Dave's
Write the rhyming words.
dime mice
10/12 Teacher Check Initial Date
page 13 (thirteen)

ACTIVITIES:
1. Children who missed more than one in the long *a* or long *e* exercise should work with the vowel cards.
2. Make up worksheets similar to the ones in the Teacher's Guide for those who missed more than one in any specific area. Work in small groups, if possible.

SPELLING WORDS:

lake
cake
game
name
mane
be
me
he
mice
hid

II. PART TWO

Page 14: Long o and u

CONCEPTS: sound of long *o*, sound of long *u*

TEACHER GOALS: To teach the children

To read words that have the long /o/ sound, and

To read words that have the long /u/ sound.

MATERIALS NEEDED: Oo and Uu cards, Worksheet 5

TEACHING PAGE 14:

Read these lists of words to the class and have the children tell which long vowel sound they hear.

Review *sounds:*

make	bike	grapes
peel	cry	train
wheat	white	me

New *sounds:*

go	you	home
few	cue	don't
gold	chose	fuel

Have the children read the title.

Have the children name the pictures and give the vowel sound for each. (nose, hose, goat, bow)

Have the children read the direction and the list of words. Help them sound out any words with which they have trouble. Point out the variations of long *o* in the words (o, oa, silent e, ow). Be sure the children know the meaning of each word. Have them use each in a sentence.

Have the children follow the same procedure for the long *u* words. Point out the variation in letters making the sound of long *u* (silent e, ou, ew). (mule, tube, cube, pew)

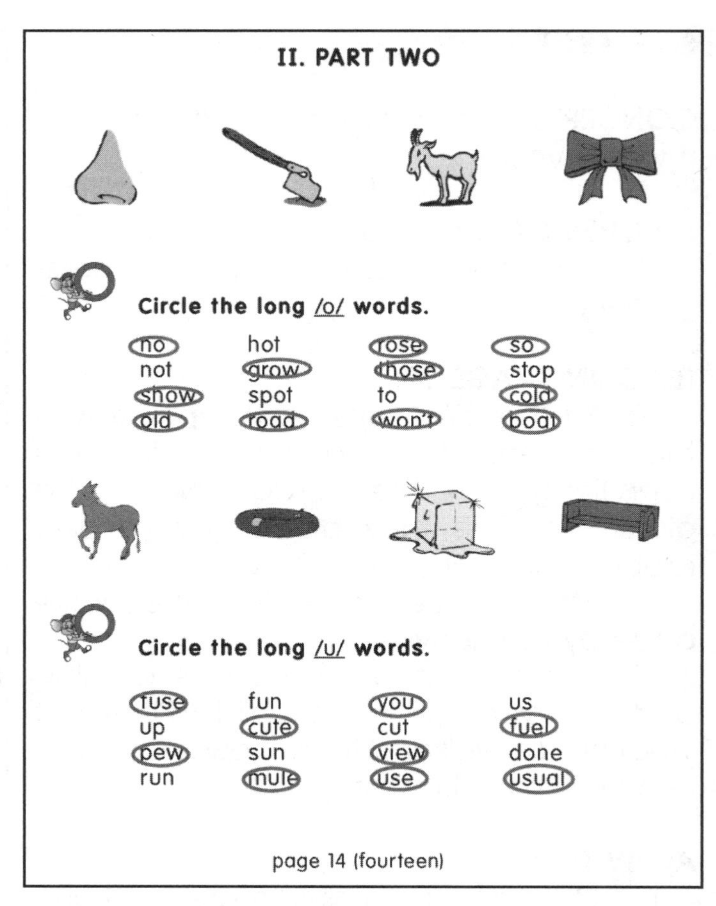

ACTIVITIES:

1. Do Worksheet 5.

Have the children read the title and first direction at the top of the page.

Do the first one or two examples together and have children repeat the words several times. Be sure the children understand that by adding the *e* to the short vowel word you are changing the vowel sound to the long sound.

Let the children finish the exercise, then read the pairs of words aloud.

Have the children read the next direction and the group of words at the bottom of the page. Tell them each word will be used once. Remind them to read carefully before they write the words. Check by having the children read the sentences.

TEACHING READING:

Have the children read the story "Adam and Eve" in *Reader 3*. Have the children read the story silently. Have them look at the picture and tell you the names of the man and the woman.

Ask questions similar to these:

"What time of day do you think it is?"

"Where are Adam and Eve?"

"What did Adam and Eve see around them?"

"Do you think they had to use sunscreen?"

"Were Adam and Eve happy?"

Ask the children if they know what happened in the garden.

Have the children find the words with long /o/. Write them on the board. Have them find the word with the short /u/ sound. Write it on the board.

Name________________

Make a New Word

Read the word. Write e on the line. Read the word you made.

rod	rod e	cub	cub e
not	not e	cut	cut e
hop	hop e	us	us e

Write a word in each sentence.

hoe **you** **grow** **used**

We can grow plants in a garden.

We must hoe our garden.

We grow our garden.

Do you know who sends the sunshine and the rain?

Language Arts 105
Worksheet 5
with page 14

Teacher check __________
Initial Date

Page 15: Activity Page

CONCEPTS: long *o*, possessives

TEACHER GOALS: To teach the children
To read words with the long *o* sound, and
To have children identify the possessive noun or pronoun.

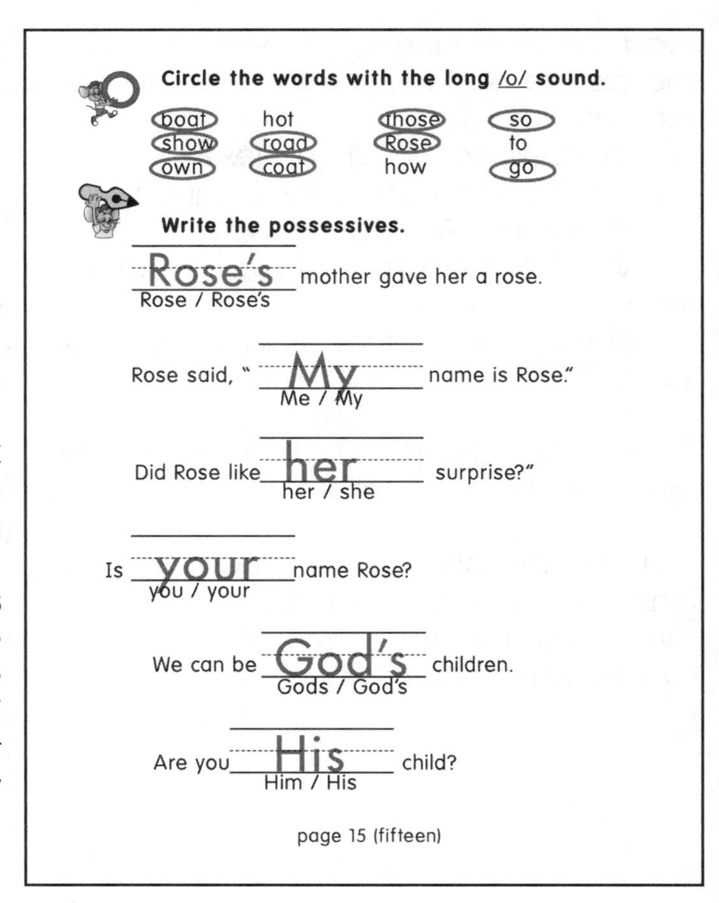

TEACHING PAGE 15:

Review the word possessives and ask the children to tell the meaning. Ask them to give examples of possessives. Ask them to give examples of possessive pronouns.

Have the children read the directions for both exercises. Have them do the page independently. Check by having the children read the words with the long /o/ sound, and the sentences using the correct word. Have the children correct any mistakes.

TEACHING READING:

Ask students how many have been close enough to a goat to touch or pet it. Where? - farm, petting zoo, back yard....etc. Ask students what goats like to eat. (just about anything) Tell them it's a common experience for a goat to grab paper out of pockets, purses and even your hand! Put the word oats on the board. Ask students if they know what oats are? (like oatmeal or cereal) Ask how many like oatmeal, cold cereal or something similar. Write Grodin on the board - teach this unusual name to students. Tell students they are going to read a story about Grodin, a goat who doesn't like to eat his oats.

Read the story "Oats Are For Goats" together, then answer the following questions:

"How did Grodin act when he was given oats in the beginning of the story?" (mad)

"What did he do first?" (put a note on the post)

"What did the note say?" (Everyone read it together): NO OATS FOR THIS GOAT!

"Did the note help?" (no)

"How do you know?" (it says, "but everyday he got oats for breakfast, lunch and dinner.")

"What did he do next?" (broke out of his pen)

"What did he find to eat?" (list from the story)

"How did Grodin feel after he ate all that stuff?" (not very well)

"How do you know?" (he groaned and said "I don't feel very well")

"Why did Grodin decide oats were good?" (the other stuff he ate made him sick)

Have students:

Find the long o words: (oh, no, oats, Grodin, groaned, goat, wrote, note, post, only, home, broke, roam, poked, nose, old, rope, broken, boat, notes, soap, slowly)

ACTIVITY:

Take the list of long o words and categorize them into groups by spelling or phonetic rule (oa, o, o_e, etc) Add more words to each group. Have students make a list of other things Grodin might like to eat (challenge - long o sounds). Use the list to make a menu for his next meal. Have students write Grodin a letter telling him why he should eat good things. Talk about the 5 food groups. Have students choose something from each food group and create a meal they would like. Have students contribute to a class list of foods they don't like....but may have to eat sometimes. Go globally – discuss situations in countries where children eat the same thing everyday.

Page 16: Activity Page

CONCEPTS: long *u*, rhyming

TEACHER GOALS: To teach the children
To read words with the long /u/ sound,
To write words that rhyme with the long /i/ sound, and
To write words in sentences.

MATERIALS NEEDED: Worksheet 6

TEACHING PAGE 16:

Have the children read the directions at the top of the page. Help them sound out and read the words in the lists. Have them listen carefully for the long /u/ sound. Point out the various spellings.

Have the children read the next direction. Have the children read the sentences aloud, then underline the long *u* words. Have different children read the sentences the second time.

Have the children read the last direction on the page. Have a child read each word and give a rhyming word. Have the children write a rhyming word for each word. You may wish to do the entire exercise with the children.

Read these words with your teacher. Listen for the long /u/ sound.

united	cube	fume	use
usual	cute	fuse	you
museum	mule	fuel	pew
music	view	humor	mew

Read these sentences.

You must sit in your usual pew.
The cute kitten said, "Mew. Mew."
The view is beautiful.
A mule uses hay for fuel.

Underline the words with the long /u/ sound. Read the sentences again.

Write rhyming words.

muse ____________ tube ____________

you ____________ plume ____________

cue ____________ you'll ____________

page 16 (sixteen)

ACTIVITIES:

1. Do Worksheet 6.

Have the children read the directions. Read through the lists of words with them and have them listen for the long /u/ sound. Read the second set of words to the children and have them listen for the sound of long *u*. In some parts of the country these words are pronounced with the *oo* sound, but the children should be aware that they are pronounced with the long /u/ sound in other parts of the country. Have them use each word in a sentence.

Have the children read the direction for the last section of the Worksheet. Tell them to read the sentences carefully. Have them circle the words that have the sound of long *u* in them. Check by having the children read the words they circled. Have each sentence read several times.

2. Dictate these words and have the children write them on a sheet of writing tablet paper. Correct the papers and have the children write each misspelled word five times on the back of the paper.

you	cube
mew	use
mule	pew
cute	fuel

TEACHING READING:

Have students think of as many kinds of machines as they can. List them. Discuss what machines do. Ask them if they could invent a machine, what would it do? Share ideas. Write Vroooooooooooooom! on the board. Practice this sound word with students. Tell them this is the sound of a machine they will read about in their story.

Read the story "Clean Machine" together, then answer the following questions:

"What is the name of the machine?" (Clean Machine)

"Why is it called the Clean Machine?" (it cleans)

List all the ways the Clean Machine cleans. (picks up, sweeps, dusts, scrubs, stacks, vacuums)

"How is this story different from other stories?" (it rhymes, it's like a poem)

"Why does it say to pull the plug and give the Clean Machine a hug?" (tired, worked hard, time to rest)

"Who do you think the Clean Machine really is?" (person, hard worker in the household)

"Who is the Clean Machine in your house?" (answers will vary)

Have students make Thank You cards to give to the "Clean Machine" at home.

Have students:

Find the long vowel words: (goes, clean, paper, sweeps, clothes, tables). Identify rhyming words: (floor-door, walls-halls, plug-hug, clean-machine)

ACTIVITY:

Have students invent their own machine. Design it and describe what it will do. Movement: Put students in groups of 3-5 and tell them they (as a group) are a machine. Have them decide what kind of machine, then each takes on a part of it. Act it out as a group and have the others guess. Make a list of other sound words machines might make.

Find books on different inventors to share with students.

Name________________

Read these words.

Listen for the long u sound.

use	you	Tuesday
used	pew	cucumber
usual	mew	excuse
usually	hew	rescue
unusual	view	useful

Use each word in a sentence.

duke	tube	due
new	stew	suit

Circle the words with the long u sound.

Can you use a saw?

Cars must have fuel to go fast.

We used up all the paint.

The kitten said, "Mew, mew."

An ice cube is cold.

Do you like music?

You'll have to come in now.

Language Arts 105
Worksheet 6
with page 16

Teacher check __________
Initial Date

Page 17: Activity Page

CONCEPT: compound words

TEACHER GOALS: To teach the children
To tell what a compound word is, and
To write compound words.

MATERIALS NEEDED: Worksheet 7

TEACHING PAGE 17:

Write the words *dog* and *house* on the chalkboard and have the children read them. Ask the children what they would have if they were to put the two words together. Write *doghouse* under the two words and have the children read it. Ask the children to give more compound words and write them on the board.

Read the direction at the top of the page with the children. Have them read the first two words and tell what the compound word is. Have them write it on the lines. Ask a child to tell what a checkup is.

Let the children finish the page by themselves. Check by having the children tell what the compound words are. Write them on the board and let children check their own work.

Have the children use each compound word in a sentence. You may have children write the sentences if you wish.

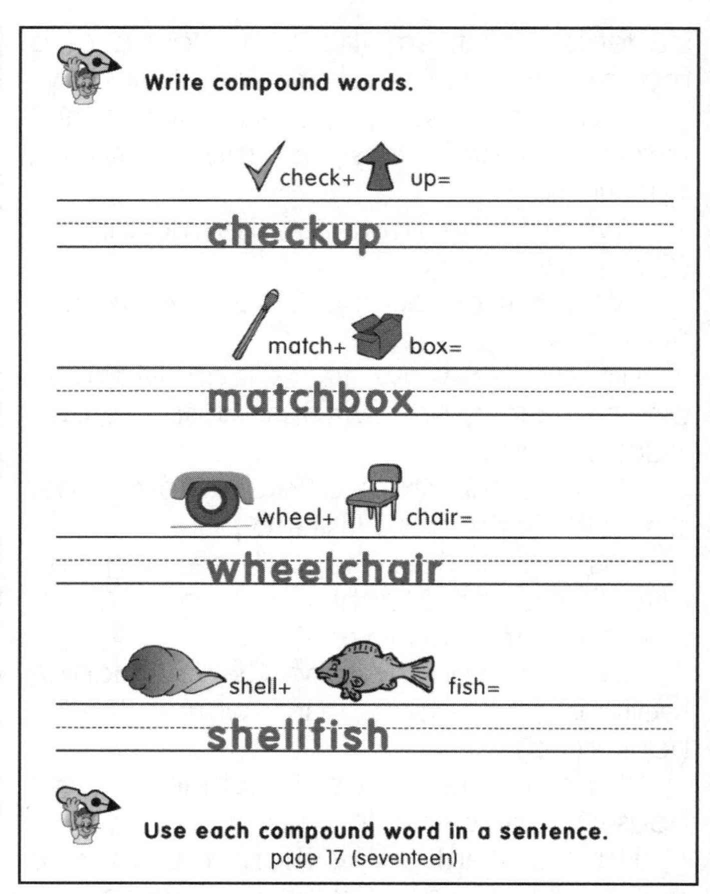

ACTIVITY:

Do Worksheet 7.

Have the children read the direction at the top of the Worksheet. Have them look at the picture and read the words. Ask the children to tell what the word checkerboard is.

Tell the children to look at the pictures on the page, to read the words, and to put the words together to get a compound word. Have them write the words on the lines.

Let the children finish the page by themselves. Check by having the children read the compound words. Write them on the board as they read them. Have the children read them again.

Have the children give other compound words and add them to the list.

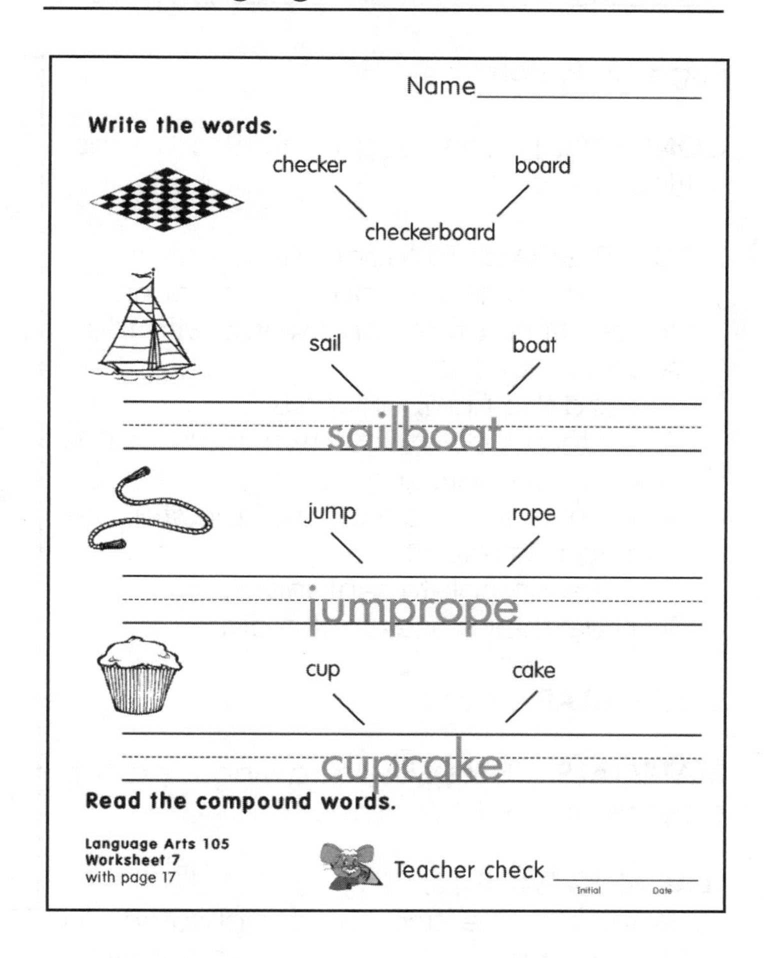

Name________________

Write the words.

checker board

checkerboard

sail boat

sailboat

jump rope

jumprope

cup cake

cupcake

Read the compound words.

Language Arts 105
Worksheet 7
with page 17

Teacher check ____________
Initial Date

Page 18: Plurals

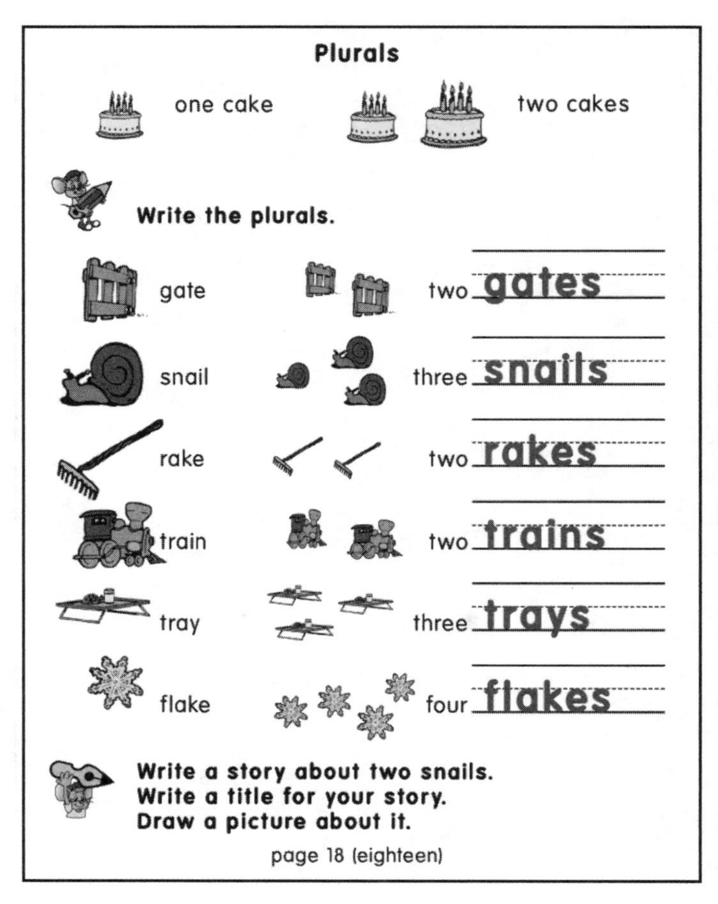

CONCEPTS: plurals, long *a*, number words, writing a story

TEACHER GOALS: To teach the children
- To write plurals by adding *s* to nouns,
- To identify pictures and words with the sound of long *a*,
- To read the number words,
- To write a story about two snails that is one or two paragraphs long,
- To identify the main idea of the story by writing a title for it,
- To write complete sentences, and
- To read their stories to the class.

VOCABULARY: snails

MATERIALS NEEDED: drawing paper, crayons or paint, Worksheet 8

TEACHING PAGE 18:

Read the title and ask the children to tell what plurals are. Ask how many ways they know to make plurals (adding s or es, some may be able to say the irregular plurals).

Have the children read the first line and tell how the plural *cakes* was made.

Read the direction with the children. Tell them to look at the pictures and words carefully, then write the plural on the lines.

The teacher should check this page. Have the children write misspelled plurals five times on a sheet of writing tablet paper.

Read the directions at the bottom of the page with the children. Tell them to write a story at least one paragraph long, two if they can. Remind them that all the sentences in the paragraph must tell about the same thing. Tell them to write neatly, to make their letters correctly, and to space their words well. When they are finished, correct their work and have them recopy it. Tell them the title should tell the main idea of the story.

ACTIVITIES:

1. Draw and color or paint a picture to go with the story. Take class time for the children to hold up their pictures and to read their stories to the class.
2. Do Worksheet 8.

Have the children read the direction at the top of the Worksheet. Have the children name the things in the pictures, then read the plurals in the boxes at the bottom.

Tell the children to cut off the bottom part of the page off along the heavy black line, then to cut the words apart. Paste the plural under the picture it matches. Give help as needed. The teacher should correct the paper and have the children correct any mistakes. The children may color the pictures when they are finished.

3. Read counting rhymes or books or stories or factual articles about snails.

TEACHING READING:

Find "The Ball Game" in *Reader 3*. Have the children read the story silently. Ask what the player's name is and what he did.

Have a child or all the children read the story aloud. Have them read the words with the long /a/ sound that they found in the story.

Ask questions similar to these:

"What time of day do you think it is? What time of year?"

"What should be in the picture that is not there? (pitcher's mound) "Where should it be?"

"What do you call each player?" "What do you think will happen next?"

"How do you think Ray feels?" "How would you feel?"

ACTIVITIES:

1. Let one child act out the story while the rest of the class reads it.
2. Have several children retell the story in their own words. They may add an ending to the story if they wish.
3. Read stories about real ball players, articles from sports magazines or newspapers about ball games and players, view films or filmstrips about playing ball, such as "Casey at the Bat."

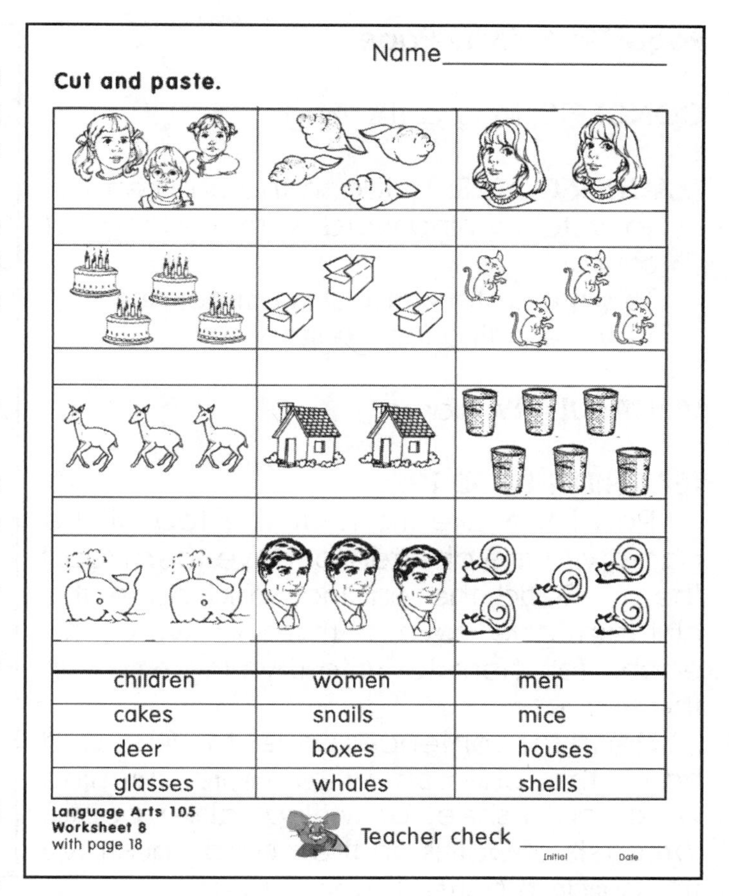

Name____________

Cut and paste.

children	women	men
cakes	snails	mice
deer	boxes	houses
glasses	whales	shells

Language Arts 105
Worksheet 8
with page 18

Teacher check ____________ Initial Date

Page 19: Activity Page

CONCEPTS: long *a*, rhyming

TEACHER GOALS: To teach the children
To write rhyming words with the long /*a*/ sound,
To write a story about a game, and
To write a title for the story.

VOCABULARY: game

TEACHING PAGE 19:

Read the directions at the top of the page with the children, or have them read them. Read the endings and have the children give several rhyming words for each. Tell them to write rhyming words in the spaces.

Read the sentences under the lines and have the children write more rhyming words on a sheet of writing tablet paper. Write lists of words on the board and have the children correct their papers.

Read the directions at the bottom of the page and talk about them. Be sure the children understand everything they are to do.

Give the children class time to write their stories or let them work on them when they finish their other work. Take class time later for the children to read their stories and show their pictures. Children should recopy their stories, after you have corrected them, before they read them aloud.

Write rhyming words. Read the words.

______ay	______ame

Can you think of more words?

Write them in your LIFEPAC Writing Tablet

What games do you like to play?

Write a story about a baseball game.
Write a title.
Draw a picture about your story.
Read your story and show your picture to the class.

page 19 (nineteen)

Page 20: Activity Page

CONCEPT: contractions

TEACHER GOALS: To teach the children
To read and write contractions, and
To match contractions with the words.

MATERIALS NEEDED: Worksheet 9

TEACHING PAGE 20 :

Read the sentence at the top of the page and the directions with the children. Have the children read each contraction, tell the words it was made from, and which letters were left out. Have the children tell why the apostrophe is there.

Read the next direction. Have the children match the words and the contraction. Check by having them read the words and the contractions that match. The teacher should check this page. Have the children correct any mistakes.

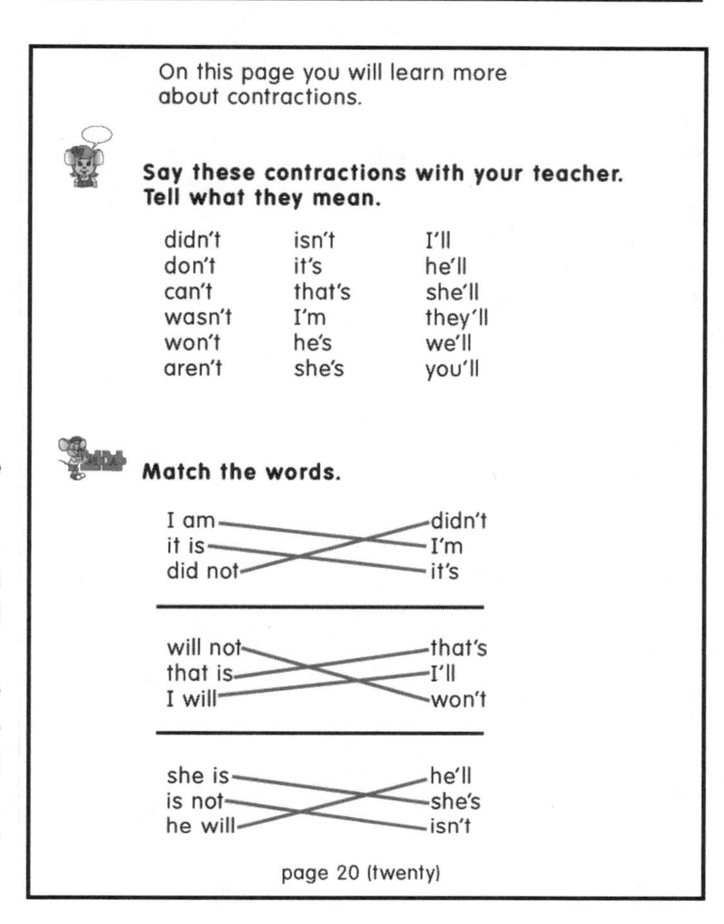

On this page you will learn more about contractions.

Say these contractions with your teacher. Tell what they mean.

didn't	isn't	I'll
don't	it's	he'll
can't	that's	she'll
wasn't	I'm	they'll
won't	he's	we'll
aren't	she's	you'll

Match the words.

I am	didn't
it is	I'm
did not	it's

will not	that's
that is	I'll
I will	won't

she is	he'll
is not	she's
he will	isn't

page 20 (twenty)

ACTIVITIES:

1. A chart posted in the classroom will help the children to learn contractions more easily. Put similar contractions in the same section of the chart.

is not...............isn't
cannot...........can't
it's....means....it is
she's.....means.....she is

Children can work with the chart alone, with a helper, or in small groups.

2. When you have a few minutes before the next class, say a contraction and have the children give the words or say the words and have the children give the contraction.

3. Do Worksheet 9.

Have the children read the direction at the top of the page. Have them read the examples, then do the page by themselves. Tell them to read the words carefully, before they write the contractions.

The last two are more difficult and some children may not be able to do them without help.

The teacher should check this page. Have the children correct any mistakes.

Have the children write a sentence for each contraction on a sheet of writing tablet paper. Tell them that they may write statements, questions, or exclamations. Remind them to write neatly and to space their words well.

The teacher should correct the papers and have the children recopy the corrected sentences. Let the children read two or three of his sentences to the class.

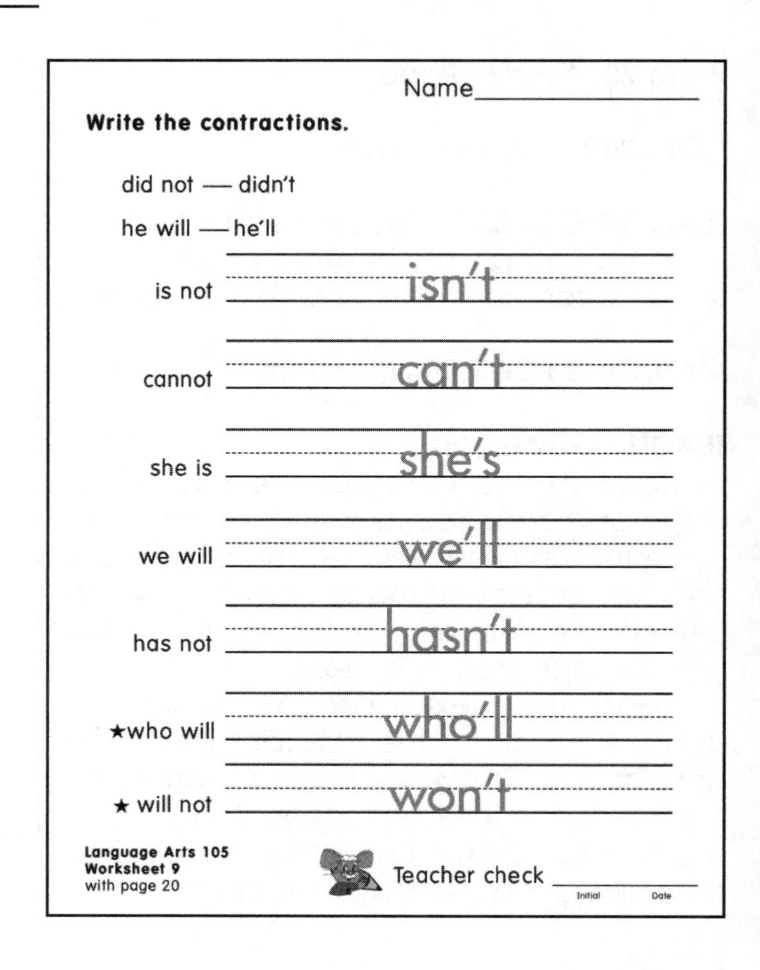

Name________________

Write the contractions.

did not — didn't

he will — he'll

is not isn't

cannot can't

she is she's

we will we'll

has not hasn't

★who will who'll

★ will not won't

Language Arts 105
Worksheet 9
with page 20

Teacher check ________
Initial Date

Jane has a balloon.
It is **Jane's** balloon.
It is **her** balloon.

Dave has a dog.
It is **Dave's** dog.
It is **his** dog.

Jane's **her** **Dave's** **his**

These words are called **possessives**.
They tell us that something belongs to someone.

Read the phrases. Tell what they mean.

Mother's house	her plate
Father's car	his nail
the girl's cat	my cake
the boy's name	our school
the dog's tail	their papers
Bill's train	your turn

page 21 (twenty-one)

Page 21: Possessives

CONCEPT: possessives

TEACHER GOALS: To teach the children
To recognize possessives and tell what they mean,
To recognize possessive pronouns and tell what they mean, and
To tell the use of the apostrophe in possessives.

MATERIALS NEEDED: Worksheets 10 and 11

TEACHING PAGE 21:

Tell the children that they will learn more about possessives on this page. Read the sentences at the top of the page and emphasize the possessives.

Note: If you have a very bright group of children, you may wish to distinguish between possessives and possessive pronouns. For the average child wait until he has learned more about pronouns before making the distinction.

Read the rest of the page and have the children repeat the phrases after you. Have the children use the phrases in sentences. Have them tell what each phrase means.

ACTIVITIES:

1. Do Worksheet 10.

Have the children read the direction at the top of the page, then look at the pictures and tell what is happening in each one.

Tell the children to write *1* under what happened first, *2* under what happened next, and *3* under what happened last. Have children tell which picture was first, next, and last.

Tell the children that the first group of sentences tells what is in the pictures. Have them read the sentences and number. Ask the children to read the sentence that happened *first*, then *next*, and *last*. Have the children correct any mistakes.

Let the children finish the page by themselves. Help any children who need help. Check by having the children read the sentences in the order they happened. Let the children tell what happened in each group of sentences in their own words (Set 1: 1, 2, 3; Set 2: 2, 1, 3; Set 3: 3, 2, 1).

2. Do Worksheet 11.

Have the children read the direction at the top of the page. Tell the children to read the sentence carefully, then to read the two words under the line. Have them circle the word that is correct, then read the sentence again using that word before they copy it on the line. Let the children do the page by themselves. Help only if needed.

Check by having the children read the completed sentence. The teacher also should check the page.

Use the last sentence in discussion with the children. Bring out the ideas that God is our Heavenly Father, that we belong to Him, and that Jesus is God's Son and our Savior. Also point out that pronouns referring to God or Jesus begin with a capital letter.

Name ______________

Write 1, 2, 3.

1 Jane's mom brings her a dress.
3 Jane is dressed.
2 Jane puts on her dress.

2 Dave runs to Father.
1 Father calls Dave.
3 Dave and Father go home.

3 Jack puts his bike away.
2 Jack rides his bike.
1 Jack gets on his bike.

Language Arts 105
Worksheet 10
with page 21

Teacher check ______________
Initial Date

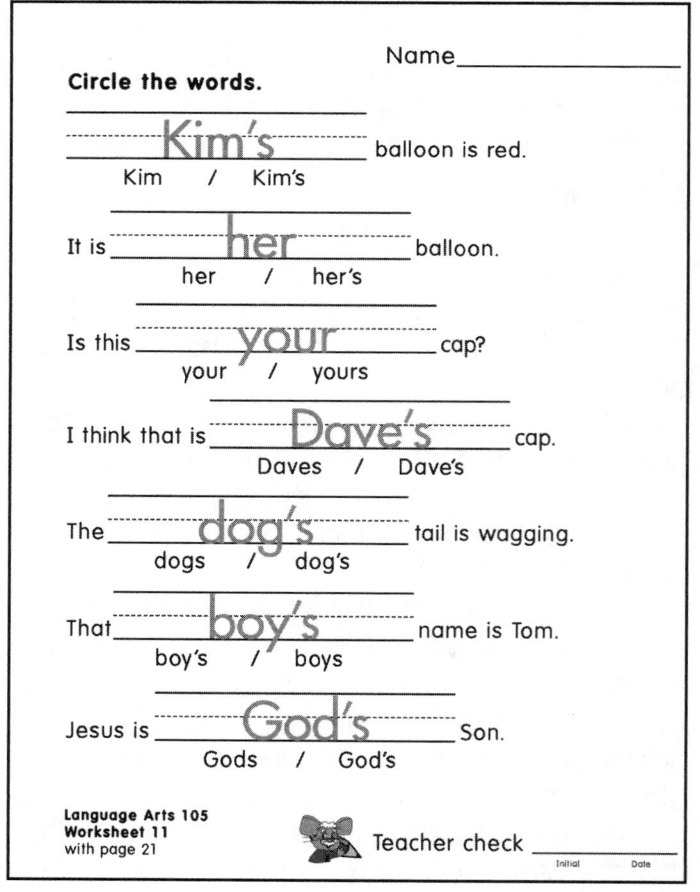

Name______________

Circle the words.

Kim's balloon is red.
Kim / Kim's

It is her balloon.
her / her's

Is this your cap?
your / yours

I think that is Dave's cap.
Daves / Dave's

The dog's tail is wagging.
dogs / dog's

That boy's name is Tom.
boy's / boys

Jesus is God's Son.
Gods / God's

Language Arts 105
Worksheet 11
with page 21

Teacher check ______________
Initial Date

Page 22: Activity Page

CONCEPTS: long *a*, rhyming, questions, possessives

TEACHER GOALS: To teach the children
To write rhyming words with the long /*a*/ sound,
To write sentences that are questions, and
To write words that show possession.

TEACHING PAGE 22:
Have the children read the direction at the top of the page. Have them read the two endings and give several rhyming words for each. Give them time to write words on the lines.

Read the directions on the rest of the page. Have the children write the endings on one side of the sheet of writing tablet paper and write rhyming words. Use the other side for the questions they are to write.

Have the children read the list of possessives and tell what each means. Use one or two in questions to illustrate the directions. Let the children write the questions.

Check the rhyming words by writing the endings on the board and by having the children give the words. Have them check their lists with the lists on the board and add to them or correct their spelling. Read the lists several times.

The teacher should correct the questions. Have children recopy them if words are misspelled, letters are poorly made, or the paper is messy.

Let the children read their questions to the class.

Write rhyming words.

______ail ______ale

Write more words in your LIFEPAC Writing Tablet.

Write a question for each of these words in your LIFEPAC Tablet.

her	snail's
their	children's
Mother's	our
mouse's	my

page 22 (twenty-two)

ACTIVITIES:
1. Dictate five *ail* words and five *ale* words and have the children write them on a sheet of writing tablet paper. Correct the papers and have the children write each misspelled word five times on the back of the paper.

Since the two endings sound the same, be sure you give the meaning of the word you want children to write. Review the meanings and spellings before you dictate the words.

2. Have the children make a scrapbook for words which have endings that sound alike. They could put a picture of each word and write the word under it for words like *mail* and *male* and *tail* and *tale*.

SELF TEST 2

CONCEPTS: sentences, punctuation, capitalization, contractions, long o, long u, compound words

TEACHER GOAL: To teach the children

To check their own progress periodically.

TEACHING PAGE 23:

Have the children read the title and tell what it means.

Read all the directions on the page with the children. Be sure they understand everything they are to do on this page. *Dictate the sentence for the children to write.*

Dictation Sentence-(Write the sentence.)

Rose is so cute.

Let them finish the rest of the page by themselves.

The teacher should check the page as soon as possible. Go over it with the child. Show him what he did well and where he needs extra work.

ACTIVITIES:

1. Give the children individual help on items missed.
2. If several miss the same things, work with them (in a small group, if possible).

SPELLING WORDS:

rose
those
so
go
use
fuse
cute
mule
cube
you

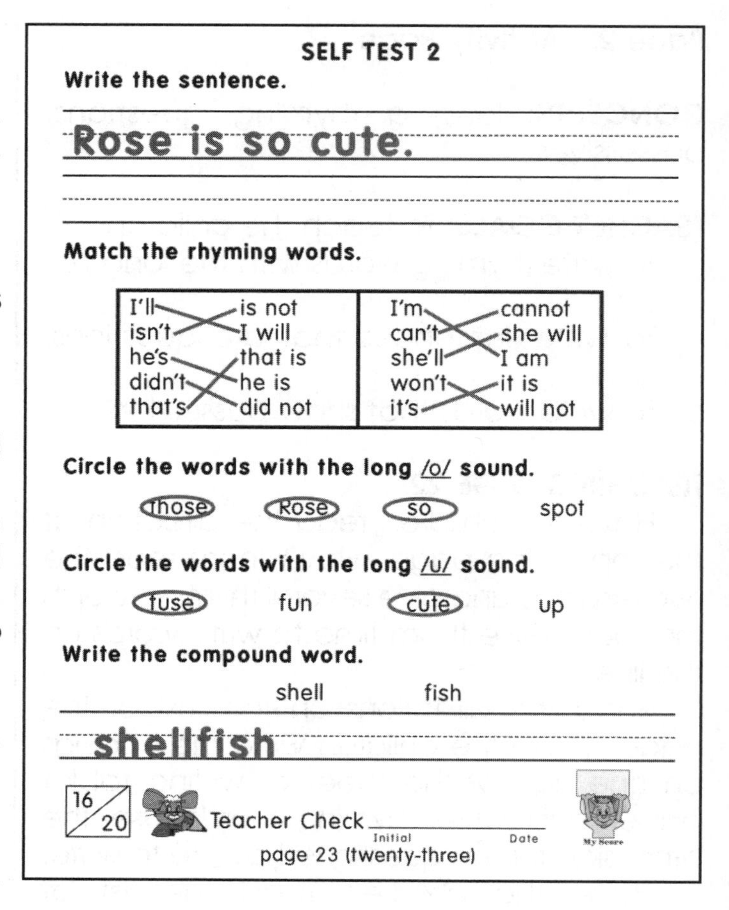

SELF TEST 2

Write the sentence.

Rose is so cute.

Match the rhyming words.

I'll	is not	I'm	cannot
isn't	I will	can't	she will
he's	that is	she'll	I am
didn't	he is	won't	it is
that's	did not	it's	will not

Circle the words with the long /o/ sound.

those Rose so spot

Circle the words with the long /u/ sound.

fuse fun cute up

Write the compound word.

shell fish

shellfish

16/20 Teacher Check ______ Initial Date

page 23 (twenty-three)

III. PART THREE

Page 24: Tell the Story

CONCEPTS: telling a story, real or make-believe

TEACHER GOALS: To teach the children
To tell a story from a picture, and
To tell if the story could be real or if it is make-believe,

TEACHING PAGE 24:

Read the title and the question at the top of the page with the children.

Tell them to look at the pictures carefully, to decide if it could really happen, and to mark the *yes* or *no*.

Have the children tell what is happening in each picture and whether they marked the *yes* or the *no*. Have them tell why they marked as they did.

In the top picture have children tell what might have happened before what they see in the picture and what might happen after.

In the bottom picture, have children tell all the story. Ask the children to tell what they would write if they could write a new ending for the story. Let several children give their versions and talk about them. Encourage the children to write different endings.

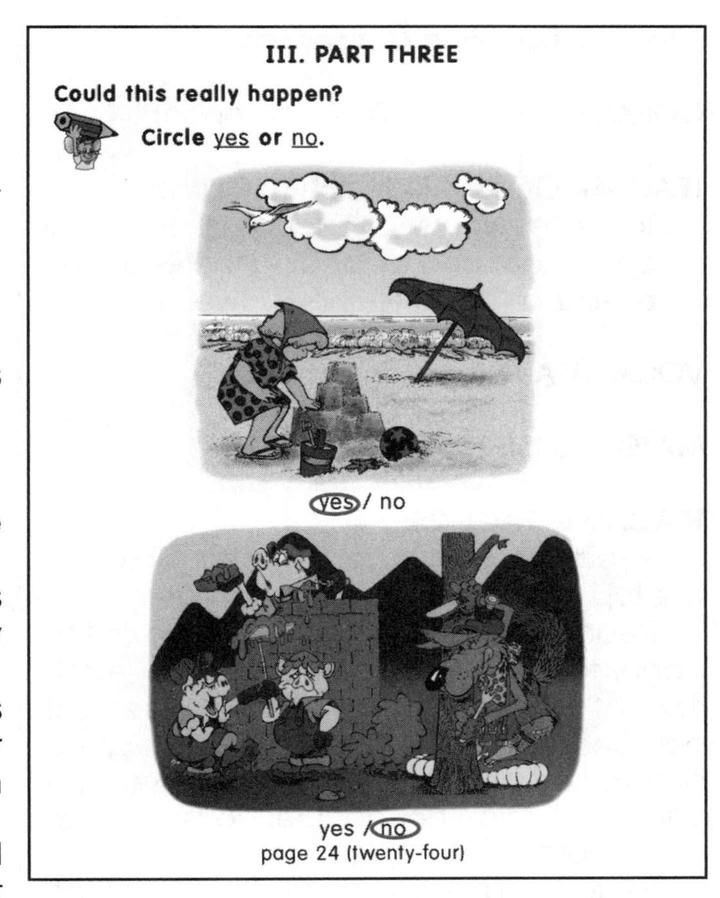

III. PART THREE

Could this really happen?

Circle yes or no.

yes / no

yes / no

page 24 (twenty-four)

Page 25: Doubling Consonants

CONCEPT: doubling final consonant

TEACHER GOALS: To teach the children

To write words by doubling the final consonant and by adding the endings -*er*, -*ed*, and -*ing* to short vowel words.

VOCABULARY: consonants

MATERIALS NEEDED: Worksheet 12

TEACHING PAGE 25:

Read the sentence and the words at the top of the page with the children.

Read the sentence in the middle of the page, then have the children read each row of words. Point out that the last consonant in each word must be doubled before adding the ending. Have the children circle the double consonant in each word on the page.

Read the question at the bottom of the page. Write the words the children give on the board. Double the consonants and add the endings on those you can and explain why other words do not have a double consonant.

Words like *win* may have the consonant doubled for the -*er* and -*ing* endings but not for the -*ed*. You will need to explain that instead of saying *winned*, the correct word is *won*.

ACTIVITY:

Do Worksheet 12.

Have the children read the direction at the top of the page, the words, and the endings.

Do the first example together. Read the word *fit*. Have the children write the word *fit*. Remind them that they must double the last consonant which is *t*, so write the *t*. Then write the *ed*. Have them read the word. Do the same with *fitting*.

Circle the double consonant.

Some words are spelled with two consonants in the middle.

When you put the <u>er</u>, <u>ed</u>, or <u>ing</u> endings on some short vowel words, you must double the last consonant.

dip	dipper	dipped	dipping
bat	batter	batted	batting
sin	sinner	sinned	sinning
bag	bagger	bagged	bagging
slip	slipper	slipped	slipping

Can you think of more?

page 25 (twenty-five)

Let the children do the pages by themselves. Check by having them read the three words in each row and tell how they wrote the word. It might help some children to remember to double the final consonant if you have them say to themselves as they write, "Write the word, double the *t* (or *d* or *b*, etc.), write the ending."

Have the children use the words in sentences.

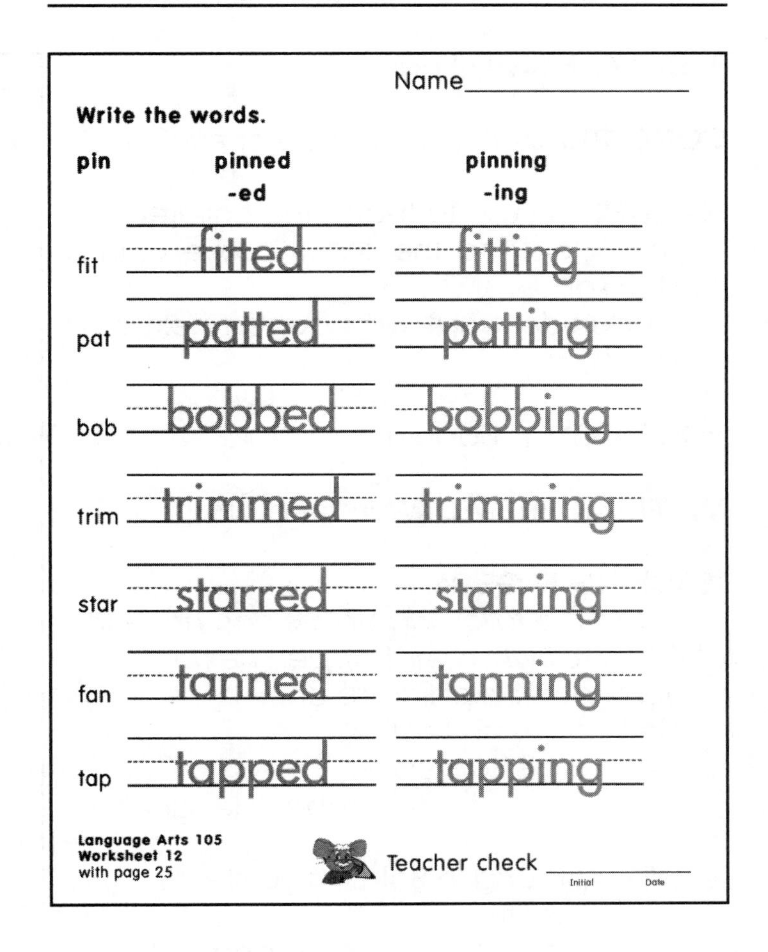
Name________________

Write the words.

pin	pinned -ed	pinning -ing
fit	fitted	fitting
pat	patted	patting
bob	bobbed	bobbing
trim	trimmed	trimming
star	starred	starring
fan	fanned	fanning
tap	tapped	tapping

Language Arts 105
Worksheet 12
with page 25

Teacher check ____________
Initial Date

Page 26: Activity Page

CONCEPTS: stories, sequence of events

TEACHER GOALS: To teach the children
To understand the order of events in a story, and
To decide what will happen next in a story.

VOCABULARY: happen

MATERIALS NEEDED: Worksheet 13

TEACHING PAGE 26:

Read the following stories and have the children tell what will happen next.

John puts his pajamas on.
He brushes his teeth.
He says his prayers.

The response should be "He goes to bed."

Billy is playing in Bobby's yard.
It is dinner time.
Mother calls Billy to come and eat.

The response should be "Billy goes home to eat."

Tell the children they will be doing the same kind of thing on this page, telling what will happen next, but they will have two sentences to choose from.

Read the direction at the top of the page with the children. Tell the children to read the first story silently. Then have them read the two sentences in the dark print and decide which one tells what will happen next.

Have a child read the story and the sentence he chose. Have a child read the other sentence and tell why it was not a good answer.

Let the children finish the page by themselves and check the same way.

It may be necessary to work through the entire page with the children.

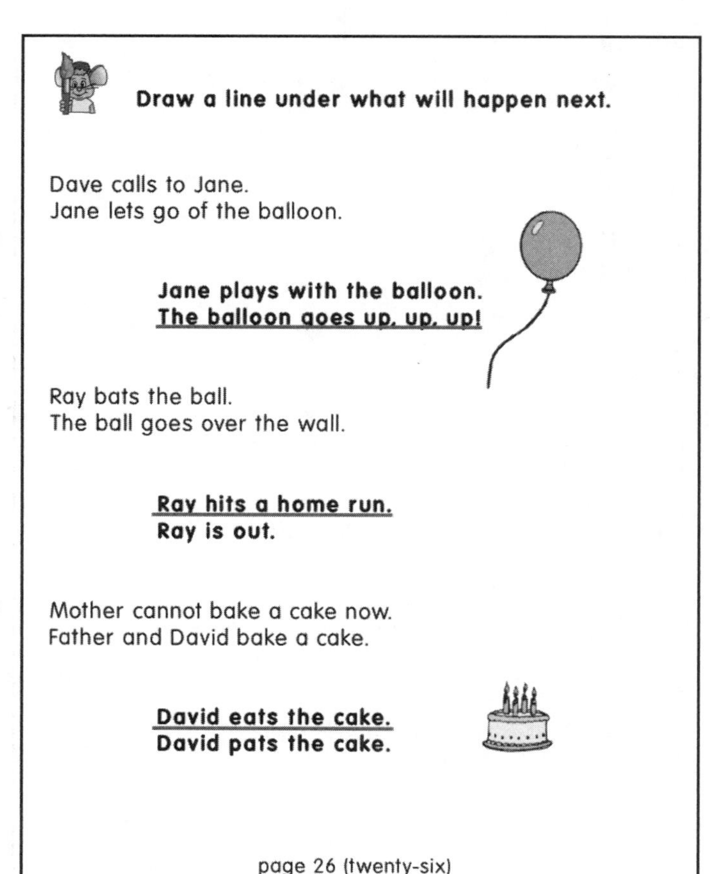

ACTIVITIES:

1. Do Worksheet 13.

Have the children read the direction at the top of the page. Tell them to read the first three lines of the story silently. Have a child read them aloud. Have the children read the next two lines silently and decide which line tells what Don will do. Have a child read it. Ask if everyone agrees.

Let the children finish the page by themselves. Check by having the children read the story and the line they underlined. Have the children correct any mistakes.

Ask the children to tell why they chose the sentence they did. Ask if it was the right thing to do and how they knew it was.

Use the last two stories in discussions with the children about sharing what we have and how our conscience makes us unhappy when we do something wrong.

2. Read stories such as "Aesop's Fables." Stop reading after the problem

has been presented and let the children tell what they think will happen next. Then finish the story and let the children decide if their endings were good ones.

Name_______________

Draw a line under what will happen next.

Don is at the lake.
He has a can of bait.
What will Don do?

He will fish.
He will play ball.

James has two cupcakes.
John hasn't any cupcakes.
What will James do?

James will give John a cupcake.
James won't give John a cupcake.

Tom did a bad thing today.
He isn't happy.
What will he do now?

Tom won't be good now.
Tom will be good now.

Language Arts 105
Worksheet 13
with page 26

Teacher check ___________
Initial Date

Page 27: Doubling Consonants

CONCEPT: doubling final consonant

TEACHER GOALS: To teach the children
To write words by doubling the final consonant and by adding the endings *-er*, *-ed*, and *-ing* to short vowel words.

TEACHING PAGE 27:
Read the sentence and the words at the top of the page, then have the children read each row of words. Point out that the last consonant in each word must be doubled before adding the ending. Have the children underline the double consonant in each word on the page.
Read the direction at the bottom of the page. Have the children double the consonants and add the endings on words.

Doubling Consonants

When you put the er, ed, or ing endings on some short vowel words, you must double the last consonant.

sag	sagged	sagging
sip	sipped	sipping
snip	snipped	snipping
knit	knitted	knitting

Write the letters.

rip	ripped	ripping
trip	tripped	tripping
tag	tagged	tagging
skip	skipped	skipping

page 27 (twenty-seven)

Page 28: My Pets

CONCEPTS: reading a story, paragraphs, recalling details

TEACHER GOALS: To teach the children

To read the story by themselves and understand it,

To identify paragraphs in the story,

To recall details of the story, and

To write a story with paragraphs and a title.

TEACHING PAGE 28:

Read the sentence and phrases at the top of the page with the children and talk about them.

Have the children look at the picture and tell what is happening. Ask what another word for animals like dogs and cats is. (pets) Have them read the title of the story.

Have the children read the story silently.

Ask the following questions.

"How many pets does Lisa have?"

"What is it?"

"What color is it?"

"What does the pet do?"

"How does the girl feel about her pet?"

Have the children point out possessives, contractions, and plurals in the story. Have several children read the story aloud.

Ask how many paragraphs are in the story. Have a child read each. Ask if all the sentences in each paragraph belong together.

Ask the children to tell who *he* refers to and who *her* refers to.

Have the children read the direction at the top of the page. Read what they are to look for and have the children repeat after you. Have the children read the story and write the words on the lines as they find them. The teacher should check this part.

Instruct the children to do the following:

Write a story about your pet.

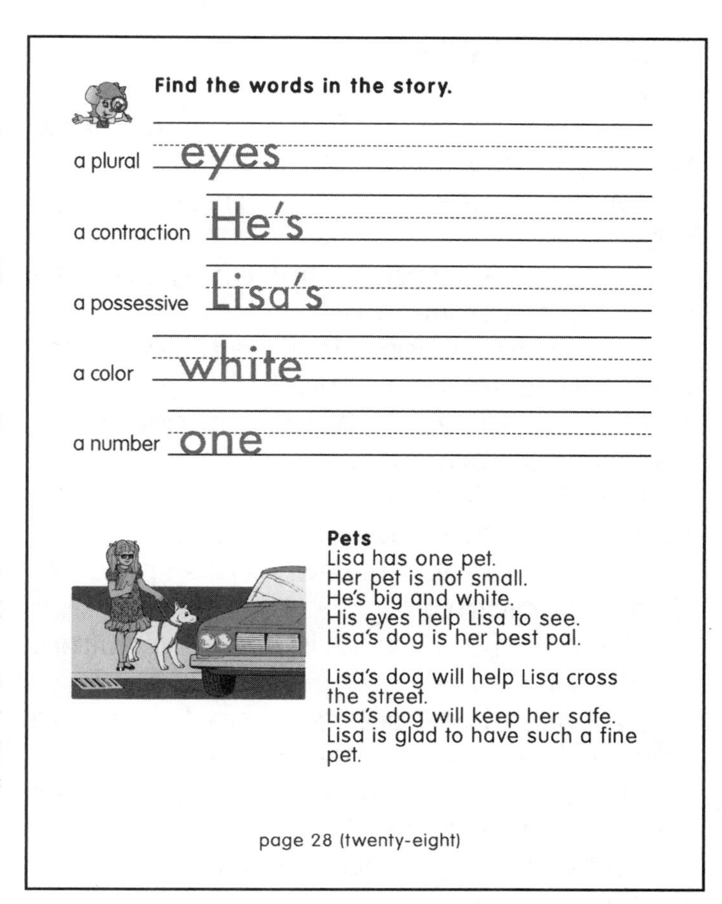

Find the words in the story.

a plural eyes

a contraction He's

a possessive Lisa's

a color white

a number one

Pets

Lisa has one pet.
Her pet is not small.
He's big and white.
His eyes help Lisa to see.
Lisa's dog is her best pal.

Lisa's dog will help Lisa cross the street.
Lisa's dog will keep her safe.
Lisa is glad to have such a fine pet.

page 28 (twenty-eight)

Write two or three paragraphs.

Write a title.

Draw a picture about your story.

Read your story and show your picture to the class.

Be sure the children understand everything they are to do. Remind them to write neatly. Help them with spelling. Children may write their stories in class or when their other work is finished. Correct the stories and have children recopy them.

Have the children practice reading their stories to an aide or another child before reading them to the class. Take one or two class periods for the children to read their stories and show their pictures.

ACTIVITY:

Read stories about pets and books or articles about caring for pets.

TEACHING READING:

Ask students:

"Who is Jesus?" (God, Son of God, Savior, teacher, friend, ...)

"What is Jesus like?" (good, loving, etc.....)

"What does Jesus want each of us to do?" (answers will vary)

Explain to students that Jesus was here on Earth to teach us many things. In the story they will read about Tony and what he learned about Jesus.

Read the story "Just Like Jesus" together, then answer the following questions:

"Where does this story take place?" (Tony's bedroom)

"What time of day is it?" (nighttime, bedtime)

"What is Tony going to do before he goes to bed?" (read the Bible)

"What does he read about?" (Jesus praying in the garden)

"Why does his dad stop by his room?" (to say goodnight)

"What did Tony want to know?" (why Jesus prayed)

"What did he learn about Jesus praying?" (Jesus prayed to teach us to pray)

"Do you think Tony understood what Jesus wanted us to learn?" (yes, he prayed before he went to bed)

Have students:

Find long vowel words: (night, Tony, sleep, read, alone, Bible, climbs, blanket, cozy, praying, Jesus, knees, peeked, say, why, He, we, so, know, pray, oh, smiled, gave, light, kneeled, like)

ACTIVITY:

Discuss other ways we can be "just like Jesus." Make a list of the ideas and post it as a reminder to everyone who sees it. Have students learn and recite The Lord's Prayer.

Tell them this is the prayer Jesus taught us so we would know how to pray. It's in the Bible! (Matt. 6) Give them a copy of it to keep. They may want to draw and color a decorative border around it. Talk about favorite Bible stories. Choose a Bible story to dramatize. Have students write a letter to Jesus, thanking Him for the things He teaches us.

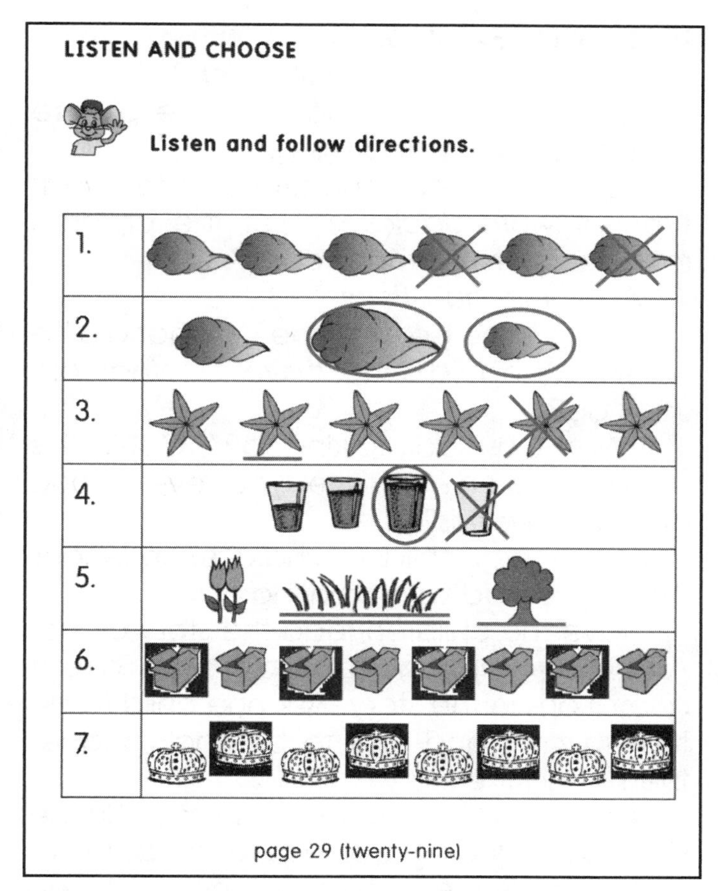

Page 29: Listen and Choose

CONCEPTS: listening, following directions, ordinal numbers, smallest-largest, shortest-tallest, full-empty, reading a story

TEACHER GOALS: To teach the children

To listen and follow oral directions given,

To understand the ordinal numbers first through eighth,

To tell the difference between smallest and largest, shortest and tallest, and full and empty, and

To read a story and tell what happened.

VOCABULARY: choose

MATERIALS NEEDED: crayons

TEACHING PAGE 29:

Read the title and the direction with the children as they follow along.

Tell the children to listen carefully and to do exactly as you say. Remind them that you will give the directions only once. Have the children lay out crayons before you begin. Have the children put their fingers on the numbers at the left to help keep their places on the page.

Read these directions:

1. Put a green X on the fourth and sixth shells.

2. Put a blue circle around the largest shell and a purple circle around the smallest shell.

3. Put a red line under the second starfish and a red X on the fifth starfish .

4. Put a brown circle around the glass you would choose if you were very thirsty. Put a brown X on the empty glass.

5. Put one yellow line under the plant that will grow tallest. Put two yellow lines under the one that father cuts so that it will not grow tall.

6. Color the first, third, fifth, and seventh boxes green.

7. Color the second, fourth, sixth, and eighth crowns blue.

The teacher should take time to check this page as soon as the children finish working. If a child has made a mistake, circle the number at the left of the row but do not tell the child which one is wrong. Let the children who had perfect scores do something else while you go through the page again and have the children correct their mistakes. Check quickly. If a child is still wrong, show him his mistake and the correct answer. Give more practice on the kinds of directions.

ACTIVITIES:

1. Use a glass and colored water to demonstrate full, empty, half full, partly filled, almost full, almost empty, and so forth.

2. Line children up in front of the room to illustrate tallest, shortest, next to tallest, next to shortest, smallest, largest, and so on.

TEACHING READING:

Find "Jack's Table" in *Reader 3*.

Tell the children to look at the picture and tell what is happening.

Have them read the title and tell what type of word *Jack's* is. Let the children read the story by themselves.

Ask these questions:

"What is the boy's name?" "What did he want?" "What did he have?" "What did Jack do?"

"Who was Jack talking to?" "Could this really happen?" "Have you ever done anything like this?"

Let several children share experiences they have had with painting.

Have the children read the story aloud. Ask the children to read the direct quotations in the story. Ask one child to be the narrator and one to be Jack and let them read the story.

Ask a child to read the possessives in the story and tell what belongs to the person.

Note: Since children have been introduced to pronouns, you may wish to begin calling *his, her, their,* and so on possessive pronouns instead of just possessives. In this case, you will need to explain that *his* is a pronoun because it means the same as Jack, but it is also a possessive because it tells who the table belongs to.

Children who are ready for this concept will learn it and use it. Children who do not understand it now will learn it later in other lessons.

Ask the children to read the contractions in the story. Have them read the sentence using the words instead of the contraction.

Have the children read all the words with the long /a/ sound.

Do page 30 in the same class period if possible.

Page 30: Activity Page

CONCEPTS: long *a*, possession, contractions

TEACHER GOALS: To teach the children
To recognize words with the long /a/ sound,
To write words that show possession, and
To write contractions

MATERIALS NEEDED: Worksheet 14

TEACHING PAGE 30:

This page should be done in the same class period as the previous page if possible.

Have the children read the direction at the top of the page and circle the words with the long /a/ sound. Check by having the children tell what they circled. Have the children tell what the vowel sound is in the other words.

Have the children read the next direction. Tell them to read the sentence carefully, to circle the word that is correct, and to copy it on the line.

Let the children do the page by themselves. Check by having the children read the sentence. Have the children correct any mistakes. As the children read each sentence, have them tell what the possessive or contraction means.

ACTIVITIES:

1. Do Worksheet 14.

Have the children read the direction at the top of this Worksheet.

Have them read the first sentence and tell which word is the possessive and what belongs to him.

Let the children finish the page by themselves. Check by having the children read the sentences. Write the possessives on the board as the children spell them. Have the children tell what belonged to each one. Have the children correct any mistakes.

Circle the long /a/ words.

train go say | the table paint | pet make have | cake hat play

Write the words.

The cat is not yours.
yours / your

My dog's house is little.
Me / My

I'll paint my table.
I'm / I'll

The table isn't red now.
isnt / isn't

page 30 (thirty)

2. Write the following list of words on the board and have the children write a sentence for each one on a sheet of writing tablet paper. Tell them they may write statements, questions, or exclamations, but that they should be sure they have the right punctuation mark. Collect the papers and correct them. Have the students recopy the corrected sentences.

they	hasn't	wasn't	our
I'm	his	she	her

Name______________

Write the words.

A dog that belongs to Tom is

Tom's dog.

A cake that belongs to Kay is

Kay's cake.

The table that belongs to Jay is

Jay's table.

The balloon that belongs to Jane is

Jane's balloon.

The LIFEPAC that belongs to Jane is

Jane's LIFEPAC.

Language Arts 105
Worksheet 14
with page 30

Teacher check ______________
Initial Date

Page 31: Activity Page

CONCEPT: syllables

TEACHER GOALS: To teach the children
To hear the parts of words, and
To understand that the parts of words are called syllables.

TEACHING PAGE 31:

Review the word *syllables* and ask what it means. Have children tell how many parts (syllables) they hear in the word *syllables* (three).

Remind the children that there are as many syllables in a word as the number of vowels that they can hear.

Have the children read the directions. Have them read the lists of words silently and write the number of syllables they hear in each word on the line behind it. Some children may need help sounding out the words. Check by having the children read the words and give the number of vowels and syllables. Remind them that *y* at the end of words with two or more syllables has the sound of long *e*.

Syllables

Say the words.

Write how many parts are in each word.

summer 2	letter 2	box 1
happy 2	walking 2	mail 1
dress 1	fence 1	sunny 2
exciting 3	pockets 2	braid 1

page 31 (thirty-one)

SELF TEST 3

CONCEPTS: predicting outcomes, syllables, contractions

TEACHER GOAL: To teach the children
To check their own progress periodically.

TEACHING PAGE 32:
Read all the directions on the page with the children. Be sure they understand everything they are to do. Let them do the entire page by themselves.
The teacher should check the page as soon as possible. Go over it with the child. Show him what he did well and where he needs to work.

ACTIVITIES:
1. Give the children individual help on items they missed.
2. If several miss the same things, reteach the skills in small groups, if possible.

SPELLING WORDS:

dipping
slipping
bagging
dipped
slipped
bagged
dipper
slipper
bagger
ladder

SELF TEST 3

Draw a line under what will happen next.

Father gets up.
He goes to work.

Father comes home from work.
Father will go to work.

Write the number of syllables.

happy 2 letter 2 summer 2

fence 1 box 1 braid 1

Add er, ed, and ing.

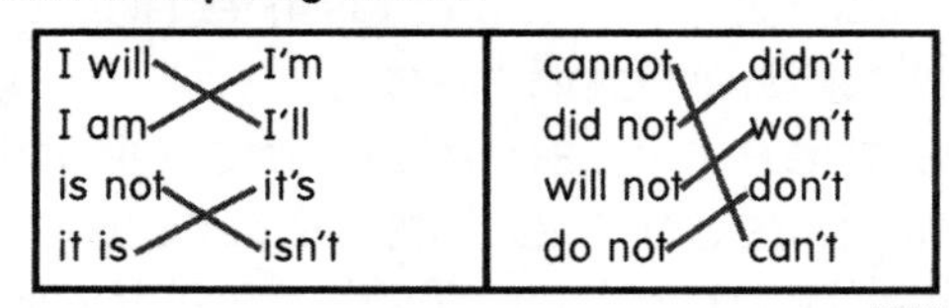

Match the rhymning words.

I will	I'm	cannot	didn't
I am	I'll	did not	won't
is not	it's	will not	don't
it is	isn't	do not	can't

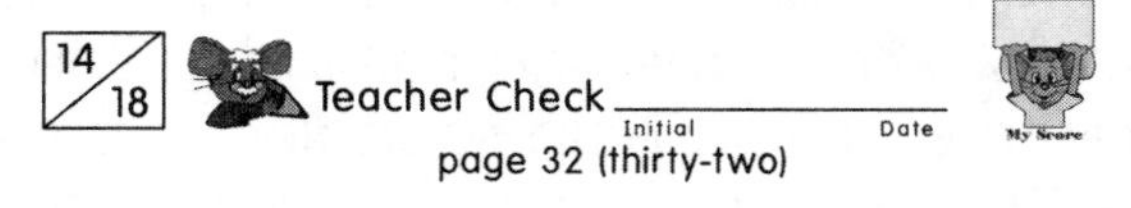

14/18 Teacher Check ______ Initial Date

page 32 (thirty-two)

LIFEPAC TEST AND ALTERNATE TEST 105

CONCEPTS: long a, long e, contractions, predicting outcomes, plurals, possessives, compound words, long i, long o, sentences, punctuation for statements, capitalization, rhyming words, and syllables

TEACHER GOAL: To teach the children

To check their own progress periodically.

TEACHING the LIFEPAC TEST:

Administer the test to the class as a group. Ask to have directions read or read them to the class. In either case, be sure that the children clearly understand. Put examples on the board if it seems necessary. Have the children name the pictures: LIFEPAC Test (cake, cat, train, skates, dog, snake, pail, cup, whale); Give ample time for each activity to be completed before going on to the next.

Dictation Sentence for LIFEPAC Test-(Write the sentence.)

We will use the dime.

Correct immediately and discuss with the child.

Review any concepts that have been missed.

Give those children who do not achieve the 80% score additional copies of the worksheets and a list of vocabulary words to study. A parent or a classroom helper may help in the review.

When the child is ready, give the Alternate LIFEPAC Test. Use the same procedure as for the LIFEPAC TEST.

Alternate LIFEPAC Test: (rain, house, table, rat, paint, snail, cap, whale, nail).

Dictation Sentence for Alternate LIFEPAC Test-(Write the sentence.)

Jane will bake the cake.

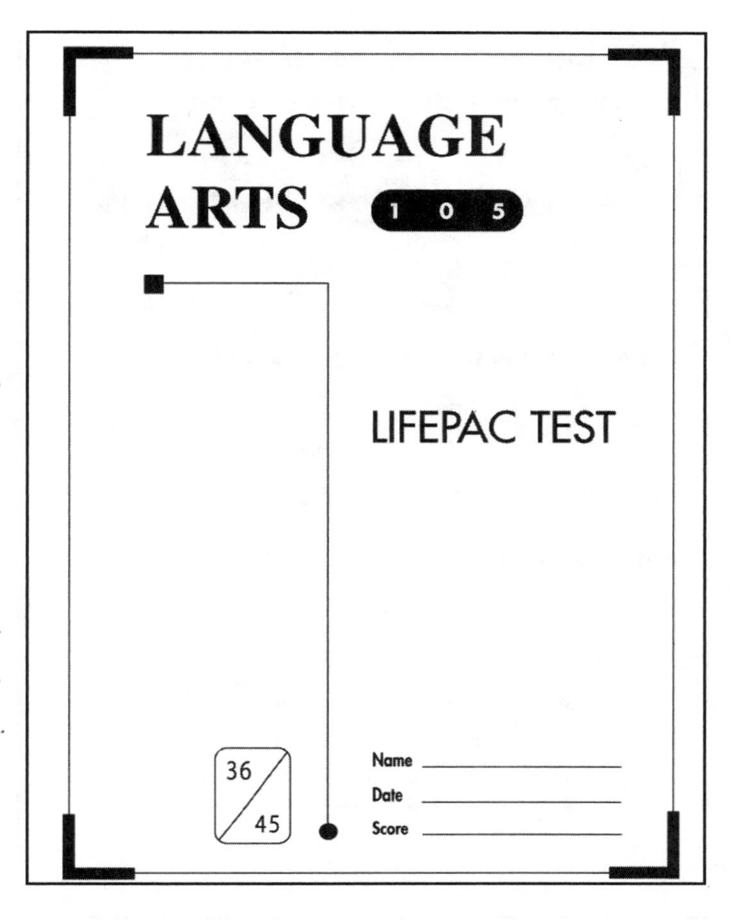

SPELLING WORDS:

LIFEPAC words	**Alternate words**
lake	game
be	he
mice	hide
rose	those
so	go
use	fuse
cute	cube
you	you
dipping	bagging
dipper	bagger

LANGUAGE ARTS 105: LIFEPAC TEST

Circle the pictures with the long /a/ sound.

Circle the words with the long /e/ sound.

(be)	pen	(see)
wet	(he)	(me)
(bee)	pet	(we)

Match the words.

I'll	is not	I'm	cannot
isn't	I will	can't	she will
he's	that is	she'll	I am
didn't	he is	won't	it is
that's	did not	it's	will not

page 1 (one)

Draw a line under what will happen next.

Jack is playing ball.
Father calls Jack.

Jack will play ball.
Jack will go to father.

Write the plurals.

cake — cakes

train — trains

Write the words.

That is David's ball.
David / David's

My cat is little.
My / Me

Write the compound word.

match box — matchbox

page 2 (two)

Circle the words with long /i/.

(dime) rim (mice) tin

Circle the words with long /o/.

(those) mop (no) (go)

Write the sentence.

We will use the dime.

Write the rhyming words.

fuse ______ cute ______

Write the number of syllables.

happy 2 box 1 sunny 2
letter 2 dress 1 fence 1

page 3 (three)

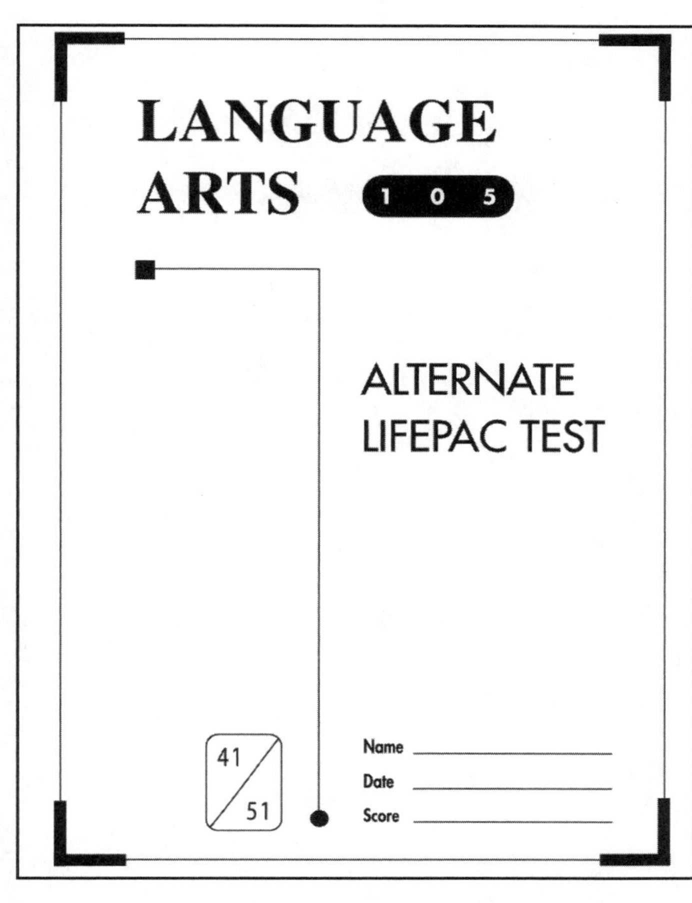

LANGUAGE ARTS 105

ALTERNATE LIFEPAC TEST

41/51

Name ____________

Date ____________

Score ____________

LANGUAGE ARTS 105
ALTERNATE LIFEPAC TEST

Circle the pictures with the long a sound.

Circle the words with the long e.

(we)	(he)	(bee)
(be)	(see)	(me)
pet	wet	pen

Write the compound word.

check up

checkup

Match the words.

didn't	do not	wasn't	we will
can't	did not	you'll	was not
don't	can not	we'll	you will
aren't	it is	won't	is not
it's	are not	isn't	will not

page 1 (one)

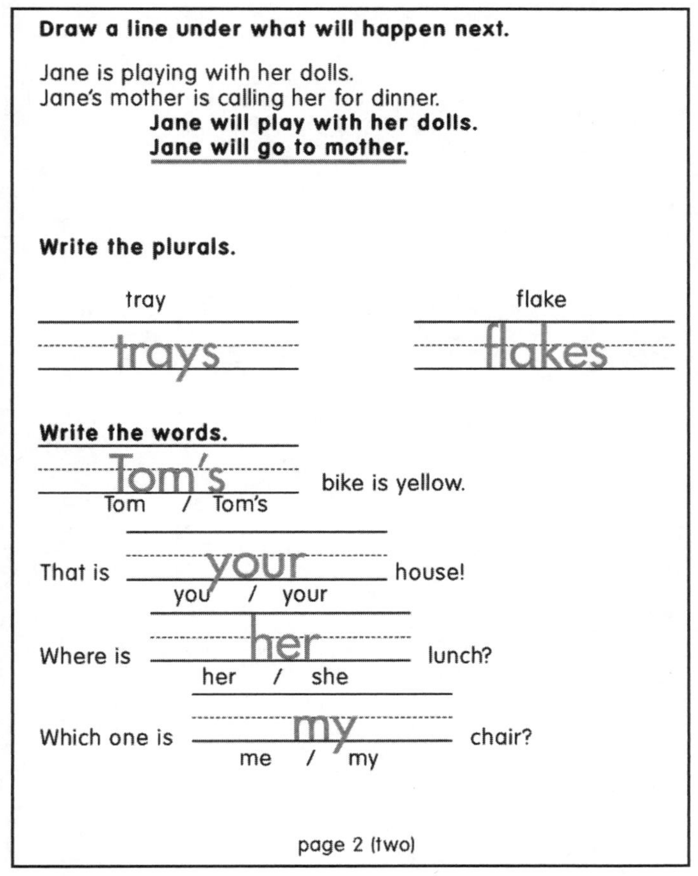

Draw a line under what will happen next.

Jane is playing with her dolls.
Jane's mother is calling her for dinner.

Jane will play with her dolls.
Jane will go to mother.

Write the plurals.

tray — trays

flake — flakes

Write the words.

Tom's bike is yellow.
Tom / Tom's

That is your house!
you / your

Where is her lunch?
her / she

Which one is my chair?
me / my

page 2 (two)

Write the sentence.

Jane will bake the cake.

Circle the words with the long i.

(hide)	(like)	(nice)
is	(hike)	hot

Write rhyming words.

those ____________ go ____________

Write the number of syllables.

sunny 2	mess 1	bunny 2
letter 2	funny 2	fence 1

Circle the words with the long u.

(muse)	mud	(use)
muff	(fuse)	(tube)
(cube)	tub	cub

page 3 (three)

LIFEPAC

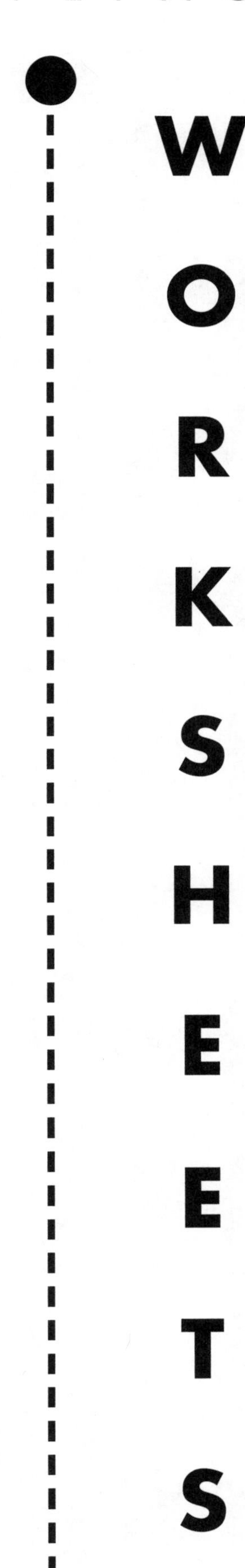

Reproducible Worksheets
for use with the Language Arts
100 Teacher Handbook

Name ____________________

Circle each picture with the short a sound.

Say each short a word with your teacher.

can	cat	ham
ran	bat	dam
pan	pat	tam
tan	rat	Sam
man	fat	ram
fan	hat	jam
dad	cab	back
pad	dab	sack
sad	jab	tack

Teacher check ____________________
Initial Date

Name ______________

Circle the sound.

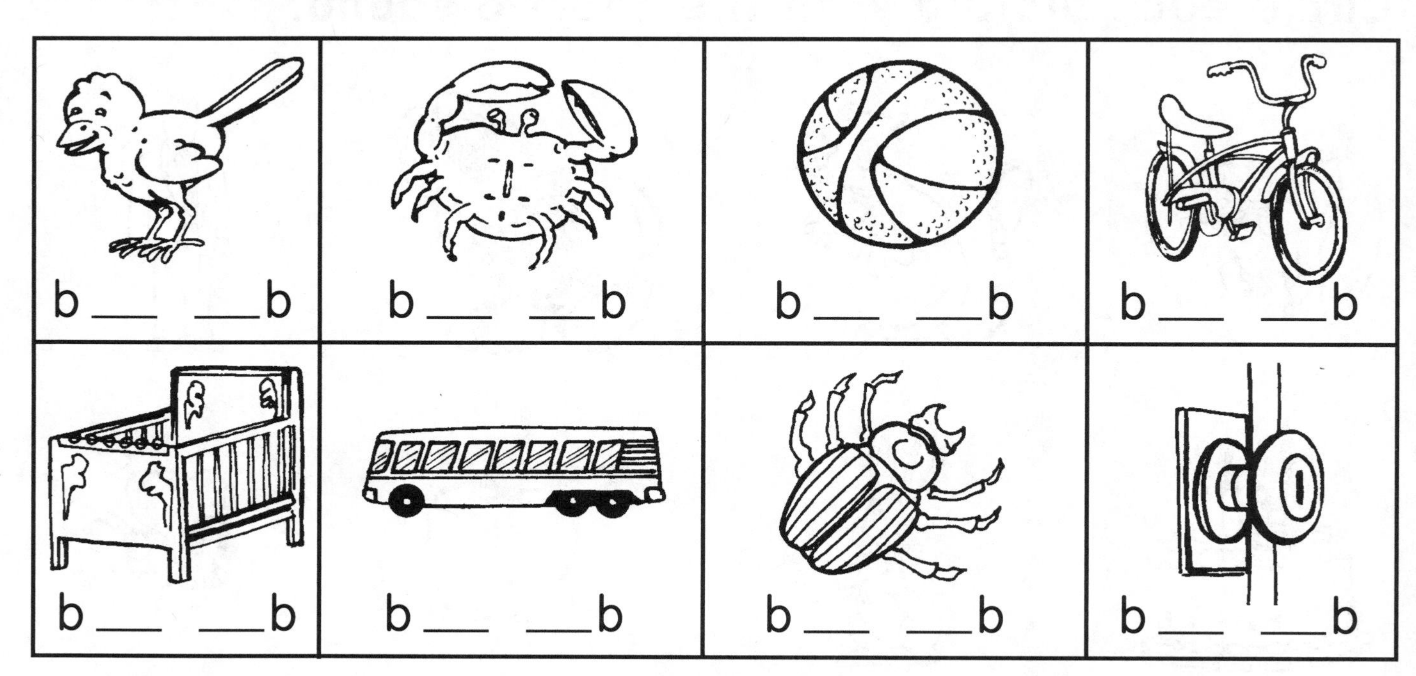

Write m under each picture that begins with the m sound.

Teacher check ______________
Initial Date

Name ____________________

Circle the pictures

Language Arts 101
Worksheet 3
with page 5

Teacher check ____________________
Initial Date

Name ____________________

Write short a to make a word.

____ m   ____ n

____ s   ____ t

am   an   as   at

Circle the pictures.

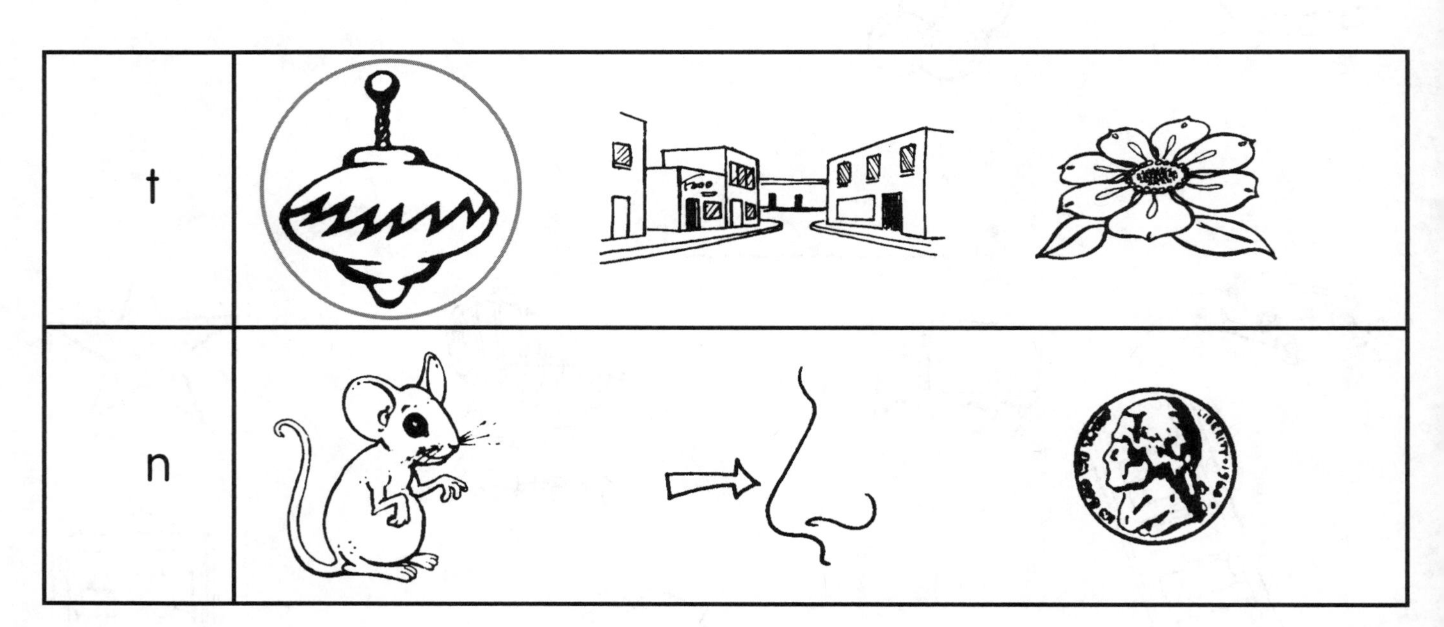

Teacher check ____________________
Initial   Date

Name ____________________

Write d.

d ______

Circle the letters.

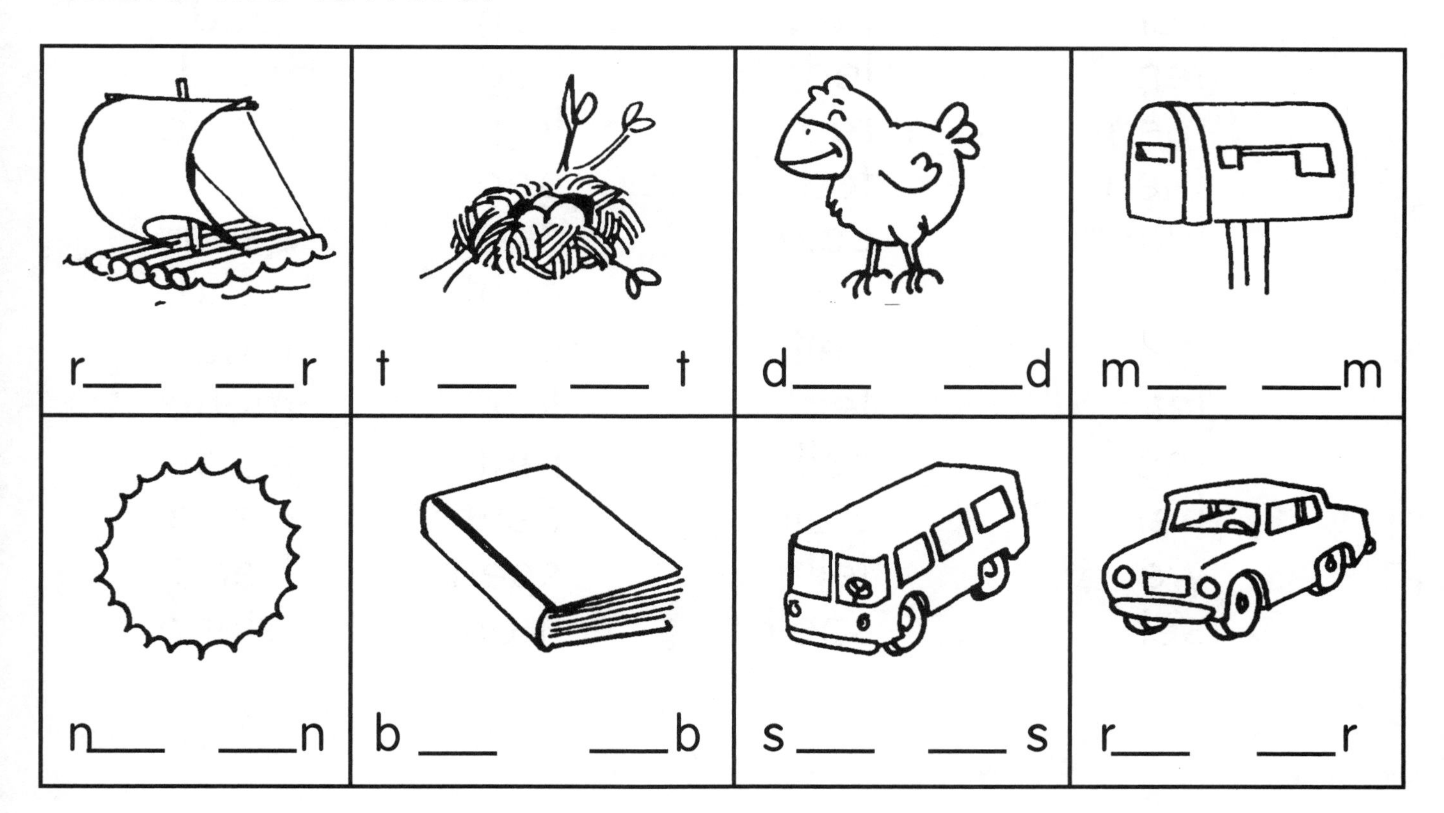

r___ ___r	t ___ ___ t	d___ ___d	m___ ___m
n___ ___n	b ___ ___b	s ___ ___ s	r___ ___r

Teacher check ____________________
Initial Date

Name ____________________

Circle the short e pictures.

Say each short e word with your teacher.

hen	bed	egg	read
ten	led	beg	head
men	red	leg	bread
then	fed	peg	
when	said		send
		bent	bend
get	bell	sent	tend
let	tell	tent	mend
met	sell	rent	lend
net	well	dent	blend
wet	fell	spent	trend
set	spell	meant	friend

Teacher check ____________________
Initial Date

Name ____________________

Circle the pictures with the p sound.

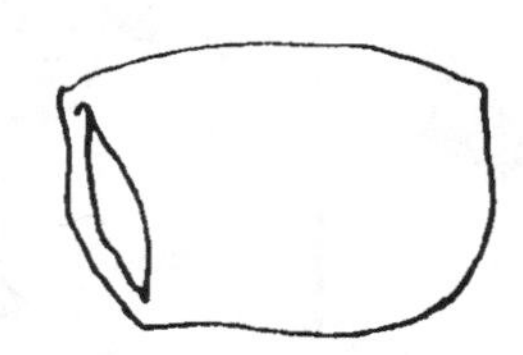

Say each short i word with your teacher.

in	him	miss	it	ill
pin	rim	kiss	bit	bill
sin	dim	this	fit	fill
tin	swim	is	hit	hill
win	trim	his	kit	kill
			lit	mill
did	big	pick	pit	pill
hid	dig	lick	sit	sill
lid	rig	sick		till
kid	wig	kick	mix	will
rid	jig	tick	fix	spill
slid	pig	stick	six	still

Teacher check ____________________
Initial Date

Name ______________________

Circle the letters.

Match the letters and words.

a	L	end	And
e	A	and	End
p	E	let	Pet
l	P	pet	Let
b	D	bent	Dent
d	B	dent	Bent

Teacher check ______________________
Initial Date

Name ______________________

Circle words that end in <u>ck</u> sound.

  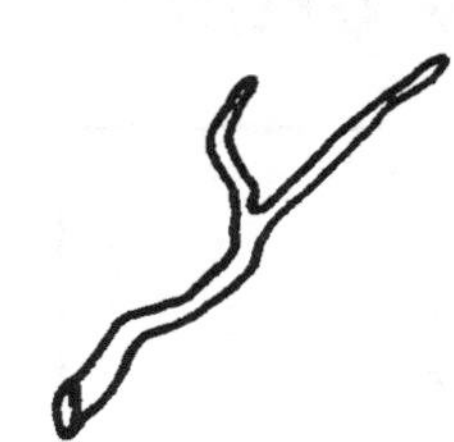  

Write the letters.

• ___	___ • ___	___ •
	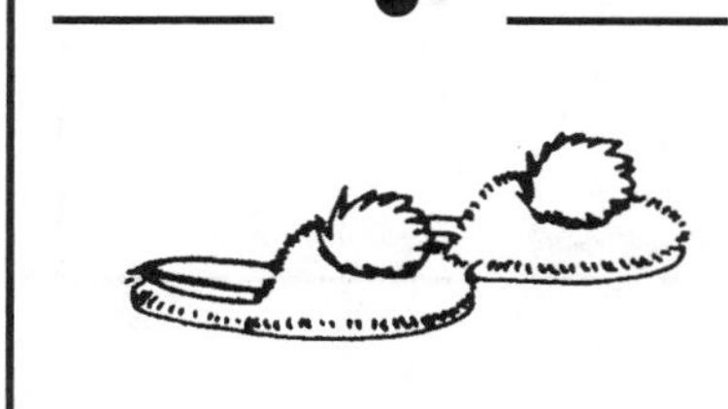	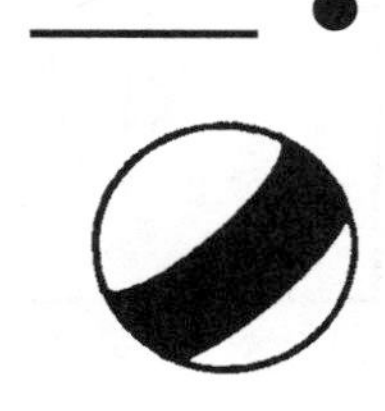

		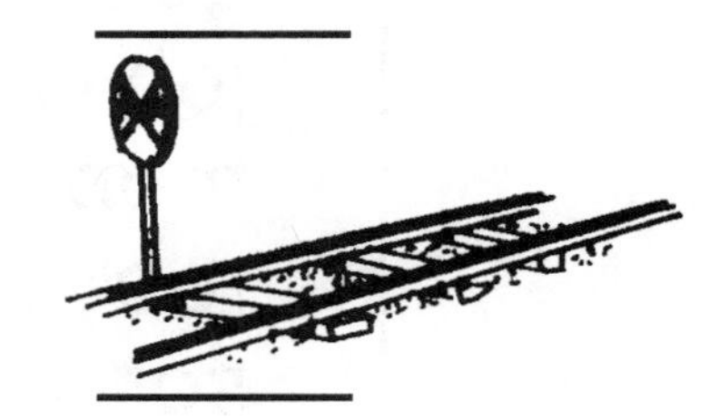
	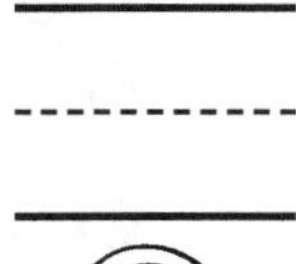 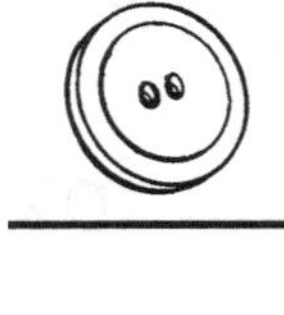	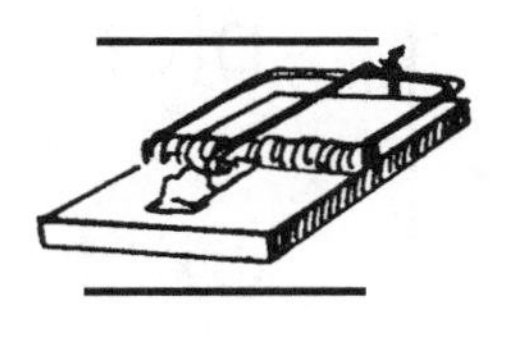

 Teacher check ______________________
Initial Date

Name ____________________

Match the letters and words.

a	O	L	i
c	A	I	l
e	C	T	m
o	E	R	n
b	D	N	r
d	B	M	t

Say the short o words with your teacher.

bob	God	hop	cock	doll	cot
cob	cod	lop	dock	Molly	dot
fob	hod	mop	hock	Polly	hot
gob	sod	pop	lock	holly	pot
job	nod	sop	mock	jolly	got
mob	rod	top	rock	folly	not
rob	pod	stop	sock		spot
sob	clod	clop	tock	Don	
knob	prod	flop	knock	Ron	cog
blob	shod	crop	block	John	jog
ox	box	fox	Mom	Tom	

Language Arts 101
Worksheet 10
with page 21

Teacher check ____________________
Initial Date

Name ____________________

Circle pictures with the g sound.

g______

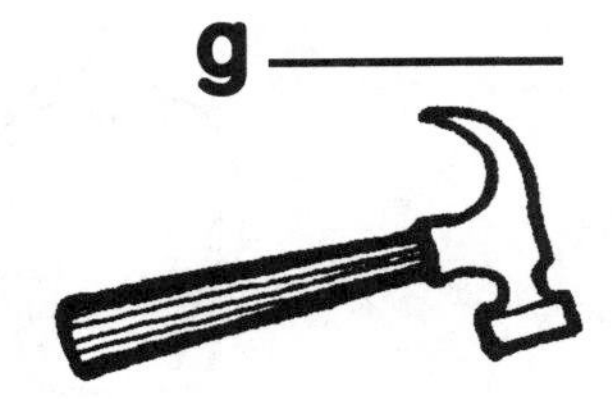
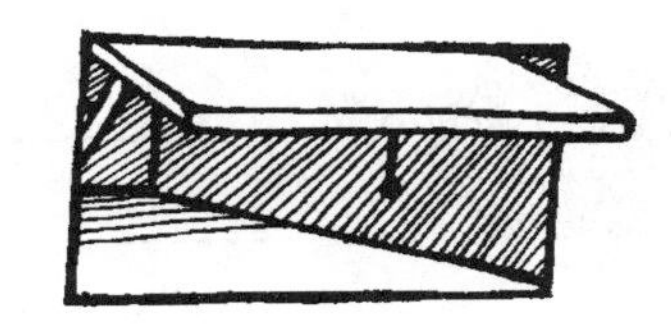

______g

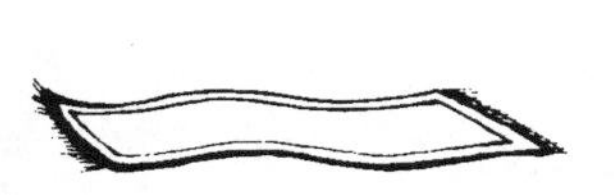

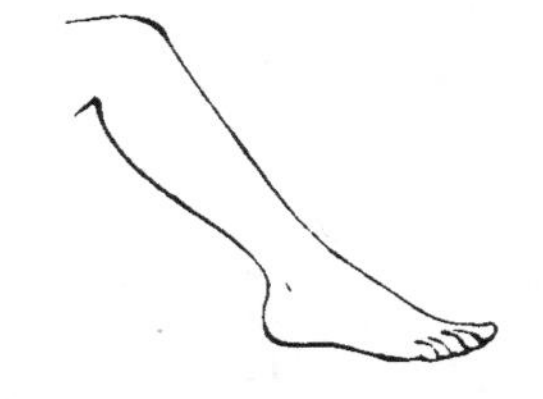

Write letters in order.

C A D B

______ ______ ______ ______

H E G F

______ ______ ______ ______

J L I K

Language Arts 101
Worksheet 11
with page 22

Teacher check ____________________
Initial Date

Write the letters.

Name ____________________

______ rass

______ ug

______ uggler

______ oat

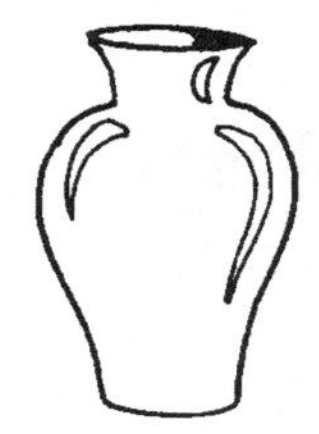

______ ase

______ ell

______ olf

______ eil

______ am

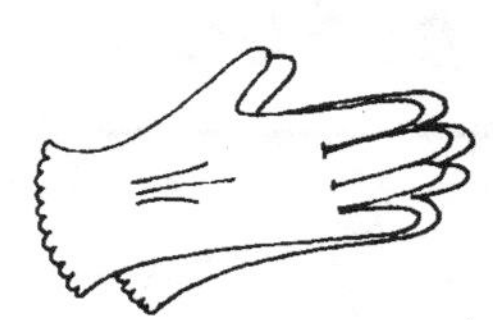

______ loves

______ est

______ indow

Teacher check ____________________
Initial Date

Circle the letters.

Name ____________________

cub	buck	buff	bug	bun	but
hub	duck	cuff	dug	fun	cut
tub	luck	huff	hug	gun	hut
club	muck	muff	lug	pun	nut
stub	puck	puff	mug	run	rut
	suck	fluff	pug	sun	shut
cud	tuck	stuff	rug	son	what
dud	cluck	bluff	tug	ton	us
mud	pluck	scuff	chug	won	bus
	stuck	tough	drug	one	thus
cup	truck	rough	slug	done	fuss
pup	chuck	enough	plug	none	muss

Teacher check ____________________
Initial Date

Name ______________________

Write letters in order.

C A D B

______ ______ ______ ______

H E G F

______ ______ ______ ______

J L I K

______ ______ ______ ______

M P O N

______ ______ ______ ______

R Q T S

______ ______ ______ ______

V X U W

______ ______ ______ ______

A B C D E F G H I J K L M N O P Q R S T U V W X Y Z

Teacher check ______________________
Initial Date

Name ________________

Circle these things in the picture.

bat **cat** **mat** **hat** **can** **match**

Color the picture.

Teacher check ________________
Initial Date

Name ______________________

Circle the things that are alike.

		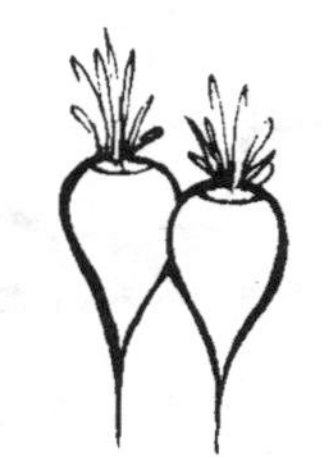

		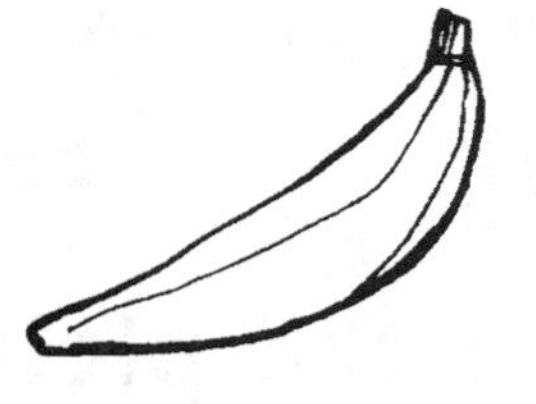

Language Arts 102
Worksheet 2
with page 3

Teacher check ______________________
Initial Date

Name ______________________

Match the rhyming words.

ten	met	can	tag
pet	peg	mat	fat
leg	pen	bag	fan

Write rhyming words.

set ______________________

beg ______________________

men ______________________

red ______________________

tell ______________________

Language Arts 102
Worksheet 3
with page 5

Teacher check ______________________
Initial Date

Name ____________________

Listen and find.

1.	
2.	
3.	
4.	
5.	
6.	
7.	
8.	

Language Arts 102
Worksheet 4
with page 8

Teacher check ____________________
Initial Date

Name ______________________

Circle the pictures.

1.			
2.			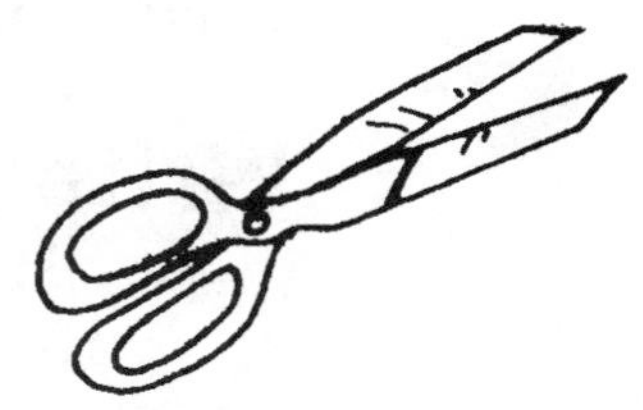
3.	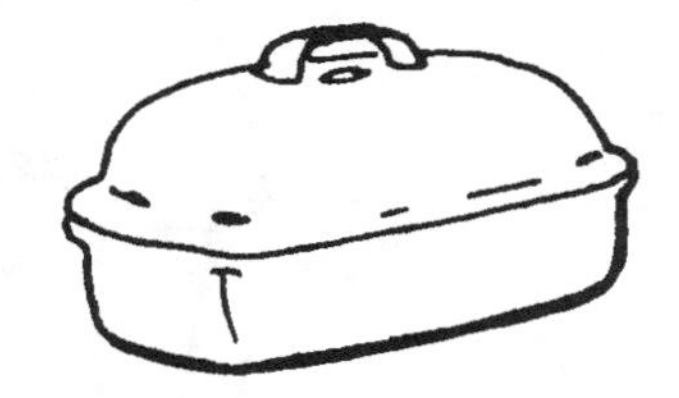		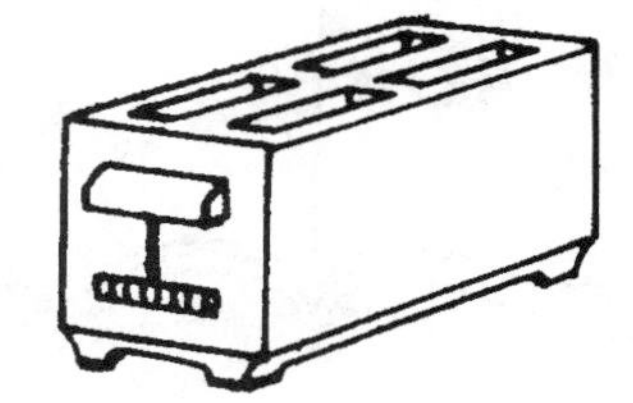
4.			
5.			
6.			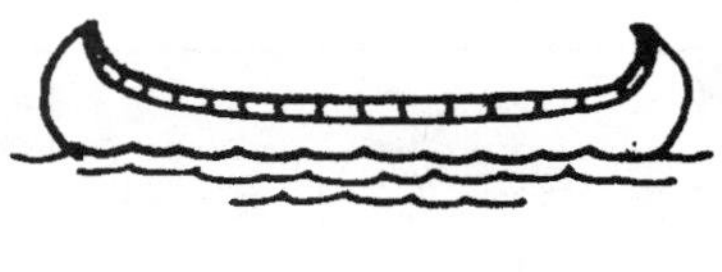

Teacher check ______________________
Initial Date

Name ______________

PUT IN ORDER

Can you tell
what comes first?
Can you tell
what comes last?

Write 1, 2, 3 **for** first, next, **and** last.

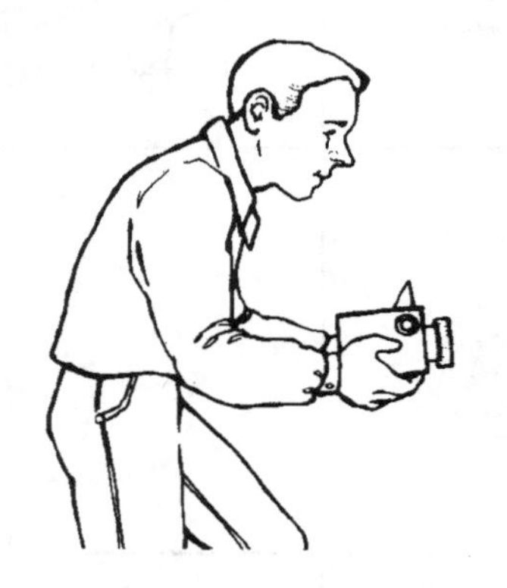

______ ______ ______

______ ______ ______

★ **morning** **night** **noon**

______ ______ ______

★ **C** **B** **A**

______ ______ ______

Teacher check ______________
Initial Date

Name ______________________

TELL THE STORY

Look at the pictures.

Tell a story about the picture.

Language Arts 102
Worksheet 7
with page 20

Teacher check ______________________
Initial Date

Name ____________________

Write the words.

● ____________________

● ● ____________________

● ● ● ____________________

● ● ● ● ____________________

two **four** **one** **three**

Match

1		three
3		one
4		two
2		four

Language Arts 102
Worksheet 8
with page 24

Teacher check ____________________
Initial Date

Name ____________

MORE SENTENCES

You will find
more ., !, and ? sentences.

Read the sentences. Write ., ?, or !.

This is a Bible ________
Is this a Bible ________
Oh ________ Oh ________
The Bible is God's Word ________

Can I swim ________
Yes, Yes ________
I can swim ________

Look, look ________
Is this a fish ________
This is a fish ________

Teacher check ____________
Initial Date

Name ____________________

Write the words.

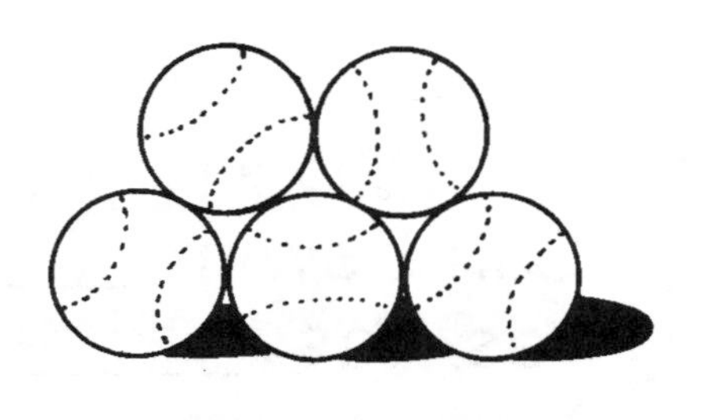

one **two** **three** **four** **five** **six**

Language Arts 102
Worksheet 10
with page 30

Teacher check ____________________
Initial Date

Name ____________________

AND MORE SENTENCES

Read more sentences.

Write ., ?, or !. Read the sentences.

Oh, look ________
Is this a six ________
This is a six ________

I can kick a ball ________
Can you kick ________
Yes, yes ________

Write a statement.

____

Write a question.

____

Write an exclamation.

____

Teacher check ____________________
Initial Date

Name ____________________

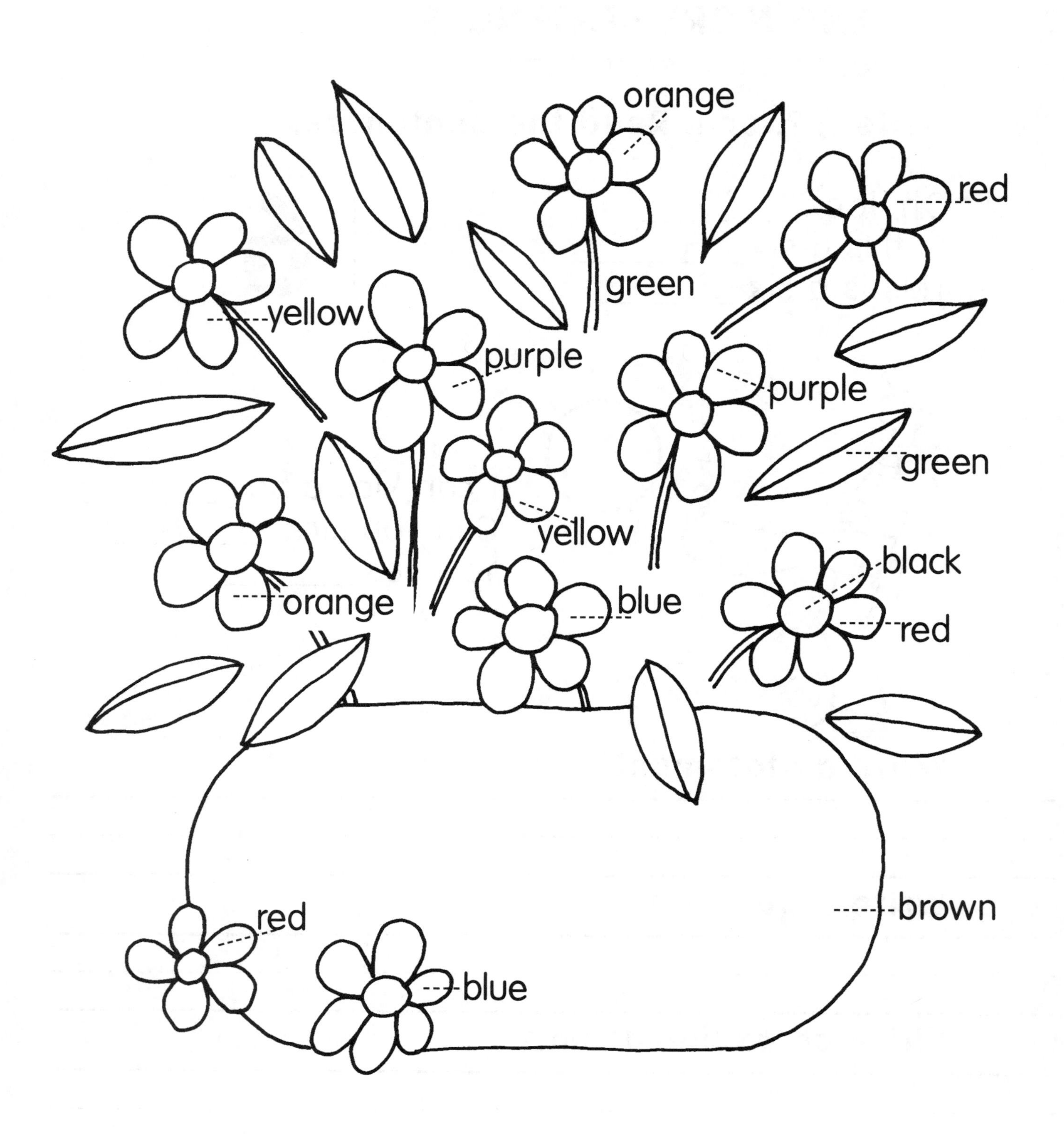

Language Arts 102
Worksheet 12
with page 32

Teacher check ____________________
Initial Date

Name ___________________________

Write th **or** wh.

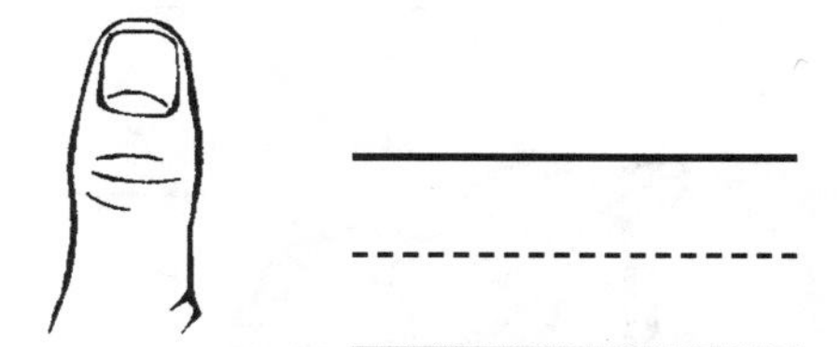

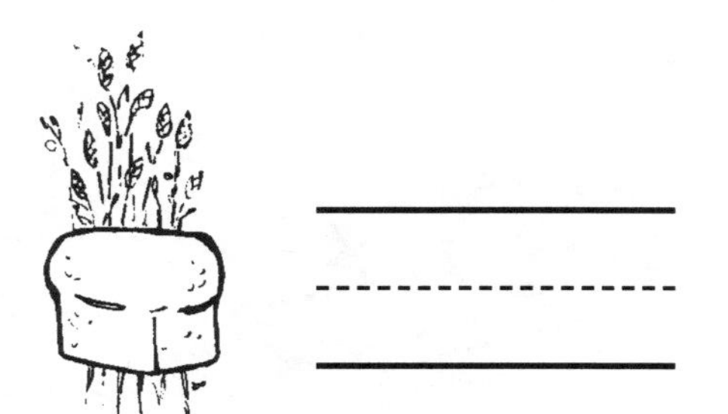

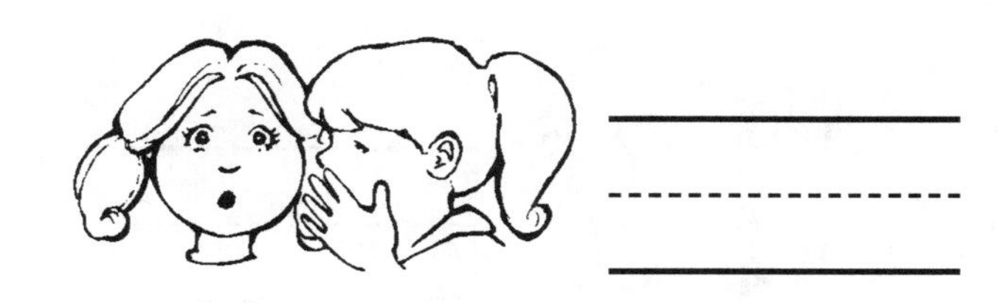

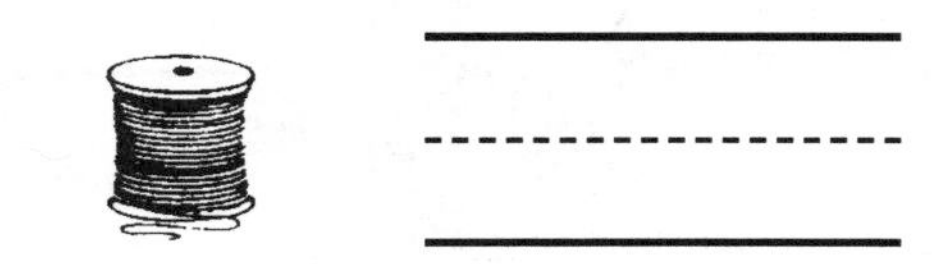

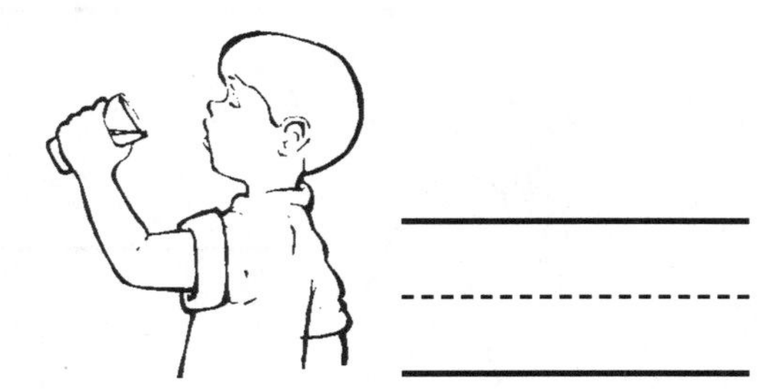

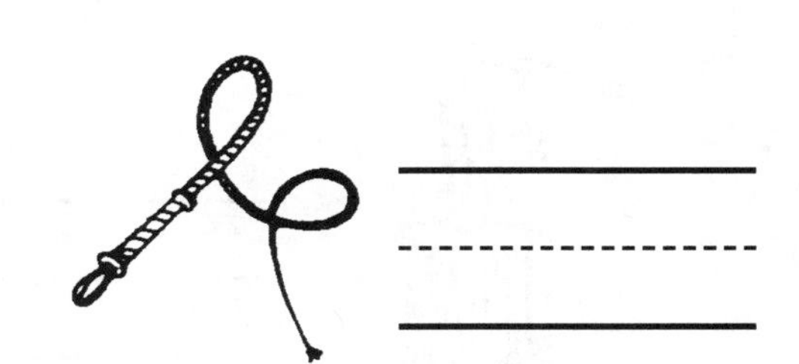

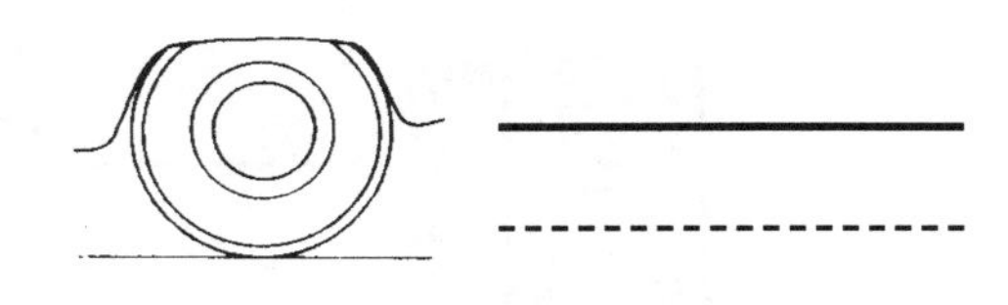

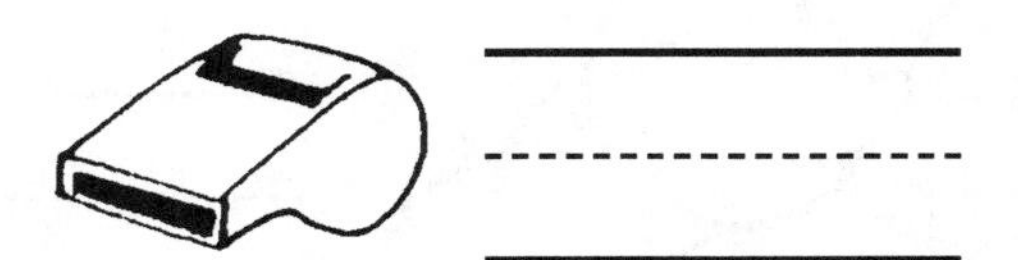

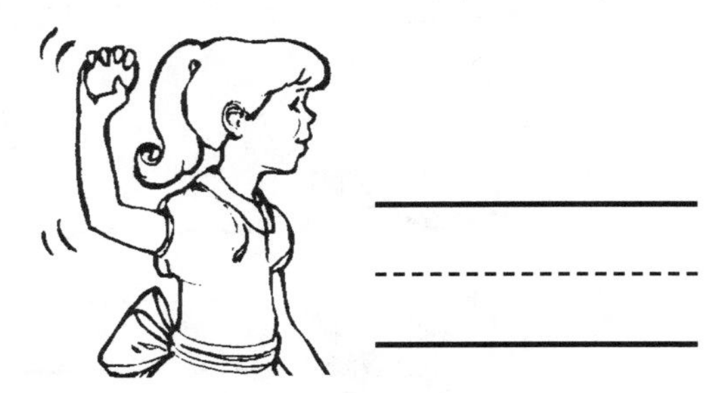

3

Language Arts 103
Worksheet 1
with page 4

Teacher check ___________________
Initial Date

Name ______________________

Write sh **or** ch.

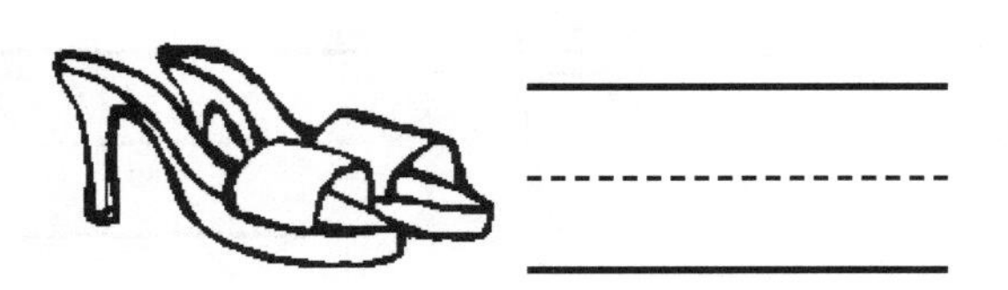

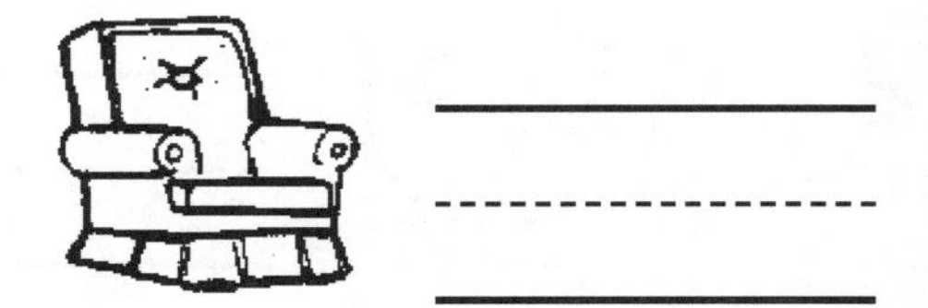

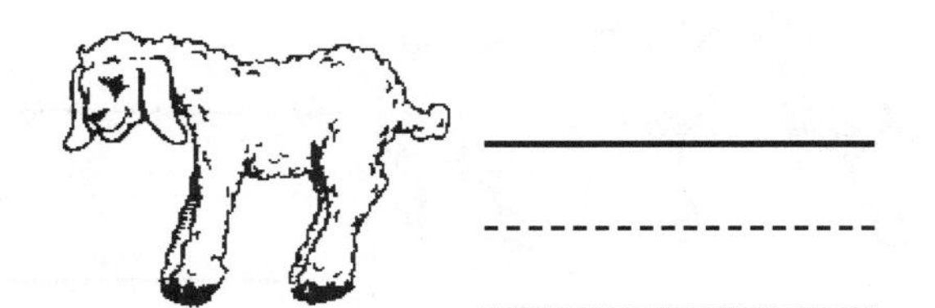

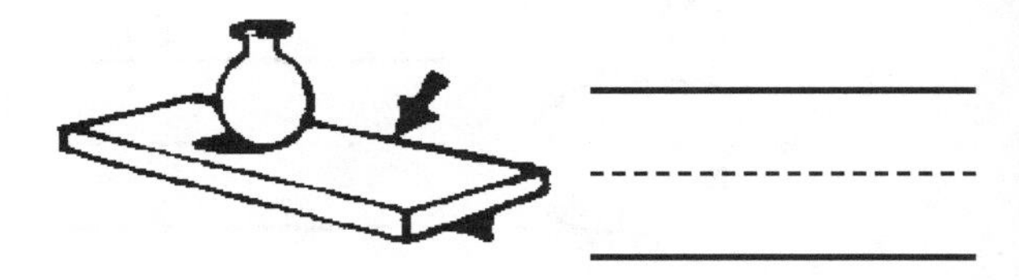

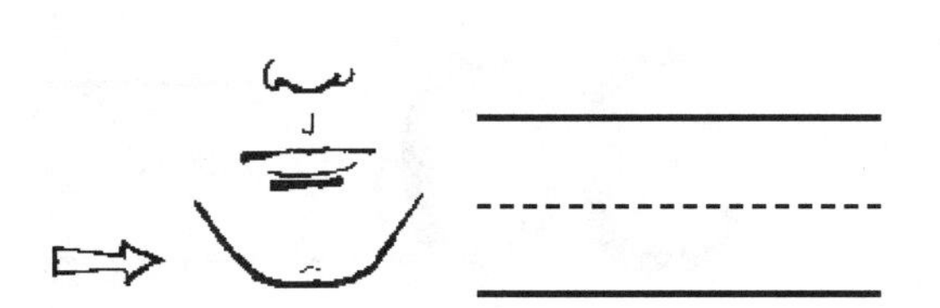

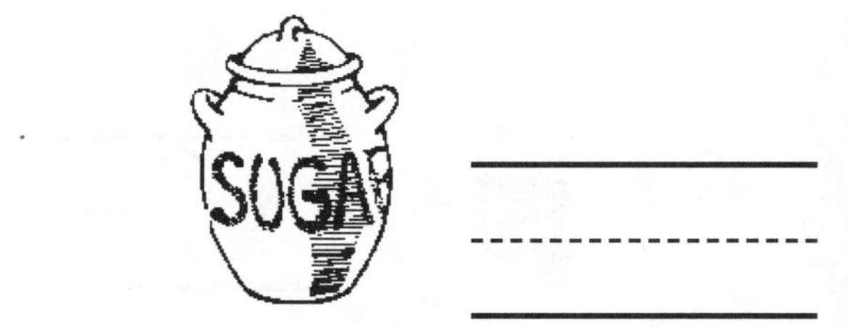

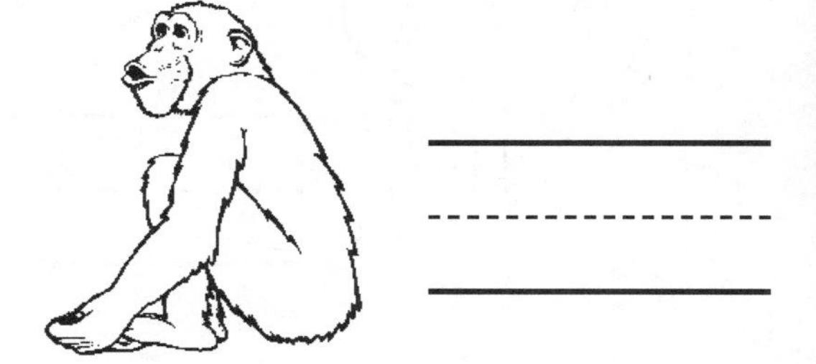

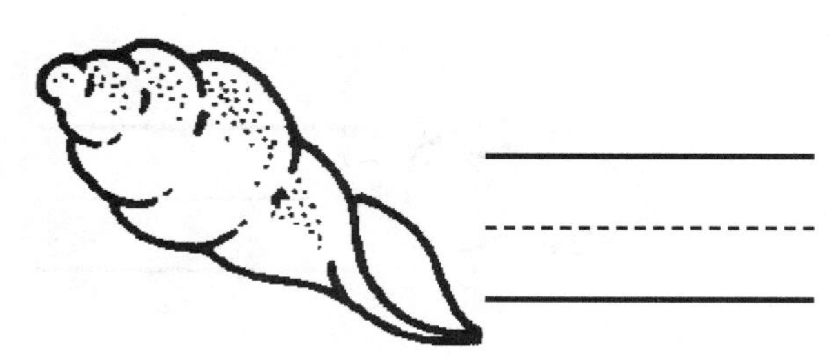

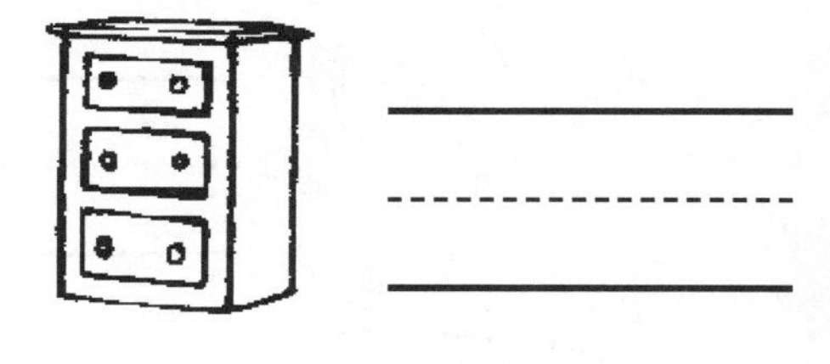

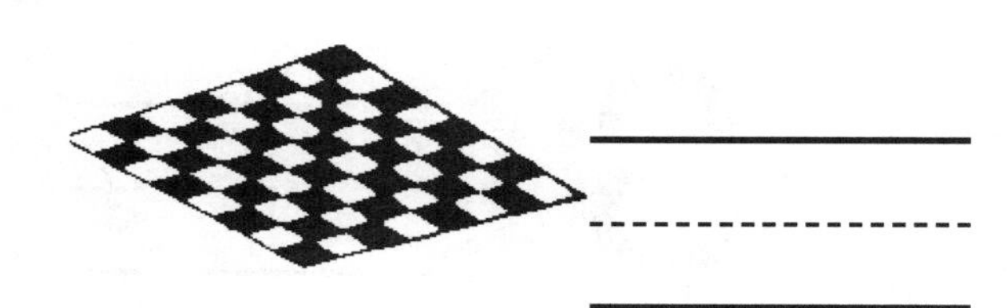

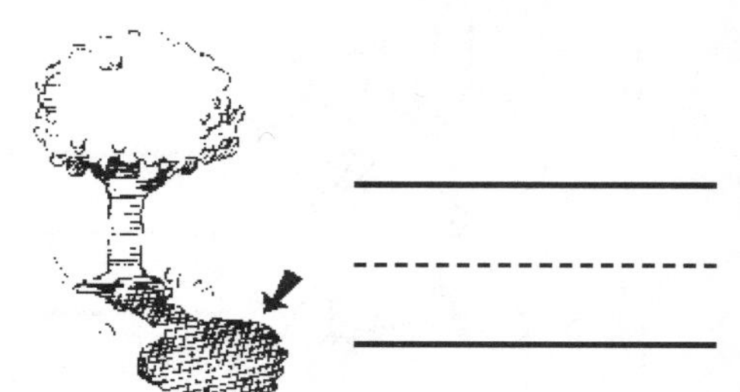

Teacher check ______________________

Initial Date

Name ____________________

Write sentences.

Is this my block?

Is this your lock?

lock ____________________

clock ____________________

box ____________________

sock ____________________

Teacher check ____________________
Initial Date

Name ______________

Match

four	5	six	2
one	4	two	8
five	7	eight	3
seven	1	three	6

Draw and color.

four red and black balls

eight blue and yellow pots

six orange and green tops

seven purple and white socks

eight little brown rocks

Language Arts 103
Worksheet 4
with page 9

Teacher check ______________
Initial Date

Name ______________________

Write the sentences.

I'm

I am a child.

I'm a child.

I'll

I will go home.

______________________ go home.

isn't

It **is not** here.

It ______________________ here.

can't

You **cannot** have it.

You ______________________ have it.

Teacher check ______________________
Initial Date

Name ______________

Write s. Read the words.

two clock	three sock ____
four lock ____	two rod ____
six circle ____	five triangle ____
eight block ____	seven stick ____
three ____	two ____

Teacher check ______________
Initial Date

Name ______________________

Write rhyming words.

cog jog

Ron ______

loll ______

Tom ______

_____op

_____ock

★**Write a word that rhymes with** stocking.

____

Language Arts 103
Worksheet 7
with page 18

Teacher check ______________
Initial Date

Name ______________

Put in the 's.

Read the sentences.

This is my house.
Is this your ball.
What is his name?
That is her mother.
Our car is blue.

Language Arts 103
Worksheet 8
with page 20

Teacher check ______________
Initial Date

Name ____________________

Circle the pictures with the soft c sound.

Write c or s.

 7 

Teacher check ____________________
Initial Date

Name ______________________

Write the words. Read the words.

six pins

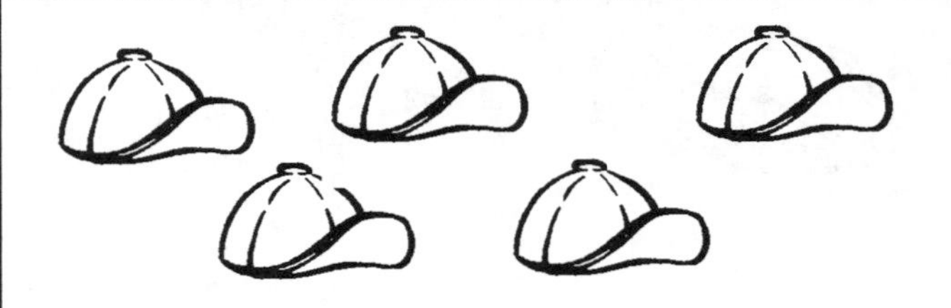

five ______________

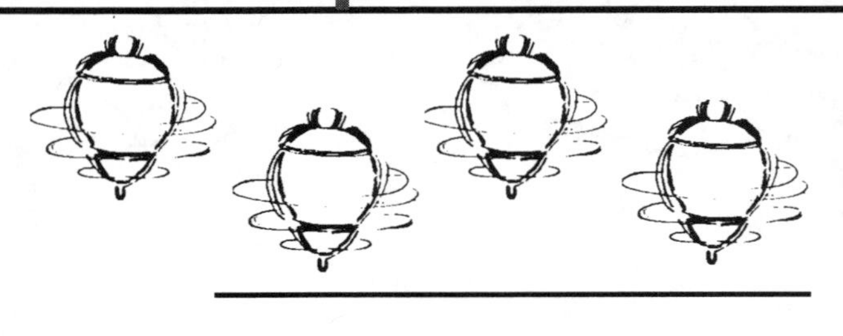

four ______________

three ______________

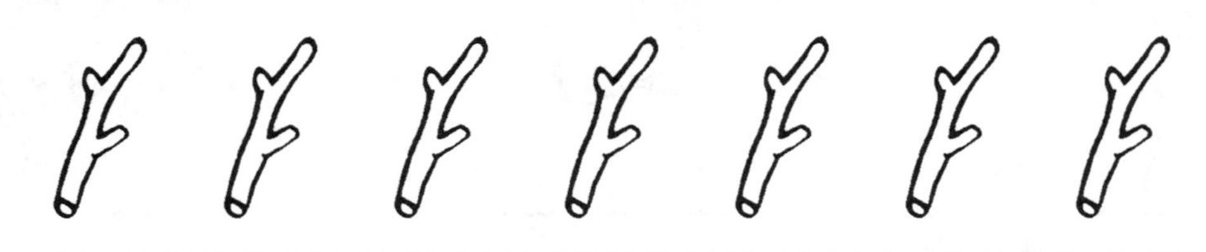

seven ______________

eight ______________

Teacher check ______________
Initial Date

Write rhyming words. Name ____________

_ill

bill

_ish

dish

Can you think of more?

Write them in your writing tablet.

Match the ryhming words.

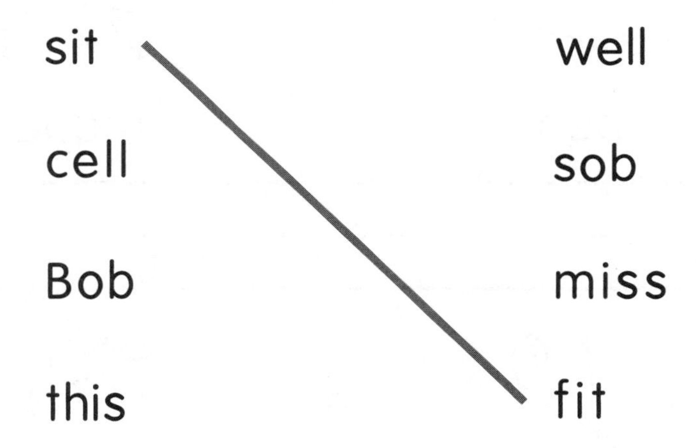

sit	well
cell	sob
Bob	miss
this	fit

Read the words.

Language Arts 103
Worksheet 11
with page 24

Teacher check ____________
Initial Date

Name ______________________

Write the words.

 +  = 

cow boy cowboy

 +   = raincoat 

rain coat raincoat

+  = 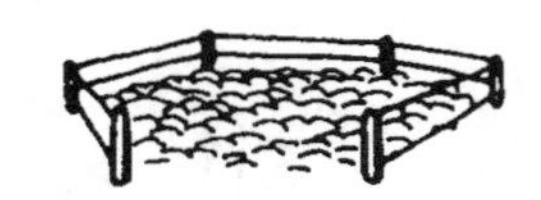

pig pen pigpen

 +  = 

finger nail fingernail

Teacher check ______________________
Initial Date

Name ____________________

Write the words.

 +  = 

rain bow

+  = 

butter fly

+  = 

cotton tail

Language Arts 103
Worksheet 13
with page 26

 Teacher check ____________________
Initial Date

Name ____________

Write 1 if you hear one part.
Write 2 if you hear two parts.

him____ the____ running____

wanted____ singing____ nod____

cab____ birthday____ Sunday____

willing____ Bible____ tug____

Read these words. How many parts do you hear?

minister____ contraction____

nursery____ banana____

dictionary____ apostrophe____

How many parts in these words?

sentences____ animal____

together____ another____

butterfly____ invitation____

Language Arts 103
Worksheet 14
with page 27

Teacher check ____________
Initial Date

Name ______________

Circle the pictures with the soft g sound.

Write g or j.

Language Arts 103
Worksheet 15
with page 29

Teacher check ______________
Initial Date

Name ______________________

Write s or es. Read the words.

two flag ______________ four fox ______________

three glass ______________ two pot ______________

Match the words and pictures.

four socks

two boxes

two buses

four dolls

three clocks

Teacher check ______________
Initial Date

Name ____________________

Cut and paste the letters.

sl	gl	pl	gl	sl	sl
pl	gl	pl	sl	pl	gl

Teacher check ____________________
Initial Date

Name ____________

Language Arts 104
Worksheet 2
with page 9

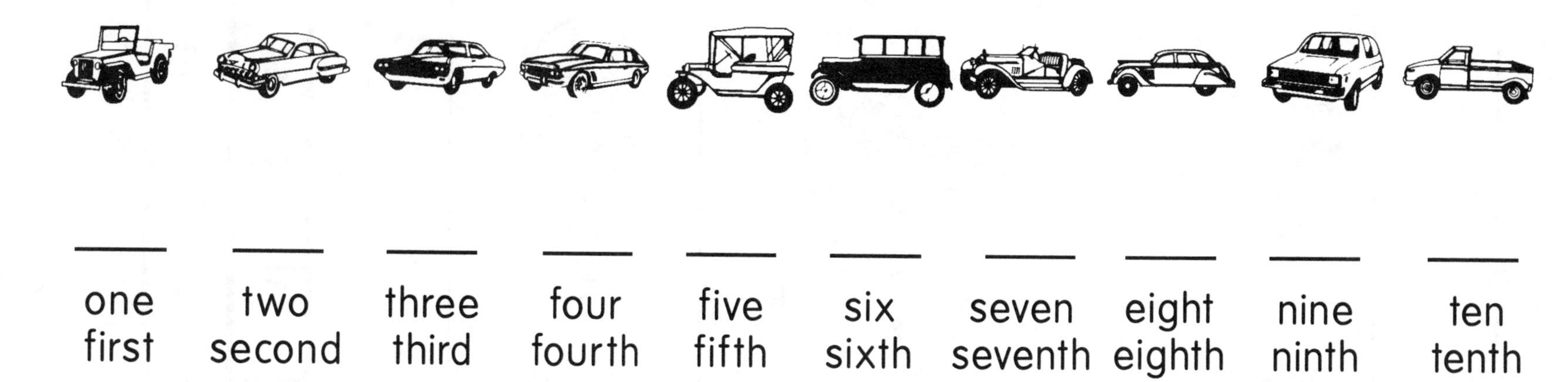

one	two	three	four	five	six	seven	eight	nine	ten
first	second	third	fourth	fifth	sixth	seventh	eighth	ninth	tenth

Write the words.

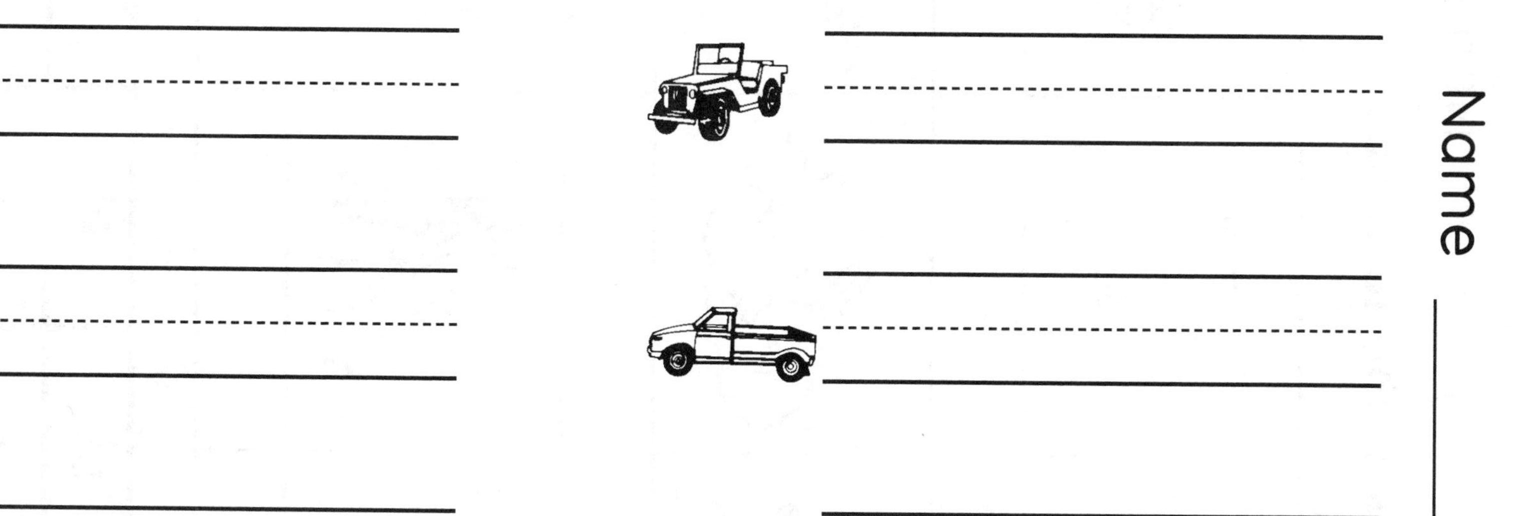

Teacher check ____________
Initial Date

Name ____________________

Circle the beginning letters.

bl cl fl	fr pr tr	gl pl sl	dr fr gr
bl pl tl	cr dr gr	tr gr pr	cl gl sl
pl bl cl	gr br dr	cl gl pl	tr dr gr
sl pl cl	bl gl fl	pr tr br	cr gr pr
br dr cr	pl bl sl	gr br dr	pr cr tr

Language Arts 104
Worksheet 3
with page 14

Teacher check ____________________
Initial Date

Name ______________

Circle the letters.

sk_ _sk _ _sk	st_ _ st _ _st	sp_ _sp_ _sp	th_ _th_ _th
sh_ _sh_ _sh	ch_ _tch_ _tch	sk_ _sk_ _sk	st_ _st_ _st
sp_ _sp_ _sp	th_ _th_ _th	sh_ _sh_ _sh	ch_ _ch_ _ch

Language Arts 104
Worksheet 4
with page 17

Teacher check ______________
Initial Date

Name ______________________

Write 1, 2, 3 **for** first, second, **and** third.

______ ______ ______

______ ______ ______

______ ______ ______

______ ______ ______

Language Arts 104
Worksheet 5
with page 25

Teacher check ______________________
Initial Date

Name ______________

What Comes Next?

Write 1, 2, 3 **for** first, second, **and** third.

______ ______ ______

Put the letters and numbers in order.

d b e c f

b ______ ______ ______ ______

w y z v x

v ______ ______ ______ ______

6 9 5 8 7

5 ______ ______ ______ ______

11 13 12 14 10

10 ______ ______ ______ ______

Teacher check ______________
Initial Date

Name ____________________

Circle the three that are alike.

□	○	△	3
Bud	big	Bob	But
one	black	eight	five
the	brick	bring	bread
jump	jam	hump	lump
pry	prop	play	pray
stump	trick	track	truck

Language Arts 104
Worksheet 7
with page 30

Teacher check ____________________
Initial Date

Name ____________________

Write the sentence.

is dog This my.

This

black is dog My.

run He can fast!

I my dog like.

you dog Do a have?

Read the story.
Draw a picture about the story.

Teacher check ____________________
Initial Date

Name ____________________

Write words that rhyme.

-ane	-ain

mane

plane

cane

Language Arts 105
Worksheet 1
with page 5

Teacher check ____________________
Initial Date

Name ______________________

Write rhyming words.

see ______________________

peal ______________________

feet ______________________

keep ______________________

Write the words.

funny **puppy** **happy**

This story is ______________________ .

My ______________________ is brown.

I am ______________________ .

Language Arts 105
Worksheet 2
with page 7

Teacher check ______________________
Initial Date

Name ____________

When you put an e at the end of a short vowel word, it changes the short vowel to a long vowel. The e is silent.

Write e on the line. Read the words.

bit	bit ____	kit	kit ____
rid	rid ____	pin	pin ____
tin	tin ____	fin	fin ____
cap	cap ____	mat	mat ____
man	man ____	plan	plan ____

Write i on the line. Read the words.

l ____ ke	wh ____ le	pr ____ ze
t ____ le	th ____ ne	kn ____ fe
b ____ te	ch ____ me	m ____ ce
r ____ de	br ____ de	B ____ ble

Language Arts 105
Worksheet 3
with page 10

Teacher check ____________
Initial Date

Name ____________________

Write i on the line. Read the words.

p ______ e   cl ______ mb   g ______ ant

m ______ ld   t ______ e   bl ______ nd

l ______ ght   m ______ ght   l ______ e

f ______ nd   w ______ ld   p ______ nt

s ______ gn   d ______ al   s ______ gh

w ______ nd   m ______ nd   n ______ ght

Write the words.

wild   **pie**   **light**

Turn the ____________________ off.

A lion is a ____________________ animal

I will eat a piece of ____________________ .

Teacher check ____________
Initial   Date

Name ____________________

Make a New Word

Read the word. Write e on the line. Read the word you made.

rod	rod ____	cub	cub ____
not	not ____	cut	cut ____
hop	hop ____	us	us ____

Write a word in each sentence.

hoe **you** **grow** **used**

We can ____________ plants in a garden.

We must ____________ our garden.

We ____________ our garden.

Do ____________ know who sends the sunshine and the rain?

Teacher check ____________
Initial Date

Name________________________

Read these words.

Listen for the long u̲ sound.

use	you	Tuesday
used	pew	cucumber
usual	mew	excuse
usually	hew	rescue
unusual	view	useful

Use each word in a sentence.

duke	tube	due
new	stew	suit

Circle the words with the long u̲ sound.

Can you use a saw?

Cars must have fuel to go fast.

We used up all the paint.

The kitten said," Mew, mew."

An ice cube is cold.

Do you like music?

You'll have to come in now.

Teacher check ______________
Initial Date

Name ____________________

Write the words.

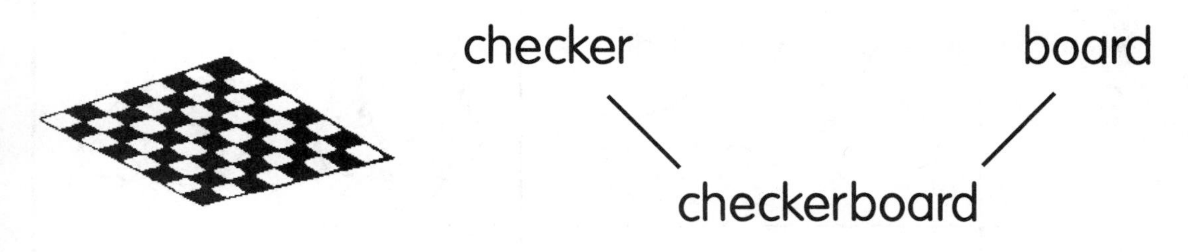

sail boat

____

jump rope

____

cup cake

____

Read the compound words.

Language Arts 105
Worksheet 7
with page 17

Teacher check ____________
Initial Date

Name____________________

Cut and paste.

children	women	men
cakes	snails	mice
deer	boxes	houses
glasses	whales	shells

Language Arts 105
Worksheet 8
with page 18

Teacher check ____________________
Initial Date

Name ____________________

Write the contractions.

did not — didn't

he will — he'll

is not ____________________

cannot ____________________

she is ____________________

we will ____________________

has not ____________________

★who will ____________________

★ will not ____________________

Language Arts 105
Worksheet 9
with page 20

Teacher check ____________________
Initial Date

Name ____________________

Write 1, 2, or 3.

_______ Jane's mom brings her a dress.
_______ Jane is dressed.
_______ Jane puts on her dress.

_______ Dave runs to Father.
_______ Father calls Dave.
_______ Dave and Father go home.

_______ Jack puts his bike away.
_______ Jack rides his bike.
_______ Jack gets on his bike.

Teacher check ____________________
Initial Date

Name ____________________

Circle the words.

______________ balloon is red.

Kim / Kim's

It is ______________ balloon.

her / her's

Is this ______________ cap?

your / yours

I think that is ______________ cap.

Daves / Dave's

The ______________ tail is wagging.

dogs / dog's

That ______________ name is Tom.

boy's / boys

Jesus is ______________ Son.

Gods / God's

Language Arts 105
Worksheet 11
with page 21

Teacher check ______________
Initial Date

Name ____________________

Write the words.

	-ed	-ing
pin	**pinned**	**pinning**
fit		
pat		
bob		
trim		
star		
fan		
tap		

Language Arts 105
Worksheet 12
with page 25

Teacher check ____________________
Initial Date

Name ____________________

Draw a line under what will happen next.

Don is at the lake.
He has a can of bait.
What will Don do?

He will fish.
He will play ball.

James has two cupcakes.
John hasn't any cupcakes.
What will James do?

James will give John a cupcake.
James won't give John a cupcake.

Tom did a bad thing today.
He isn't happy.
What will he do now?

Tom won't be good now.
Tom will be good now.

Teacher check ____________________
Initial Date

Name ____________________

Write the words.

A dog that belongs to Tom is

____________________ dog.

A cake that belongs to Kay is

____________________ cake.

The table that belongs to Jay is

____________________ table.

The balloon that belongs to Jane is

____________________ balloon.

The LIFEPAC that belongs to Jane is

____________________ LIFEPAC.

Language Arts 105
Worksheet 14
with page 30

Teacher check ____________________
Initial Date

Name

Reproducible page.

Name

Reproducible page.

Name

Reproducible page.

Name

ALTERNATE

TESTS

Reproducible Tests
for use with the Language Arts
100 Teacher Handbook

LANGUAGE ARTS 101

ALTERNATE LIFEPAC TEST

Name ______________________

Date ______________________

Score ______________________

Match the letters and words.

A	b	hill	Tan
B	d	pet	Hill
D	a	bob	Pet
N	m	lamb	Bob
M	n	tan	Lamb

Match the rhyming words.

Jack	well
sell	rack
got	pot

Put the letters in order.

Z V W X Y

V_____ W_____ X_____ Y_____ Z_____

Match the letters and words.

f	H	dad	And
h	P	boy	Dad
p	K	man	Boy
k	C	no	Man
c	L	and	No
l	F		

Circle the pictures with the short i sound.

Circle the pictures with the short o sound.

Circle the pictures with the short u sound.

Circle the letters.

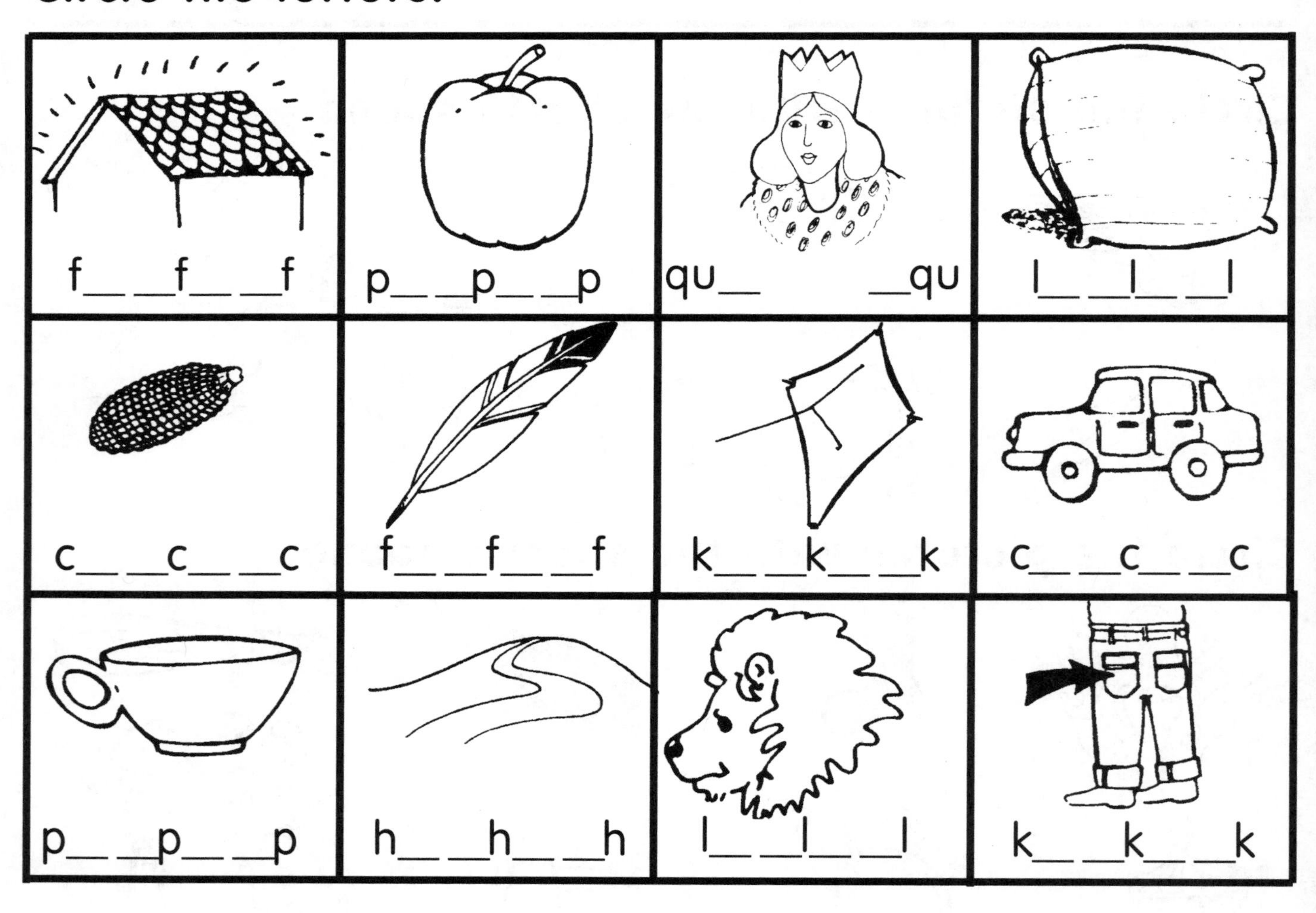

LANGUAGE ARTS 102

ALTERNATE LIFEPAC TEST

Name ____________________

Date ____________________

Score ____________________

LANGUAGE ARTS 102:
ALTERNATE LIFEPAC TEST

Match the letters and words.

f	H	Ten	hem
h	P	Let	ten
p	K	Hem	let
k	C	Pet	can
c	L	Can	pet
l	F		

Write the plurals.

cat ____________ dog ____________

Circle the picture.

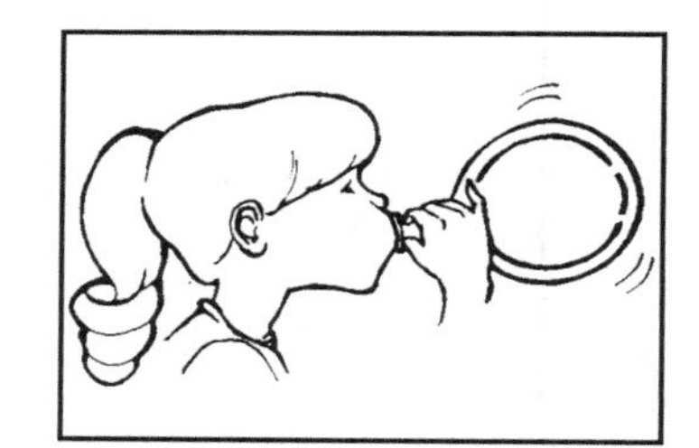

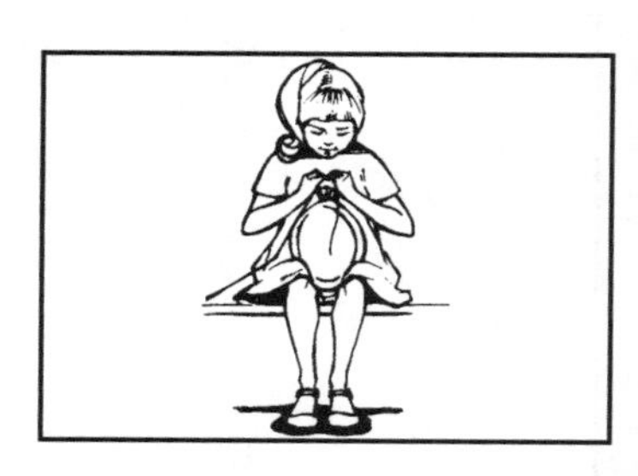

Could this really happen? Circle yes **or** no.

Write the punctuation.

This is a cat ____________

Is this a cat ____________

Look at that cat ____________

Circle the three which are alike.

dog	big	dig	rig
six	four	yes	five
g	g	g	G

Match the rhyming words.

fish	pin
thin	this
hiss	bill
sill	dish
bit	dig
fig	sit

Write 1, 2, 3 **for** first, next, **and** last.

______ ______ ______

Add ing.

stick ______________

make ______________

Fill in the missing letters.

a ___ d ___ f ___ h i ___ k ___ m n o ___ q

s ___ u ___ w x ___ z

LANGUAGE ARTS 1 0 3

ALTERNATE LIFEPAC TEST

Name ____________________

Date ____________________

Score ____________________

LANGUAGE ARTS 103
ALTERNATE LIFEPAC TEST

Write the letters ch, sh, wh, or th.

Match the contractions.

I am — don't

do not — I'm

Write rhyming words.

bob

box

Listen and do.

Circle the pictures with the soft g sound.

Circle the pictures that begin with the soft c sound.

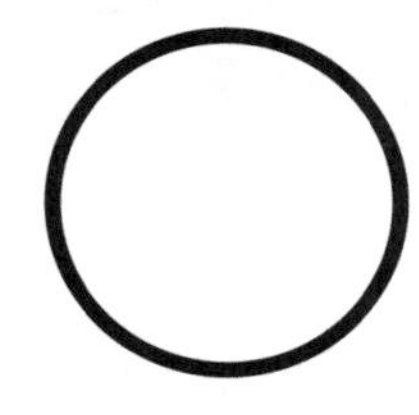

Write s or es.

three dot ________	four top ________
two doll ________	two fox ________

Match the rhyming words.

Rick	bell
maps	tips
rips	naps
shell	Nick

---

when	miss
this	sat
that	hop
chop	Ben

Write a sentence. Use the correct punctuation.

hot am i

LANGUAGE ARTS 104

ALTERNATE LIFEPAC TEST

Name ____________________

Date ____________________

Score ____________________

LANGUAGE ARTS 104
ALTERNATE LIFEPAC TEST

Write bl, cl, fl, gl, pl, **or** sl.

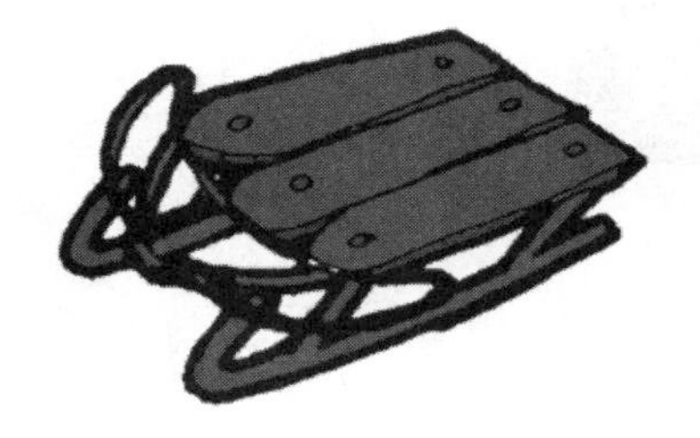
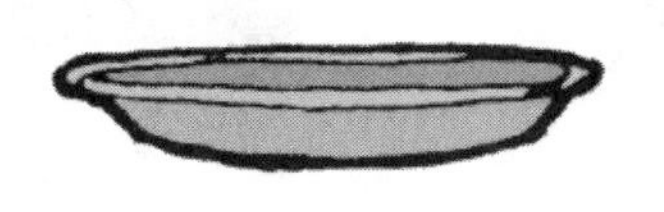

Write br, cr, dr, gr, fr, pr, **or** tr.

Put an X **on the one that does not belong.**

brick	brush	bring	tray
drive	black	drink	drum
crayon	crack	frog	crane
grapes	frog	fresh	fry
trip	trap	flap	try

Circle the words.

I can __________ fast.

ran / run

The ______________ are playing house.

girl / girls

That ball ________ Tom's

is / are

The men ____________ cars.

has / have

I am ________________ rope.

jump / jumping

Write 1, 2, 3 **for** first, next, **and** last.

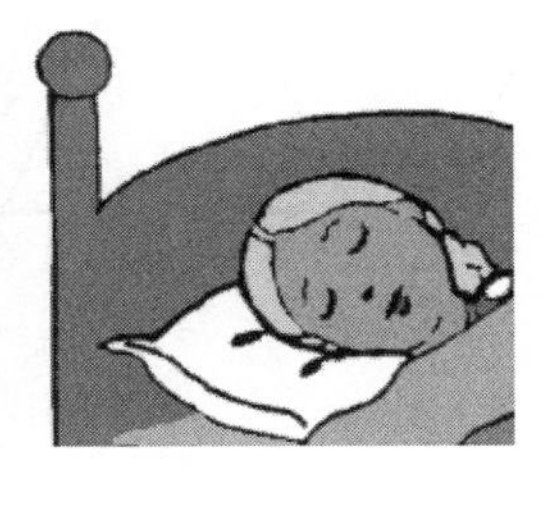

____

____

____

Match rhyming words.

rocks	jog
Polly	tops
mops	dolly
cog	socks

Circle the silent letters.

knee walk lamb

Circle the f sound.

laugh telephone tough

Write a sentence.

hot am i

____

Circle the pictures.

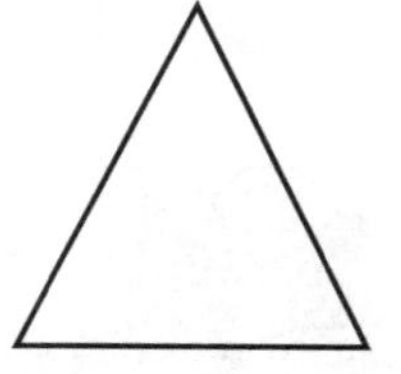 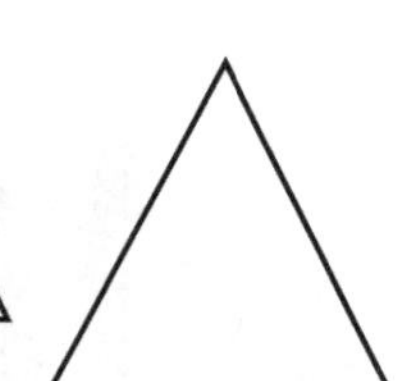 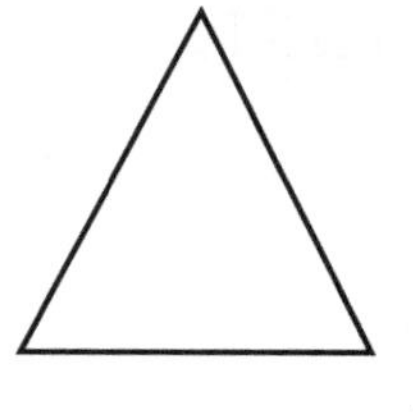 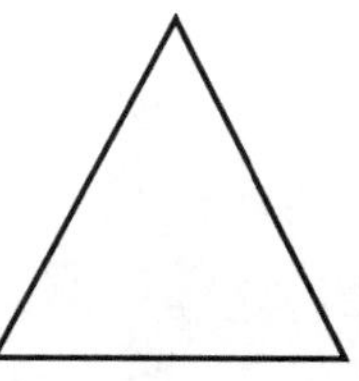 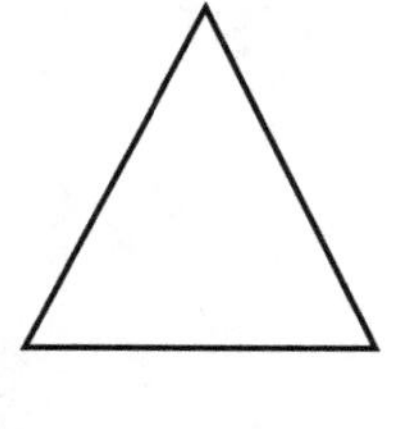  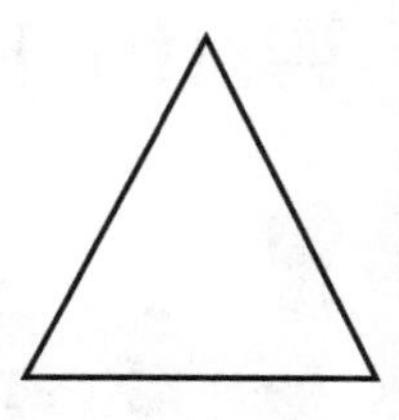

LANGUAGE ARTS 1 0 5

ALTERNATE LIFEPAC TEST

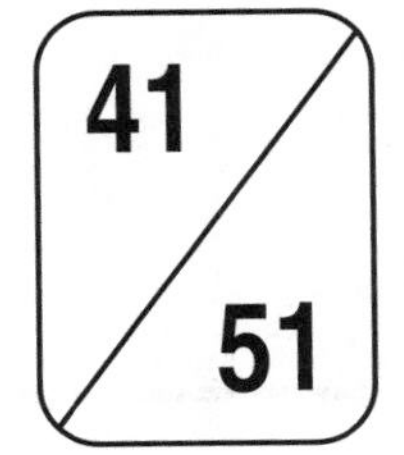

Name ____________________

Date ____________________

Score ____________________

LANGUAGE ARTS 105
ALTERNATE LIFEPAC TEST

Circle the pictures with the long a sound.

Circle the words with the long e.

we	he	bee
be	see	me
pet	wet	pen

Write the compound word.

check up

____

Match the words.

didn't	do not	wasn't	we will
can't	did not	you'll	was not
don't	can not	we'll	you will
aren't	it is	won't	is not
it's	are not	isn't	will not

Draw a line under what will happen next.

Jane is playing with her dolls.
Jane's mother is calling her for dinner.

Jane will play with her dolls.
Jane will go to mother.

Write the plurals.

tray ____________________

flake ____________________

Write the words.

____________________ bike is yellow.
Tom / Tom's

That is ____________________ house!
you / your

Where is ____________________ lunch?
her / she

Which one is ____________________ chair?
me / my

page 2 (two)

Write the sentence.

Circle the words with the long i.

hide	like	nice
is	hike	hot

Write rhyming words.

those ____________ go ____________

Write the number of syllables.

sunny_____	mess_____	bunny_____
letter_____	funny_____	fence_____

Circle the words with the long u.

muse	mud	use
muff	fuse	tube
cube	tub	cub